Aspects of Language Development in an Intensive English Program

While there is much in the literature on ESL development, this book is the first of its kind to track the development of specific language abilities in an intensive English program (IEP) longitudinally, and it highlights the implications of this particular study's findings for future IEP implementation and practice and ESL and SLA research. The volume draws on many years' worth of data from learners at an IEP at the University of Pittsburgh to explore selected aspects of language development, including lexical, grammatical, speaking, and writing abilities, in addition to placement assessment practices and student learning outcomes. A concluding chapter points to the ways in which these findings can be applied to decision-making around IEP curriculum development and the future role of IEPs in higher education more broadly. With its focus on students in IEP settings and the concentration on data from students evaluated over multiple semesters, this volume offers a unique opportunity in which to examine longitudinal developmental patterns of different L1 groups on a variety of measures from the same learners and will be key reading for students and researchers in second language acquisition, English for academic purposes, language education, and applied linguistics.

Alan Juffs is Professor of Linguistics and Director of the English Language Institute at the University of Pittsburgh. He has also taught English in Asia, Europe, and North America. His research focuses on formal linguistic approaches to second language acquisition, the lexicon (*Learnability and the Lexicon: Theories and Second Language Acquisition Research*, 1996), and sentence processing (*Second Language Sentence Processing*, 2014).

Routledge Studies in Applied Linguistics

The Social Lives of Study Abroad
Understanding Second Language Learners' Experiences through Social Network Analysis and Conversation Analysis
Atsushi Hasegawa

Defining and Assessing Lexical Proficiency
Agnieszka Leńko-Szymańska

Global Perspectives on Project-based Language Learning, Teaching, and Assessment
Key Approaches, Technology Tools, and Frameworks
Edited by Gulbahar H. Beckett and Tammy Slater

Referring in a Second Language
Studies on Reference to Person in a Multilingual World
Edited by Jonothan Ryan and Peter Crosthwaite

Aspects of Language Development in an Intensive English Program
Alan Juffs

First Language Influences on Multilingual Lexicons
Edited by Paul Booth and Jon Clenton

Corpus Analysis in Different Genres
Academic Discourse and Learner Corpora
Edited by María Luisa Carrió-Pastor

Vocabulary and the Four Skills
Pedagogy, Practice, and Implications for Teaching Vocabulary
Edited by Jon Clenton and Paul Booth

For more information about this series, please visit: https://www.routledge.com/Routledge-Studies-in-Applied-Linguistics/book-series/RSAL

Aspects of Language Development in an Intensive English Program

Alan Juffs

LONDON AND NEW YORK

First published 2020 by Routledge

2 Park Square, Milton Park, Abingdon, Oxon OX14 4RN
605 Third Avenue, New York, NY 10017

Routledge is an imprint of the Taylor & Francis Group, an informa business

First issued in paperback 2021

Copyright © 2020 Taylor & Francis

The right of Alan Juffs to be identified as author of this work has
been asserted by him in accordance with sections 77 and 78 of
the Copyright, Designs and Patents Act 1988.

All rights reserved. No part of this book may be reprinted or reproduced or
utilised in any form or by any electronic, mechanical, or other means, now
known or hereafter invented, including photocopying and recording, or in
any information storage or retrieval system, without permission in writing
from the publishers.

Notice:
Product or corporate names may be trademarks or registered trademarks,
and are used only for identification and explanation without intent to
infringe.

Publisher's Note

The publisher has gone to great lengths to ensure the quality of this reprint
but points out that some imperfections in the original copies may be apparent.

Library of Congress Cataloging-in-Publication Data
Names: Juffs, Alan, author.
Title: Aspects of language development in an intensive English
    program / Alan Juffs.
Description: 1. | New York : Taylor and Francis, 2020. |
    Series: Routledge studies in applied linguistics | Includes
    bibliographical references and index.
Identifiers: LCCN 2019056028 | ISBN 9781138048362 (hardback) |
    ISBN 9781315170190 (ebook)
Subjects: LCSH: English language—Study and teaching. | Second
    language acquisition—Study and teaching.
Classification: LCC PE1128 .J84 2020 | DDC 428.0071—dc23
LC record available at https://lccn.loc.gov/2019056028

ISBN: 978-1-138-04836-2 (hbk)
ISBN: 978-1-03-217305-4 (pbk)
DOI: 10.4324/9781315170190

Typeset in Sabon
by Apex CoVantage, LLC

Contents

List of Figures	xi
List of Tables	xii
Acknowledgments	xiv
Preface	xv

**1   Intensive English Programs and Second Language
Teaching Research**   **1**

1.1 *Intensive English Language Programs: Early
Beginnings and Professionalization 1*

1.2 *The Spread of English as a World Lingua Franca
and Economic Impact 2*

1.3 *The Economic and Political Context of the Intensive
English Program 4*

1.4 *Wider Context in Research and Second Language
Teaching 7*

    1.4.1 *Second Language Acquisition as Theoretical
Research 8*

    1.4.2 *Second Language Acquisition and Language
Teaching Research 10*

    1.4.3 *The Role of Instruction in Language
Development 10*

1.5 *Goals and Role of Intensive English Programs in the
Wider Context of English for Academic Purposes
and English for Specific Purposes 11*

1.6 *The Research in This Book: Mixed Methods and
in the Spirit of 'Design-Based' Research 12*

1.7 *Summary 13*

1.8 *Topics for Administrators and Teachers
to Reflect On 13*

    1.8.1 *Questions and Issues Mainly for Program
Administrators and Curriculum Supervisors 13*

vi *Contents*

    1.8.2 Questions and Issues for Classroom
       Teachers 14
  References 15

2 The Intensive English Program at the University of
    Pittsburgh: Methods and Curriculum   19
  2.1 Methodology – The Communicative Approach
    (CLT) 20
  2.2 The Faculty and the Design and Implementation
    of the Curriculum 22
  2.3 The Students: National Origins, Proficiency, and
    Goals 26
  2.4 The Curriculum 28
    2.4.1 The Speaking Curriculum – Goals, Objectives,
      Student Learning Outcomes 30
    2.4.2 The Writing Curriculum – Goals, Objectives,
      Student Learning Outcomes 31
    2.4.3 The Grammar Curriculum – Goals,
      Objectives, Student Learning Outcomes 32
  2.5 Summary 33
  References 33
  Appendix I English Language Institute General Best
    Practices 36
  Appendix II Level 3 Horizontal Articulation 38
  Appendix III Level 4 Horizontal Articulation 45
  Appendix IV Level 5 Horizontal Articulation 52

3 Placement Assessment and Developmental Measures in
    an Intensive English Program   58
  3.1 Introduction 58
  3.2 Background to Assessment 60
  3.3 Placement Assessment 63
    3.3.1 Description of the Placement Tools in the
      Intensive English Program 63
    3.3.2 Determining and Justifying Cut Scores 66
  3.4 Data Visualization and Analysis 69
    3.4.1 Central Tendency and Dispersion 69
    3.4.2 Cluster Analysis 70
  3.5 A Case Study From the Pitt Intensive English
    Program 71
    3.5.1 Participants 72
    3.5.2 Data Visualization 74
    3.5.3 K-Cluster Analysis 75

Contents vii

3.6 *Rubrics for Assessing Development* 84
3.7 *Final Exams* 85
   3.7.1 *Reading* 85
   3.7.2 *Writing* 86
   3.7.3 *Listening* 86
   3.7.4 *Speaking* 86
   3.7.5 *Grammar* 87
3.8 *Summary* 87
3.9 *Topics for Administrators and Teachers*
   to Reflect On 87
   3.9.1 *Questions and Issues Mainly for*
      Program Administrators and Curriculum
      Supervisors 87
   3.9.2 *Questions and Issues for Classroom*
      Teachers 88
References 89
Appendix I Writing Sample Rubric 93

4 Lexical Development in an Intensive English Program   **94**
4.1 *Introduction* 94
4.2 *Some Terminology for the Lexicon* 95
4.3 *Which Words Should and Do the Students Know at*
   Each Proficiency Level? 97
4.4 *How Does Lexical Knowledge Develop? Diversity,*
   Sophistication, and Depth 98
   4.4.1 *Comparing vocD and Advanced Guiraud for*
      Advanced Writing 102
   4.4.2 *Naismith et al. (2018): Which List Is Better*
      for Calculating Advanced Guiraud: The Role
      of L1 and L2 Experience 103
   4.4.3 *Differences Among Regions With the Same*
      First Language 105
4.5 *Instructional Approaches to Vocabulary*
   Teaching 106
   4.5.1 *Teaching Vocabulary: Decisions for the*
      Approach, Method, and Technique 106
   4.5.2 *Using Technology to Teach Vocabulary: The*
      Role of Learners' Motivation, Culture, and
      Teachers' Perceptions 108
4.7 *Collocations and Formulaic Sequences* 113
4.6 *Conclusion* 114
4.8 *Topics for Administrators and Teachers*
   to Reflect On 115

viii *Contents*

4.8.1 *Questions and Issues Mainly for Program Administrators and Curriculum Supervisors 115*

4.8.2 *Questions and Issues for Classroom Teachers 115*

References 117

Appendix I English Language Institute Vocabulary List 122

5 **Grammatical Development in an Intensive English Program**   127

5.1 *Introduction: Theories of Grammar and Learning 127*

5.2 *Background: Grammatical 'Functors' in English, Developmental Orders, and First Language Influence 129*

5.3 *Acquisition Orders in Functors and L1 Influence Revisited 130*

5.4 *Development of Clause Structure in Recorded Speaking Activities 135*

5.5 *Word Frequency Ranking Changes Reflect Morpho-Syntactic Development in English as a Second Language Writing 137*

5.5 *Specific Structures and L1 Development: Two Case Studies 157*

5.5.1 *Articles 157*

5.5.2 *Development of Passive in the Intensive English Program 159*

5.6 *Summary 160*

5.7 *Topics for Administrators and Teachers to Reflect On 161*

5.7.1 *Questions and Issues Mainly for Program Administrators and Curriculum Supervisors 161*

5.7.2 *Questions and Issues for Classroom Teachers 162*

References 163

6 **Spoken Language: Pronunciation and the Development of Complexity, Accuracy, and Fluency in an Intensive English Program**   170

6.1 *A Brief Review of Topics in Pronunciation: Phonetics and Phonology 171*

Contents ix

6.2 *Complexity, Accuracy, and Fluency in L2 Speaking 174*

    6.2.1 *Recorded Speaking Activities in the Pitt Intensive English Program 176*

    6.2.2 *Do Self-Correction Notes Make a Difference? 180*

    6.2.3 *The Development of Fluency in the Intensive English Program – An Example Intervention Study 181*

    6.2.4 *A Comment on Task-Based Language Instruction and Complexity, Accuracy, and Fluency Research 184*

6.3 *The Influence of L1 Phonology and Orthography on L2 Reading and Writing 186*

6.4 *Summary 187*

6.5 *Topics for Administrators and Teachers to Reflect On 188*

    6.5.1 *Questions and Issues Mainly for Program Administrators and Curriculum Supervisors 188*

    6.5.2 *Questions and Issues Mainly for Classroom Teachers 189*

References 190

7 Some Features of the Development of Writing in an Intensive English Program   **194**

7.1 *Introduction 194*

7.2 *Research on L2 Writing Development – Selected Key Highlights 195*

    7.2.1 *Writing: Taking Account of the Potential Reader 195*

    7.2.2 *The Learner-Centered Curriculum 196*

    7.2.3 *Awareness of Genre 197*

    7.2.4 *Contrastive Rhetoric: L1 Influence in L2 Writing 198*

    7.2.5 *Corrective Feedback: Second Language Acquisition Research 199*

    7.2.6 *Corpus-Based Studies of Writing: Quantitative Measurements 199*

    7.2.7 *The Big Picture 203*

7.3 *Case Studies From the Intensive English Program – Tracking Development of Eight Students Over Three Semesters 204*

x Contents

7.3.1 Review of Curriculum Goals and Background of Selected Students 204

7.3.2 Quantitative Overview of the Learners' Texts 208

7.3.3 Qualitative Analysis 212

7.3.3.1 Content Evaluation 212

7.3.3.2 Do Quantitative Ratings and Qualitative Teacher Evaluations Align? 216

7.4 Summary and Conclusion 219

7.5 Topics for Administrators and Teachers to Reflect On 220

7.5.1 Questions and Issues Mainly for Program Administrators and Curriculum Supervisors 220

7.5.2 Questions and Issues Mainly for Teachers 220

References 221

Appendix I. AF3 Arabic L1. Writing Texts 225

Appendix II. BN7 Arabic L1. Writing Texts 230

Appendix III. AQ1 Chinese L1. Writing Texts 237

Appendix IV. BL7. Chinese L1. Writing Texts 242

Appendix V. AY3 Japanese L1. Writing Texts 248

Appendix VI. FW1 Japanese L1. Writing Texts 254

Appendix VII. CC4 Korean L1. Writing Texts 260

Appendix VIII. EQ8 Korean L1. Writing Texts 267

8 Epilogue 273

8.1 The Wider Context of the Intensive English Program 273

8.2 Tracking Development: Providing Quantitative Support for Qualitative Judgments 274

8.3 Aspects Not Covered 275

8.4 Prospects for Intensive English Programs 275

8.4.1 In the United States 275

8.4.2 Around the World 276

References 276

Index 277

Figures

2.1	Numbers and Levels of Students in the Pittsburgh English Language Corpus (PELIC)	27
3.1	The Normal Curve (c.f. Brown, 1988)	69
3.2	Normal and Non-Normal Distributions in a Boxplot	70
3.3	Boxplot of EPT Total Scores	74
3.4	K-Cluster Means Centroids and Actual Level Placement Using EPT Listening and Structure	77
3.5	K-Cluster Means and Actual Level Placement Using EPT Structure and IEP Listening Test	79
3.6	Quality of Model and Size of Clusters for IEP Placement	81
3.7	Z-Score Distribution and Importance of Predictors in IEP Placement	82
3.8	Comparison of Mean Scores of Initial IEP Placement and Clusters	83
4.1	Gains in Advanced Guiraud Scores by First Language and Level Using Pitt IEP Frequency List	104
4.2	Gains in Advanced Guiraud Scores by First Language and Level Using NGSL Frequency List	105
5.1	Putative Universal Development Order of English Functors	130
5.2	L1 Development of Nominal Functors by Chinese and Arabic Learners by Level	132
5.3	Accuracy on Verbal Functors, Chinese and Arabic Learners by Level	133
5.4	Emergence of Clause Types by Proficiency Level	136
5.5	Frequency Rank of Selected Functional Categories by Level	147
5.6	Estimated Frequency per Million of 'whether' by L1 and Level	148
5.7	Level 3: NP vs. CP Verb Frequency per Million by L1	151
5.8	Level 4: NP vs. CP Verb Frequency per Million by L1	152
5.9	Level 5: NP vs. CP Verb Frequency per Million by L1	153
7.1	Complex NPs per Clause for Each Learner's Sample of Two Texts	211
7.2	Mean Length of Clause for Each Learners' Two Texts From Levels 3–5	211

Tables

2.1	ELI Administrative Structure: Responsibilities of Administrative Faculty	23
2.2	Other Essential Faculty Administrators	25
3.1	Pitt IEP Placement Test Scores – Historical Viewpoint	64
3.2	Pitt IEP Cut Scores (Note Level 6 Added After 2015)	66
3.3	Test Scores by Initial Placement Level	75
3.4	Placement Test Results by L1 Typological Group	75
3.5	K-Means Cluster and Level Means With Michigan EPT vs. Actual Placement (Only EPT)	76
3.6	Correlations Among Scores Used in Placement Assessment	78
3.7	K-Means Cluster and Level Means With EPT Structure and IEP Listening vs. Actual Placement	78
4.1	Coverage of the Most Frequent Words in Various Genres	97
4.2	Lexical Diversity and Lexical Sophistication Scores of IEP Level 4 and 5 Students: Arabic, Chinese, and Korean	103
4.3	Results of Paired *t*-Tests on % Scores of Receptive and Productive Skills	110
5.1	English Inflectional Morphemes	129
5.2	Verbs and Approximate Complement Preferences (NP vs. CP) Based on Kennison (1999) or Google N-Gram if Absent (in Alphabetical Order)	143
5.3	Descriptive Data by L1 and by Level	144
5.4	Frequency Rank of Functional Category Words (FCW) in Top 2000 Most Frequent Words by Language and Level. (COCA Rank in Header). Rank/Frequency per Million. (Lower Rank and Higher Frequency per Million Indicate Increased Use)	144
5.5	Frequency Rank of Verbs Permitting CP (V-CP), but Preferring NP or CP (Kennison, 1999) by Language and Level. Rank/Estimated Frequency per Million. (Lower Rank and Higher Frequency per Million Indicate Increased Use)	145

6.1	Results of the Number of Preserved and Deleted Consonant Codas	172
6.2	Results of the Number of Errors From Preserved Consonant Codas	172
6.3	Basic Statistics: Initial Measure and Subsequent Growth Rates	178
6.4	Reliable Differences Among CAF Measures on Picture Prompt	183
7.1	Lu and Ai (2015) Selected Syntactic Complexity Indices (Averaged Across Proficiency Levels)	202
7.2	Curriculum Objectives and Features, Levels 3–5	205
7.3	Summary of Students in the IEP Contributing Writing With Number of Texts Over 50 Words Long	206
7.4	Quantitative Scores of Learners' Lexical Richness: AG and vocD Scores of All Texts of 50 Words or More	208
7.5	Mean Lexical Richness Scores by L1 for All Writing Texts in PELIC	209
7.6	Level 3 Syntactic Complexity Measures	210
7.7	Level 4 Syntactic Complexity Measures	210
7.8	Level 5 Syntactic Complexity Measures	210
7.9	Topics Chosen by Students	213
7.10	Correlations Among Average Essay Rating and Measures of Syntactic Complexity ($N = 48$ in All Cases)	217
7.11	Impersonal and Personal Texts by Level in the Sample	219

Acknowledgments

The number of people who contributed time and expertise to this project are too numerous to mention all by name, but I would like to thank all the students, teachers, researchers, and programmers in the Intensive English program at Pitt. They made this book possible. Very special thanks are due to Associate Director Dawn E. McCormick and Associate Director Dorolyn Smith for their help and support in the 22 years that I have been Director of the English Language Institute. Dorolyn Smith also cast her expert eye on the manuscript and helped get it ready for publication. Ben Naismith also read and made comments on the manuscript. ELI faculty members Lois Wilson and Christine O'Neill deserve special mention, as they were a large part of the research during the data collection. Greg Mizera assisted in collecting and storing the informed consent forms required by Pitt's Institutional Review Board (IRB0509152: English as a Second Language Base Course). More recently, Na-Rae Han helped to make much of the data useable for analysis in Python through her expert knowledge of computational linguistics and the incredible amounts of time that she has spent with us processing the data. She has patiently guided me in my clunky attempts at learning and using Python. Of course, I take responsibility for all errors that occur in the book.

I would also like to acknowledge the two previous directors of the ELI at the University of Pittsburgh, Professor Edward M. Anthony, Jr., and Professor Christina Bratt Paulston, who established a culture of collaboration and scholarship in the institute. I am only the third director in the 55 years that the IEP at Pitt has been in existence, and I owe a debt to them for making Pitt a center of applied linguistics. They are both much missed.

This research was supported in part by a grant from the Pittsburgh Science of Learning Center (www.learnlab.org) to Alan Juffs. The Pittsburgh Science of Learning Center was funded by the United States National Science Foundation award number SBE-0836012. Previously, it was NSF award number SBE-0354420. I am very grateful to Professor Kenneth Koedinger of Carnegie Mellon University and Professor Charles Perfetti of the University of Pittsburgh for including our IEP in their plans for the Pittsburgh Science of Learning Center.

Preface

This book is the product of collaboration, conversations, observations, and analysis with the help of many colleagues and students over the years I have spent as Director of the English Language Institute and Professor of Linguistics at the University of Pittsburgh.

The work here is presented as 'aspects' of language development in an intensive English program (IEP). This title is meant to indicate that it is absolutely not a complete picture of one program, let alone how other programs should be. Rather, I present a series of 'snapshots' or illustrations of various facets of the administration of the program and the language development of the students.

The book provides the context of the IEP in education for international students in general and specifically at the University of Pittsburgh. Each chapter seeks to provide IEP administrators and teachers with a refresher in the research underpinning language education in IEPs in order to contextualize the data analysis that is provided. Subsequently, selected data of an aspect of the learners' language are analyzed followed by some discussion. A section at the end of each chapter raises issues for administrators and teachers to reflect on in light of the theory and data presented in the chapter.

Chapter 1 provides some national and global context of IEPs, while Chapter 2 offers insights into the organization and curriculum of the IEP at Pitt. The topic of Chapter 3 concerns assessment in the IEP, focusing particularly on the Pitt IEP's experience with the challenge of placement testing. Subsequent chapters illustrate the language development of the students in the areas of lexis (Chapter 4), grammar (Chapter 5), spoken language (Chapter 6), and writing (Chapter 7). In Chapter 8, I reflect briefly on what we have learned and point out other areas that we need to invest time and energy in tracking in the future. To a great extent, the discussion in Chapters 3 through 7 is dependent on the data that we have been able to collect and analyze to date and should by no means be seen as making definitive claims about development in the Pitt IEP.

The book can be seen as a series of case studies of issues that have come up in one IEP. The selected aspects of language development are those evidenced

xvi *Preface*

by the learner data collected during the typical two to three semesters that learners spend in our IEP before they either return to their home countries or go on to academic studies. The analysis concentrates primarily on Arabic-speaking, Chinese-speaking, Korean-speaking, and Japanese-speaking learners. In Pittsburgh, Spanish-speaking learners are rather scarce in the IEP, and there are not enough speakers of other languages to even attempt to look at the first language influence among those students.

The work in this volume attempts to address two audiences at the same time. This goal is a risky undertaking, as it could 'fall between two stools', satisfying neither constituency. On the one hand, the goal is to describe language development in enough detail so that students and researchers in second language acquisition might find it of some value in generating future research questions and topics of inquiry. On the other hand, the style and level of detail should be such that teachers in IEPs will find most sections in each chapter accessible and thought provoking enough to stimulate action research projects. Although most teachers in IEPs have at least a master's degree, many Master's degrees in the Teaching of Speakers to Other Languages (MA TESOL) programs do not focus a great deal on quantitative research and experimental design (Gass, Juffs, Starfield, & Hyland, 2018), and so very sophisticated quantitative analysis will not always be immediately accessible. Where the chapter gets too detailed in terms of statistics and analysis, the reader is invited to skip to the main points that the chapter is trying to make.

The data and analysis that are presented may be unique in several respects. One advantage of the data is that it was collected 'in the wild'. This means that much of the data are not the result of an experimental intervention (although some are) but rather an account of what the students were doing in the IEP as part of their routine studies; data have been collected over many years (2003–2016), in part as a component of a project funded by the United States National Science Foundation. The second advantage is that the data are in many cases longitudinal. Such documentation of longitudinal language development is rare (Ortega, 2011) and constitutes a major gap in the literature both from a second language acquisition and a pedagogical perspective.

Of course, the background scholarship on L2 development is of high quality and very extensive. What is different in this book is the focus on the setting of an IEP (rather than students matriculated in an academic degree program) and the concentration on data from the students who are tracked over multiple semesters. Thus, the volume does not include a review of the work that the English Language Institute does for students who are already in degree programs at the University of Pittsburgh.

Most analysis is based on production data collected from students' assignments in the day-to-day course of their studies and are therefore less controlled than rigorous quasi-experimental interventions. However, some chapters do draw on published experimental data (e.g., de Jong & Perfetti, 2011), corpus data (Vercellotti, 2017), and unpublished thesis

Preface xvii

data (e.g., Schepps, 2014), but all of these data were collected from students in the Pitt IEP.

Therefore, the focus is on a group of learners who are perhaps less well studied than non-native English-speaking students enrolled in degree programs. (Although see the work of Bardovi-Harlig (2000) and many of her other articles for examples of data from learners in an IEP.) However, in my literature searches, I have found very few studies – even in journals – that *explicitly* address longitudinal development by adult students in *intensive English programs*. For very good reasons of experimental design, second language acquisition studies tend to focus intensely on one or two structures and are less able to cover larger numbers of the same students' production data from a variety of sources over time (written exam data being an exception, e.g., Murakami & Alexopoulou, 2016). In these data, we are able to cover a wide variety of structures and discourse abilities in speaking and writing over periods of 8–12 months.

It is hoped that second language acquisition researchers might be interested in the more detailed analyses of the data, but they are not the principal target audience. Instead, members of organizations such as International TESOL and its local affiliates, UCIEP (www.uciep.org), and EnglishUSA (www.EnglishUSA.org) might find the reports of learner development to be of some value. In addition, the book could be relevant to teachers and administrators in intensive English programs across the world, for example, in the United Kingdom, Australia, New Zealand, Canada, the Middle East, Latin America, and Asia.

The detailed overview of an IEP would be relevant to a variety of graduate and undergraduate TESOL programs, including teacher preparation courses in higher education such as M.Ed. TESOL, and program administration, as well as teaching and learning courses.

References

Bardovi-Harlig, K. (2000). *Tense and aspect in second language acquisition: Form, meaning, and use.* Oxford: Blackwell.

de Jong, N., & Perfetti, C. (2011). Fluency training in the ESL classroom: An experimental study of fluency development and proceduralization. *Language Learning, 61*(2), 533–568.

Gass, S. M., Juffs, A., Starfield, S., & Hyland, K. L. (2018). Conducting research at language centers: Perspectives from the field. *TESOL Quarterly, 54*(2), 1108–1119. doi:10.1002/tesq.484

Juffs, A. (1996). *Learnability and the lexicon: Theories and second language acquisition research.* Philadelphia, PA: John Benjamins.

Juffs, A., & Rodríguez, G. A. (2014). *Second language sentence processing.* New York: Routledge.

Murakami, A., & Alexopoulou, T. (2016). L1 influence on the acquisition order of English grammatical morphemes. *Studies in Second Language Acquisition, 38*(3), 365–401. doi: 10.1017/S0272263115000352

Ortega, L. (2011). *Second language acquisition.* New York: Routledge.

xviii *Preface*

Schepps, H. (2014). *The emergence of complexity, accuracy, and fluency as dynamic systems in the spoken output of Arabic and Chinese learners of English* (MA thesis), ETD University of Pittsburgh, Pittsburgh.

Vercellotti, M. L. (2017). The development of complexity, accuracy and fluency in second language performance. *Applied Linguistics, 38*(1), 90–111.

1 Intensive English Programs and Second Language Teaching Research

1.1 Intensive English Language Programs: Early Beginnings and Professionalization

Intensive English programs have officially existed for over 70 years in the United States to serve the needs of learners who wish to study various subjects through the medium of English at universities and colleges. It is generally accepted that the first program was established in 1941 at the University of Michigan in Ann Arbor (https://lsa.umich.edu/eli/about-us.html).[1] Its founder, the linguist Charles Carpenter Fries (1887–1967) (Anthony, 1968), sought to combine teaching English as a second language (ESL), materials writing, and research on ESL learning as part of his broader work as a linguist (Anthony, 1968). According to some accounts, Fries can also be considered one of the originators of modern construction grammar, but his ideas were eclipsed by the paradigm shift in linguistics triggered by Chomsky's generative approach to grammar (Zwicky, 2006, languagelog/archives/003743.html). This background history is important because it underpins one of the goals of this book, which is to show that knowledge of theories of language and descriptive linguistics is a vital component of understanding instructed language development. Such understanding is the basis for creating materials to make development more efficient in instructed contexts (Juffs, 2017).

After the founding of the English Language Institute (ELI) at the University of Michigan, other institutes quickly followed in the 1950s and 1960s. In 1964, one of Fries' students, Edward Mason Anthony, Jr., was recruited from Michigan to the University of Pittsburgh. He founded the ELI as part of a program of internationalization at the university (www.utimes.pitt.edu/?p=36498). The Department of Linguistics was founded concurrently, in part as a way to train teachers for the institute. Hence, Fries' influence extended from English language teaching to teacher training and linguistics itself.

From these early beginnings, IEPs have increased in importance and in their professional standing as the field of teaching English to speakers of other languages (TESOL) has evolved into a mature profession. In

2 *IEPs and Second Language Teaching Research*

1967, at a conference for international student advisors, administrators and teachers (NAFSA), a group of individuals from 13 intensive English programs, including the one at the University of Pittsburgh, realized that they had many issues in common, and so the association College Intensive English Program (CIEP) was founded, later to become University and College Intensive English Programs (UCIEP) (www.uciep.org/). Subsequently, other organizations were created that included private language schools. The most well known of these organizations is now called EnglishUSA (www.englishusa.org) but was founded as the American Association of Intensive English Programs. Many IEPs belong to both organizations. In 2019, there are well over 400 intensive English programs in the United States.

The field of English as a second language is now an established profession, with international professional organizations for teaching practice and research (www.tesol.org; www.aaal.org). One of the most recent developments in the professionalization of the field was the establishment of program standards for accreditation and an organization to monitor the adherence to these standards. The Commission on English Language Program Accreditation (CEA) (www.cea-accredit.org) is one organization that is recognized by the US Department of Education as an approved accrediting body for US IEPs, as well as IEPs overseas, including in Greece, Peru, Qatar, Turkey, Kuwait, and Saudi Arabia. As immigration policy and border control in the United States have increased in importance, accreditation has become required for all intensive programs in the United States (www.ice.gov/sevis/accreditation-act). The enactment of this legislation was in part the result of advocacy by UCIEP, EnglishUSA, and TESOL.

1.2 The Spread of English as a World Lingua Franca and Economic Impact

As the second half of the twentieth century unfolded, and as the United States succeeded the United Kingdom as the English-speaking military and economic global power, the teaching and learning of English as a second language developed into a true industry itself. One key reason for this development is that technological and economic success continued to be linked to knowledge of English. Proficiency in English remained the gateway to acquiring expertise in science and technology in higher education and consequently to both personal and national economic advancement.

In the aftermath of World War II, the United States was the leader in science, technology, and industrial capacity. As other countries rebuilt from the devastation of the war, globalization began with the economic dominance of the United States and its leading research universities and industries, in addition to higher education in English-speaking democracies that include the United Kingdom, Ireland, Canada, Australia, and New Zealand. Access to education and professional training provides economic benefits to students, but these benefits could only be accessed through English-medium education. Thus, the range and influence of English as a lingua franca has continued to expand (Graddol, 1997; Melitz, 2016). For example, it was estimated in 1997 that over 750 million people world-wide are learning English as a foreign language, which was nearly twice the number of 'native' speakers of English (Graddol, 1997, p. 10).[2] For this reason, as a gateway to the benefits of higher education, learning English is a core component to the programs of many universities that seek to recruit students.

However, it is not only international students who benefit from university education overseas; the institutions where they study also benefit. For institutions in English-speaking countries, the motivation to recruit international students is both economic and cultural. One primary reason is that universities around the world increasingly need the funds that international students bring in the form of tuition dollars and services paid for; in addition, international students provide cultural diversity on campus that enriches the educational experience of the locally resident students. Because of these long-term benefits, universities provide English language training both before and during degree programs to help students succeed as well as to attract highly qualified students whose English might otherwise not be quite proficient enough for university coursework.

An added benefit is that the economic life of the towns and cities around campus benefit greatly from this educational activity. For example, the money spent on housing, food, and services had a total impact on the US economy estimated to be worth over $42 billion in 2017 (www. iie.org/Research-and-Insights/Open-Doors/Data/Economic-Impact-of-International-Students). After graduation, international students add to the talent pool in the workforce. These factors make local and national governments view international students favorably.

This context, then, is the one in which the research in this book is situated: economic goals of international students lead them to learn English to access higher education; higher education institutions need their dollars to support their academic and cultural diversity goals in an increasingly globalized economy. All of this activity is occurring in a wider context of globalization – a trend that brings both benefits and challenges.

The role of an intensive English program is to provide a bridge for students to cross from their educational system into the world of English-medium education. Acting as a bridge – a *means* rather than an *end goal* – can be a challenge for teachers and administrators in IEPs (dePetro Orlando, 2016; Hoekje & Stevens, 2017). For some students, the IEP and standardized tests, such as the Internet-Based Test of English as a Foreign

4 *IEPs and Second Language Teaching Research*

Language (TOEFL) (iBT) and the International English Language Testing System (IELTS), constitute barriers instead of a pathway to success in coursework. The IEP can be perceived as a block to students' access to their ultimate goals of enrollment in a degree program and successful completion of that program. From the point of view of the university, the IEP can be seen as a unit that is not part of their central mission of delivering degree programs and research output funded by government and industry (Algren, 2016). Often, English language learning and teaching are seen as simply a 'support' enterprise, such as a computer support or some other 'ancillary' unit. As a result, the domain expertise that applied linguists bring to the IEP can sometimes be ignored or discounted by academic units that are ignorant about the knowledge base ESL professionals have of linguistics, language development patterns, and instructional methodology.

The hope is that this book can serve as a source of reference and documentation of how learners can improve their English in IEPs. Examples of student output are intended to allow administrators and teachers to compare what is happening in their programs with the data in this book and online at https://github.com/ELI-Data-Mining-Group/Pitt-ELI-Corpus. The more data administrators of programs can present to sponsors and learners regarding the effectiveness of their programs, the better equipped they will be to convince students and higher administrators of the importance of the education that IEPs provide and of the scientific basis of our discipline.

1.3 The Economic and Political Context of the Intensive English Program

Pennington and Hoekje (2010)'s Chapter 1 provides an excellent overview of the economic and political landscape in which IEPs operate. Although their book was written nine years ago, most of their observations remain relevant today. The international political economy of the world changes constantly, and these changes have direct impacts on IEPs. The election of Donald Trump as US president in 2016 and the tide against globalization as represented by the UK voting to leave the European Union (BREXIT) makes predicting future developments even more challenging than during usual economic cycles around the world. Because their overview of the context of intensive English programs is an important background, it is worth summarizing their main points here.

First, international students make up a significant proportion of all students in higher education in the US and other English-speaking countries. Thus, an important fact is that many English-speaking universities depend on international students for a substantial part of their tuition revenue. Some numbers that were relevant in 2010 have not changed a great deal. In Australia, from 20% in 2006, now 23% of students in higher education are international students (https://docs.education.gov. au/node/39321). The United Kingdom reported 436,585 international students in 2014–2015 (http://institutions.ukcisa.org.uk/). In the United States, data from Open Doors (www.iie.org/Research-and-Insights/Open-Doors/Data/International-Students/Enrollment) in late 2017 showed that the number of international students increased by 1.5% to 1,094,793 students, making up 5.5% of all students in the United States. This is an increase of 2% of total students since 2008, the top five countries being China (33.2%), India (17.9%), Saudi Arabia (4.1%), South Korea (5.0%), and Canada (2.4%). While most countries have increased the numbers that they send to the United States, economic and political turmoil in countries sending students abroad can create large fluctuations. For example, the number of students from Brazil decreased 18.2% from 23,675 in 2015 to 19,370 in 2016, and students from Saudi Arabia decreased by 15.5% from 52,611 in 2016/2017 to 44,432 in 2017/2018. Changes in Saudi scholarship policy have had a particularly severe effect on US IEP enrollments.

As Pennington and Hoekje (2010) pointed out, the web of international exchanges is increasingly complex and connected. It is no longer a one-way street to English-speaking countries. Students learning Chinese as a second language, for example, are increasing as China promotes its language and culture through the Confucius Institutes (http://english.hanban.org/). In addition, of the almost half-million students in the United Kingdom, over 16,000 were from the United States and presumably speakers of some variety of English. Moreover, a recent development is that many UK and US universities now have established 'international' campuses, especially in China, because of population and demand. For example, Duke University (https://dukekunshan.edu.cn), New York University (https://shanghai.nyu.edu), and the University of Pittsburgh (http://scupi.scu.edu.cn/en/) all have campuses and/or programs in China with different levels of collaboration. The United Kingdom has also established international presence in China; for example, the University of Nottingham (www.nottingham.edu.cn/en/index.aspx) is in Ningbo and the University of Liverpool in Xi'An in cooperation with Xi'An Jiaotong University (www.liverpool.ac.uk/xjtlu/).

This growth in English-medium education in countries where English is a *foreign* language is not limited to degree courses. Although the British Council has long been involved in English language teaching around the world, IEPs are increasingly being set up by institutions to support English-medium education in their own countries. An early example in Japan in the 1980s was at the International University of Japan (www.iuj.ac.jp/), where students from many countries continue to study international relations and business through the medium of English. The increase in CEA-accredited IEPs outside the United States indicates that countries in the Middle East are now trying to raise the level of ESL

6 *IEPs and Second Language Teaching Research*

in their students before they depart overseas for specialized degree programs. It is also noteworthy that Malaysia, a former British colony that reduced the importance of English, has now reemphasized the importance of English (e.g., Gill, 2006), demonstrating the *economic* power of knowing English. These developments mean that English as a medium of instruction is important not only in the English-speaking countries but also internationally.

In addition to the global historical background and economic developments noted by Graddol (1997) and others, Pennington and Hoekje (2010) draw attention to increased *electronic* connectivity that has arisen: the world wide web and the advent of smartphones enable students to connect with each other and with institutions very rapidly and from almost any location in the world. Technology developers have used these developments to create language learning programs (Duolingo.com) that are available wherever the learners may be on their smartphones. Some of these online, web-based companies are trying to break into the ESL market for testing (https://englishtest.duolingo.com/) and online education through partnerships with media companies (e.g., https://onlineenglish.pearson.com).

As we have seen, the teaching and learning of English as a second and foreign language is a multi-billion-dollar industry in the United States alone. The Open Doors website's figure of $39.4 billion applies only to the United States, so of course globally, the impact must be even higher. While the sale of textbooks by major publishers and private language schools has always been part of international language teaching commerce, learners are increasingly seen as 'customers' to be vied for as education moves to more and more of a business footing. The internet-based companies just mentioned are one aspect of this trend.

Another recent development is the outsourcing of English as a second language instruction by US and British universities to companies whose core business may not be education. Such decisions by higher level university administrators reflect their lack of understanding of the academic basis of language instruction; that is, they wrongly treat language teaching as a *service* rather than an academic endeavor with a scientific basis that belongs under the umbrella of the university rather than a private company. One example is a provider called INTO (www.intostudy.com/en-gb/) that bundles the search for degree programs via agents and their own website with immigration, accommodation, and 'pathway' programs in the United States, the United Kingdom, and China. Such outsourcing proved very attractive to some institutions in the United States after the crash of 2008, when funding for public universities from US state governments collapsed due to declines in tax revenue. This opportunity for outside vendors arose in part because state governments, required to cut budgets, viewed a large influx of international students as a solution to funding shortfalls. International students pay higher tuition than domestic students and come from wealthy families who neither need nor qualify for financial aid. In some cases, these students prefer studying overseas to attending institutions in their home countries. While such 'for-profit' outsourcing is of concern to some educators (www.tesol.org/docs/pdf/13029.pdf?sfvrsn=2), they seem to have established a firm foothold in the United States, as INTO now has eight US universities in its system.

This context of the monetary value of students means that IEP educators need to be even more aware of the quality of education that we provide and be able to demonstrate to students the benefit that they receive for the investment that they and their families make to their education. Second language teaching is often called a caring profession because teachers are mediators of language and culture (Watson-Gegeo, 1988), and part of that caring is that we know how best to provide instruction that will help students meet their life goals and not put the bottom line of a for-profit company as a priority. To achieve this goal of helping our students, we need to have an increasingly clear idea of exactly what and how our students learn during their time in the intensive English program.

1.4 Wider Context in Research and Second Language Teaching

Human beings, and with them their languages and cultures, have been coming into contact with each other for as long as recorded history, and so, presumably, have issues of language learning. Languages of wider communication – lingua francas – have been documented at least since the Achaemenid Empire (550–330 BCE), where Imperial Aramaic (a Semitic language) was used in an empire dominated by the Persian-speaking ruling class (https://en.wikipedia.org/wiki/Achaemenid_Empire#Languages). English is thus merely the most recent in the history of changing languages of wider communication. The difference is that how to teach modern languages to speakers of other languages is now the focus of significant academic study in its own right.

The modern discipline of second language studies itself now consists of many subfields. Some of these subfields are more theoretically related to representation and cognitive science; some are more applied in terms of how instruction can be delivered in real time either in classrooms or increasingly via computer-assisted instruction. Other research looks into the social underpinnings of language teaching in a wider social context. The body of research of relevance to second language acquisition (SLA) spans time and space from uninstructed language learning via language contact (Thomason & Kaufman, 1988) to attrition in heritage speakers (e.g., Montrul, 2008; Nagy, 2018) to the cultural, political, and economic forces that drive language maintenance and shift and language policy

8 IEPs and Second Language Teaching Research

(Paulston, 1994, 1997; Paulston et al., 2007). Instruction and learning in IEPs fits into this wider context of research on second language acquisition and teaching that is by now well documented but can be considered divided into two main areas, which are theory and application.

1.4.1 Second Language Acquisition as Theoretical Research

Instruction in IEPs relies on a solid foundation of research in second language learning and teaching, which is itself founded on linguistic theory. Indeed, the relationship between language learning and linguistic theory has a long history (Lightbown & White, 1987). At times, this relationship has been very close, as during the early period of audiolingualism (Bloomfield, 1942; Castagnaro, 2006). At other times, the study of second language acquisition and classroom instruction have drifted apart because abstract theoretical concerns were seen as less relevant to classroom practice and the development of knowledge of academic literacy that students need to succeed in their programs.

Thus, some researchers hold the view that SLA can be *purely theoretical*, without any classroom applications as a goal of the research in mind (Juffs, 2017; White, 1990). Indeed, it is important to understand what the cognitive (mental) state of knowing another language is and how that state comes into being like any other natural phenomenon. It is clear that theoretical second language acquisition has now emerged as an independent discipline outside the practical concerns of foreign and second language classroom teaching. In fact, since the late 1960s (Corder, 1967), the study of second language development has become an important part of linguistics and psychology and not necessarily *directly* related to classroom language instruction at all. The precise extent to which SLA can be considered an independent discipline remains a complex issue in the field (Long, 2007), but many researchers would argue that second language acquisition must in fact be studied as discipline that is independent of education, albeit part of the wider field of cognitive science. This position does not mean that the results of pure SLA research are not useful or in fact vital in improving educational practice. Indeed, this book will consider the implications of SLA research in classroom contexts, but a direct application of research findings is not always obvious or desirable even if the research is classroom based. This caution is especially needed if results are based only on a single study (Plonsky & Oswald, 2014). In this book, the focus will be on the specific context of language development in intensive English programs as evidenced by corpus data and experimental data in one specific IEP and how observed developmental patterns *could be* informed by a wide range of theoretical approaches, which I discuss briefly in the following paragraph. The point is that research in applied linguistics can and should be relevant to language centers and IEPs (Gass, Juffs, Starfield & Hyland, 2018).

It is important to emphasize that this book concerns *aspects* of language development, and in no sense is it intended to be comprehensive. The focus will be mainly on lexical development, the development of morphosyntactic accuracy, writing for academic purposes, and to some extent fluency. We will not address in detail reading comprehension of extended texts, even though this is a very important skill for students to master.

The current approaches to second language acquisition that this book will draw on reflect the developments in the fields of linguistics, psychology, anthropology, and education. These perspectives vary quite widely, as the summary articles in different handbooks of SLA demonstrate (e.g., Hinkel, 2005; Doughty & Long, 2003; Ritchie & Bhatia, 2009). The first approach to research is that carried out in the tradition of formal linguistics. This approach seeks to understand how abstract knowledge constrains the hypothesis space in acquisition and processing (White, 2003), but it also provides a detailed theory to describe learner development. In contrast, approaches that are grounded in connectionist psychology put much more emphasis on input and frequency than abstract structures (e.g., Robinson & Ellis, 2008). Sociocultural theory focuses on understanding how learners interact and co-construct knowledge and may be more directly relevant to how learners actually behave in classrooms and with technology that we introduce (e.g., Lantolf & Thorne, 2006; Juffs & Friedline, 2014).

The IEP that is the subject of this volume provides focused instruction, not only on linguistic forms but also literacy in the broadest sense in terms of reading skills (bottom-up and top-down) and written output that would be appropriate in an academic context in US higher education. SLA research has not always considered 'literacy' part of its core focus because the subfield of English for academic purposes (EAP) has occupied that niche to some extent. It is worth re-emphasizing Larsen-Freeman & Long's (1991, pp. 169–170) call for more nuanced approaches to SLA. Researchers and teachers need to bear in mind the concerns of basic interpersonal communication skills (BICS) and cognitive and academic language skills (CALP) proposed by Cummins (1979, 2003). Such differences must be taken seriously when preparing students for academic work and following their progress toward those goals. In other words, some (but certainly not all) differences of opinion in SLA stem from researchers trying to account for language acquisition at the level of basic sentence structure and pronunciation versus high-level skills in academic settings. However, as recent discussion in the literature has shown (c.f., De Bot, Lowie & Verspoor, 2007; Ionin, 2007), scholars are engaging more with each other and clearly delineating areas where each can excel (see also Shirai & Juffs, 2017).

10 *IEPs and Second Language Teaching Research*

1.4.2 *Second Language Acquisition and Language Teaching Research*

Naturally, the divisions of labor that have been created between 'theoretical' SLA, with its different theoretical paradigms, and classroom-based research sometimes result in a view of language, proficiency, and identity that is 'reified' (e.g., Brumfit, 1997). 'Reification' means that definitions are created and *artificial boundaries* set up between users of language, formal descriptions of language systems, language researchers, and educators. Consequently, competition among approaches is promoted that is not helpful in establishing evidence for learning that directly assists teachers as they help learners to achieve their goals. Thus, in this book, I draw on multiple perspectives, reflecting what has become one guiding principle in the University of Pittsburgh's ELI, which is 'principled eclecticism' (Larsen-Freeman, 2000). This means that we take the best insights from theories of grammar, pedagogical grammar, corpus research, classroom-based research, sociocultural theory, curriculum design, and methodology and apply them to what we perceive our learners' needs to be in the best way we are able.

1.4.3 *The Role of Instruction in Language Development*

It seems odd to address this issue in a volume that is about IEPs, where teaching is paramount, but the influence of some researchers who claim that explicit instruction is of reduced value persists. In brief, some confusion remains regarding such topics as the 'natural approach' propounded by Krashen (1987), who has denied a direct link between instruction and what he called 'acquisition' in contrast to 'learning'. I assume here that by 'acquisition' Krashen meant the acquisition of the abstract structures of language that formal linguists assume is the basis of knowledge of language and vocabulary learning. This issue remains one of debate among applied linguists. However, the approach taken in the Pitt IEP is that instruction is vital in speeding learners through developmental stages and avoiding 'fossilization' or reaching a plateau in learning (Larsen-Freeman & Long, 1991, pp. 321–322). However, aspects of language use other than abstract knowledge, such as the appropriate way to construct an academic research paper, must be taught through explicit example and instruction. Thus, this knowledge is clearly amenable to manipulation through instruction, as indicated in the following paragraphs.

The logical next question is what kind of instruction is most appropriate. As communicative language teaching evolved and was added to the drills of audiolingualism (Paulston, 1974, pp. 352–353), the influence of Krashen's monitor model (Krashen, 1987), and subsequent research on interaction (e.g., Mackey [2008]), it is clear that syllabi devoted to instruction on a progression through a list of forms alone is untenable in *basic* language instruction (Larsen-Freeman & Long, 1991, p. 322). We will address communicative language teaching and its relation to form-based instruction in more detail in Chapter 2. However, recent meta-analyses seem to suggest that no matter the form and regardless of the difficulty level of the structure, explicit instruction that is form-focused in communicative settings is superior to implicit instruction (Spada & Tomita, 2010). This finding relates pronunciation, morphology, and syntax.

In contrast to debates regarding grammar instruction, especially for beginning to intermediate language learners, instruction regarding cultural norms and conventions in academic writing has never been questioned (to my knowledge). Such skills will of necessity be explicitly instructed and practiced in classrooms. There is no reason to assume that structured progression of this type of content should not be organized and formal, building on skills one at a time. Thus, an approach to second language instruction and learning must be nuanced as regards language and content in ways that 'basic language' instruction might not be. This feature of the Pitt IEP program and how learners make progress will be taken up specifically in the chapter on writing, and we will consider how instruction affects the development of these skills.

1.5 Goals and Role of Intensive English Programs in the Wider Context of English for Academic Purposes and English for Specific Purposes

One important practical contribution of applied linguists over the past 50 years has been the establishment of the subdisciplines of English for academic purposes and English for specific purposes (ESP). EAP refers to the general preparation of students for participation in university or advanced programs of study. It would be impossible to discuss all of these authors' contributions here, but linguists such as Widdowson have for a long time written both scholarly articles on academic English and edited EAP textbook series (e.g., Widdowson's [1979] series *Reading and Thinking in English*, published by OUP). These textbooks applied research in written academic discourse to ESL textbooks in order to help learners participate in the academic culture(s) that they aspired to join. More recently, several researchers have contributed to the specific lexical items required in EAP (e.g., Coxhead, 2000; Gardner & Davies, 2014) and other academic and vocational contexts; handbooks of research in the area have also appeared (Stoller, 2016).

For more specific contexts, Swales (e.g., Swales, 1990; Swales & Feak, 1994) has been a major contributor in the area of ESP, which focuses on language required in special fields such as engineering, science, and technology – the so-called 'STEM' fields. Corpus linguists such as Biber (Biber, Conrad, & Cortes, 2004; Pan, Reppen, & Biber, 2016) and Hyland (e.g., Hyland, 2008, 2012) have concentrated on the language used in

12 IEPs and Second Language Teaching Research

specific scientific contexts, developing not only lists of lexical items but also set phrases that are useful for learners entering different fields of study.

Both of these fields now have academic journals devoted to improving our understanding of the needs and development trajectories of learners in these domains: in EAP (www.journals.elsevier.com/journal-of-english-for-academic-purposes) and in ESP (www.journals.elsevier.com/english-for-specific-purposes/). These professional resources form the basis for the goals of IEPs in addition to those provided by more general professional associations such as Teaching English to Speakers of Other Languages (www.tesol.org/).

All of this very important research forms the background to the kinds of English genres that students in an IEP need to be made familiar with. Thus, the task of many IEPs is to bring students from a low intermediate level of English to a very high level of literacy in a relatively short time. Some students are constrained by their own finances or restricted by their government's support of their language learning prior to beginning degree courses.

However, not all students desire to study in an English-medium degree course. Many students want to spend time in an English-speaking environment, study some English for personal or professional purposes, and then return to their home countries, enriched by their study abroad, in order to continue their lives. These students are often in the same classes as students who desire to enroll in degree programs, and IEPs also have to be sensitive to their needs.

1.6 The Research in This Book: Mixed Methods and in the Spirit of 'Design-Based' Research

As Gass et al. (2018) point out, research related to language development can take many forms: psycholinguistic experiments in the laboratory, corpus analysis, teacher-initiated action. The studies in this book includes all three of these approaches. In addition, it is in the spirit of 'design-based' research, which is discussed by Cumming (2015). Citing Anderson and Shattuck (2012), Cumming notes the following six characteristics of design-based research, which are worth listing in full:

1. Real educational contexts
2. Design and testing of significant intervention
3. Mixed research methods (quantitative and qualitative)
4. Multiple iterations
5. Collaborative partnerships
6. Practical impact on practice

The IEP is a real educational context in which design and intervention take place. In some cases, as with the fluency training discussed in

Chapter 5, interventions were designed. The methods used to analyze the data are both quantitative and qualitative (quantitative syntactic complexity and lexical sophistication metrics are used, but so are interviews with students and opinions about the effectiveness of student writing). There are multiple iterations in that many of the students provided data over several semesters or various aspects of a reading tutor were investigated. The data were collected in a collaborative partnership with researchers, teachers, graduate students, and the ESL students themselves. Finally, the research has led the IEP teachers to changes in their practice, as will be discussed in Chapter 8.

1.7 Summary

IEPs face challenges in a global context that is changing rapidly in terms of international political economy. The dominance of the United States in higher education is less overwhelming than before as other countries develop their own scientific and research infrastructure. Competition among world powers has made the world a less predictable place, and this can directly impact IEPs.

In addition, research in second language learning and teaching is evolving, but probably has stabilized around communicative learning supported by technology and increasing understanding of the tasks that IEP learners will face in their studies and daily lives. Thus, this book seeks to provide a volume of snapshots on various aspects of development in an IEP that is intended to provoke reflection on the part of administrators, curriculum supervisors, and teachers.

Each chapter begins with some review of relevant literature in the field on the topic of the chapter in order to provide some background for the questions being asked about the development of students in the program. These sections are designed for teachers to review recent research and to provide a schema to read about the type of research from the data in the IEP. Each chapter also contains a section that is designed as a framework or guide for administrators and teachers to consider the research background and findings presented in the chapter.

1.8 Topics for Administrators and Teachers to Reflect On

1.8.1 Questions and Issues Mainly for Program Administrators and Curriculum Supervisors

1. How do you keep up with international political developments that may affect your IEP?
2. Consult www.iie.org/opendoors for your region or state if you are in the United States: www.iie.org/en/Research-and-Insights/Open-Doors/Fact-Sheets-and-Infographics/Data-by-State-Fact-Sheets.

14   *IEPs and Second Language Teaching Research*

3. Download the .pdf for your state and fill out these questions:

    a. Total number of international students in the state: _____
    b. The dollar amount of international student expenditure in the state: $ _____
    c. The top three countries of origin of international students
    d. The number of American students studying abroad: _____ (remember it's not a one-way street)

4. What unit is your IEP housed in? Possibilities are:

    a. Academic department
    b. Provost area
    c. Continuing education
    d. Other

5. How does the reporting structure/administrative unit affect your operation as an IEP?
6. Is your IEP accredited by an accrediting agency such as CEA? If not, how is the IEP accredited?
7. What is the marketing plan for the IEP? What are the internal markets (if you're a college- or university-based IEP), and what are the external markets?
8. Is the IEP a member of UCIEP or EnglishUSA? How does the administration of the IEP benefit from and/or contribute to the membership of these organizations?
9. Does the IEP have a written policy for its approach to second language learning and teaching? What research background does the policy refer to in order to justify its approach?

1.8.2 *Questions and Issues for Classroom Teachers*

1. Do you know if your IEP has a set of 'best practices'? If so, what steps do you take to make sure you're up to date with them and their basis in research?
2. What kinds of professional development activities do you engage in to keep up to date with developments in the field? Possibilities are:

    a. Attending or presenting at International TESOL conferences
    b. Attending or presenting at local TESOL affiliate workshops
    c. Reading articles and/or books
    d. Listening to/participating in webinars
    e. Other
    f. How many of the above have you done this year?

3. In the survey of IEP teachers reported in Gass et al. (2018, p. 1111), teachers reported a variety of responses to engaging in research

that included both personal and programmatic advantages, for example:

a. 'Helped improve my own teaching'
b. 'Feeling of accomplishment'
c. 'See disconnect between student needs and curriculum'
d. 'Helped my department understand student learning and possible ways of accelerating learning'

For you and your colleagues, reflect on how research helps both in your personal professional growth and in your program development. Can you list any specific examples in these two categories?

Notes

1. It is certain that programs for teaching English for academic purposes existed even before this time. For example, English medium universities existed in China as early as the late nineteenth century (https://en.wikipedia.org/wiki/St._John's_University,_Shanghai). My Chinese teacher and English teaching colleague in Hunan Province in the early 1980s, Zhang Zijing [张梓敬], was a graduate of St. John's and a fluent English speaker. The famous architect I.M. Pei was an alum also. In addition, the Yale Mission in China established a medical school in Changsha, Hunan Province, in the early twentieth century. The legacy of their English medium education extended into the 1980s at Hunan Medical College, where the older teachers and professors still taught classes for medical students in fluent English (White & Juffs, 1998).
2. The term 'native' speaker has become problematic for many reasons (e.g., Graddol, 2003; Kumaravadivelu, 2016; Rampton, 1990). The term remains in use as a short-hand for a speaker of the very highest level of proficiency, but henceforward I will use Rampton's (1990) term: 'expert speaker'.

References

Algren, M. (2016). How intensive English programs contribute to campus internationalization. *Evolution.com*. Retrieved from http://evolllution.com/revenue-streams/global_learning/how-intensive-english-program-contribute-to-campus-internationalization/

Anderson, T., & Shattuck, J. (2012). Design-based research: A decade of progress in education research? *Educational Researcher, 41*(1), 16–25.

Anthony, E. M. (1968). Charles Carpenter Fries. *English Language Teaching Journal, 23*, 3–4. doi:10.1093/elt/XXIII.1.3

Biber, D., Conrad, S., & Cortes, V. (2004). If you look at. . .: Lexical bundles in university teaching and textbooks. *Applied Linguistics, 25*(3), 371–405. Retrieved from https://doi-org.pitt.idm.oclc.org/10.1093/applin/25.3.371

Bloomfield, L. (1942). *Outline guide for the practical study of foreign languages.* Baltimore, MD: Linguistic Society of America, Waverly Press.

Brumfit, C. (1997). How applied linguistics is the same as any other science. *International Journal of Applied Linguistics, 7*(1), 86–94. doi:10.1111/j.1473-4192.1997.tb00107.x

16 IEPs and Second Language Teaching Research

Castagnaro, P. J. (2006). Audiolingual method and behaviorism: From misunderstanding to myth. *Applied Linguistics, 27*(3), 519–526. doi:10.1093/applin/aml023

Corder, S. P. (1967). The significance of learners' errors. *International Review of Applied Linguistics, 5*, 161–169.

Coxhead, A. (2000). A new academic word list. *TESOL Quarterly, 34*, 213–238.

Cumming, A. (2015). Design in four diagnostic assessments. *Language Testing, 32*(3), 407–416. doi:10.1177/0265532214559115

Cummins, J. (1979/2003). BICS and CALP: Origins and rationale for the distinction. In C. B. Paulston & G. R. Tucker (Eds.), *Sociolinguistics: The essential readings* (pp. 322–328). New York: Wiley.

De Bot, K., Lowie, W., & Verspoor, M. (2007). A dynamic view as a complementary perspective. *Bilingualism: Language and Cognition, 10*(1), 51–55.

dePetro Orlando, R. (2016). *Perspectives on US university intensive English programs*. New York: TESOL International Association.

Doughty, C., & Long, M. (Eds.). (2003). *Handbook of second language acquisition*. Malden, MA: Blackwell.

Gardner, D., & Davies, M. (2014). A new academic word list. *Applied Linguistics, 35*(3), 305–327. doi:10.1093/applin/amt015

Gass, S. M., Juffs, A., Starfield, S., & Hyland, K. L. (2018). Conducting research at language centers: Perspectives from the field. *TESOL Quarterly, 54*(2), 1108–1119. doi:10.1002/tesq.484

Gill, S. K. (2006). Change in language policy in Malaysia: The reality of implementation in public universities. *Current Issues in Language Planning, 7*(1), 82–94.

Graddol, D. (1997). *The future of English? A guide to forecasting the popularity of English in the 21st century*. London: The British Council.

Graddol, D. (2003). The decline of the native speaker. In G. Anderman & M. Rogers (Eds.), *Translation today: Trends and perspectives* (pp. 152–167). Clevedon: Multilingual Matters.

Hinkel, E. (Ed.). (2005). *Handbook of research in second language teaching and learning*. Mahwah, NJ: Erlbaum.

Hoekje, B. J., & Stevens, S. G. (2017). *Creating a culturally inclusive campus: A guide to supporting international students*. New York: Routledge.

Hyland, K. (2008). As can be seen: Lexical bundles and disciplinary variation. *English for Specific Purposes, 27*, 4–21. doi:10.1016/j.esp.2007.06.001

Hyland, K. (2012). Bundles in academic discourse. *Annual Review of Applied Linguistics, 32*, 150–169.

Ionin, T. (2007). DST vs. UG: Can DST account for purely linguistic phenomena? *Bilingualism: Language and Cognition, 10*(1), 27–29.

Juffs, A. (2017). Moving generative SLA from knowledge of constraints to production data in educational settings. *Second Language. Journal of the Japanese Second Language Association, 16*, 19–38. Retrieved from https://doi.org/10.11431/secondlanguage.16.0_19

Juffs, A., & Friedline, B. E. (2014). Sociocultural influences on the use of a web-based tool for learning English vocabulary. *System, 42*(2), 137–166. Retrieved from http://dx.doi.org/10.1016/j.system.2013.10.015

Krashen, S. D. (1987). *Principles and practice in second language acquisition* (Chapter 4: The role of grammar). Englewood Cliffs, NJ: Prentice-Hall.

IEPs and Second Language Teaching Research   17

Kumaravadivelu, B. (2016). The decolonial option in English teaching: Can the subaltern act? *TESOL Quarterly, 50*(1), 66–85. doi:10.1002/tesq.202

Lantolf, J., & Thorne, S. (2006). *Sociocultural theory and the genesis of second language development*. Oxford: Oxford University Press.

Larsen-Freeman, D. (2000). Techniques and principles in language teaching (Teaching Techniques in English as a Second Language) (2nd ed.). Oxford, UK: Oxford University Press.

Larsen-Freeman, D., & Long, M. H. (1991). *An introduction to second language acquisition research*. London: Longman.

Lightbown, P. M., & White, L. (1987). The influence of linguistic theories on language acquisition research: Description and explanation. *Language Learning, 37*(4), 483–510.

Long, M. H. (2007). *Problems in SLA*. New York: Lawrence Erlbaum.

Mackey, A. (Ed.). (2008). *Conversational interaction in second language acquisition*. New York: Oxford University Press.

Melitz, J. (2016). English as a global language. In *The Palgrave handbook of economics and language* (pp. 583–615). Basingstoke: Palgrave Macmillan.

Montrul, S. (2008). *Incomplete acquisition in bilingualism: Re-examining the age factor*. Philadelphia: John Benjamins.

Nagy, N. (2018). Heritage language speakers in the university classroom, doing research. In P. Trifonas & T. Aravossitas (Eds.), *International handbook on research and practice in heritage language education*. New York: Springer.

Pan, F., Reppen, R., & Biber, D. (2016). Comparing patterns of L1 vs. L2 academic professionals: Lexical bundles in telecommunications research journals. *Journal of English for Academic Purposes, 21*, 60–71. Retrieved from https://doi.org/10.1016/j.jeap.2015.11.003

Paulston, C. B. (1974). Linguistics and communicative competence. *TESOL Quarterly, 8*, 347–362. Retrieved from www.jstor.org/stable/3585467

Paulston, C. B. (1994). *Linguistic minorities in multilingual settings: Implications for language policies*. Amsterdam: John Benjamins.

Paulston, C. B. (1997). Language policies and language rights. *Annual Review of Anthropology, 26*(1), 73–85.

Paulston, C. B., Haragos, S., Lifrieri, V., & Martelle, W. (2007). Some thoughts on extrinsic linguistic minorities. *Journal of Multilingual and Multicultural Development, 28*(5), 385–399.

Pennington, M. C., & Hoekje, B. J. (2010). *Language program leadership in a changing world: An ecological model*. New York: Emerald.

Plonsky, L., & Oswald, F. L. (2014). How big is "big"? Interpreting effect sizes in L2 research. *Language Learning, 64*(4), 878–912. doi:10.1111/lang.12079

Rampton, M. B. H. (1990). Displacing the "native speaker": Expertise, affiliation, and inheritance. *ELT Journal, 44*(2), 97–101. doi:10.1093/eltj/44.2.97

Ritchie, W., & Bhatia, T. (Eds.). (2009). *New handbook of second language acquisition*. Leeds: Emerald.

Robinson, P., & Ellis, N. C. (Eds.). (2008). *Handbook of cognitive linguistics and second language acquisition*. New York: Routledge.

Shirai, Y., & Juffs, A. (2017). Introduction: Convergence and divergence in functional and formal approaches to SLA. *Second Language Research, 33*(1), 3–12. doi:10.1177/0267658316681046

18 IEPs and Second Language Teaching Research

Spada, N., & Tomita, Y. (2010). Interactions between type of instruction and type of language feature: A meta-analysis. *Language Learning, 60*(2), 263–308. doi:10.1111/j.1467-9922.2010.00562.x

Stoller, F. L. (2016). *The Routledge handbook of English for academic purposes.* New York: Taylor & Francis.

Swales, J. (1990). *Genre analysis: English in academic research settings.* Cambridge: Cambridge University Press.

Swales, J., & Feak, C. (1994). *Academic writing for graduate students: Essential tasks and skills.* Ann Arbor, MI: University of Michigan Press/ELT. (Second edition, 2004).

Thomason, S. G., & Kaufmann, T. (1988). *Language contact, creolization, and genetic linguistics.* Berkeley, CA: California University Press.

Watson-Gegeo, K. A. (1988). Ethnography in ESL: Defining the essentials. *TESOL Quarterly, 22*(4), 575–592. doi:10.2307/3587257

White, L. (1990). Implications of learnability theories for second language acquisition research and teaching. In M. A. K. Halliday, J. Gibbons, & H. Nicholas (Eds.), *Learning, keeping and using language* (pp. 271–286). Amsterdam: John Benjamins.

White, L. (2003). *Second language acquisition and universal grammar.* New York: Cambridge University Press.

White, L., & Juffs, A. (1998). Constraints on Wh-movement in two different contexts of non-native language acquisition: Competence and processing. In S. Flynn, G. Martohardjono, & W. O'Neill (Eds.), *The generative study of second language acquisition* (pp. 111–130). Hillsdale, NJ: Erlbaum.

Widdowson, H. G. (1979). *Reading and thinking in English* (4 vols.). Oxford: Oxford University Press.

Zwicky, A. (2006). Charles Carpenter Fries. *Language Log.* Accessed December 29, 2019. http://itre.cis.upenn.edu/~myl/languagelog/archives/003743.html

2 The Intensive English Program at the University of Pittsburgh

Methods and Curriculum

This chapter provides an overview of the IEP at the University of Pittsburgh from 2005–2013. This is the period during which the data in the subsequent chapters were collected; the chapter therefore provides the background to those data. In addition, this description should be useful as a stand-alone description of an IEP in terms of its pedagogical approach, administrative structure, and curriculum. As far as I am aware, no detailed record, in either article or book form, presents a description of the organization of an IEP's complete structure. Thus, this chapter serves as a record of one IEP for other administrators and teachers to compare with their own organizations. Based on the strengths and weaknesses of the Pitt IEP for their own context, the account in this chapter may provide an impetus for discussion and review of what occurs at other institutions. At a minimum, the chapter provides a snapshot of one IEP at one point in time as a reference for the field. As we shall see in Chapter 8, the IEP has evolved over the years and no longer has the structure described in this chapter.

When data collection began in 2005 as part of the Pittsburgh Science of Learning Project (www.learnlab.org), the IEP routinely offered classes at three levels of proficiency: low intermediate (Level 3), intermediate (Level 4), and advanced (Level 5).[1] The classes were organized according to a 'traditional', separate skills (speaking, listening, reading, writing) plus grammar format. Hence, each level had 5 classes that were integrated both vertically (e.g., Writing Level 3 → Level 4 → Level 5) and horizontally across skills in one level (Reading, Writing, Speaking, Listening, Grammar). (Many IEPs combine reading and writing classes and also combine listening and speaking classes for solid pedagogical reasons. This approach takes reading as a basis for models of student writing and listening as a basis for student spoken output.) The Pitt IEP does not combine such skills classes into two-hour blocks, in part to accommodate the needs of part-time students who may not be able to participate in combined classes. Moreover, the IEP operated a 'split level' policy in which students could place into a Level 4 speaking class but a Level 3 reading class depending on their strengths in different skill areas.

20   *The IEP at the University of Pittsburgh*

The chapter is organized as follows. First, the overall methodological approach is presented, followed by a description of the administrative structure. The curricula are then discussed, with full details of the curricula at each level and for each class provided in Appendices I–III.

2.1 Methodology – The Communicative Approach (CLT)

Since its founding in 1964, the English Language Institute at the University of Pittsburgh has adopted an approach that its faculty have dubbed 'principled eclecticism' following Larsen-Freeman (2000). This 'philosophy' reflects how the program perceives the current state of the field of applied linguistics with regard to methods of instruction. Approaches to language teaching for adults have developed certain basic tenets, but the field has not yet agreed on a single 'method'. This view relies on a conceptualization of *language* as a multi-modal (spoken and written) construct, consisting of various sub-constructs. *Language teaching* is itself based on a variety of disciplines, including linguistics, psychology, anthropology, and education. Given this complex view of language and teaching, it is highly unlikely that any 'single method' for a domain as complex as language and second language instruction could ever be developed. Earlier 'complete methods' (e.g., grammar-translation, the audiolingual method [Richards & Rodgers, 1986]) certainly tried to provide a single solution, but perhaps such approaches only addressed beginning to intermediate language learning and not the complex, higher-level skills that advanced learners need for academic success.

It is useful to unpack the construct 'language' a little to explain the Pitt IEP's approach. First, from a linguistic point of view, language is an abstract cognitive system, which is not directly observable by the conscious mind. This property is true whether one adheres to a view that language is acquired through frequent exposure to sounds and sentence structures that match forms to functions (e.g., MacWhinney, 2008) or whether a more formal, specifically linguistic, core sub-component is also assumed (e.g., White, 2003). The important point here is that speakers are *not aware* of the many levels of representation in phonology, syntax, and semantics that make the complex systems of language work; the most they may be aware of are relationships among words and levels of appropriate use and so-called 'accent'. For example, until someone has a linguistics class, expert English speakers usually are not aware of the 'rule' of aspiration for voiceless sounds /p,t,k/ in syllable initial position. They may think that phonetically, the /t/ in 'top', 'stop' and 'total', are the same – which they are phonologically, but not phonetically; however, only the initial /t/ in 'top', and 'total' are aspirated. (The second /t/ in 'total' in American English is a tap.) Similarly, they are not aware of the complex conditions on the use of the auxiliary 'do'. When students learn a second language, they may or may not find conscious knowledge

The IEP at the University of Pittsburgh   21

useful and be able to reflect on the complex linguistic knowledge that they are developing, but some aspects will never be available for conscious reflection.

The key discipline of psychology informs the field in a variety of ways, such as where the subconscious processes of reading (Perfetti, 2003; Koda, 2005; Martin, 2017) and writing systems come into play. The roles of frequency, saliency, and the timing of practice intervals in output practice (DeKeyser, 2007) is also important. Anthropology and sociology are perhaps less *directly* involved in the language classroom, but they can help in understanding how culture and society influence classroom behaviors, attitudes to learning, and motivation regarding how cultures interact (e.g., Bourdieu, 2018; Csizér & Dörnyei, 2005). As Paulston (1974) made clear, not only must a student know the 'rules' of a language but also how to say the appropriate thing at the right time. Part of being bilingual is being bicultural, after all, and Paulston suggests the bicultural aspect may be even harder than the bilingual aspect.

Educational theories are also vital in explaining how language is used and learned in classrooms. Particularly influential in this regard is the work of second language scholars who work in a Vygotskyan paradigm (Lantolf & Thorne, 2006), who focus on the role of teacher as the expert informant, guiding the development of the learner.

Language knowledge for use in higher education is *also* a skill that is learned consciously due to the academic conventions of scholarship, which have nothing directly to do with abstract structures that are *specific* to the morpho-syntax and phonological systems of learner language. Consequently, an instructional approach to the nuances of tense and aspect in English, which may include implicit as well as explicit 'rules', will not always be directly applicable for the teaching of rhetorical structure in a formal essay or social science research paper.

In this context, it is useful to recall a distinction made by the founder of the ELI and the Department of Linguistics at Pitt: Anthony (1963) pointed out the difference between an 'approach', a 'method', and a 'technique'. An overall approach refers to a theoretical stance on the nature of language – for example, language is a set of structures to be learned; such a stance might lead to a method, for example, the audiolingual method; a technique related to this method would be a listen-and-repeat 'drill'. The point is that given the complexity of language as a phenomenon, no single 'set' of approach-method-techniques is going to be adequate. Moreover, techniques may be appropriate for many methods, not just one.

Since the late 1970s, the 'communicative approach' to language teaching has been recognized as the overall guiding framework most appropriate to classroom language instruction (Canale & Swain, 1980). Anyone reading this book will be well aware of the origins and factors that led to the adoption of this framework, dating from the insights of Hymes' (1972) communicative competence being incorporated into the field by

22 *The IEP at the University of Pittsburgh*

applied linguists such as another director of the Pitt ELI, Christina Bratt Paulston (1974). Mention should also be made of the functional-notional approach (Wilkins, 1976), which derived from advances in the field of pragmatics, most specifically Speech Act theory (Searle, 1969).

By now, it is also well known that a theory of communicative competence – focusing on meaning and achieving goals students want to accomplish with language – has developed a set of methods and techniques called 'the task-based approach' to language learning (e.g., Nunan [1989, 2004]; Skehan [1998]). Within this approach, the role of focus on grammar (form) has been controversial due to the influence of Krashen's (Krashen, Long, & Scarcella, 1979; Krashen, 1987) distinctions between acquisition and learning (but see Gregg's [1984] and McLaughlin's [1987] critiques of Krashen). The IEP at Pitt holds that there is sufficient evidence that explicit, targeted instruction on form is useful for students (e.g., Spada & Tomita, 2010), and thus a separate grammar class is provided. However, this grammar class employs a communicative methodology consistent with task-based learning approaches and fits with the goals and objectives of the skills classes.

Based on these considerations, the IEP provides a set of 'best practices' to the teachers, which is provided in Appendix I of this chapter.

2.2 The Faculty and the Design and Implementation of the Curriculum

The core of the permanent ELI faculty consists of those teachers who have been selected on the basis of competitive searches in which teachers with knowledge and experience are sought – usually a minimum of three years' experience for a full-time teacher. (This open search in recruitment is required by the university, but it is also important because the quality of the delivery of instruction depends on the expertise of those in the classroom.) These faculty members are given responsibility for the development of the curriculum described in the rest of this chapter and in detail in Appendices I–III. They hold meetings to write, review, and edit the curricula. They also provide guidance for the teachers who teach the curriculum at the beginning and end of the term. Further revision is then often made based on the feedback from how well the semester went in terms of the textbook exercises and pace of the class. Thus, the orientation and end-of-term meetings allow for constant review and adjustment of the curriculum. Teaching loads for full-time faculty who carry out administration vary from one to two classes per semester, with contact hours being about eight per week. For full-time faculty with no administrative load, there is usually a maximum of 12 contact hours per week, although this can increase to 16 if an overload is needed.

The research in the IEP that is presented in the following chapters crucially depends not just on one researcher or even a team of researchers

The IEP at the University of Pittsburgh 23

but also on a group of dedicated, collaborative faculty, graduate students, and part-time instructors.

As part of an academic department, the Pitt IEP employs and supports a limited number of graduate teaching assistants (TAs). These graduate students are usually MA in applied linguistics students, but some of them are PhD students who carry out research on language development in the IEP. (Recent examples are Li & Juffs, 2015; Martin, 2017; Naismith, Han, Juffs, Hill, & Zheng, 2018; Spinner, 2011; Vercellotti, 2017.) Graduate student involvement in the IEP is a great strength. Once students have had at least the basic training in the linguistics methods class, they bring new views into the IEP and provide a stimulus to full-time IEP faculty to think about the curriculum as they explain it to the graduate students and guide them in its implementation.

Last, and by no means least, part-time instructors are a vital resource for the IEP. These instructors are hired on an as-needed basis. All are fully qualified with appropriate master's-level training, but some teachers (for one reason or another) either do not desire full-time employment or the IEP cannot financially guarantee full-time employment due to the unpredictable rise and fall in enrollments. The part-time instructor pool constitutes a vital part of many IEPs.

An administrative overview is provided in Tables 2.1 through 2.2. These tables have changed since the research for the corpus was originally collected, but they are an illustration of how an IEP can be organized in terms of administration and teaching. In the case of the Pitt IEP,

Table 2.1 ELI Administrative Structure: Responsibilities of Administrative Faculty

	ELI Director
	• ELI budget
	• Liaison with university (Dean, administrators, offices)
	• Works with
Administrative responsibilities	o Associate Director-Operations (Associate Director-O) & Marketing/Activities Coordinator)
	o Requests for new programs/courses from within the University (works with Associate Director-O and Marketing/Activities Coordinator)
	o ELI publications
	• Reports on ELI accomplishments to the Dean
	• Research Co-Ordinator
	• Representative for professional organizations, for example, UCIEP
	• Supervises MA and PhD graduate students.
Teaching responsibilities	Teaches three linguistics classes (not in the IEP) per year
	Supervision of graduate student research

(Continued)

Table 2.1 (Continued)

	ELI Associate Director (O = Operations)	ELI Associate Director (T = Teachers)

Administrative Responsibilities	• Employment: point of contact for new part-time instructors; arranges interviews; maintains faculty résumés and verifies academic credentials
	• ELI schedule: devises ELI teaching schedule for each term
	• ELI database: interfaces with designer, trains ELI admin. and faculty, oversees implementation and management
	• ELI registration: overall organization (including signage)
	• Overall operations – arranges . . .
	  o Major ELI admin meetings, sets agenda, leads meetings
	  o Major ELI faculty meetings for beginning and end of term: sets agendas, leads meetings
	  o Repairs to classrooms/Ts office or equipment
	• Visitors to ELI
	• Assists with design of new programs as needed (works with Director, Marketing Coordinator, and assigned faculty)
		• Helps to ensure that Ts are following university policies (e.g., sexual harassment training)
		• ELI Faculty Handbook
		• Approves ELI T requests for substitutes for non-medical reasons
		• T training and supervision:
		  o New T orientation (organizes – works with all ELI admin)
		  o New TA videos
		  o Organizes T observations
		  o Organizes peer observations
		  o Organizes T mtgs to facilitate institutional communication
		  o Works with T representative
		• Linguistics responsibilities:
		  o TESOL Certificate Coordinator
		  o Advising
		  o Serves on MA and PhD committees
		  o Attends faculty meetings
		• ELI Technology/
		  o Oversees ELI Technology Asst. and equipment/CALL
		• Attends closing ceremonies – speech 1×/yr

Teaching responsibilities	One class per term	One class per term
Supervision responsibilities	Three curricula, for example, Grammar 3, 4, 5	Two curricula Technology Coordinator

The IEP at the University of Pittsburgh   25

Table 2.2 Other Essential Faculty Administrators

Role	Main Functions	Other details
Assessment Supervisor	Placement testing IEP Registration for standardized tests	Teaches two classes and supervises three curricula
Accreditation Supervisor	CEA accreditation coordinator/ UCIEP membership Curriculum meeting planner	Teaches two classes and supervises three curricula
Student Services Supervisor	Student Exchange and Visitor Information System (SEVIS) record manager Student admissions: process applications to IEP, letters of recommendation, sponsor letters, and applications to university • Liaison with university Office of International Services	Teaches one class
Marketing and Activities Coordinator	Marketing Special programs Activities	Teaches two classes per term
Technology Supervisor	Assists students and teachers with classroom technology Provides support for software and smartphone learning applications	Teaches two classes per term
	ELI Administrator II Assists with applications Marketing Agent contracts General office coordination and ordering of supplies	**Administrative Assistant** Answers inquiries by telephone and email; data entry; ensures supplies are complete; supervises work studies

the director is also a tenured professor and SLA researcher. This situation has been the case since the founding of the institute, and it also provides a link to graduate education in the Department of Linguistics.

The Director and the Associate Directors work closely together, with the Director having extensive interactions with upper administration and budget, while the Associate Directors are responsible for the day-to-day operation of the IEP. In addition to the director group, essential curriculum planning and teaching is done by other members of the administrative faculty. The list of these positions and very basic responsibilities is in Table 2.2.

In addition to these major functions, other full-time or part-time faculty may take on other ad hoc roles in administration. The total number

26 *The IEP at the University of Pittsburgh*

of faculty members for the IEP, which teaches between 250–350 full- and part-time students annually, including the Director, are 12 full-time faculty, 1 to 3 graduate students (varies with financial commitments), and approximately 12 part-time instructors, who may teach between one and three courses per semester either in the IEP or in the classes that the ELI provides to support matriculated students. (The part of the ELI that supports matriculated students is not part of the discussion in this book, but the IEP is integrated into the university and the department in several complex ways, including testing and ESP courses. These activities are not immediately relevant to language development in the IEP but provide a framework in which it can thrive.)

An important aspect of the professional training and status of the IEP faculty is that the IEP belongs to two professional organizations: University and College Intensive English Programs (UCIEP) (www.uciep.org/) and English USA (www.EnglishUSA.org). The Pitt ELI was a founding member of UCIEP in 1967. UCIEP requires its member institutions to employ faculty with at least an MA in a field related to linguistics and language teaching. Some supervised teaching by students in an MA program is permitted. Similarly, the CEA standards for faculty (Faculty Standard 1, http://cea-accredit.org/images/pdfs/2018_CEA_Standards.pdf) also state that for higher education, the MA with TESOL training is the appropriate level of education. Thus, the teaching staff of the IEP follows standards set by recognized professional organizations.

2.3 The Students: National Origins, Proficiency, and Goals

Students who study in intensive English programs come from countries all over the world. Changes in the home countries of IEP students in the USA (and perhaps international students in general) reflect trends in international politics and economics. In the 1970s, many students in the United States were from Iran – a trend that changed abruptly with the Iranian Revolution and collapse in the relationship between the United States and Iran in 1979. The 1980s saw an increase in students from Japan as a result of the strength of Japan's economy. In the 1990s, the economic development of the so-called Asian Tiger economies (Hong Kong, Singapore, South Korea, and Taiwan, but especially South Korea for IEPs) drove enrollments from those countries up. After the 9–11–2001 attack on the United States, students from the Middle East, who had been a regular source of IEP students, obviously declined precipitously; however, they again increased after the agreements between King Abdullah and George Bush in 2006. The 2000s also marked a dramatic increase in students from the People's Republic of China as that economy became more important and an affluent middle class emerged in China. Thus, countries whose economies are developing, have a rising middle class with disposable income large enough to fund international education, and have larger populations of young people who aspire to higher education are usually the source of (international) students.

The students in the IEP during the period of data collection reflect these populations of students. Thus, over about 10 years, the majority of students were from Arabic-speaking countries, principally Saudi Arabia, but also other Gulf states, as well as a minority from Libya. Other large groups included students from S. Korea, Japan, mainland China, and Taiwan. Figure 2.1 illustrates the approximate numbers of students with different first languages in the database, reflecting the international political forces that affected IEP enrollment in the early part of the twenty-first century.

An important point to be made here is that the IEP accepts both full-time and part-time students. It is *legal* for a non-immigrant to the USA to study without a student visa (F-1 or J-1) if the study is 'incidental' to that individual's stay. For example, a spouse (F-2 visa) of a full-time student or someone visiting as a tourist (B-1 or B-2 visa) may want to study under the 'avocational' or 'recreational' clause referred to in footnote 1 of the document referred to in the US Immigration and Customs Enforcement (ICE) web document: www.ice.gov/doclib/sevis/pdf/Nonimmigrant%20 Class%20Who%20Can%20Study.pdf.

The Pitt IEP allows such students to study, and so the data in the rest of the book may derive from full- or part-time students. Thus, not all students who contributed data in writing classes will have contributed data in other classes and may not have had instruction in the curricula described in Section 2.4. Moreover, not all students are on track to

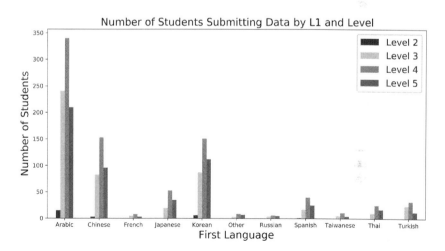

Figure 2.1 Numbers and Levels of Students in the Pittsburgh English Language Corpus (PELIC)

28   *The IEP at the University of Pittsburgh*

enroll in a degree program, a fact the IEP curriculum must take into account.

The IEP also admits full-time students who have different goals. The majority of Arabic-speaking students seek to enter a degree program either at the undergraduate or graduate level. Many other students have similar aspirations. However, a significant proportion of students study full or part time in order to improve their English for their professional development in their home country or for social reasons in the United States.

The IEP at Pitt does not accept absolute beginner students or even students who have very low proficiency. Entry requirements are described in more detail in Chapter 3, but in general, students whose internet-based TOEFL score (iBT) would be below 24 are not eligible for admission (www.eli.pitt.edu/admission-english-language-institute/). To some extent, this requirement reflects the program's position that it is not possible to gain sufficient proficiency to enter a degree program within one year if the student starts at the complete beginner level. In addition, numbers of complete beginner students are not high enough to warrant a class. Following UCIEP guidelines, class size is limited to an average of 15 students, with classes being split into two sections of the same class if enrollment approaches 25, which is the maximum allowed by UCIEP guidelines.

2.4 The Curriculum

As mentioned in Chapter 1, the IEP at the University of Pittsburgh has been accredited by the Commission on English Language Program Accreditation since 2005. The accreditation process requires programs to provide very detailed accounts of the planning and implementation of assessment practices (described in Chapter 3), as well as a range of other requirements with regard to administration, facilities, faculty, and student-related standards.

In order to be a full-time student, visa regulations require students to be in class a minimum of 18 hours a week. Full-time students at Pitt's ELI are enrolled 20 hours per week in five courses that meet four days per week, Monday, Tuesday, Thursday, and Friday. Wednesdays are reserved for homework, laboratory work, and extra-curricular activities. Examples of these are engagement with community organizations, trips to local museums and sites of interest, and conversation partner activities with University of Pittsburgh students.

In the pages that follow, a description of the intended progression in the program in each skill, from Level 3 to Level 5, is provided. In the Appendices to this chapter, the 'horizontal' or integration of each skill at each LEVEL is provided, including details of textbooks, grading criteria, exit criteria, and typical activities. The descriptions follow CEA requirements, which are posted online (http://cea-accredit.org/about-cea/standards). In this context, all three curriculum standards are relevant:

Curriculum:

Curriculum Standard 1:

The curriculum is consistent with the mission of the program or language institution, appropriate to achieve the organization's goals and meet assessed student needs, and available in writing.

Curriculum Standard 2:

Course goals, course objectives, and student learning outcomes are written, appropriate for the curriculum, and aligned with each other. The student learning outcomes within the curriculum represent significant progress or accomplishment.

Curriculum Standard 3:

The instructional materials and methodologies are appropriate and supportive of course objectives.

It is important to understand the differences among 'goals', 'objectives', and 'student learning outcomes'. The CEA notes for this standard (http://cea-accredit.org/images/pdfs/2018_CEA_Standards.pdf) state that 'goals' are the *overall* intended outcome of the course, 'objectives' are 'what will be taught', and the 'student learning outcomes' (SLOs) are stated in terms of 'what the student will be able to do' as a result of the course – namely a *functional* outcome. Thus, these SLOs must 'be written, observable, measurable, and able to be expressed in terms of academic readiness or practical applications'. These guidelines are consistent with language learning for a purpose – in our case, language for use in academic and professional settings. As might be expected, Level 3 goals are to build knowledge adding a range of linguistic tools (vocabulary, structure) in more constrained contexts. Level 4 involves consolidation of what is learned at Level 3, adding increased task demands and enhanced control of complex language. Level 5 focuses on refining and extending what is learned at Levels 3 and 4 to contexts not directly familiar to the student. Verbs used in the goals and objectives reflect these aims: Level 3 – '*develop*', Level 4 – '*improve*', and Level 5 – '*refine*'.

As the data will derive mainly from speaking, grammar, and writing classes, this section will concentrate on those curricula, but the goals, objectives, and SLOs for listening and reading are provided in the Appendices to this chapter.

30 *The IEP at the University of Pittsburgh*

2.4.1 *The Speaking Curriculum – Goals, Objectives, Student Learning Outcomes*

The Speaking curriculum from Levels 3 to 5 in the ELI concentrates on encouraging the development of accurate and fluent monologues and dialogs. The goals, objectives, and SLOs are extensive for each level, so this section will concentrate on the main points.

At Level 3, one goal states that 'Students will learn to create short written and spoken texts to express their own ideas and to represent the ideas of others'. At this level, more emphasis is on basic structure and pronunciation. Level 3 SLOs state that students will be able to create short spoken texts that include topic sentences and supporting ideas, describe a chart or series of pictures, and create an oral summary of a text. In addition, they will be able to engage in dialogs on topics of personal relevance. The goals and objectives discuss the linguistic means (question formation, simple embedded clauses, target vocabulary from the Academic Word List, and pronunciation foci).

At Level 4, one principal goal is that 'Students will interact via responding to written texts and interlocutors & eliciting written or spoken information on personal, practical, social, and general academic topics. Interaction will include clarifying and negotiating meaning. Students also will be introduced to abstract topics'. The SLOs are similar, but stipulate longer text length (three to seven minutes for a prepared, original spoken text, with an appropriate structure that includes an introduction, appropriate support, and a conclusion. The added features include the control of appropriate transitions, which indicate comparison/contrast, opinion, and a summary. Linguistic tools included at this level include awareness of register for social and academic topics, control of *do*-support with question formation and negation, and control of the modal system. Overall, the Level 4 curriculum SLOs are much more specific regarding the linguistic goals than are the SLOs of Level 3.

For Level 5, one principal goal is that 'Students will learn to create medium-length and long multi-paragraph written and spoken texts to express, extend, and elaborate their own ideas, to represent, extend, and elaborate on the ideas of others'. Thus, by Level 5, the focus is on *reporting* complex ideas of others and expressing an *evaluation* of those ideas. The linguistic focus is similar to Level 4, but the requirement is an extension of variety of structure and more focused control of accuracy.

One particularly important part of the curriculum during this period was the 'Recorded Speaking Activity' (RSA), details of which were published by McCormick and Vercellotti (2013). The RSA is still used in the IEP as of 2019–2020. As part of a focus on feedback and self-correction, this activity involved the students recording a two-minute monologue in the laboratory using *Runtime Revolution* software; then the students transcribed the speech and were encouraged to write down exactly what they had said without corrections. The next step was to correct any errors that they had noticed in notes. Finally, the students were asked to re-record the speech, incorporating the corrections that they had noticed. These data will be discussed in much greater depth in Chapter 6 on speaking.

2.4.2 The Writing Curriculum – Goals, Objectives, Student Learning Outcomes

The writing curriculum is ultimately designed to help students achieve the ability to write texts that are acceptable in humanities and social science research. Level 3 begins with a focus on the paragraph level and helping students to understand that writing is a process of creation and revision, including planning, writing, editing, and revising. At this stage, objectives include being able to write definitions, basic information, and narrative. Writing a definition involves supporting the definition with examples, comparisons, and opinions; past time narratives require command of chronological organizers. Descriptive writing requires using details for support and the cohesion devices that support such writing.

Level 4 introduces more concepts regarding providing support for a thesis statement in terms of data and outside references to support points that the writer wishes to make. Functions include explaining, evaluating, and summarizing. Student writing topics include writing clear, organized instructions; writing a memo; writing detailed explanations of ideas and concepts; and making an evaluation based on accepted criteria. Students are asked to use a variety of types of evidence to support their evaluation. Finally, some assignments might require students to summarize and respond to reading passages. Sentence-level grammar highlighting simple, compound, and complex (embedded) sentence types are highlighted at this level, even though they may be introduced in Level 3.

Level 5 progresses to the level of a research paper, including the mechanics of references and appropriate rhetorical patterns. This is a typical essay that is described, for example, in Atkinson and Ramanathan's (1995) account of IEP writing classes rather than the type of essay written in freshman composition classes. The typical IEP writing class essay focuses on developing a thesis statement, followed by paragraphs organized along the lines of topic sentences and supporting ideas, and ending with a concluding paragraph. It also includes details of citing references in text and providing a reference list at the end of the paper. Essays that are developed according to particular organizational patterns include: comparison and contrast, cause and effect, and 'argumentative' essays, which means proposing and supporting a point of view. Optionally, students could write classification essays and/or process analysis essays.

32 *The IEP at the University of Pittsburgh*

2.4.3 *The Grammar Curriculum – Goals, Objectives, Student Learning Outcomes*

The grammar curriculum was designed to support the other curricula at various levels. In that sense, the idea to provide students and teachers with a set of grammar points that might come up for 'focus on form' (singular). This notion is in contrast to a grammar syllabus that 'focuses on *forms*' (plural), which Long (2007, pp. 121–122) describes thus: 'Focus on forms attempts the impossible: to impose a pre-set, external linguistic syllabus on the learners, riding roughshod over individual differences in readiness to learn'. In contrast, Long (2007, p. 122) defines 'focus on form' as follows:

> Focus on form . . . involves briefly drawing students' attention to problematic linguistic targets, when certain conditions are met, in context, in an otherwise communicatively oriented lesson. It can help learners "notice" items in the input (in the sense of Schmidt, 2001, and elsewhere) that otherwise may escape them, as well as mismatches between the input and deviant forms in their output, especially where there is no resulting communication breakdown that might serve the purpose.

In other words, rather than teaching a set of step-by-step grammar points in each class that the learners are supposed to learn and create a system with, the grammar curriculum is used to assist in noticing form in general and to serve as a resource for in-class corrective feedback when the appropriate *opportunity* for feedback arises. The grammar curriculum is also designed to raise awareness of structures that the learners have been exposed to either before attending the IEP or as support for the rhetorical patterns that they will need in the course of their other classes. The development of grammatical accuracy in speaking and writing classes uses the grammar points that are covered at each level (simple sentence structures and principal parts of speech). More generally, the goals are to develop spoken and written fluency in communicative situations using the target grammar points, improve listening comprehension of texts including the target grammar structures, and develop the ability to identify and such structures in reading texts. Finally, and very importantly for the advanced students, they should develop the ability to monitor their own errors in speaking and writing and be able to correct them.

Thus, at Level 3, examples of verb phrase structures that are reviewed include the contrast between simple past and present, present/future-time modals to express ability, requests, possibility and necessity, adverbial clauses of time, and gerunds and infinitives. For noun phrases, articles are reviewed, as well as basic quantifiers. At Level 4, for verb phrase grammar, the challenging topics of event aspect and tense are reviewed, along with passive. In noun phrases, relative (adjective) clauses including subject and object relatives and 'where' and 'when' clauses are covered. At Level 5, review for verb phrase grammar includes more complex and nuanced work with modals, unreal conditionals, embedded clauses (noun clauses), and passive. For noun phrases, articles, adjective order, and quantifiers are reviewed.

To sum up, if students have been in a grammar class, the teacher can more easily make reference to important metalanguage and awareness on the part of the student to speedily draw a student's attention to their output at the right moment. This approach is part of the whole view of methods. Although some researchers would not be in favor of explicit teaching about grammar, more recently, some research has shown that contrastive teaching that compares the L1 system to the L2 system can be beneficial (McManus & Marsden, 2017, 2019). Such recent research findings lend support to the IEP view that final conclusions have not been reached with regard to explicit instruction of grammar points. Thus, even if only some students can benefit from explicit instruction in grammar, they should be provided with such opportunities to learn from it.

2.5 Summary

The IEP at Pitt has a history of 55 years and is unusual in that it is housed in a Department of Linguistics and closely associated with a program that trains teachers and conducts research as part of its mission. The methodologies used rely on insights from second language acquisition research that is both theoretical and classroom based, which is itself grounded in diverse basic disciplines. The teachers in the ELI are trained and experienced teachers with appropriate graduate degrees (MA and PhD). Almost all have some kind of overseas experience, which enhances their ability to empathize and understand the students' challenges in a new culture. The student body is composed of mostly younger people from various countries around the world who are seeking higher education in English. The curriculum is based on a separate skills approach that takes communicative competence as a goal to be achieved through language task-based activities that may combine all skills at various points in a class and include explicit grammar instruction.

Note

1. Where enrollment numbers are adequate, the IEP has a Level 2 – low beginning. The IEP now has five levels, from 2–6.

References

Anthony, E. M. (1963). Approach, method and technique. *English Language Teaching Journal*, 17(2), 63–67.

Atkinson, D., & Ramanathan, V. (1995). Cultures of writing: An ethnographic comparison of L1 and L2 university writing/language programs. *TESOL Quarterly*, 29, 539–568.

34 *The IEP at the University of Pittsburgh*

Bourdieu, P. (2018). Cultural reproduction and social reproduction. In D. Grusky (Ed.), *Inequality: Classic readings in race, class, and gender* (pp. 257–272). New York: Routledge.

Canale, M., & Swain, M. (1980). Theoretical bases of communicative approaches to second language teaching and testing. *Applied Linguistics, 1,* 1–17.

Csizér, K., & Dörnyei, Z. (2005). The internal structure of language learning motivation and its relationship with language choice and learning effort. *Modern Language Journal, 89,* 19–36.

DeKeyser, R. M. (Ed.). (2007). *Practice in a second language: Perspectives from applied linguistics and cognitive psychology.* Cambridge: Cambridge University Press.

Gregg, K. (1984). Krashen's monitor and Occam's razor. *Applied Linguistics, 5,* 79–100.

Hymes, D. (1972). On communicative competence. In P. John & J. Holmes (Eds.), *Sociolinguistics* (pp. 269–293). Harmondsworth: Penguin.

Koda, K. (2005). *Insights into second language reading: A crosslinguistic approach.* Cambridge: Cambridge University Press.

Krashen, S. D. (1987). The role of grammar. In *Principles and practice in second language acquisition.* Englewood Cliffs, NJ: Prentice-Hall.

Krashen, S. D., Long, M., & Scarcella, R. (1979). Accounting for child-adult differences in second language rate and attainment. *TESOL Quarterly, 13,* 573–582.

Lantolf, J. P., & Thorne, S. L. (2006). *Sociocultural theory and the genesis of second language development.* Oxford: Oxford University Press.

Larsen-Freeman, D. (2000). *Techniques and principles in language teaching (Teaching techniques in English as a second language)* (2nd ed.). Oxford, UK: Oxford University Press.

Li, N., & Juffs, A. (2015). The influence of moraic structure on English L2 syllable final consonants. *Annual Meeting on Phonology.* doi:10.3765/amp.v2i0.3767

Long, M. H. (2007). *Problems in SLA.* New York: Lawrence Erlbaum.

MacWhinney, B. (2008). A unified model. In P. Robinson & N. C. Ellis (Eds.), *Handbook of cognitive linguistics and second language acquisition* (pp. 341–371). New York: Routledge.

Martin, K. I. (2017). The impact of L1 writing system on ESL knowledge of vowel and consonant spellings. *Reading and Writing, 30,* 279–298. doi:10.1007/s11145-016-9673-5

McCormick, D. E., & Vercellotti, M. L. (2013). Examining the impact of self-correction notes on grammatical accuracy in speaking. *TESOL Quarterly, 47*(2), 410–420. doi:10.1002/tesq.92

McLaughlin, B. (1987). *Theories of second language learning.* London: Edward Arnold.

McManus, K., & Marsden, E. (2017). L1 explicit instruction can improve L2 online and offline performance. *Studies in Second Language Acquisition, 39*(3), 459–492.

McManus, K., & Marsden, E. (2019). Using explicit instruction about L1 to reduce crosslinguistic effects in L2 grammar learning: Evidence from oral production in L2 French. *The Modern Language Journal, 103*(2), 459–480.

Naismith, B., Han, N-R., Juffs, A., Hill, B. L., & Zheng, D. (2018). Accurate measurement of lexical sophistication with reference to ESL learner data.

In K. E. Boyer & M. Yudelson (Eds.), *Proceedings of the 11th International Conference on Educational Data Mining* (pp. 259–265). Buffalo, NY. Retrieved from http://educationaldatamining.org/EDM2018/

Nunan, D. (1989). Sequencing and integrating tasks. In *Designing tasks for the communicative classroom*. Cambridge: Cambridge University Press.

Nunan, D. (2004). *Task-based language teaching*. New York: Cambridge University Press.

Paulston, C. B. (1974). Linguistic and communicative competence. *TESOL Quarterly, 8*, 347–362.

Perfetti, C. (2003). The universal grammar of reading. *Scientific Studies of Reading, 7*(1), 3–24.

Richards, J., & Rodgers, T. S. (1986). *Approaches and methods in language teaching*. Cambridge: Cambridge University Press.

Schmidt, R. W. (2001). Attention. In P. Robinson (Ed.), *Cognition and second language instruction* (pp. 3–32). Cambridge: Cambridge University Press.

Searle, J. R. (1969). *Speech acts: An essay in the philosophy of language*. Cambridge: Cambridge University Press.

Skehan, P. (1998). Task-based instruction. *Annual Review of Applied Linguistics, 18*, 268–286.

Spada, N., & Tomita, Y. (2010). Interactions between type of instruction and type of language feature: A meta-analysis. *Language Learning, 60*(2), 263–308. doi:10.1111/j.1467-9922.2010.00562.x

Spinner, P. (2011). Second language assessment and morphosyntactic development. *Studies in Second Language Acquisition, 33*, 529–561.

Vercellotti, M. L. (2017). The development of complexity, accuracy and fluency in second language performance. *Applied Linguistics, 38*(1), 90–111. Retrieved from https://academic.oup.com/applij/article-abstract/38/1/90/2951570

White, L. (2003). *Second language acquisition and universal grammar*. New York: Cambridge University Press.

Wilkins, D. A. (1976). Notional syllabuses. *Bulletin CILA* (Commission interuniversitaire suisse de linguistique appliquée) ("Bulletin VALS-ASLA" Depuis 1994), *24*, 5–17.

Appendix I
English Language Institute
General Best Practices

1. Explain the purpose/language focus of the activity so that students understand the purpose/focus and how it connects to other class content and activities:
   - for example, the purpose of this prelistening activity is to identify what you know about the topic before you listen to the lecture.
   - for example, the purpose of this activity is to practice using indirect questions in a conversation with a partner.

2. Use visual support when teaching new points, eliciting and/or providing information/answers/examples in order to:
   - attend to auditory and visual learners
   - support sound/symbol correspondence
   - ensure accuracy of information/answers/examples

3. Focus on the targeted skill when planning or implementing a lesson (i.e., writing in writing class, listening in listening class, etc.).
   - for example, do not spend an entire listening class on vocabulary prelistening – include some listening.
   - for example, when explaining the writing process, be sure to do some writing.

4. Encourage students to work though language or knowledge gaps rather than always filling in the gaps for the students. For example:
   - encourage circumlocution in speaking
   - ask students to correct errors based on correction feedback
   - ask students what they heard/read/know that is related to a topic/question when they cannot "answer" a question
   - elicit answers to students' questions from other students

5. Provide positive and negative feedback during or after activities, especially when practice is focused on accuracy.
   - for example, positive: Yes, that's correct.
   - for example, negative: No. That's a good guess but not correct; Recast

The IEP at the University of Pittsburgh   37

6. Maximize student interaction with the language:

    - for example, ask students to read directions
    - for example, ask students to define key words before reading/listening
    - for example, use pair/group work
    - for example, minimize teacher talk

7. Model directions, activities, homework, etc. as needed, but in particular when something new is introduced.

8. Adjust your level of teacher talk, especially directions, explanations, and feedback, to the level of the class to maximize comprehensibility; perhaps:

    - rate
    - complexity
    - vocabulary, including idioms

Appendix II
Level 3 Horizontal Articulation

Level 3	Listening	Speaking	Reading
Text(s)	▪ Hartmann and Blass, 2000. *Quest 1: Listening and Speaking in the Academic World*, McGraw-Hill	▪ Baker and Goldstein, 1990. *Pronunciation Pairs*, Cambridge Univ. Press ▪ Rost, 1998. *Strategies in Speaking*, Longman	▪ Ediger and Pavlik, 2000 *Reading Connections: Intermediate (RC-I)* ▪ Rogerson et al., 1988. *Words for Students of English Vol. 4*. Michigan Univ. Press ▪ *Newbury House Dictionary of American English*). Newbury House.

Goals	• Build listening comprehension of conversational American English
	• Introduce effective listening comprehension strategies
	• Develop fundamental academic note-taking skills
		▪ Increase awareness of American pronunciation of English vowels and consonants
		▪ Develop fundamental oral language skills that will prepare students to participate in:
		  • social discourse
		  ▪ class discussions
		  ▪ individual and group oral presentations
		• Introduce discourse strategies
		Pronunciation:
			▪ Develop the ability to read and comprehend simplified and abridged texts in English on topics of general interest with reasonable speed and efficiency
			▪ Increase vocabulary to a level that permits high intermediate reading
			▪ Introduce reading strategies for different purposes.
			▪ Use an English language dictionary with skill

Objectives (Objectives continued)	• Apply pre, while, and post listening comprehension skills (e.g., predict, infer, summarize) • Guess vocabulary meaning from context • Recognize meaning from tone of voice	▪ Utilize pronunciation illustrations and explanations ▪ Aurally discriminate phonemes in limited contexts • Produce phonemes in controlled speech with increasing accuracy	▪ Do exercises and participate in discussions to demonstrate comprehension of simplified and easier authentic texts. ▪ Apply specific pre-reading strategies ▪ Apply specific strategies to identify the main idea of a paragraph. ▪ Scan material for specific information

(*Continued*)

Leve 3	Listening	Speaking	Reading
	• Identify main ideas and supporting details • Apply introductory note-taking skills (e.g., outlining, using abbreviations) • Construct questions about listening text content ▪ Identify definitions, comparisons, reasons ▪ Distinguish textual relationships ▪ Identify a speaker's point of view	**Speaking:** ▪ Produce target grammar structures in spoken English ▪ Build on practiced phrases and model expressions in spontaneous speech ▪ Recognize formal and informal spoken English ▪ Prepare and present formal and informal speeches and presentations ▪ Participate in class discussions	▪ Do exercises to determine the organization of a text • Write short answers that summarize the text to answer questions. ▪ Recognize and use new vocabulary from the textbooks ▪ Use context cues to understand word meaning ▪ Make inferences from reading material ▪ Use an English dictionary to find, pronounce, spell and use words
Exit criteria	Students must pass the course with a grade of C- or better. • Students with grades below C- may exit into Level 4 at the discretion of the student advisor in consultation with their Listening 3 teacher & supervisor and/or a Michigan test score at the Level 4 placement level.	Students must pass the course with a grade of C- or better. • Students with grades below C- may exit into Level 4 at the discretion of the student advisor in consultation with their Speaking 3 teacher & supervisor and/or a Michigan test score at the Level 4 placement Level.	Students must pass the course with a grade of C- or better. ▪ Students with grades below C- may exit into Level 4 at the discretion of the student advisor in consultation with their Reading 3 teacher & supervisor and/or a Michigan test score at the Level 4 placement Level.
Grading policy	60% Listening comprehension exercises from *Quest 1* and other materials 30% Note-taking and quizzes from *Quest 1* and other materials 10% Participation	20% General in-class speaking activities 40% Impromptu speeches, seminar speeches, and panel discussions 30% Pronunciation practice 10% Participation	70% Reading skills exercises and tests 20% Vocabulary exercises and quizzes 10% Class Participation

Activities	**Intensive reading component**
	▪ Short articles from FYI
	▪ Abridged or edited for ESL learners
	▪ Some articles from publications aimed at K-12
	▪ Equal in emphasis in the curricula with extensive reading
Activities	**Extensive reading component**
	• Graded readers
	▪ Tom Sawyer
	▪ Frankenstein
	▪ Tale of Two Cities
	▪ Read as a class
	• Two per term
	• Equal in emphasis in the curricula with intensive reading
Supplemental Activities (optional)	▪ Clips from movie videos to accompany the graded readers.
	• Teacher may, with approval of the curriculum supervisor, choose additional texts for students to read and work with in class.

(*Continued*)

Level 3	Writing	Grammar
Text(s)	▪ Cavusgil, 1998. *Looking Ahead 1*, Heinle & Heinle. **Chapters covered: 1–5 & 7** ▪ 2000. *Newbury House Dictionary*, Heinle & Heinle.	● Fuchs, Bonner & Westheimer 2000. *Focus on Grammar: An Intermediate Course for Reference and Practice*, Longman

Goals	● Compose meaningful sentences and paragraphs that focus on a central idea with appropriate support and conclusion
	 ● Introduce the concept that writing is a process
	 ● Express ideas in writing to the reader in as clear a way as possible
	 ● Increase fluency in writing
		● For simple sentences and the principal parts of speech, students will. . .
		   ● Develop grammatical accuracy in speaking and writing
		   ● Develop spoken and written fluency in communicative situations
		   ● Improve listening comprehension
		   ● Develop ability to identify and understand the target grammar structures in reading texts
		   ● Develop ability to monitor own errors in speaking and writing

Objectives	● Compose logical paragraphs and short compositions conforming to the patterns presented in the text ● Do free-writing to increase fluency in writing ● Learn and use systematic steps in writing: planning, writing, editing, revising, rewriting and proofreading ● Practice the basic grammar structures of informational writing, persuasive writing, written definitions, and narratives ● Edit for correct mechanics (punctuation, capitalization, spelling)	● Use target grammar structures in focused practice for accuracy ● Use the target grammar structures in communicative activities with a partner or a small group ● Write short (3–5 sentences) paragraphs or dialogues using the target grammar structures appropriately and correctly ▪ Understand the grammar structures in listening passages ▪ Identify the grammar structures in short passages in the textbook ▪ Recognize and correct errors of the target grammar structures in the textbook passages and the student's own speech and writing.

Exit criteria	Students must pass the course with a grade of C- or better. • Students with grades below C- may exit into Level 4 at the discretion of the student advisor in consultation with their Writing 3 teacher & supervisor and/or a Michigan test score and writing sample at the Level 4 placement level.	Students must pass the course with a grade of C- or better. • Students with grades below C- may exit into Level 4 at the discretion of the student advisor in consultation with their Grammar 3 teacher & supervisor and/or a Michigan test score or cumulative test score at the Grammar 3 level.
Grading policy	50% Compositions and revisions outside of class 40% Other writing assignments 10% Class participation	• 55% Written work (tests 40%, HW and written quizzes 15%) • 20% Listening work • 15% Speaking accuracy • 10% Participation

Grammar Structures Covered	• Intro to parts of complete sentences
	• Punctuation following logical connectors
	• Opinion structures
	• Adverbs of frequency
	• Modals – *may & might* in generalizations
	• Expressions of quantity
	• Connecting clauses with *and, but, so*
	• Comparison structures
	• Contrastive connectors
	• Conditional Sentences (real)
	• Present tense verbs
	• Generic articles and nouns
	• Adjective clauses (subject relatives in restrictive relative clauses)
	• Past tense verbs
	• Prepositional phrases in descriptions
	• Pronouns of interactive communication (*we* vs. *you*)
	• Indirect speech
		• Verb tenses:
		  • Present: simple, perfect and progressive
		  • Past: simple and progressive
		  • Future (*be going to* and *will*)
		• Modals: present – by function
		• Adjectives and adverbs (including comparatives/superlatives)
		• Gerunds & infinitives
		• Nouns and articles, basic uses

(*Continued*)

Activities	**Writing Skills covered in the text chapters assigned**	Students should:
	▪ Organizing ideas from general to specific	▪ Read the introduction and explanation before class
	▪ Supporting generalizations with examples from personal experience	▪ Participate in grammar explanations with the teacher at the beginning of each new grammar point
	▪ Extended comparison and contrast	▪ Do written homework and study mistakes
	▪ Cohesion devices	▪ Pay attention to grammar as they speak
	▪ Writing a definition	▪ Actively participate in grammar practice with the teacher, a partner or a group every day
	▪ Supporting a definition with examples, comparisons, and opinions	▪ Do recorded speeches in the lab
	▪ Past time narratives	▪ Take quizzes and tests and study the teacher's corrections
	▪ Chronological organizers	
	▪ Description	
	▪ Using details for support	
	▪ Writing a survey	
	▪ Summarizing information	
Supplemental activities (optional)		▪ Keep an error progress chart

Appendix III
Level 4 Horizontal Articulation

Level 4	Listening	Speaking	Reading
Text(s)	• Lebauer, 2000. *Learn to Listen, Listen to Learn, 2nd Ed.*, Longman	• Orion, 1997. *Pronouncing American English, 2nd ed.*, Heinle & Heinle • Dale & Wolf, 2000. *Speech Communication Made Simple, 2nd ed.*, Longman	• Ediger and Pavlik, 2000 *Reading Connections: High Intermediate (RC-HI)* • Rogerson et al., 1989. *Words for Students of English* Vol. 6, Michigan Univ. Press. • *Newbury House Dictionary of American English* (recommended). Newbury House.

Goals	• Improve listening comprehension of authentic American English discourse
	• Practice and improve academic note-taking skills
	• Improve effective listening comprehension strategies
		• Improve accuracy of pronunciation of American English vowels and consonants
		• Improve oral language skills needed to participate in:
		  • individual and group oral presentations
		  • class discussions
		  • social discourse
		• Develop self-assessment skills
			• Improve overall reading comprehension so that student is ready to begin working with authentic texts.
			• Significantly increase the number of English words student can understand in a written context.
			• Develop reading strategies for different purposes.

Objectives (Objectives continued)	• Apply pre, while, and post listening comprehension skills (e.g., predict, infer, summarize) • Guess vocabulary meaning from context • Recognize meaning from tone of voice • Identify main ideas and supporting details	**Pronunciation:** • Consistently aurally discriminate phonemes • Produce phonemes in prepared and spontaneous speech with increasing accuracy **Speaking:** • Utilize common grammatical forms with increasing accuracy	• Do exercises and participate in discussions to demonstrate comprehension of simplified and easier authentic texts. • Apply specific pre-reading strategies. • Apply specific strategies to identify the main idea of a paragraph

	Listening	Speaking	Reading
	<ul><li>Apply note-taking standards (e.g., outlining, using abbreviations)</li><li>Apply note content to other activities (e.g., discussions, content quizzes) to emphasize the importance of meaningful notes</li><li>Construct questions about listening text content</li><li>Refine identification of definitions, comparisons, reasons</li><li>Distinguish textual relationships</li><li>Attend to meaning during extended listening texts</li></ul>	<ul><li>Use an expanded vocabulary</li><li>Use language appropriate for different discourse patterns in social and formal settings</li><li>Participate in class discussions with a high level of comprehension</li><li>Reduce hesitations during prepared and spontaneous speech</li><li>Self-correct language samples</li></ul>	<ul><li>Recognize and use specific vocabulary to understand different organization patterns in the text</li><li>Write simple summaries of readings from the text and from unabridged readings chosen by the student</li><li>Recognize and use new vocabulary from the textbooks</li><li>Use context cues to understand word meaning</li><li>Evaluate websites on topics related to those in the reading text</li></ul>
Exit criteria	Students must pass the course with a grade of C- or better. Students with grades below C- may exit into Level 5 at the discretion of the student advisor in consultation with their Listening 4 teacher & supervisor and/or a Michigan test score at the Level 5 placement level.	Students must pass the course with a grade of C- or better. Students with grades below C- may exit into Level 5 at the discretion of the student advisor in consultation with their Speaking 4 teacher & supervisor and/or a Michigan test score at the Level 5 placement level.	Students must pass the course with a grade of C- or better. Students with grades below C- may exit into Level 5 at the discretion of the student advisor in consultation with their Reading 4 teacher & supervisor and/or a Michigan test score at the Level 5 placement level.
Grading policy	45% Listening comprehension (exercises from *LLLL*, CNN and NPR News, videos and other materials) 45% Note-taking (lectures from *LLLL* and other materials) and activities based on students' notes 10% Participation	15% General in-class speaking activities 75% Speeches and other structured activities 10% Participation	55% Reading skills exercises and tests 20% Vocabulary exercises and quizzes 15% Outside Reading reports 10% Class Participation

(*Continued*)

Activities	**Intensive reading component**
	▪ Readings in Reading Connections
	▪ Abridged or edited for ESL learners
	Extensive reading component
	▪ Students choose readings from the WWW or periodicals on topics covered in MC
	▪ Approved by the teacher
	• Mainly homework
	• Dictionary activities
Other activities	• Teacher may, with approval of the curriculum supervisor, choose additional texts for students to read and work with in class.

Level 4	Writing	Grammar
Text(s)	• Byleen, 1998. *Looking Ahead 3*, Heinle & Heinle. **Chapters covered: 1–5** • 2000. *Newbury House Dictionary*, Heinle & Heinle. (Recommended)	• Fuchs & Bonner, 2000. *Focus on Grammar: A High Intermediate Course for Reference and Practice*, Longman.

Goals	▪ Compose meaningful sentences, paragraphs, and essays that focus on a central idea with appropriate support and conclusion
	▪ Understand and use the writing process
	▪ Express ideas in writing to the reader in as clear a way as possible
		▪ For simple sentences, the principal parts of speech, and some complex sentences (adjective clauses and conditionals), students will. . .
		  ▪ Develop grammatical accuracy in speaking and writing
		  • Develop spoken and written fluency in communicative situations
		  • Improve listening comprehension
		  • Develop ability to identify and understand the target grammar structures in reading texts
		▪ Develop ability to monitor errors in speaking and writing

Objectives	• Compose meaningful paragraphs and essays conforming to the patterns presented in the text • Follow the steps in the writing process • Use cohesion devices in paragraphs and essays • Practice basic grammar structures of informational writing, giving instructions, explaining, evaluating, and summarizing ▪ Incorporate information from an outside source (especially in the form of a quotation) into an essay that the student has written ▪ Edit for correct mechanics (punctuation, capitalization, spelling) ▪ Correctly format and type essays on the word processor	• Use target grammar structures in focused practice for accuracy • Use the target grammar structures in communicative activities with a partner or a small group • Write dialogues or compositions of 1 or 2 paragraphs using the target grammar structures appropriately and correctly ▪ Understand the grammar structures in listening passages ▪ Identify the grammar structures in textbook passages, newspaper articles and readings ▪ Recognize and correct errors of the target grammar structures in the textbook passages, the student's own production, and in the production of others

(*Continued*)

Level 4	Writing	Grammar
Exit criteria	Students must pass the course with a grade of C- or better. • Students with grades below C- may exit into Level 5 at the discretion of the student advisor in consultation with their Writing 4 teacher & supervisor and/or a Michigan test score and writing sample at the Level 5 placement level.	Students must pass the course with a grade of C- or better. • Students with grades below C- may exit into Level 5 at the discretion of the student advisor in consultation with their Grammar 4 teacher & supervisor and/or a Michigan test score or cumulative test score at the Grammar 4 level.
Grading policy	60% Longer paragraphs and compositions 20% Shorter written assignments done-in class 10% Shorter homework assignments 10% Class participation	55% Written work (tests 40%, HW and written quizzes 15%) 20% Listening work 15% Speaking accuracy 10% Participation
Grammar Structures Covered	• Identifying cohesion devices • Simple, compound, complex, and compound-complex sentences • Commands • Conditional sentences (present real) • Modals in instructions • Definition structures • Cause and effect sentences • Punctuation of direct speech • Modals to control the strength of generalizations • Punctuation of in-text and end-of-text citations • Passive sentences in informational writing • Using comparatives and superlatives to give evidence in an evaluation • Using a variety of verb tense to show effects over a period of time • Subject-verb agreement	Verb tenses: 　Present: simple, perfect and progressive 　Past: simple, perfect and progressive 　Future (*be going to*, *will*, present & present progressive) Modals: present & past Adjective clauses Conditionals (real & unreal) Gerunds & infinitives Passive: present & past tense

Activities	**Writing Skills covered in the text chapters assigned**	Students should:
	• Practice four basic sentence structures	▪ Read the introduction and explanation before class
	• Review paragraph organization and cohesion devices	▪ Participate in grammar explanations with the teacher at the beginning of each new grammar point
	• Write clear, organized instructions	▪ Do written homework and study mistakes
	• Essay organization	▪ Pay attention to grammar as they speak
	• Write a memo	▪ Actively participate in grammar practice with the teacher, a partner or a group every day
	• Write detailed explanations of ideas and concepts	▪ Do recorded speeches in the lab
	• Make an evaluation based on accepted criteria	▪ Take quizzes and tests and study the teacher's corrections
	• Use a variety of types of evidence to support your evaluation	
	• Summarize and respond to reading passages	
	▪ Distinguish main ideas from supporting details and examples	
Supplemental activities (optional)		• Keep an error progress chart
		• Bring in or find examples of the grammar structure in reading texts or newspaper articles

Appendix IV
Level 5 Horizontal Articulation

Level 5	Speaking/Listening (Listening component)	(Speaking component)	Reading
Text(s)	• Hartmann & Blass, 2000. *Quest 3: Listening and Speaking in the Academic World*, McGraw-Hill • Orion, 1997. *Pronouncing American English, 2nd ed.*, Heinle & Heinle	• Hartmann & Blass, 2000. *Quest 3: Listening and Speaking in the Academic World*, McGraw-Hill • Orion, 1997. *Pronouncing American English, 2nd ed.*, Heinle & Heinle	▪ Baudoin, et.al., 1994. *Reader's Choice*, 2nd edition. Michigan. (*RC*) ▪ Rogerson, *Words for Students of English Vol.7*. Michigan.

Goals	▪ Refine aural language skills needed to participate as an interlocutor in:
	  ▪ individual and group oral presentations in academic, business, or personal arenas
	  ▪ discussions in formal settings (e. g., classrooms, business and public meetings)
	▪ Refine focused aural language skills needed to participate in:
	  • comprehending content of authentic listening materials
	  • note-taking of lectures and reports
		▪ Improve pronunciation, stress, and intonation at the discourse level
		▪ Refine oral language skills needed to participate in:
		  • individual and group oral presentations in academic, business, or personal arenas
		  • discussions in formal settings (e. g., classrooms, business and public meetings)
		• Develop self-assessment skills
		• Self-select language learning strategies
			▪ Develop reading comprehension to an advanced level, focusing on authentic texts, in order to handle professional and academic reading tasks
			▪ Increase vocabulary to an advanced level
			▪ Use reading strategies effectively for different purposes
			▪ Improve reading fluency

Objectives (Objectives continued)	• Apply pre, while, and post listening comprehension skills (e.g., predict, infer, summarize) ▪ Guess vocabulary meaning from context ▪ Recognize meaning from tone of voice ▪ Identify main ideas and supporting details	**Pronunciation:** ▪ Recognize English stress and intonation patterns ▪ Increase use of appropriate syllable, word, and phrasal stress ▪ Consistently aurally discriminate phonemes	• Do exercises and participate in discussion to demonstrate comprehension of authentic texts • Practice critical reading for restatement, inferences, personal opinions

(Continued)

Level 5	Speaking/Listening (Listening component)	(Speaking component)	Reading
	▪ Personalize note-taking skills (e.g., key words, abbreviations, symbols, outlining, indenting) ▪ Construct questions about listening text content ▪ Distinguish textual relationships ▪ Identify a speaker's point of view ▪ Apply note content to other activities (e.g., discussions, content quizzes) to emphasize the importance of meaningful notes ▪ Increase understanding of complex grammatical forms ▪ Increase understanding of complex vocabulary ▪ Listen to self-selected materials outside of the classroom	▪ Produce phonemes in prepared and spontaneous speech with increasing accuracy **Speaking:** ▪ Increase accurate use of complex grammatical forms • Increase accurate use of context-specific vocabulary • Reduce hesitations during prepared and spontaneous speech • Increase comprehensibility ▪ Prepare and present formal and informal speeches • Create appropriate visual materials to support formal speeches • Organize and execute a debate or panel • Consistently and actively participate in in-class speaking activities • Self-correct language samples • Self-select or create language learning strategies based on self-correction	• Apply specific pre-reading strategies • Identify main ideas and supporting details of paragraphs and longer texts • Skim for main ideas • Scan for specific information • Use context clues to understand word meanings • Recognize and use advanced, topic-based vocabulary sets • Use word analysis (stems and affixes) to understand word meanings • Read tables and graphs • Do timed reading in class and extensive reading out of class for fluency improvement • Summarize reading passages and write personal opinions on them, using short passages in class and book-length extensive reading out of class
Exit criteria	Students must pass the course with a grade of C- or better.	Students must pass the course with a grade of C- or better.	

Grading policy	Teacher determines specifics: 40–50% Listening comprehension exercises from *Quest 3* and other materials 40–50% Note-taking related activities (notes, quizzes from notes, etc.) 10% Participation	Teacher determines specifics: 40–60% Performance on debates, panels, leading class activities, final project, and other in-class speaking activities 30–50% Performance on speeches (impromptu and seminar) 10% Participation	50% Comprehension 25% Vocabulary 15% Outside Reading 10% Participation
Activities			**Intensive reading component** ▪ Readings from *RC* ▪ Authentic texts of different genres ▪ Nonprose readings ▪ Vocabulary units in WSE 7 ▪ Intensive vocabulary study **Extensive reading component** • Students choose one or more books, approved by the instructor, to read during the term

(*Continued*)

Level 5	Writing	Grammar
Text(s)	• Smalley, Ruetten, and Kozyrev, *Refining Composition Skills* (5th edition). Heinle & Heinle, 2000 (RCS) **Chapters covered: 1, 2, 5, 6, 7, 8, 11, 12; optional: 9 or 10** • Menasche,1997. *Writing a Research Paper* (2nd edition) (WRP)	▪ Maurer, 2000. *Focus on Grammar: An Advanced Course for Reference and Practice*, Longman

Goals	• Compose expository essays in preparation for professional or academic writing tasks
	• Compose a term or research paper to prepare for this academic writing task
	• Understand and use the composing process effectively in all writing tasks
	• Express ideas in writing in as clear a way as possible for the reader
		▪ For all sentence types, both simple and complex, with full or reduced dependent clauses, students will. . .
		  • Develop grammatical accuracy in speaking and writing
		  • Develop spoken and written fluency in communicative situations
		  • Improve listening comprehension
		  • Develop ability to identify and understand the target grammar structures in reading texts
		▪ Develop ability to monitor errors in speaking and writing

Objectives	▪ Compose expository essays conforming to patterns in the text ▪ Practice writing larger amounts more quickly to develop fluency in out-of-class writing and in timed, in-class sessions for essay exams ▪ Follow the steps of the composing process to generate ideas, draft, revise, and edit ▪ Use cohesive elements appropriately, particularly transitions, key words, and reference words ▪ Use organizational (rhetorical) patterns appropriately ▪ Compose paragraphs with effective main ideas and support sentences ▪ Edit for correct sentence-level grammar ▪ Edit for correct mechanics: punctuation, capitalization, spelling, indentation ▪ Practice academic writing conventions for a term paper or research paper	• Use target grammar structures in focused practice for accuracy • Use the target grammar structures in communicative activities with a partner or a small group • Write extended dialogues or essays of multiple paragraphs using the grammar structures appropriately and with good form. • Understand the grammar structures in listening passages • Identify the grammar structure in textbook passages, newspaper articles and readings • Recognize and correct errors of the target grammar structures in the textbook passages, the student's own production, and in the production of others.

Exit criteria		Students must attain a grade of C- or better on the work done in this course.
Grading policy	40% Research Paper	55% Written work (tests 40%, HW and written quizzes 15%)
	40% Compositions (homework and in-class writing)	20% Listening work
	10% Journal and other writing, grammar. and mechanics exercises	15% Speaking accuracy
	10% Class participation	10% Participation
Grammar Structures Covered	Review some grammar patterns, at teacher's discretion, based on observed students' needs in particular classes	Verb tenses:
		Present: simple, perfect and progressive
		Past: simple, perfect and progressive
		Future (*be going to*, *will*, present & present progressive) + future perfect & future perfect progressive
		Modals: present & past
		Adjective clauses, including reduced clauses
		Unreal Conditionals, including subjunctives & inverted subject
		Gerunds & infinitives
		Passive: present & past tense
		Adverb clauses, including reduced clauses
Activities	**Writing Skills covered in the text chapters assigned**	Students should:
	▪ Writing process	▪ Read the introduction and explanation before class
	▪ General paragraph structure	▪ Participate in grammar explanations with the teacher at the beginning of each new grammar point
	▪ Expository paragraphs	▪ Do written homework and study mistakes
	▪ Expository essay structure	▪ Pay attention to grammar as they speak
	▪ Essays developed according to particular organizational patterns	▪ Actively participate in grammar practice with the teacher, a partner or a group every day
	▪ Examples	▪ Do recorded speeches in the lab
	▪ Comparison and Contrast	▪ Take quizzes and tests and study the teacher's corrections
	▪ Cause and effect essay	
	▪ Argumentative essay	
	▪ Classification essay (optional)	
	▪ Process analysis essay (optional)	
Supplemental activities (optional)		▪ Keep an error progress chart
		▪ Bring in or find examples of the grammar structure in reading texts, newspaper articles or conversations

3 Placement Assessment and Developmental Measures in an Intensive English Program

3.1 Introduction

Assessment is a vital part of the administration of an IEP for placement of students on entry, measuring their progress through the program, and evaluating their academic readiness. Teachers know that they need to assess students' development at different points, and students expect that their proficiency will be judged. The importance of assessment is also stressed by agencies that recognize the quality of language programs. For example, the Commission on English Language Program Accreditation makes assessment a key component of its **Student Achievement Standards.** This focus is to ensure that students who enroll in language programs are receiving education that clearly indicates to them how they can make progress in their language ability and informs them of that progress in terms that they can understand. For example, CEA Student Achievement Standard 1 focuses on placement systems:

http://cea-accredit.org/images/pdfs/2018_CEA_Standards.pdf

> **Student Achievement Standard 1:** The program or language institution has a placement system that is consistent with its admission requirements and allows valid and reliable placement of students into levels.

The subsequent Student Achievement Standards (2–4) require that written documentation be in place for valid and reliable evaluation of students' achievement, how students can progress through the program (or not), and how students are informed of the assessment of their development in the program. Failure to meet such standards will result in accreditation being withheld from an IEP. In the context of the United States, we have already seen that accreditation is required by the US government for the right to issue documents for student visas (I-20s), so this area is not only important for program quality but also for maintaining a program's accreditation status.

This focus on assessment is reflected in recent scholarship and demonstrates that language program assessment practices and learning outcomes are scrutinized as part of program evaluation in the wider research community, and not just for accreditation purposes (Norris, 2009). While such review does not always mean that quantitative details and analysis are better than qualitative program review (Kiely, 2009), some universities have used such programmatic evaluation in high-stakes decisions concerning whether programs are even allowed to continue in operation (Shawer, 2012).

Moreover, assessment is necessary to make decisions concerning, among other things: (a) whether general English or more specific English is more effective in preparing students for admission to a university (Cumming, 2015, pp. 414–415) or work in their academic field (Chostelidou, 2011); (b) whether simpler placement tools such as lexical decision tasks could be used (Harrington & Carey, 2009; Roche & Harrington, 2013); and (c) how placement might relate to later development and academic achievement both in English as a second language and English as a foreign language (EFL)-medium academic programs (Harrington & Roche, 2014).

Although this chapter provides some theoretical background for assessment, it cannot present a single 'best' version of how placement and assessment of development should be carried out based on the most up-to-date quantitative analyses.[1] Instead, this chapter concentrates on various aspects of how placement and writing assessment *actually worked* in this IEP and how it has evolved based on experience, data analysis, and discussion among faculty members. The account in this chapter thus describes a real situation, with all its challenges. The main goal of this chapter is to outline a process of analysis of placement data, which is why this is by far the longest section. However, the later portion of the chapter describes our current exam policies and reviews issues related to rubrics.

The section on placement testing introduces several statistical concerns, which may be challenging for some teachers. (See Brown (2013) for an overview of topics that teachers may find useful.) Based on my experience, the reality in most IEPs is that many teachers and administrators often do not have time to consider carefully all the recent developments in sophisticated statistical models and testing theory. Moreover, professionals with the depth of expertise in the rapidly developing field of assessment and the quantitative methods used in large testing companies such as Educational Testing Service (ETS), which runs the internet-based Test of English as a Foreign Language, or the Cambridge Exam syndicate, are rarely available in IEPs. Even if they were, the sample sizes in most IEPs would make statistical analysis difficult. Based on the 'true story' analysis of the Pitt IEP, we may make recommendations for practical decision-making in other IEPs. Therefore, this chapter is conceived of as a practical reflection of what actually happens in one IEP rather

60 *Placement and Assessment in an IEP*

than a theoretical and quantitative justification of what *should* happen based on up-to-date theory. (This position is not to doubt or discount quantitative research, as such work is very important for the field in general. For example, Gu [2014] conducted a recent analysis of TOEFL iBT scores that examined the contexts in which learners had prepared for the TOEFL and was able to conclude that study in an English-speaking country vs. a non-English-speaking country had little effect on TOEFL iBT scores.)

As we shall see, placement decisions may run counter to students' uneven stages in linguistic and literacy development and may not always 'fit' into a program in the way that language center administrators might hope. Often, students are stronger in one skill and weaker in another, but that is not a reason to be pessimistic about placement decisions. Many readers of this chapter will recognize the challenges that they have faced in making placement and assessment decisions in their own programs. The data presented in this chapter might inform practices in other programs: either for confirmation of local decision-making processes or for adapting procedures to make them more or less flexible depending on the needs of the program. The chapter also provides some suggestions for how programs might *visualize* data as a part of a documentation process for an accreditation agency or for internal discussions. Before plunging into the IEP data, the next section provides some reminders that concerns about testing and assessment are warranted.

3.2 Background to Assessment

Lyle Bachmann has been one of the leading figures in second language assessment in recent decades. In an article that provided a historical overview, Bachman (2000) traced the recent history of approaches to language testing. Much like the recent history of language teaching, the theory and practice of assessment have evolved as our understanding of language as a complex cognitive linguistic system and set of literacy skills has improved.

In early years, during the 1970s in the United States, the construct 'proficiency' was seen by the testing research community more as a 'single trait'.[2] This characterization meant that the different skill areas (reading, writing, speaking, listening, and grammar) could be viewed as deriving from a unitary 'whole' single source of proficiency. The result of this view was that knowledge was assessable via discrete point item tests, rather than longer texts produced by learners. Recall that a discrete-point item is one in which a single grammatical or lexical point could be measured in one question. For example, in the paper-based version of the TOEFL, the structure that required subject-verb inversion after a negative word at the beginning of the sentence was frequently part of the grammar section, for example: 'Not only does Kris drink milk, but she also drinks tea',

Placement and Assessment in an IEP   61

compared with the ungrammatical '*Not only Mary drinks milk, she also drinks tea'. This kind of test was common when multiple-choice sections in listening, grammar, and reading were the means of determining a learner's proficiency. At its inception, the TOEFL had no tests of productive skills, and only later did tests in speaking (Test of Spoken English) and writing (Test of Written English) become available as supplementary components. The paper-based standard TOEFL was an achievement test that was primarily designed to determine whether someone was ready to begin study in an English-medium higher education institution. The Michigan Test of English Language Proficiency (MTELP) (Corrigan et al., 1978) was a similar test. In fact, the 'constructs' underlying the skills of reading, writing, speaking, and listening remain a focus of underlying trait analysis, now called 'components'. For example, Gu (2014) analyzed TOEFL iBT scores and concluded that scores on the four sections could be 'reduced' to two 'latent components', where 'the ability to listen, read and write' constituted one component and 'the ability to speak' a second and clearly separate component.

The 1980s witnessed the emergence of more sophisticated views of the complexity of language proficiency, due in large part to the notion of communicative competence (Hymes, 1972) and its introduction into language teaching theory and methods (Paulston, 1974; Canale & Swain, 1980). One can broadly characterize this change from a specialized focus on accuracy of forms (grammar and vocabulary) at the sentence level to a broader view of how language is used to achieve communicative goals in different contexts and in longer discourse beyond the sentence level. Moreover, it was recognized that exact grammatical accuracy was not the sole criterion for judging proficiency as it had been under the controlled view of language training of patterns in the audio-lingual method, where error was to be corrected (Lado & Fries, 1957, p. xv). Despite these theoretical advances, by the end of the 1980s, many testing organizations had not adapted their basic test format, and it was not until 2005 that ETS incorporated mixed skills into the TOEFL, which it did in its internet-based test (www.ets.org/s/toefl/pdf/toefl_ibt_insight_s1v6.pdf). This development relied in part on work by Biber and colleagues (e.g., Biber et al., 2004), who analyzed language that was used in various academic contexts and resulted in a test that measured a student's ability to function in that language environment.

In a test developed outside the United States, the IELTS (first developed by Cambridge University and the British Council and later in collaboration with Australian universities and colleges) adapted earlier to changes in views of communicative competence and produced a test that was widely available by the late 1980s. Their use of information transfer tasks, for example, describing a graph in a writing assessment task, was already a common pedagogical practice advocated by British applied linguists in the 1980s. Examples of such tasks can be found in Brumfit and

62 Placement and Assessment in an IEP

Johnson (1979)'s book on communicative language teaching. Widdowson's (1979) textbook series on reading and thinking skills was another example of interactive text and information transfer exercises. (The British Council had made this series available to teachers supervised by them when I arrived in China as a volunteer English teacher in the autumn of 1982.)

Bachman recounts that during the 1990s and 2000s, research and development on testing increased its use of results of second language acquisition theory and developmental stages, making the gap between second language acquisition research and language assessment narrower. The important insight from Corder's (1967) and Selinker's (1972) work on interlanguage is that while instruction *is* important (Long, 2007; Spada & Tomita, 2010), learners also exhibit '*internally regulated*' developmental patterns that do not directly and immediately reflect instruction about rules. Indeed, there may be developmental patterns, processing routines or bottle-necks, and abstract constraints from the first or other languages that influence a learners' perception of language input either in spoken or written form (e.g., Harrington, 1987; Juffs & Rodríguez, 2014; Martin, 2017). A very specific example of such a constraint emerged in research by White, Spada, Lightbown, and Ranta (1991) on question formation among French-speaking elementary school learners in Quebec. Although the learners acquired 'Can you eat pizza?', moving the auxiliary in front of a pronoun to form a *yes-no* question, they were challenged by the auxiliary in front of a full noun phrase in sentences such as 'Can Garfield eat pizza?' (p. 429). This reflects a constraint on question formation in French that they applied to English in spite of the instruction that they received. At the beginning to intermediate stages of language development, basic structures of the language may develop based on these (internal) constraints. An example of an approach to assessment based on these processing considerations is Pienemann's work on his 'Rapid Profile' tool (Pienemann, Johnston, & Brindley, 1988; Pienemann, 1998, 2005; Spinner, 2011). In teaching methods in Spanish as a second language, VanPatten's Processing Instruction Approach (VanPatten, 2002) reflects these insights and related findings from processing in Spanish L2.

In sum, language testing practices have evolved from multiple-choice formats that focus on discrete points of grammar and vocabulary to task-based formats that include longer assessments of spoken and written production with portfolios (e.g., Barootchi & Keshavarz, 2002), insights from SLA theory, corpus-based analyses of tasks that learners face (e.g., Lee, 2007; Mislevy, Steinberg, & Almond, 2002), and vocabulary assessments that measure lexical knowledge more precisely (Read, 2007, 2013).[3] In sociocultural theory, assessment can be integrated into instructional activities (Poehner & Lantolf, 2005). Finally, advances in data science have allowed researchers to track the development of learners' language use both in classroom data (e.g., Juffs, 2019; Naismith,

Han, Juffs, Hill, & Zheng, 2018) and production data in standardized tests (e.g., three million test-takers for IELTS in 2017 (www.ielts.org/news/2017/ielts-numbers-rise-to-three-million-a-year).[4]

In the light of these considerations, we will first address issues of placement assessment and then consider other forms of assessment.

3.3 Placement Assessment

In this section, we consider the following specific questions:

1. What theoretical and empirical assessment tools can inform IEP administrators' decisions?
2. What kinds of *statistics* and *qualitative* evaluation can be used for assessment?
3. Is there a justification for relying more or less on one placement tool?

3.3.1 Description of the Placement Tools in the Intensive English Program

The first decision that a program must make concerns which level to place students in based on their proficiency at entry. This process is an important one for both students and administrators. The placement test is a high-stakes task for the student because this evaluation affects the time that they must spend studying English before they enter an academic program or feel ready to enter the workforce using English. (Students who are sponsored by their government may also have time limits for reaching a particular level. This situation may make them either eager to be in a higher or lower level depending on their specific circumstances. However, placement decisions should be made on the basis of proficiency fit with the curriculum level and not on time and funding available.)

It is also a high-stakes activity for the IEP administration. IEP students are not like international students who are going to take university degree courses, have made a large tuition deposit, and are therefore almost guaranteed to come to campus for their programs. For an IEP, it is possible that only 60–80% of students who have been issued I-20s to get a student visa will actually attend the institution. Thus, the Pitt IEP usually does not even know how many students will arrive to study or what their level will be on the first day because they are not required to present proficiency scores before they arrive. In this context, placement testing, subsequent decisions on splitting a class that is over-enrolled, and the consequent need to hire part-time instructors is an intense process. Student testing, placement, and orientation must be accomplished within a short turn-around time, often no longer than two days. A key factor is that placement cannot result in students clamoring to change

64 Placement and Assessment in an IEP

levels – either because they think they should be in a higher level or because they want to be in a lower level for some other reason. Some testing researchers suggest consulting learners themselves as part of the diagnostic process (e.g., Harding, Alderson, & Brunfaut, 2015), but student self-assessment is not, and probably could not be, part of the process in the Pitt IEP.

Until 2012, the IEP used the MTELP for placement into three levels. For information purposes and for context for the data in later chapters, Table 3.1 lists the range of scores and cut scores (see Section 3.3.2) that

Table 3.1 Pitt IEP Placement Test Scores – Historical Viewpoint

Level	MTELP	IEP List. Comp. Test	Writing Sample	CEFR Equiv.	Descriptor – Typical Beginning Student
ELI 3	40–59	11–18	2	A2–B1 Waystage	• Can communicate only with much difficulty in most situations. • Fluency is very limited. • Comprehension is very limited. • Makes very many errors that lead to misunderstanding. • Can produce some discourse of several sentences (speaking and writing).
ELI 4	55–79	19–25	3	B2–C1 Threshold	• Can communicate with limited success in many situations. • Fluency is limited. • Comprehension is limited. • Makes frequent errors that lead to misunderstanding. • Can produce extended discourse beyond several sentences but still limited (speaking and writing).
ELI 5	70–100	26–32	4–5	C1 and Above	• Can communicate with success in many situations. • Has several weaknesses in fluency. • Has several weaknesses in comprehension. • Difficulties with accuracy cause some misunderstandings. • Can produce some extended discourse beyond the paragraph level (speaking and writing); writing shows some organizational awareness.

Placement and Assessment in an IEP 65

were used until 2015 during the period of data collection described in Chapters 4–7.

The MTELP was originally designed to test higher-level students' readiness for academic study and to distinguish among higher-level students; it is a discrete point test, and contained rather dated language that sometimes might appear in a nineteenth-century novel. Thus, the IEP found that this test did not distinguish adequately at the lower levels. In other words, there were 'floor effects', which means too many learners scored low and made it difficult to make level-placement decisions distinguishing Level 3 from Level 4, even though large proficiency differences exist between those two levels. This issue is a very important one for programs because it is necessary to sort learners into manageable groups that match the materials prepared for different proficiency levels of students and the associated student learning outcomes that were discussed in Chapter 2.

Therefore, in order to address this problem, the IEP added the use of an IEP in-house writing test in order to 'finesse' the placement of students into appropriate levels. This test took the form of two writing prompts. Possible topics were:

1. Describe the place you grew up in. What are the advantages and disadvantages of XYZ for children?
2. Describe how you use X in your daily life. How has X changed people's lives?

These writing tasks were designed to assist in determining students' writing skills that would indicate where in the program a student might best start. Only 30 minutes were allowed for this task, so not a great deal of output was possible. These writing samples were scored on a range of 1–6, based on the following categories:

1. Grammar and punctuation, capitalization
2. Spelling, appropriate meaning, correct derivational form, variety
3. Content: does the sample address the prompt, are ideas fully developed (not formulaic), and is meaning clear?
4. Organization: main ideas supported with details and examples (includes reference to topic/support and cohesive devices)

The writing rubric thus targets the components of writing that are the focus of coursework in the IEP. This rubric is provided in Appendix I.

Subsequently, the IEP also developed a listening test that was matched to the tasks that the students would complete in the curriculum as tasks became progressively more sophisticated and more linguistically demanding from Level 3 to 4 to 5. There were four sections in the test:

1. General listening: 3 passages and 6 questions
2. Short academic lectures: 4 passages and 12 questions

66 Placement and Assessment in an IEP

3. Conversation, 6 conversations: 12 questions
4. Picture interpretation (listening and observing a picture): 2 pictures and 2 questions

All answers were multiple choice, with 32 possible points, converted to a percentage. Thus, the MTELP, the writing sample, and the listening tests scores were then used for placement.

As new tests became available, the IEP adapted its approach to placement assessment beginning in 2013, with cut scores revised in 2015 as additional levels were created. The IEP now uses a newer test, specifically designed for placement: The Michigan English Placement Test (Michigan EPT), https://michiganassessment.org/institutions/products-services/michigan-ept/. (The test, previously known as CaMLA ept, was originally developed by Cambridge Assessment English and the University of Michigan's English Language Institute Testing and Certificate Division.) The IEP uses the following parts of this test: the ept Listening (25 points), the ept Grammar (20 points), Reading (15 points), and Vocabulary (20 points). A combined listening and grammar-reading-vocabulary ept score out of 80 is used primarily to place students. The new established cut scores for the program are set out in Table 3.2.

After the adoption of the EPT, the IEP continued to use the in-house writing and listening tests with the EPT for several years. The analysis in Section 3.4 includes both scores from the EPT and these two tests and will show how the IEP made decisions to change its placement practice based on the analysis.

3.3.2 Determining and Justifying Cut Scores

A 'cut score' is a score used to create a 'break' score among levels of proficiency in placement decisions. One question administrators face is

Table 3.2 Pitt IEP Cut Scores (Note Level 6 Added After 2015)

Level	Ept Combined Maximum = 80	Writing Maximum = 6	CEFR Equivalent and Language 'Ability'
Not accepted	Below 38	Below 3	A1 Breakthrough
Low Intermediate Level 3	38–47	3.1–3.9	A2–B1 Waystage
Intermediate Level 4	48–59	4.0–4.9	B1 Threshold
High Intermediate Level 5	60–68	5.0–5.9	B2–Edge of C1
Low Advanced Level 6	69+	6.0	Low C2 Effective

how to know which specific scores are appropriate cut scores for each proficiency level. Comparisons among tests, for example, Michigan EPT, TOEFL iBT, and CEFR, are one way to start, but a program may have more than three or four levels. Many commercial IEPs have entry once a month for flexibility. Some university-based programs have admissions twice a semester, making six 'levels' over the course of an academic year, or even eight if the program operates on a quarter system. There are various ways of determining these scores and demonstrating to an outside entity – a dean's office or accrediting agency – that the groups cohere in terms of proficiency and either justify smaller classes or represent acceptable practice. In this section, we will review some published reports of methods of confirming cut scores and compare the ELI data to these reports.[5]

Shin and Lidster (2016) looked at three ways of establishing cut scores for levels that make reference both to quantitative data and the expertise of language faculty: the bookmark method, the borderline method, and cluster analysis.

The bookmark method is based on item response theory, which assesses how likely it is for a test taker to be correct depending on the place of a specific test item on a difficulty range. The researchers ranked test items on an in-house multiple-choice test in a list – one per page – from 'most easy' to 'most difficult'. For example, the item G.20 involved a counter factual 'if clause' and G.21 a clause with 'since/for', but G.22 was an object relative clause.

G.20 If there ___ so much traffic yesterday, I would have arrived on time. A: (hadn't been)
G.21. Eric studied Japanese ___ four years. (A: for)
G.22 The case ____ was very luxurious. (A: which she wanted)

They asked teachers to indicate where the cut-off should be for each level. The teachers were instructed not to flip ahead or to skip back.

The researchers discovered that teachers found this task difficult. Indeed, the ranking for the G.21 versus the other two items would seem problematic – the 'for/since' distinction of G.21 is somewhat lexical, whereas the counter-factual and object relatives are much more complex than G.21, depending perhaps on first language influence. Moreover, the teachers disobeyed instructions not to flip back and ahead. Insufficient low-level items were also a problem for this method.

Another issue with this approach is that it is solely based on grammar and ignores the more communicative approach to language proficiency. While it is true that higher-level communicative functions normally require more complex grammar, this is not always the case. For example, expressing a possibility using complex grammar is one way of communicating: 'The man might be a manager, as he wears a suit to work', but a

68 Placement and Assessment in an IEP

similar idea could also be conveyed with a simpler structure: 'Perhaps the man is a manager because he's wearing a suit'. In this latter sentence, the uncertainty is expressed with the adverb *perhaps*, rather than the more difficult modal verb phrase 'might be'. (It is generally a mark of lower-level learners that they use adverbials to express concepts determined by complex verb phrases in higher-level students, e.g., VanPatten, 2002.)

A second method that Shin and Lidster explored was the 'borderline method'. In this approach, teachers identify the median (50th percentile) scores of the lowest and highest students in a level. This score then becomes a cut score for determining students in the level below and the level above that particular level. The issue in this case for an IEP is that some levels often have lower numbers of students, which makes it impossible to identity a large enough group of lower and higher students, and, because of these low numbers, the cut scores are unstable. Such an approach also does not fully take into account the kinds of skills and functions that each level is designed to teach.

The final method that Shin and Lidster discuss is the k-cluster approach, which we will discuss in the next section on data analysis and presentation. This approach is also a possibility discussed by Winke (2013), who found it useful in organizing groups. In her study, she combined self-assessment, a listening test, and group oral test scores in a k-means cluster analysis to place learners into seven classes. Only 4 out of 128 test takers asked to be moved to a different class, one to be with his wife, one to have a different teacher, and two to have more challenging classes. Thus, this placement test with group orals was a success (Winke, 2013, p. 261).

Another potential placement method that has emerged recently is one that relies almost entirely on vocabulary recognition and speed of recognition (reaction time) (e.g., Harrington & Carey, 2009; Roche & Harrington, 2013). The assumption in this approach is that vocabulary size will correlate very well with proficiency and could be a reliable proxy for measurement of other skills such as academic writing and thus ultimately achievement in an academic context. On this basis, the claim might be that placement decisions can be made through a rapid and automatic timed *yes-no* (Y/N) test. Harrington and Carey (2009) investigated placement and scores on the Y/N test in a commercial language program in Australia, an English as second language context. They found that it correlated well with listening and grammar tests.

In an English as a foreign language context, Roche and Harrington (2013) investigated an academic English-medium program in Oman. Their study relied on scores on a writing sample based on an IELTS prompt (scored from 1–10 points), scores from grade point average at the university, and scores on a simple vocabulary recognition test based on the 1000 to 3000, the 5000, and the 10,000 frequency bands in the British National Corpus.[6] Distractors in the Y/N test included phonologically/orthographically possible words such as 'blurge' and impossible words such as 'rgbuel'. The Y/N test required participants to answer within 5 seconds (5000 milliseconds). Vocabulary scores were calculated based on a ratio of correct responses on the possible and impossible words. Overall, the authors are cautiously optimistic that the results they found with the Y/N test are predictive of academic performance. However, the students in their study – Arabic speakers – accepted more non-words than students who studied in Australia. This effect may have been due to well-known problems Arabic-speaking students have with vowels or perhaps students not taking the activity as seriously as they needed to. In general, Harrington's work suggests that the Y/N test needs some work to monitor response rates to the 'false alarms' or acceptances of non-words. However, the task clearly has the potential to be used as a placement tool. It may be especially useful for online pre-screening for placement (Harrington & Carey, 2009, p. 625). This procedure would be useful for institutes that may wish to gain an insight into students' proficiency before they arrive at the program and thus be able to estimate how many sections at each level may be needed.

3.4 Data Visualization and Analysis

3.4.1 Central Tendency and Dispersion

Most teachers and administrators have a good idea of measures of central tendency: mean (=average), median (=50th percentile, or the score that marks the central point above which and below which half of the scores occur), and mode (most frequently occurring score). In addition, there are measures of dispersion, which are the range (lowest to highest score) and standard deviation (the average distance of all the scores from the mean). This latter statistic is important in understanding the 'normal distribution' or bell curve. In a normal distribution, one standard deviation above and below accounts for 34.1% of the data on each side of the mean:

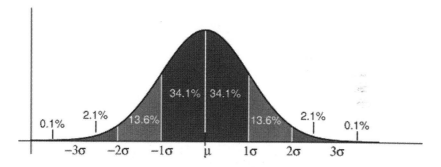

Figure 3.1 The Normal Curve (c.f. Brown, 1988)
Source: https://commons.wikimedia.org/w/index.php?curid=1788643

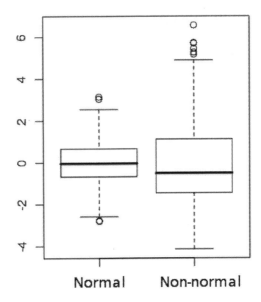

Figure 3.2 Normal and Non-Normal Distributions in a Boxplot
Source: https://commons.wikimedia.org/wiki/File:Normality_box-plot.png

Based on this notion of distribution of scores, many other different ways of visualizing data exist that will help administrators understand the distribution of their data. One important and useful way of visualizing data is the boxplot (Larson-Hall, 2017). A boxplot is informative in that it shows the group center and the spread (dispersion). In addition, the shape of the boxplot is very useful, as the central line shows the 50th percentile: a normal distribution should have equal portions above and below the central line. The shaded part of the box shows the interquartile range from the 25th to the 75th percentiles. Boxplots also identify outliers, which are data points that are very far from the average. These scores could be truly extreme or the result of data entry error, which can be checked. The lines extend to the minimum and max of data set, with outliers being mapped separately. A boxplot is illustrated in Figure 3.2, showing the 50th percentile on the right boxplot, with many scores higher than the 50th percentile, including outliers.

3.4.2 Cluster Analysis

The statistics of central tendency and dispersion allow an administrator to see descriptive patterns. Cluster analysis uses a statistical procedure that goes beyond description, however (Staples & Biber, 2015).

Jain (2010) identified three main goals of cluster analysis. The first is to understand 'underlying structure': to gain insight into data, generate hypotheses, detect anomalies, and identify salient features. The second is 'natural classification': to identify the degree of similarity among forms or organisms (phylogenetic relationships). The third reason has the most potential for use in IEP contexts: this is 'compression', which is a method for 'organizing the data and summarizing it through cluster prototypes'.

One of the problems that IEPs face is that learners may have strengths in one area but weaknesses in another. For example, some learners may have some oral fluency with a limited range of vocabulary and syntax but be less competent in reading and/or writing. However, the strengths and weaknesses can potentially be summed together to form a central point; this 'summation' is the goal of a cluster analysis. The analysis will take account of the strengths and weaknesses and will group students based on their most similar characteristics.

Most statistical software packages have a k-means (or kernel) cluster analysis function, which is the specific statistical procedure that looks at many data points from a large group and then tries to establish subgroups that are as different from each other as possible based on these multiple data points. In other words, 'high dimensional data are transformed into lower dimensional data' (Ding & He, 2004, p. 29). An important first step is to convert the scores to Z scores (that is, scores with a mean of 0 and standard deviation of 1.) This conversion is important because the scores must be on the same scale/range for the program to make the correct calculations. The package SPSS, which is available to most university faculties, will carry out these calculations, under the 'Classify' menu and choosing k-means. (In statistics, 'k' stands for 'group'.) This method allows the researcher to specify the number of desired groups that reflect levels in an IEP. A second method is called the 'two step' cluster, which does *not* allow the researcher to specify the number of groups but instead provides a strictly statistical look at how the data may best be classified.

3.5 A Case Study From the Pitt Intensive English Program

In order to provide a practical example of how data can be displayed, visualized, and analyzed with k-cluster analysis, this section will present an example analysis from the University of Pittsburgh IEP placement data over several semesters. The analysis focuses on answering the following questions:

1. Are students in each level *homogeneous* subgroups for that level?
2. If there are outliers, what might explain these students' placement?

72 *Placement and Assessment in an IEP*

3. Does the Michigan EPT placement test correlate with the in-house ELI listening test (graded on a large range interval) and the in-house writing test (graded by rubric on a narrower range of scores)?
4. Are there similar homogeneous subgroups for the in-house tests?

3.5.1 Participants

Placement data from five semesters were accessed from the ELI database: summer 2014, fall 2015, spring 2015, summer 2015, and fall 2016. A total of 359 records were selected from the IEP database. (The database had been designed to make administration of the IEP more efficient in processing applications and for registration. Subsequently, the database has been invaluable in tracking records and creating reports for CEA accreditation.) All records for the semesters (374 records) were downloaded. These data were screened by removing non-IEP students (students who took one course in the evening, for example, were removed), and a check was made for duplicate records and that a student had not been registered in a previous term. This screening resulted in the removal of 15 records. Because not all students took all tests, students who had EPT records + writing scores totaled 294, and students who had an EPT, ELI writing, and in-house listening totaled 219. The first languages of the students were approximately: Arabic 43%, Chinese 12%, Spanish 8%, Japanese 7%, Korean 7%, Thai 3%, Turkish 3%, Kazakh 3%, Other: 10%.

There are several points to note from these data on initial inspection. Obviously, the score means in each level are what is expected from the cut scores listed in Table 3.2. For the EPT, the test showed reliable differences among the groups ($F(3, 358) = 406.88$, $p \leq .0001$). However, it is striking that the ELI writing test resulted in identical scores for Levels 5 and 6. When the writing scores are compared, a difference among the groups is found ($F(3, 353) = 29.5$, $p \leq .0001$), but Levels 5 and 6 are not different, as the means clearly suggest. The ELI listening test does reliably differentiate each group ($F(3, 275) = 124.16$, $p \leq .0001$).

One issue that is rarely addressed quantitatively, although much discussed by teachers, is the effect of first language of the learners when they first register in the IEP. This issue has to be considered carefully, because the 'first language' includes not only the typological characteristics of the L1 (syntax, phonology, etc.) but also issues related to orthography and the educational system of the learners. Most IEPs have a heterogeneous learner population, although, as we saw in Chapter 1, this may depend on their location in the United States. Most IEP students in the United States come from the Middle East (Gulf States in particular), China, Korea, and Japan and fewer speakers from Latin America. In looking at our proficiency data, if languages were grouped by language family, the following region of origin/L1 typologies can be observed: Arabic

Placement and Assessment in an IEP   73

(n = 126), Japanese/Korean (n = 39),[7] Chinese (n =40), and Romance (n = 31). These groupings serve as a proxy for their overall language structure and possibly cultural influences. Bearing in mind Bachmann's admonition regarding numbers (they don't tell the whole story), it is worth considering a more fine-grained analysis to investigate whether perceptions of teachers have any quantitative support.

Repeated-measures ANOVA showed a reliable proficiency by L1 typological group interaction (F(6, 504) = 8.78, $p \leq$ .0001), with the Romance group being reliably different from the Arabic-speaking group, while no other differences are reliable. Separate analyses show that the source of this interaction is that the Arabic-speaking group is different from the Romance speakers in ELI writing and the grammar-vocabulary-reading part of the Michigan EPT but not the listening component.

Further exploration of the data, based on the interaction between scores on writing and listening in a repeated-measures ANOVA, was that we know intuitively that the Arabic speakers are more aurally/orally oriented, in contrast to the other groups, who perform somewhat better on 'literacy' measures (writing, reading, and grammar). For the Arabic speakers, the relationship between the Michigan EPT listening and ELI writing is (r = .39, p = .0001), and the EPT grammar and ELI writing is (r = .39, p = .0001), which is the same. However, for the Romance speakers, while a relationship between the Michigan EPT listening and ELI writing exists (r = .36, p = .0001), the EPT grammar and ELI writing relationship is stronger (r = .44, p = .0001). Analogous correlations for the Chinese were r = .410 listening-writing and r = .50 grammar-writing, and for the Japan-Korean group, r = .31 and r = .54. Regression analysis confirms that for all groups *except* the Arabic-speaking learners, performance on the ELI writing task is more strongly related to grammar-reading and vocabulary (25% of variance explained for the other groups combined) than listening ability, as one might expect. In contrast, the Arabic-speaking learners show a stronger relationship between listening ability and the ELI writing, albeit a weak one (15%) of writing ability variance explained by listening.

These results confirm a frequently noted tendency for Arabic speaking learners' spoken skills to be more developed than their written skills, whereas other language groups show a more expected relationship among the skills. One implication is that in our testing and instruction, we might give less weight to Arabic speakers for their listening scores in placement for programs that lead to academic preparation. It could be useful to think of this in terms of the Basic Interpersonal Skills/Cognitive and Academic Language Proficiency (Cummins, 2003). Our Arabic-speaking students are fluent communicators (strong BICS) but as yet have not developed CALP.

The results show that the Arabic-speaking group does not differ from the other two large groups typically enrolled in IEPs, however. This result

74 *Placement and Assessment in an IEP*

is important, as it shows that classes combining L1 typological groups in each level are fully justified and that the L1 effects, while real, can be dealt with within the classes at each level.

3.5.2 Data Visualization

Given that we have reported the descriptive and first language statistics, we can now move to visualize the data in boxplots. Figure 3.3 demonstrates the combined Michigan EPT scores for the data set represented in Table 3.3.

Recall that the upper and lower whiskers represent scores outside the middle 50% of scores. Whiskers often (but not always) stretch over a wider range of scores than the middle quartile groups. Notice that in addition to central tendency (the 50th percentile bar in the center of each box), now it is possible to see outliers identified in this case by the L1. This visualization can immediately alert a placement reviewer to potential errors in data entry, placement, or other issues in a way that simple means and standard deviation cannot.

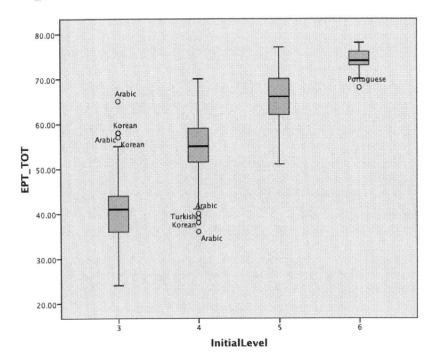

Figure 3.3 Boxplot of EPT Total Scores

Placement and Assessment in an IEP 75

Table 3.3 Test Scores by Initial Placement Level

Level	Combined EPT: Mean (SD)	Writing: Mean SD/6	Listening: Mean SD/100%
3	40.91 (6.4) ($n = 124$)	3.26 (.73) ($n = 101$)	43.79 (12.26) ($n =98$)
4	54.16 (6.47) ($n = 126$)	3.81 (.85) ($n = 108$)	60.08 (11.88) ($n = 101$)
5	65.22 (5.18) ($n = 77$)	4.41 (.92) ($n = 59$)	74.87 (10.01) ($n = 57$)
6	73.43 (2.75) ($n = 32$)	4.41 (.94) ($n = 26$)	83.90 (9.97) ($n = 20$)
Total	359	294	276

Table 3.4 Placement Test Results by L1 Typological Group

$N = 256$	Arabic ($n = 126$)	Japanese/ Korean ($n = 39$)	Chinese ($n = 40$)	Romance ($n = 51$)
EPT Listening	18.56 (4.06)	18.90 (4.2)	19.18 (3.79)	19.61 (3.78)
EPT Grammar, Reading, Vocabulary	32.88[a] (9.56)	36.69 (8.33)	35.97 (8.80)	40.59[a] (8.48)
ELI Writing	3.6[b] (.89)	3.82 (.97)	3.99 (.81)	4.07[b] (.91)

*Means that have the same superscript[a/b] are reliably different.

In this case, Level 3 shows outliers above the range, and Level 4 show outliers below that range. For Level 3, the Korean speaker had a very low writing score – 1.7/6 – and another only 3.5. The two Arabic speakers in Level 3 who had higher EPT scores also had low writing – 3.5, 3.6, which is why they were in Level 3. In Level 4, the Arabic speakers had low scores on all measures; the Korean speaker had low scores on all measures – 2.65; the Turkish speaker had low scores and 2.35 on writing. In Level 6, the Portuguese speaker had a writing score of 4.5 (which would be Level 4) and a total EPT score of 69.

3.5.3 K-Cluster Analysis

As outlined already, students are currently placed into one of four levels: Low Intermediate (Level 3), Intermediate (Level 4), High Intermediate (Level 5), and Advanced (Level 6). The data used are from five semesters ($N = 294$ students) of level placement and three placement scores: Cambridge-Michigan Placement Tests (EPT) of Structure and Listening and the IEP in-house writing test.

76 *Placement and Assessment in an IEP*

The first analysis that was carried out was based on five semesters of data that included writing scores. All scores were converted to z scores to ensure comparability. (Note that z scores are transformed scores, such that 0 is the mean, +1 is one standard deviation above the mean, and −1 one standard deviation below the mean. See https://en.wikipedia.org/wiki/Standard_score for further information.) The values reported in the graphs are cluster centers and mean z scores from actual placement levels. For example, in column 1, the average score for the EPT structure for level 3 is −1.00 SD below the mean of all students who took the EPT, whereas the mean for advanced students is on average 1.5 SD above the mean of all the students who took the test.

If writing scores are part of the model, the results for Structure and Listening make some sense, although the listening k-means cluster center scores are consistently lower than actual placement z-score means. What appears to be really odd is that the Level 4 z-score cluster center is actually higher than that of Level 5 in writing. This result is further confirmation that the writing test is not terribly useful in placing learners in appropriate classes based on intended student learning outcomes.

If writing is removed from the model and only EPT scores are used, the k-means cluster centers again do not fit our program placement decisions. These are reported in Table 3.5.

Significantly, learners were grouped with k-means based on *lower* overall z scores, especially listening z scores, than the actual placement levels. The clusters would have resulted in very uneven level sizes (e.g., 45 students in Level 3, 134 students in Level 6). These distributions are illustrated in Figure 3.4. Comparison of the scatter plots and centroids of the EPT data show in visual form how the k-means cluster analysis would group learners together differently than the IEP did in reality.

Table 3.5 *K*-Means Cluster and Level Means With Michigan EPT vs. Actual Placement (Only EPT)

	Final cluster center and placement level z scores: Structure	*Final cluster center and placement level z scores: Listening*	*Number in cluster/level placement*
Cluster 2	−1.17	−1.72	45
Low Inter. (3)	−1.00	−0.89	124
Cluster 4	−0.78	−0.20	121
Interm. (4)	0.03	0.17	126
Cluster 1	*0.23*	*−0.64*	*59*
High Int. (5)	*0.91*	*0.66*	*77*
Cluster 3	1.00	0.88	134
Advanced (6)	1.5	1.21	32

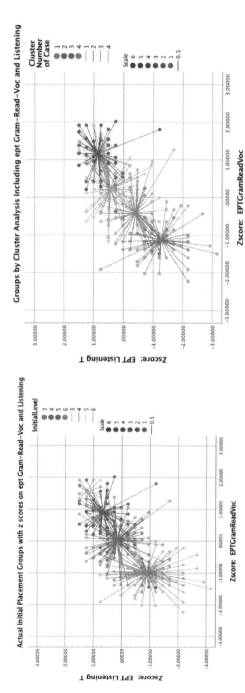

Figure 3.4 K-Cluster Means Centroids and Actual Level Placement Using EPT Listening and Structure

78 *Placement and Assessment in an IEP*

The ELI listening test (ELLPCT) is now used for confirmation one week into the term, but correlations among the various tests used for placement for these learners are provided in Table 3.6.

Because the EPT Structure and the ELLPCT correlate the most strongly at $r = 0.73$, $p = 0001$, it seemed reasonable to look at whether the ELLPCT might match placement groups better. The results of k-means cluster analysis of these two scores compared to actual placement are provided in Table 3.7.

However, this analysis was no better than the two EPT scores. Scatter plots with centroid distribution are provided in Figure 3.5. The scatter plot in the left box reveals that the low-level students are (a) very few and (b) scoring higher than the next level of student on the grammar test (the x axis). This finding suggests that the k-means analysis is weighting the listening score too high and creating uneven group sizes.

It is noteworthy that the EPT listening test is negatively skewed, even after conversion to z scores. This means that more students scored very well, resulting in a 'tail' of low scores. One problem could have been

Table 3.6 Correlations Among Scores Used in Placement Assessment

	EPT Listening	*EPT Gram/Read/ Vocab*	*IEP Writing*	*IEP Listening*
EPT Listening	1			
EPT Gram/Read/Vocab	.658** (359)	1		
IEP Writing	.434** (294)	.517** (294)	1	
IEP Listening	.661** (276)	.730** (276)	.416 (221)	1

**Significant at p ≤ .01

Table 3.7 K-Means Cluster and Level Means With EPT Structure and IEP Listening vs. Actual Placement

	z Score Grammar Vocab	*z Score IEP Listening*	*Number in Group*
Cluster 1	−0.82	−1.92	12
Level 3 LI	−1.0	−0.93	76
Cluster 4	−1.25	−0.81	68
Level 4 I	0.03	0.08	87
Cluster 3	*0.14*	*.08*	*150*
Level 5 Hi	*0.91*	*1.01*	*42*
Cluster 2	1.24	1.42	46
Level 6 Adv	1.5	1.4	16

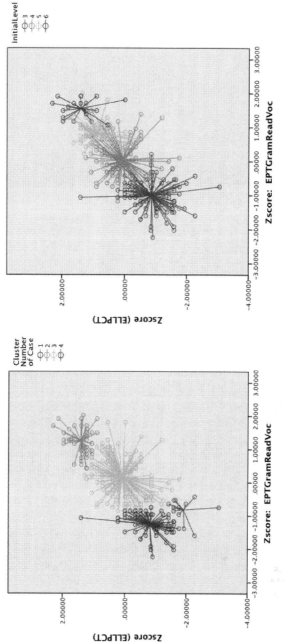

Figure 3.5 K-Cluster Means and Actual Level Placement Using EPT Structure and IEP Listening Test

80 *Placement and Assessment in an IEP*

with outliers (because k-means can take an outlier as a cluster center). Nevertheless, a boxplot analysis suggests there are very few outliers, and this is unlikely to be the case.

Another analysis possible is called a two-step cluster analysis. Two-step cluster analysis is similar to k-means cluster analysis in that it carries out the k-means procedure first and then creates homogeneous clusters based on that analysis. The difference is that the researchers do not specify how many clusters to create (Mooi & Sarstedt, 2011) but instead allow the statistical model to create clusters based on four data points – two from the Michigan EPT and one each from the writing sample and the IEP listening test.

The results are reported in SPSS output in Figures 3.6 and 3.7. Figure 3.6 shows that the analysis breaks down all the data into three rather than four groups needed by the ELI placement.

Figure 3.7 demonstrates the importance of the scores in determining the groups. Consistent with current practice in the IEP, this analysis ranks the EPT structure as the most important factor in determining group membership, but the EPT listening is less important than the IEP listening confirmation test. We have already discussed the fact that the IEP listening test, correlated with the EPT Structure and our curriculum SLOs, requires more reading that the EPT listening, so this is not surprising. This analysis suggests that, *statistically*, the spread of scores might justify fewer groups than we actually have, although this does not undermine our ultimate placement decisions. Decisions should not be made on quantitative data alone, as the professional experience of the faculty must be accorded value in interpreting the data.

Finally, when only the mean scores and standard deviations of the k-cluster analysis on only the EPT listening and grammar-vocabulary-reading components are calculated (and ignoring the group sizes created by the k-clusters), very similar mean scores are found when the means are calculated for the four groups created by the program. The comparison is shown in Figure 3.8.

The mean scores for the IEP levels are slightly higher than the groups that the k-cluster analysis created. However, they are fairly close. The main difference between the k-cluster analysis and the IEP placement was the number of participants in each group. It appears that the k-cluster procedure attempted to create groups of equal sizes, whereas the IEP does not seek to create equal group sizes. Thus, in terms of cut scores, the cluster analysis means and group centers support the IEP cut scores.

In conclusion, using z scores from these data sources, the analysis showed that k-means clusters created groups that were very different from initial placement groups but with similar ranges of scores. Clearly, this result was due to writing scores not being very useful in distinguishing among the levels for actual placement decisions, as the final cluster center z scores were much lower than placement grouping for Advanced

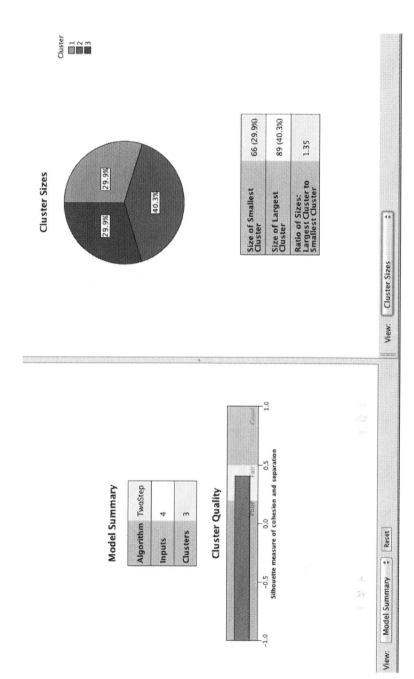

Figure 3.6 Quality of Model and Size of Clusters for IEP Placement

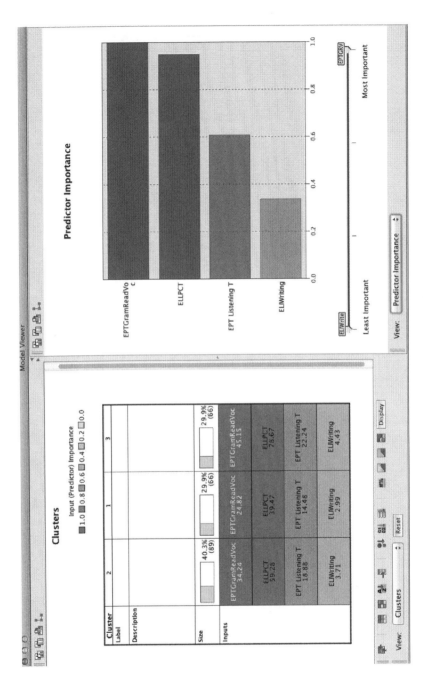

Figure 3.7 Z-Score Distribution and Importance of Predictors in IEP Placement

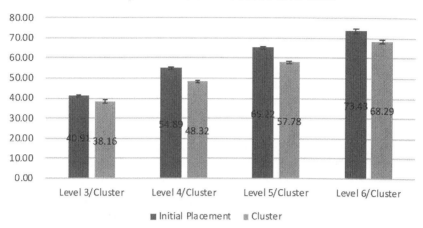

Figure 3.8 Comparison of Mean Scores of Initial IEP Placement and Clusters

students, especially in listening. Moreover, the cluster center z scores for the IEP in-house writing test varied wildly compared to level placement. This result could derive from an L1 effect from the many Arabic-speaking learners in the program, who, it will be recalled, score much higher in listening than structure and writing, necessitating expert qualitative interpretation of scores.

Thus, the IEP's having changed its practice of treating in-house listening and writing scores in placement decisions appears justified. The time spent on administering a writing test and extra listening test is not warranted by the role it plays in placement. If there are borderline decisions, it *may* be worth converting a student's score to a z score based on historical data, as expert opinion and experience with previous students at each level is probably more important than a single number. (It is important to note that z scores will be based on each testing session, so, like percentiles, they will change for each test because they are based on that sample.) The IEP could calculate an IEP 'population' set of z scores, but this analysis has not included students not placed before data collection. A more reasonable approach may be to pay special attention to distributions and graphing the data with boxplots, which can also help raise awareness of students who may be misplaced. The IEP currently confirms placement in each level and skill with placement confirmation activities 2–3 days after classes start.

These findings confirm Shin and Lidster's (2016, p. 20) caution that cluster analysis may not correspond well with matching students to the intended level's student learning outcomes at different levels and Winke's

84 Placement and Assessment in an IEP

(2013, p. 257) observation that teachers have concerns that go beyond statistical analysis. Finally, the data support Harding et al.'s (2015, p. 333) call for more research on accurately diagnosing listening skill, especially at higher levels of proficiency.

3.6 Rubrics for Assessing Development

In each of the skill areas, the IEP uses rubrics for evaluating student performance. Rubrics have become standard tools in ESL and IEPs to assess and encourage development (Becker, 2010). Holistic rubrics tend to be used in summative assessment (e.g., www.ets.org/Media/Tests/TOEFL/pdf/Writing_Rubrics.pdf), whereas analytical rubrics may be better adapted for formative assessment. The balance of each one in different tasks remains the focus of research (see Knoch, 2011, for a recent research article and overview of types of scale). More recently, Yamanishi, Ono, and Hijikata (2019) compared rubrics that required holistic assessments (which take less time and are more useful for summative assessment with larger numbers of test-takers) and analytic assessments (which take more time but are more helpful for providing developmental feedback). A version of the ETS rubric is used by the IEP. Yamanishi et al. (2019) carried out both qualitative and quantitative analysis of a hybrid rubric for evaluating summary writing for EFL learners in Japan, focusing in particular on paraphrasing. They found that the scoring on the two aspects was significantly related, produced inter-rater reliability, and allowed teachers to provide both holistic and developmental feedback.

As with most assessment tools, Vercellotti and McCormick (2019) point out that validity, reliability, practicality, and beneficial consequences (positive washback) are important. We can unpack these terms briefly. Validity refers to what the test is measuring – that is, whether the construct, skill, or knowledge that the test seeks to assess is actually being measured by the test. The old paper-based TOEFL test, for example, may not have been a very valid test of 'readiness to succeed in an English-speaking university degree course' (=construct) because simple discrete point items are not able to measure the ability to understand and respond to longer spoken and written texts. Reliability refers to the potential for the assessment to produce similar scores based on the performance of the test-taker no matter who is grading and that similar performances by different students receive similar scores. Rubrics may be deficient and unreliable if they are too vague and permit impressionistic and subjective rater opinions to influence scoring (Knoch, 2009, p. 277). Practicality is very important for IEPs in which large numbers of students are enrolled and that have significant numbers of teachers: Can all the teachers apply the rubric well (that is, with good reliability) and with a degree of ease under time pressure? Finally, the impact of the rubric on the classroom instruction and student learning should be beneficial.

Goodrich Andrade (2001) provides useful criteria when considering the quality of instructional rubrics that effectively assist students in their learning. Rubrics should be written in language the students understand, define and describe quality work, refer to common weaknesses, and assess work in progress and guide revision and improvement. The criteria should list what counts and describe strong, average, and weak work. These descriptors should take account of student developmental readiness. In her study of high school students in the United States, Goodrich Andrade found that providing students with a rubric enhanced their awareness of the qualities of good writing, but the students had more challenges transferring that knowledge into good writing. The IEP rubrics currently in use provide a stage in which scores are not provided in order to focus students' attention on the writing rather than the scores.

3.7 Final Exams

The final exams in the Pitt IEP are coordinated across sections of the same skill and the same level. Wherever possible, teachers do not evaluate their own sections but rather grade students from other sections. Scores on final exams have a very high impact on whether students can advance to the next level in the program.

The testing formats and exact test questions and prompts cannot be published for the obvious reason that (a) they must remain confidential from students and (b) they change over time. However, some general guidelines can be shared for teachers and administrators to compare with the exam systems in their IEPs.

3.7.1 Reading

Reading exams consist of both comprehension and vocabulary sections. The comprehension passages have to be checked for appropriateness with *https://readability-score.com/* by comparing the examination text with a text at the end of term for that level. (Levels 3 and 4 typically have a passage from a textbook, whereas Levels 5 and above have an authentic text that may be slightly edited.) The texts are chosen to be of a length that would allow a student to read a passage twice in 20 minutes. Assuming a reading speed of 60 words per minute for Level 3 students, a Level 3 final exam text might be 1000 words long, for example. (For comparison, Rayner, Slattery, and Bélanger (2010) report that typical expert college-age speakers of English read on average between 207 (slow readers) and 337 (fast readers) wpm.) Higher levels would require longer texts, perhaps up to 200 wpm at the highest level. IEP guidelines state that questions on the texts to be included should be related to topic/main ideas (15%), inferencing (10%), and details (25%), with other skills and comprehension strategies from the course being targeted (50%).

86   *Placement and Assessment in an IEP*

The vocabulary that is assessed as part of reading includes both core IEP academic word list vocabulary (see Chapter 4), as well as vocabulary from the textbooks. The ratio of the AWL and textbook vocabulary increases in favor of AWL words as the levels get higher, from 25% to 50%. In addition to the basic words, collocations are also assessed. Both fill-in-the-blank and matching words with definitions question types are used.

3.7.2 *Writing*

Vocabulary is also part of the writing assessment. Students are provided with a word bank of 15 words and required to use at least 3 of them in their essays. Students are permitted paper dictionaries but no electronic resources. Students are provided with several topics and required to write as follows: (a) Level 3 is required to write one essay of two paragraphs. (b) Level 4 is given one essay type with three topic options, and students chose one. (c) Level 5 students are given three types of essay with one topic each and required to choose one. The type of essay required at Levels 4 and 5 is a traditional five-paragraph essay, with each paragraph required to be at least five sentences long.

While this approach seems highly structured, it is necessary to provide students with very clear guidelines on how to prepare and to ensure that students write enough to be evaluated.

3.7.3 *Listening*

In general, the listening finals consist of three sections: (a) 60-second listening segments that are loosely related to subject or topics that have been covered during the course of the semester. Many of them are drawn from National Geographic programs. Students are familiar with the format of these 60-second segments, as they are done throughout the term as a listening exercise. (b) Longer listening segments that are designed to include 'social listening', for example, conversations and/or interviews and 'lecture' texts. (c) A dictation component of ten sentences that includes items from the vocabulary of each level. Level 3 students are not required to take notes, but all other levels are required to provide notes from their listening. Levels 5 and 6 may be required to write a summary from their notes.

3.7.4 *Speaking*

In speaking, the evaluation consists of two activities, both of which are recorded: a conversation roleplay and a monologue. The roleplays require pairs of students to engage in a conversation, the topic for which is based on a prompt. Students in Levels 3 and 4 receive two prompts; students in Levels 5 and 6 receive three. Interviews at Levels 3 and 4 usually take about 4–5 minutes, while those in Levels 5–6 would take a little longer time. Their recorded monologue is called a 'recorded speaking activity' and is described and analyzed more fully in Chapter 6 (McCormick & Vercellotti, 2013). Students record two versions of their monologue and can choose which one they submit for evaluation.

3.7.5 Grammar

Grammar is assessed in two modes: listening and writing. Both modes for each level probe knowledge of all grammar points (AGP) taught at that level. The written grammar test consists of a variety of item types: traditional multiple choice, fill-in-the-blank, sentence completion, answering questions, and writing a short paragraph. The listening part of the grammar test begins with a comprehension 'True or False' section that taps students' understanding of grammatical points and is followed by a test of cloze items. The listening section is played twice for each subsection.

3.8 Summary

This chapter has focused on various aspects of assessment: placement, rubrics, and final exams. It is important for an IEP to have a faculty member who is competent in basic descriptive statistics and software that can be used to describe students' progress through the program, both to outside stakeholders, be they university administrators or sponsors, and to the IEP administrators and teachers themselves.

3.9 Topics for Administrators and Teachers to Reflect On

3.9.1 Questions and Issues Mainly for Program Administrators and Curriculum Supervisors

1. Consult the websites of the language assessment journals and review the titles of articles from the past two years. Note any titles of interest and skim the abstracts for an article you may read later.

   a. *Language Testing*: https://journals.sagepub.com/home/ltj
   b. *Language Assessment Quarterly*: www.tandfonline.com/toc/hlaq20/current

2. Download a recent research report from a major testing organization and share it with your team:

   a. TOEFL, ETS: www.ets.org/toefl/research/
   b. IELTS: www.ielts.org/en-us/teaching-and-research/research-reports

88 *Placement and Assessment in an IEP*

3. What information from your reviews in 1 and 2 might cause you to change any assessment procedure in your IEP?

    a. Placement
    b. In-class assessment
    c. Academic readiness
    d. Other professional readiness

4. How do you share test results with your faculty? What kinds of feedback do you solicit from faculty on assessment?
5. How do you share test results with students?
6. Do you have any placement confirmation procedures? How often do students change a level after initial placement?

3.9.2 *Questions and Issues for Classroom Teachers*

1. What do you know about the research basis of your IEP's placement, level, and final exam policies? Can you easily find out more if you need to?
2. Choose a skill that you like to teach most. How do you think proficiency should be assessed in that skill? How is it assessed in your IEP and when?
3. One method of assessment that was not discussed in this chapter was portfolio assessment for writing. Is this method of assessment used in your IEP? What do you and your colleagues think about this approach?
4. Hamp-Lyons (2007, p. 480) summarizes 'two ends of the assessment cultures continuum. For example, a learning culture would focus more on fluency, whereas a classical testing culture might focus more on accuracy'. Brainstorm some other possible features of these two cultures and then check Hamp-Lyons' article and see if you agree with her list. What kind of assessment cultures does your IEP embrace?

Notes

1. As we shall see in Chapter 7, quantitative assessment may not always be the only way to judge student writing.
2. See Furnham (1990) for a discussion of single and multiple trait theory in psychology as it relates to personality.
3. Chapter 4 discusses vocabulary development in much more detail.
4. I have not been able to find total numbers for the TOEFL iBT. I assume that they must be larger than IELTS, but that assumption is not based on data.
5. It should be noted that a cut score may be appropriate for the beginning of a semester for a level, but for mid-term admission, students may need to be placed in a lower level because the students in the level have progressed in their learning.

Placement and Assessment in an IEP 89

6. We will discuss frequency bands and corpora in much greater detail in Chapter 4.
7. Both Japanese and Korean have Subject-Object-Verb (SOV) word order, particles indicating grammatical relations, and somewhat similar phonological constraints on syllable structure. In terms of writing, however, Korean Hangul is an alphabet and Japanese relies on a three-part writing system, including kanji (characters borrowed from Chinese), a syllabary for morphology in Japanese (*hiragana*), and a syllabary for foreign loanwords (*katakana*).

References

Bachman, L. F. (2000). Modern language testing at the turn of the century: Assuring that what we count counts. *Language Testing, 17*(1), 1–42.

Barootchi, N., & Keshavarz, M. H. (2002). Assessment of achievement through portfolios and teacher-made tests. *Educational Research, 44*(3), 279–288.

Becker, A. (2010). Examining rubrics used to measure writing performance in US intensive English programs. *The CATESOL Journal, 22*(1), 113–130.

Biber, D., Conrad, S. M., Reppen, R., Byrd, P., Helt, M., Clark, V., & Urzua, A. (2004). *Representing language use in the university: Analysis of the TOEFL 2000 spoken and written academic language corpus*. Princeton, NJ: Educational Testing Services.

Brown, J. D. (1988). *Understanding research in second language learning*. Cambridge and New York: Cambridge University Press.

Brown, J. D. (2013). Teaching statistics in language testing courses. *Language Assessment Quarterly, 10*(3), 351–369.

Brumfit, C. J., & Johnson, K. (1979). *The communicative approach to language teaching*. Oxford: Oxford University Press.

Canale, M., & Swain, M. (1980). Theoretical bases of communicative approaches to second language teaching and testing. *Applied Linguistics, 1*, 1–17.

Chostelidou, D. (2011). Needs-based course design: The impact of general English knowledge on the effectiveness of an ESP teaching intervention. *Procedia Social and Behaviorial Sciences, 15*, 403–409. doi:10.1016/j.sbspro.2011.03.112

Corder, S. P. (1967). The significance of learners' errors. *International Review of Applied Linguistics, 5*, 161–169.

Corrigan, A., Dobson, B., Kellman, E., Palmer, A., Peterson, J., Spaan, M., & Upshur, J. (1978). *English placement test: University of Michigan English Language Institute*. Ann Arbor, MI: University of Michigan, University of Michigan English Language Institute.

Cumming, A. (2015). Design in four diagnostic assessments. *Language Testing, 32*(3), 407–416. doi:10.1177/0265532214559115

Cummins, J. (2003). BICS and CALP: Origins and rationale for the distinction. In C. B. Paulston & G. R. Tucker (Eds.), *Sociolinguistics: The essential readings* (pp. 322–328). New York: Wiley.

Ding, C., & He, X. (2004, July 29). *K-means clustering via principal component analysis*. Proceedings of the 21st International Conference on Machine Learning.

Furnham, A. (1990). The development of single trait personality theories. *Personality and Individual Differences, 11*(9), 923–929. Retrieved from https://doi.org/10.1016/0191-8869(90)90273-T

Goodrich Andrade, H. (2001). The effects of instructional rubrics on learning to write. *Current Issues in Education, 4*(4). Retrieved from http://scholarsarchive.library.albany.edu/etap_fac_scholar/6

Gu, L. (2014). At the interface between testing and second language acquisition: Language ability and context of learning. *Language Testing, 31*(1), 111–133. doi:10.1177/0265532212469177

Hamp-Lyons, L. (2007). The influence of testing practices on teaching: Ideologies and alternatives. In J. Cummins & C. Davison (Eds.), *International handbook of English language teaching* (pp. 473–490). Boston, MA: Springer.

Harding, L., Alderson, J. C., & Brunfaut, T. (2015). Diagnostic assessment of reading and listening in a foreign language. *Language Testing, 32*(3), 317–336. doi:10.1177/0265532214564505

Harrington, M. W. (1987). Processing transfer: Language-specific processing strategies as a source of interlanguage variation. *Applied Psycholinguistics, 8*, 351–377.

Harrington, M. W., & Carey, M. (2009). The on-line yes/no test as a placement tool. *System, 37*, 614–626. doi:10.1016/j.system.2009.09.006

Harrington, M. W., & Roche, T. (2014). Identifying academically at-risk students in an English-as-a-lingua-franca university setting. *Journal of English for Academic Purposes, 15*, 37–47. doi:10.1016/j.jeap.2014.05.003

Hymes, D. (1972). On communicative competence. In P. John & J. Holmes (Eds.), *Sociolinguistics* (pp. 269–293). Harmondsworth: Penguin.

Jain, A. K. (2010). Data clustering: 50 years beyond k-means. *Pattern Recognition Letters, 31*, 651–666.

Juffs, A. (2019). The development of lexical diversity in the writing of intensive English program students. In R. M. DeKeyser & P. B. Goretti (Eds.), *Reconciling methodological demands with pedagogical applicability* (pp. 179–200). Amsterdam: John Benjamins.

Juffs, A., & Rodríguez, G. A. (2014). *Second language sentence processing.* New York: Routledge.

Kiely, R. (2009). Small answers to the big question: Learning from language programme evaluation. *Language Teaching Research, 13*(1), 99–116. doi:10.1177/1362168808095525

Knoch, U. (2009). *Diagnostic writing assessment: The development and validation of a rating scale.* Frankfurt-am-Main: Peter Lang.

Knoch, U. (2011). Rating scales for diagnostic assessment of writing: What should they look like and where should the criteria come from? *Assessing Writing, 16*(2), 81–96.

Lado, R., & Fries, C. (1957). *English sentence patterns: Understanding and producing English grammatical structures. An oral approach.* Ann Arbor, MI: University of Michigan Press.

Larson-Hall, J. (2017). Moving beyond the bar plot and the line graph to create informative and attractive graphics. *The Modern Language Journal, 101*(1), 244–270.

Lee, I. (2007). Assessment for learning: Integrating assessment, teaching, and learning in the ESL/EFL writing classroom. *Canadian Modern Language Review, 64*(1), 199–213.

Long, M. H. (2007). *Problems in SLA.* New York: Lawrence Erlbaum.

Martin, K. I. (2017). The impact of L1 writing system on ESL knowledge of vowel and consonant spellings. *Reading and Writing, 30*, 279–298. doi:10.1007/s11145-016-9673-5

McCormick, D. E., & Vercellotti, M. L. (2013). Examining the impact of self-correction notes on grammatical accuracy in speaking. *TESOL Quarterly, 47*(2), 410–420. doi:10.1002/tesq.92

Mislevy, R. J., Steinberg, L. S., & Almond, R. G. (2002). Design and analysis in task-based language assessment. *Language Testing, 19*(4), 477–496.

Mooi, E., & Sarstedt, M. (2011). *A concise guide to market analysis.* Berlin: Springer.

Naismith, B., Han, N-R., Juffs, A., Hill, B. L., & Zheng, D. (2018). Accurate measurement of lexical sophistication with reference to ESL learner data. In K. E. Boyer & M. Yudelson (Eds.), *Proceedings of the 11th international conference on educational data mining* (pp. 259–265). Buffalo, NY. Retrieved from http://educationaldatamining.org/EDM2018/

Norris, J. M. (2009). Understanding and improving language education through program evaluation: Introduction to the special issue. *Language Teaching Research, 13*(1), 7–13. doi:10.1177/1362168808095520

Paulston, C. B. (1974). Linguistics and communicative competence. *TESOL Quarterly, 8*, 347–362.

Pienemann, M. (1998). *Language processing and second language development: Processability theory.* Amsterdam: John Benjamins.

Pienemann, M. (Ed.). (2005). *Cross-linguistic aspects of processability theory* (Vol. 30). Amsterdam: John Benjamins Publishing.

Pienemann, M., Johnston, M., & Brindley, G. (1988). Constructing an acquisition-based procedure for second language assessment. *Studies in Second Language Acquisition, 10*, 217–243.

Poehner, M. E., & Lantolf, J. P. (2005). Dynamic assessment in the language classroom. *Language Teaching Research, 9*(3), 233–265.

Rayner, K., Slattery, T. J., & Bélanger, N. N. (2010). Eye movements, the perceptual span, and reading speed. *Psychonomic Bulletin and Review, 17*(6), 834–839. doi:10.3758/PBR.17.6.834

Read, J. (2007). Second language vocabulary assessment: Current practices and new directions. *International Journal of English Studies (IJES), 7*(2), 105–126. doi:10.6018/ijes.7.2.49021

Read, J. (2013). Second language vocabulary assessment. *Language Teaching, 46*(1), 41–52.

Roche, T., & Harrington, M. W. (2013). Recognition vocabulary knowledge as a predictor of academic performance in an English as a foreign language setting. *Language Testing in Asia, 3*(12). Retrieved from https://doi.org/10.1186/2229-0443-3-12

Selinker, L. (1972). Interlanguage. *International Review of Applied Linguistics, 10*, 209–231.

Shawer, S. F. (2012). Accreditation and standards-driven program evaluation? Implications for program quality assurance and stakeholder professional development. *Qual Quant, 47*, 2883–2913. doi:10.1007/s11135-012-9696-1

Shin, S-Y., & Lidster, R. (2016). Evaluating different standard-setting methods in an ESL placement testing context. *Language Testing.* doi:10.1177/0265532216646605

Spada, N., & Tomita, Y. (2010). Interactions between type of instruction and type of language feature: A meta-analysis. *Language Learning, 60*(2), 263–308. doi:10.1111/j.1467-9922.2010.00562.x

92 Placement and Assessment in an IEP

Spinner, P. (2011). Second language assessment and morphosyntactic development. *Studies in Second Language Acquisition, 33*, 529–561.

Staples, S., & Biber, D. (2015). Cluster analysis. In L. Plonsky (Ed.), *Advancing quantitative methods in second language research* (pp. 243–275). New York: Routledge.

VanPatten, B. (2002). Processing instruction: An update. *Language Learning, 52*, 755–803.

Vercellotti, M. L., & McCormick, D. E. (2019). *Creating rubrics for assessing language performance in the TESOL classroom.* Workshop presented at the TESOL International Preconvention Institute, Atlanta, GA, March 11, 2019.

White, L., Spada, N., Lightbown, P., & Ranta, L. (1991). Input enhancement and L2 question formation. *Applied Linguistics, 12*, 416–432.

Widdowson, H. G. (1979). *Reading and thinking in English.* Oxford: Oxford University Press.

Winke, P. (2013). The effectiveness of interactive group orals for placement testing. In K. McDonough & A. Mackey (Eds.), *Second language interaction in diverse educational contexts* (pp. 247–268). Amsterdam: John Benjamins.

Yamanishi, H., Ono, M., & Hijikata, Y. (2019). Developing a scoring rubric for L2 summary writing: A hybrid approach combining analytic and holistic assessment. *Language Testing in Asia, 9*(1), 13. doi:10.1186/s40468-019-0087-6

Appendix I
Writing Sample Rubric

Scores	Descriptors
6	Very good writing proficiency. The writer fulfills all requirements of the writing prompts. The writing is well organized with main ideas supported by appropriate details and/or examples. There is a variety of sentence types, very few or no grammar errors, and very few errors in word choice or word form. There is no confusion about meaning.
5	Good writing proficiency. The writer fulfills all requirements of at least one writing prompt and at least the general requirements of the second prompt. The writing is generally organized with main points and at least some support with details and/or examples. There is a variety of sentence types. There are some grammar, word choice, and/or word form errors. There is little or no confusion about meaning.
4	Fair writing proficiency. The writer addresses one or both prompts in a general way. There may be details and general statements, but no clear organization. There is little sentence variety, and sometimes more complex sentences with errors in grammar, word choice, and word form. There may be occasional confusion about word meaning.
3	Poor writing proficiency. The writer may address one or both of the writing prompts, but only in the most general way. There is little organization and little or no distinction between generalizations and specifics. There are only simple sentences, some of which have errors in grammar, word choice, and word form. There may be confusion about meaning.
2	Very poor writing proficiency. The writer may address one or both of the writing prompts, but only in the most general way. There is only a list of simple sentences, with many errors in grammar, word choice, and word form. There may be confusion about meaning.
1	No writing proficiency. The writer may not address either of the writing prompts, and may write only a few unconnected words.

(Adapted from the Test of Written English, TWE Scoring Guide, Educational Testing Service, Princeton, NJ. 1986, revised 2/90)

4 Lexical Development in an Intensive English Program

4.1 Introduction

Teachers and learners of second languages need no reminders about the importance of vocabulary in second language learning. It is surprising, then, that in early thinking in *theoretical* linguistics and even language teaching, researchers considered the rules of sentence structure ('grammar') much more important and completely separate from vocabulary. Partly for this reason, until the 1990s, vocabulary received less attention than 'rules' in research and theorizing about language learning (Nation, 2001, p. xiii). More recently, in some theories of language, 'vocabulary' (understood as everything from a bound morpheme to an idiomatic phrase or proverb [Juffs, 2009]), has come to be considered the foundation of almost all learning, including providing the basis of sentence structure itself. In this chapter, we will not engage in theoretical debates regarding the separation of vocabulary from 'grammar rules', but rather we will focus on vocabulary development simply as a vital part of any instructional program in an IEP. Lexical knowledge may be the easiest component of proficiency to evaluate because vocabulary tests can target single words fairly easily. In compositions that have been written with a computer, computational tools can identify and count items separated by 'white' spaces in electronic texts fairly efficiently, provided that the texts are in certain formats. However, while researchers can easily count words with computers, the issue of correct usage is harder to measure this way. Thus, Crossley and Kyle (2018), when describing TAALES, their complex and powerful tool for measuring lexical sophistication, caution that it 'does not distinguish the context in which words are used and whether or not they are used appropriately (e.g., it does not identify discourse structures)'. Usage, of course, may ultimately be much more important in determining whether a student is ready for academic study than word recognition. Indeed, Laufer, Elder, Hill, and Congdon (2004, p. 203) emphasize that correct 'free production reflects the highest level of lexical knowledge'. This issue will be addressed more deeply in Chapter 7 on writing development.

Setting aside the important challenges regarding usage, the choice of which specific vocabulary items to focus on in a curriculum as well as understanding the measurement of lexical development are still of great importance for administrators and teachers in IEPs. Knowledge of the nature of vocabulary learning has increased a great deal in recent decades, in large part due to the work of Paul Nation (Nation, 1990, 2001) and others whose work is discussed in later sections in this chapter, for example, Cobb (2006, 2016), Coxhead (2000), Laufer and Hulstijn (2001), Read (2004), and Schmitt and Schmitt (2014), to mention only a very few.

This chapter will address two aspects of vocabulary development. First, we will focus on the growth of lexical knowledge, concentrating on the growth of lexical sophistication. The later part of the chapter will discuss the way vocabulary has been taught both in the Pitt IEP and with other similar groups of learners.

4.2 Some Terminology for the Lexicon

Before a consideration of the research itself, it is useful to review some terminology in order to understand the nature of word learning in sufficient detail. The term 'word', it turns out, is actually not a very useful one except as 'short-hand' when talking about lexical items, which consist of a 'bundle' linked system of meaning, orthographic form, and phonology (Perfetti & Hart, 2002). Instead, linguists prefer the term 'morpheme' because various form-meaning connections can be made with units smaller than a string of letters (or sounds) on a written page that are separated by white space in alphabetic languages such as English.

First, let us consider basic morphological terminology. A *lemma* is the basic word form, frequently used as the headword in a dictionary; the term *lexeme* refers to a specific form of a lemma. A set of lexemes makes up a *word family*. For example, the word *modern* is a two-syllable adjective, consisting of one morpheme. It can appear on its own – it's a 'free' morpheme. If a speaker also knows the verb *modernize*, then they actually know two things: the adjective form and the causative suffix -*ize*, which creates the verb that means 'to make modern'. Adding a bound affix (a bound morpheme, which must attach to another word) to a word that can change its part of speech is referred to as 'derivation'. The relationship between *modern* and *modernize* is clear. However, other words, the word *ignore*, for example, pose different problems. The form *ignore-s*, as in 'She ignores junk email', is an inflected form and doesn't change the core meaning of the word, which might be paraphrased as 'to not pay attention to' or 'disregard'. However, the noun form *ignorance* means something a little different – it means 'lack of knowledge' as in 'ignorance of the law is no defense'. The word in this sentence does not

96   *Lexical Development in an IEP*

mean 'not paying attention to the law is no defense'. Thus, we might treat the two derived words as two separate 'words' but not two inflected forms. Hence, *ignore, ignores, ignoring, ignored* all count as knowing ONE 'word', whereas *ignore* and *ignorance* would count as knowing two words. In some dialects of English, the additional derived adjective form *ignorant* actually means 'rude'. We would say that the learner knows three lemmas: the four inflected forms of *ignore*, plus *ignorance*, and *ignorant*. All six are 'lexemes' and would count as one 'word family'. In general, the lemma is considered a useful level of analysis for measuring vocabulary and making instructional decisions. In other words, derived forms are considered separate lemmas and different points of word knowledge.

One final word of caution is that the role a morpheme plays in one word, such as *de-* meaning *un-*, as in *de-act-iv-ate*, may not actually be a morpheme but part of the root in another word. For instance, the *de-* in *delight* does not mean 'un-light', so *delight* is actually a single morpheme (c.f., also *debrief*). Similarly, the suffix *-er* in *worker* forms a noun from a verb, but not in the single morpheme *corner*, and forms the inflected comparative form when attached to an adjective, for example, *dark-er*.

In the Pitt IEP, we have recognized that a persistent issue with derived words is that learners face challenges with which form of a word to use in a particular syntactic context; in fact, learners often fail to see the relationship among derived words or lemmas from the same word family (Friedline, 2011). We will address some of the reasons for this problem in this chapter. For now, it should be noted that English poses a challenge because the part of speech for many words can actually only be determined by the morpho-syntactic contexts in which they occur. For example, in the two sentences 'the hunter wanted to duck under the tree' and 'the duck paddled away quickly', the word *duck* is a different part of speech and also has different meanings. (One could argue that the relationship is one of polysemy. That is, the verb 'duck' is perhaps being used figuratively if one can link what ducks do when they dip under water with a human getting lower under a tree branch.) The first is identifiable as a verb because it is preceded by the infinitive marker *to* and followed by a prepositional phrase. The second is a noun, as it is preceded by a definite article, *the*. In contrast, with the word *butter* in 'Mary wanted to butter the toast' and 'John softened the butter', the meanings are much closer even though they are different parts of speech in those clauses. Thus, derived words are especially challenging for learners in terms of their forms, their various polysemous meanings, and how easily these can be identified.

'Words' can also be larger than a single free morpheme. For example, *by and large* is a set phrase that means 'in general' and is derived from sailing, referring to a ship that could do well whether it was sailing into the wind ('by the wind') or with the wind behind ('large').[1] In fact, many

Lexical Development in an IEP 97

phrases in everyday use have drifted from their original meanings and can be traced back to older uses in specific trades or contexts. (e.g., https://blog.oxforddictionaries.com/2014/06/30/nautical-language/). However, we will continue to use the term *word* in its non-technical sense.

4.3 Which Words Should and Do the Students Know at Each Proficiency Level?

Due to the extensive research that they have done on word lists and word frequency, applied linguists and publishers are an important source of information regarding which words students ought to know and should be taught (Youngblood & Folse, 2017). One early list is West's (1953) general service list, and most scholars since West (1953) agree that knowledge of the 2000 most frequent words in English constitutes a vital base on which to build up more sophisticated lexical knowledge. Some frequencies of a word remain relatively stable over time, for example, articles in English tend not to change in frequency, and, unsurprisingly, *the* is the most frequent word in both expert user English and learner English corpora. However, with changes in technology and other aspects of life, frequencies and meanings of some words evolve over time. Browne, Culligan, and Philips (2013) report on the New General Service List (NGSL, www.newgeneralservicelist.org/), which takes account of changes in frequency since West's (1953) original list was developed. They propose a new core of 2800 words, including 700 for spoken English. The website that Browne and colleagues have developed is based on a very large corpus of 273 million words and also provides smaller sublists relevant to different genres, including Business (1700 words) and Academic English (960 words). Word lists are often grouped into 'bands' of 1000 words, so that the '1000' frequency band is a list of the 1000 most frequent words, the '2000' band the next most frequent, and so on.

Nation (2001, p. 17) provided a good idea of the coverage of the most frequent 1000 and 2000 words in English, in Table 4.1.

Table 4.1 shows that in conversation, the 1000 and 2000 frequency bands in English account for 90.3% of the vocabulary used (84.3% 1000

Table 4.1 Coverage of the Most Frequent Words in Various Genres

Frequency	Conversation	Fiction	Newspapers	Academic
1000	84.3%	82.3%	75.6%	73.5%
2000	6%	5.1%	4.7%	4.6%
Academic Word List	1.9%	1.7%	3.9%	8.5%
Other	7.8%	10.9%	15.7%	13.3%

98 *Lexical Development in an IEP*

frequency band + 6% 2000 frequency band). Even in academic texts, 78.1% of the words come from the most frequent 2000 words. However, Nation estimates that a learner needs to know about 98% of words in a text for 'guessing from context' to work efficiently in comprehension. Thus, beyond the most frequent 2000 and the academic word lists (AWLs) of Coxhead (2000) and Gardner and Davies (2014), learners in an IEP who are preparing to study other subjects in English also need to focus on the 'Other' 13.3% for academic texts.

The base of words in the productive lexicon of each learner in the IEP is one important factor. It would not be economical to list all the frequent words used by students in a book. The reason for this is that (a) there is immense overlap in the most frequent 2000 lemmas per level; (b) the online lists allow us to efficiently provide lists by level and by L1 that go as far as the 3000–9000 level that could be most useful for teachers and programs. Thus, the frequency lists of each level with combined L1s and for each language by level are provided online at: https://github.com/ELI-Data-Mining-Group/Pitt-ELI-Corpus, or by contacting the author. They are available in spreadsheet format. Each word is ranked for frequency, e.g., 'the' is the most frequent word for most intermediate learners and is ranked '1' in the list. In addition to raw frequencies in the texts, they are also listed with estimated frequencies per million words so that frequencies from level to level can be more easily compared. Curriculum planners might use these lists to develop their own lists for instructional intervention based on which words students may not be using enough. In Chapter 5, further suggestions are made about which verbs might receive more instructional intervention. Obviously, the most frequent words in English texts are function words, for example, *the, or, and,* and *but,* and then frequent lexical items for daily life such as *have, go, friend,* and *job.* This frequency is reflected in the learner data, but there are some differences between learner frequency lists and native speaker lists. For example, the word *visa* does not appear at all on www.wordfrequency.info and is listed as a 5000-level BNC-COCA-25 word at https://lextutor.ca/. However, it is ranked approximately 1000 in frequency for the Level 3 IEP students: obviously, an international student needs a 'visa' to be a student in the United States, and therefore they know and use this word. Students thus use some words more frequently than expert speakers do, and they know those words earlier in their acquisition trajectory than expert native speaker frequency lists might suggest. We will see that this second language–specific lexical knowledge has implications for measuring vocabulary growth in an IEP.

4.4 How Does Lexical Knowledge Develop? Diversity, Sophistication, and Depth

In Section 4.3, we discussed lists of basic words that students need or are likely to know early on in their development so that vocabulary learning

Lexical Development in an IEP 99

can be supported by extensive reading. While it is true that learners must eventually learn many low frequency words, it is difficult to know *which* less frequent words should be targeted by an ESL program. Certainly, various academic words lists are an important start. Coxhead's (2000) AWL drew attention to words often used in social science research and Todd (2017) to vocabulary for engineering. However, Gardner and Davies (2014) pointed out that 236 of Coxhead's 570 word families (41%) overlap with the most frequent 1000 and 2000 words in the Corpus of Contemporary American English (COCA). They argue that because the 570 AWL families overlap with the GSL, they may not need to be taught. In contrast, many words with specific *academic* meanings on the GSL are not on the AWL (e.g., the business meanings of *account, exchange*, and *rate*), and so students may miss out on instructional intervention where their domain-specific meanings are concerned in business. The issue of polysemy (related but different meanings of a word across contexts or disciplines) is another issue that they raise. For example, the word *pipe* can mean a 'conduit for liquid', a 'smoking instrument', 'a musical instrument', or even a very specific meaning in computer science as a *Unix* command. (It means 'redirect the output of one computational process to another'.) An example of the importance of context is clear in a sentence such as 'He took out his pipe, and began to play', where the meaning of *pipe* is only clearer when the second half of the sentence is read, and the interpretation of *pipe* as a smoking instrument becomes much less probable. Adding the phrase *a beautiful melody* would confirm the 'instrument' interpretation.

Thus, Gardner and Davies (2014) propose a new academic vocabulary list (AVL) that addresses some of the issues raised by word families and lemmas while taking into account both frequency and dispersion. The dispersion measure looked at frequency in various contexts and tried to ensure that the words chosen are not just frequent in one context. Therefore, in the AVL, *restorative* is omitted (presumably too specific to clinical settings), whereas *detect* and *simulated* are included because they frequently occur in scientific usage but also more 'general' contexts. Nation (2013) also describes what he means by specifically 'academic words' and shows that they account for 9% of vocabulary in academic texts.

The question of which list, or lists, is optimal has therefore become one of considerable debate (see Youngblood and Folse [2017] for a review of learner lists). However, the debate is often carried out on the basis of expert speaker corpora, and such lists often do not attempt to measure what learners actually know before they enter an IEP as opposed to what expert speaker corpora suggest they *should* know. As we saw in Chapter 2, students come to IEPs with various L1 backgrounds (if you're a speaker of a Romance language, you have a great advantage because of educational backgrounds and the many words of similar form [cognates]).

100   *Lexical Development in an IEP*

The curricula and experience of students from different countries varies greatly, but with regard to the choices of words to focus on, Schmitt and Schmitt (2014, p. 496) pointed out that the 3000 to the 9000 frequency bands contain important words for students who need to use English to learn other subjects as well as for a range of 'authentic purposes'. For example, the following words appear in those bands:

3001–4000: academic, consist, exploit, rapid, vocabulary
4001–5000: agricultural, contemporary, dense, insight, particle
5001–6000: cumulative, default, penguin, rigorous, schoolchildren
6001–7000: axis, comprehension, peripheral, sinister, taper
7001–8000: authentic, conversely, latitude, mediation, undergraduate
8001–9000: anthropology, fruitful, hypothesis, semester, virulent

Presumably, students should be taught these kinds of words rather than very low frequency words. However, the 6000 words in these lists still present an impossible number for instruction in class, even over three semesters of 16 weeks, as Cobb (2016) has pointed out. Thus, applied linguists need to establish how class time can be best used to focus on key items that will give learners 'the biggest bang for their buck'.

In general, learners take classes at IEPs in order to get help learning the less frequent words that they need to know to succeed in their academic or professional life. Knowing and using less frequent words obviously contributes to making the learners' vocabulary 'richer'. Most work on lexical 'richness' in vocabulary has been done with their written output because writing can be collected, stored, and analyzed more easily. (Another reason is that spoken language is less lexically sophisticated in general – see Table 4.1.) Lexical development can encompass increases in *lexical diversity*, *lexical sophistication*, and *lexical depth* (Bulté & Housen, 2014; Jarvis, 2013a, 2013b; papers in Jarvis & Daller, 2013; Sisková, 2012; van Hout & Vermeer, 2007). This chapter will focus on the first two of these measures.

The first kind of measure, referred to as 'lexical diversity', only considers the words used in the text written by the learner. This measure is a special type of type/token ratio. A type/token ratio considers the variety of words in a text: for example, in the sentence 'The woman saw the tall tree'. There are five different types (five because *the* occurs twice) and six different tokens. Therefore, the type/token ratio is 5/6 = .83. In contrast, in 'the woman saw the other woman', *the* and *woman* occur twice, making the number of tokens four: 4/6 = .67. Obviously, .83 is higher and indicates greater variety. A simple type/token ratio is very sensitive to text length, and so other measures of lexical diversity have been developed to control for text length.

A widely used measure to describe diversity is a calculation known as 'vocD', which presents a statistic called '*D*'. The use of this measure is designed to allow researchers to demonstrate developmental trends independently of text length. McCarthy and Jarvis (2010, p. 383) summarize the procedure to calculate D thus: 100 random samples of 35 words are taken and a type/token ratio (TTR) calculated. This process is repeated twice again with a larger sample of words, producing a TTR curve that results in a final score, which usually ranges from 10 to 100.[2] Some research has indicated that D is in fact sensitive to length (McCarthy & Jarvis, 2007). Nevertheless, because previous research has shown vocD to be a robust measure and because computer programs such as CLAN (MacWhinney, 2000) and websites (e.g., www.textinspector.com) provide vocD, Juffs (2019) used this measure for lexical diversity. As reported on *Textinspector.com* and in Duràn, Malvern, Richards, and Chipere (2004, Figure 4.1, p. 238) a D score 25 would be typical of an English-speaking child, who by 5 years old would reach a score of about 65. In contrast, an adult ESL learner might have a D score of about 55. Academic texts tend to be 90 and over. (Another less complex measure mathematically that has been used is a simple Guiraud index, which is the number of types simply divided by the square root of the total number of tokens. This procedure is also said to control [somewhat?] for text length [Daller, Turlik, & Weir, 2013]).

The second kind of measure is known as 'lexical sophistication'. This term refers to the *proportion* of words in a text that are from lower frequency bands, that is, below the 2000 most frequent words. A useful and humorous example comes from the first film in the series *Pirates of the Caribbean*. The aristocratic daughter of the governor requests that the pirate captain release her after the pirates had kidnapped her and taken her to their ship; the pirate captain, a rough man, ironically and mockingly replies, 'I am disinclined to acquiesce to your request: means "no"'. His answer could be paraphrased as 'I don't agree'. The word *acquiesce* is in the 7000 band of most frequent words in English, and *disinclined* is in the 11,000 band, while *agree* is among the 1000 most common words. Obviously, the lexical sophistication of the pirate captain's reply is the reason for humor and even has led to a meme based on this answer (https://memegenerator.net/instance/45838080/captain-barbossa-is-disinclined-to-acquiesce-your-request). Lexical sophistication is often measured by 'Advanced Guiraud'. Advanced Guiraud is based on excluding the 2000 most frequent words from the types that a student uses and then dividing the remaining number of types by the square root of the tokens to control for text length: advanced types/√tokens. More recently, other suggestions have been made on how to measure this feature (Crossley & Kyle, 2018).

Thus, statistical measures that do and do not refer to word frequencies have been important in research on lexical development. Based on our IEP data, we have published two papers on the topic of lexical diversity and sophistication: Juffs (2019) and Naismith, Han, Juffs, Hill, and

102 *Lexical Development in an IEP*

Zheng (2018). Juffs (2019) was actually the first paper on the IEP vocabulary data and consisted of an analysis of Level 4 and 5 writing based on a subset of individually selected writing samples. Naismith et al. (2018) was a follow-up study that analyzed 4.2 million words in the database. We will focus on Juffs (2019) first, as it set up some groundwork for Naismith et al. (2018).

4.4.1 Comparing vocD and Advanced Guiraud for Advanced Writing

Juffs (2019) compared two methods of lexical richness: the within-text 'lexical diversity' measure and the 'lexical sophistication' measure, which refers to corpus frequency data. Three groups of learners contributed a significant enough amount of data that their essays could be tracked over two semesters from Level 4 (intermediate) to Level 5 (high intermediate/advanced): 22 Arabic, 20 Chinese, and 19 Korean speakers. Demographic details are provided in detail in Juffs (2019), but of note were two characteristics: first, more Chinese (15) and Korean speakers (10) tested directly into Level 4, whereas only 6 Arabic speakers started at that level, with the other 16 moving up from Level 3. While their global proficiency on entering the program was different as measured by MTELP, their writing scores were not different – a factor which reflects the discussion of placement assessment in Chapter 3.

Of direct relevance to the topic of this paper is the focus in all levels and all classes on words from the AWL (Coxhead, 2000). IEP 'Core Vocabulary' lists had been created for weeks 2–12 of the semester, 5–8 words for each week for a total of up to 55 to 80 lexemes per week. Level 3 words (55) ranged only from BNC-COCA frequency 1000–4000, Level 4 words (93) from frequency bands 1–6, with most being BNC-COCA level 3000, and level 5 words (122) again concentrated in the BNC-COCA 3000 range. Hence, the maximum number of words students were consistently instructed on over three semesters would have been 270. Students at each level are provided with a list of words for that level to study.

Recall from Chapter 2 that the IEP values a focus on vocabulary at all levels and in all skills. Teachers are encouraged to write the words on a 'word wall' in class and elicit definitions, examples, and morphological variants for about the first five minutes of each class, although it can't be guaranteed that teachers stick to this recommendation. It can be said that instruction sought to raise awareness of lexical development and the correct usage of different forms of a word.

The writing curriculum at Level 4 states that 'Students will produce medium-length, original written texts (≤500 words) responding to information on personal, practical, social, and general academic topics' and use words in BNC 3000–4000 frequency bands. Writing assignment genres include 'Process', 'Classification', and 'Cause-effect'. Students were free to choose their own topics within those types.

The Level 5 writing curriculum goals states that 'Students will produce medium-length and long, original written texts (500–2000 words) on personal, practical, social, and general academic topics' with a focus on BNC 5000+ word lists. Essay topics included 'Explanation', 'Narrative', 'Argument/persuasive essay', and 'Comparison/contrast essay'.

Juffs (2019) found that vocD did not reliably capture differences in lexical richness between Levels 4 and 5, whereas Advanced Guiraud did capture this difference. Table 4.2 provides the basic descriptive statistics, but Juffs (2019) provides the complete details of the statistical analysis.

The statistics showed that vocD scores were not statistically reliably different from Level 4 to 5. One reason for this is that the texts were already reaching a level of D that approximates native speaker texts of some complexity, that is, scores of between 70 and 120. In other words, the Level 4 and Level 5 lexical diversity scores were at ceiling, whereas once the increased use of lower frequency words was taken into account, it appears that the Level 5 students had indeed improved compared to the Level 4 students.

4.4.2 Naismith et al. (2018): Which List Is Better for Calculating Advanced Guiraud: The Role of L1 and L2 Experience

Following up on Juffs' (2019) analysis of a small number of texts (632 texts total and 254,055 words), Naismith et al. (2018) used techniques from data science to carry out a preliminary analysis of the whole corpus of written texts: a total of 4.2 million words from all levels. Naismith et al. (2018) took up an earlier observation by Juffs, Petrich, and Han

Table 4.2 Lexical Diversity and Lexical Sophistication Scores of IEP Level 4 and 5 Students: Arabic, Chinese, and Korean

L1 and Level (N)	Measure	Tokens	Level 4 Mean (SD)	Level 5 Mean (SD)
Arabic 4 (22)	D	31,357	69.06 (9.53)	74.72 (12.61)
Arabic 5 (22)	Advanced Guiraud	60,522	1.32 (0.55)	2.12 (1.07)
Chinese 4 (20)	D	37,404	77.48 (14.34)	80.94 (16.16)
Chinese 5 (20)	Advanced Guiraud	49,987	1.53 (0.79)	2.07 (1.22)
Korean 4 (19)	D	31,531	72.45 (13.24	77.01 (13.27)
Korean 5 (19)	Advanced Guiraud	43,254	1.38 (0.68)	1.90 (1.07)

(2013) that learners knew some very low frequency words. They pointed out that the first language culture and the experience which students have with higher education mean that they often use words that only appear in lower frequency bands for native speakers (e.g., *spicy, camel, dumpling; semester, visa*). Naismith et al. (2018)'s analysis is based on all of the words in the learners' writing, including writing assignments, grammar exercises, and reading reports.

Naismith et al. (2018) found that a better measure for the calculation of lexical sophistication was a list of low frequency words that did not give students credit for words such as *semester* and *camel* as part of their 'advanced' word knowledge. They calculated the frequency ranks of the most frequent 2000 words in the Level 3 student writing and used that list as the basis of the 'most frequent 2000' to exclude in calculating Advanced Guiraud. The result of this calculation is shown in Figure 4.1. The data showed that all L1 groups increased reliably at each proficiency level, starting at a fairly low level for the Arabic-speaking learners.

In contrast, Figure 4.2 shows that using the New General Service list resulted in higher scores overall and a 'false' finding that Korean-speaking learners did not improve at all from Level 3 to Level 4, which is highly counter-intuitive. IEP teachers have a good sense that some of the largest gains made by students occur from Levels 3 to 4, and a finding that the Korean speakers' lexical sophistication makes no progress between these levels is hard to accept.

Advanced Guiraud, then, seems to be a good indicator of progress that students make in their lexical development as long as prior vocabulary knowledge is accounted for. It might be possible, with further research, to suggest benchmarks for students' writing that approach that required for academic papers. The data from Naismith et al. (2018) and Juffs

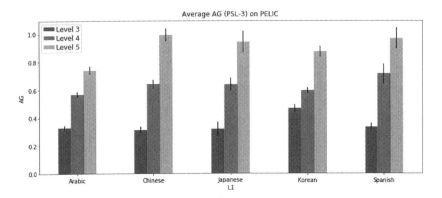

Figure 4.1 Gains in Advanced Guiraud Scores by First Language and Level Using Pitt IEP Frequency List

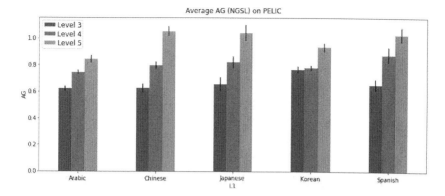

Figure 4.2 Gains in Advanced Guiraud Scores by First Language and Level Using NGSL Frequency List

(2019) would suggest that an Advanced Guiraud score of between 1 and 2 would be appropriate for learners to be 'academically ready'. As a point of comparison, Lincoln's Gettysburg address (Bliss version) is 272 words long; 90.8% of the words are in the K-1 and K2 BNC-COCA-25 frequency bands, and we estimated the speech to have an AG score of 1.15 based on the NGSL list.

4.4.3 Differences Among Regions With the Same First Language

It should also be noted that differences may exist for speakers of the *same* language from different sub-regions of the world where that language is spoken. For example, speakers of Chinese from Taiwan may have different exposure to English than those from Hong Kong, Singapore, and mainland China. Each group could be different even though they speak different varieties of one 'language', Chinese. In the IEP data, this possibility arose with students from Libya and from the Gulf States, principally Saudi Arabia. Andrews (2009) carried out a study into any potential differences between the students from Libya and those from Saudi Arabia. Initially, the impression was that the Libyan students' writing might have greater lexical richness because they were older students, they had had some professional training in Libya, and were from a country that had been colonized by a European country (Italy), potentially exposing them to more Latinate words. In contrast, the Saudi students were younger, not exposed to a colonial language, and less experienced. In the small sample that Andrews studied, she suggested that the Libyan students did not in fact have an advantage and that topic choice of essay

106 *Lexical Development in an IEP*

and focus on the task (motivation) more likely explained the small differences in observed lexical development.

4.5 Instructional Approaches to Vocabulary Teaching

4.5.1 *Teaching Vocabulary: Decisions for the Approach, Method, and Technique*

Deciding which lemmas and phrases are appropriate to teach at each level is one task that a curriculum planner must decide on. (The actual lists for the IEP during the research period are provided in Appendix I to this chapter.) However, the question of *how* to implement vocabulary instruction in a university-based IEP is also a topic that is very important. Although it is clear that extensive reading, or implicit vocabulary learning (Krashen, 1989; Nagy & Herman,1987), must absolutely be the key element in acquiring a larger vocabulary, the question of whether targeted, in-class instruction has an effect at all remains a matter of highly charged debate (Cobb, 2016; Nagy & Townsend, 2012). Questions arise as to whether *instruction* is even a worthwhile endeavor at all. In a series of publications dating from the 1970s, Krashen has cast doubt on the role of explicit instruction in language learning, maintaining that it has a role only for 'monitoring' output when there is time for metalinguistic knowledge to be used. He has extended this position to the teaching of vocabulary, and specifically more advanced vocabulary. For example, Krashen (2012, p. 233) stated 'I doubt that any member of the human race has ever consciously learned more than very modest amounts of academic language. This claim, of course, is subject to empirical investigation'. In my view, IEP students expect and deserve to be guided in their learning, so the option of no instructional intervention at all is simply indefensible.

Even if one concedes that some explicit instruction is important, however, other questions focus on the *type* of (written) output practice that might be best for lexical learning. For example, some teachers believe that writing new sentences using the target word is important. Hulstijn and Laufer (2001) have suggested that activities that require deeper processing through involvement from need to know a word, a search for the word, and subsequent evaluation of the word in context lead to improved retention. They have called this approach 'the involvement load hypothesis'.

However, whether writing sentences and output is worth the time spent on it remains a question for research (Barcroft, 2004, 2006; Folse, 2006). Folse (2006) carried out a study that examined the effectiveness of 'fill-in-the-blank' versus sentence writing exercises. In a carefully controlled study, he provided three conditions in a design where the students practiced 18 words once with a fill-in-the-blank from a list, three times with fill-in-the-blank from a list, and also a sentence writing task. A modified version of the Vocabulary Knowledge Scale (Paribakht & Wesche, 1997) was used in the pre- and post-tests: 0 for no knowledge, 1 for a synonym or translation, and 2 for *both* the translation/synonym and a sentence that included the word. His results suggested an approach in which 'fill-in-the-blank' exercises are the most efficient way to practice words.

In a more recent study, Zou (2017) considered Hulstijn and Laufer's (2001) involvement load hypothesis in greater depth as part of a study on academic writing. Zou (2017) reviewed the recent literature and comes to a somewhat different conclusion than Folse (2006) with regard to fill-in-the-blank type exercises. Zou's study considered fill-in-the-blank exercises and two kinds of writing exercises in which the involvement load was manipulated by means of creating contexts for vocabulary in sentence writing and compositions that required respectively higher levels of evaluation. The one issue that Zou conceded was a weakness of this study was that time on task could have affected the outcomes, although the 30 minutes for the fill-in-the-blank group vs. 35 minutes for the two writing output groups does not seem particularly different. Perhaps more significant was that the composition group was required to plan a discourse in which to put the words, whereas the sentence writing group was not. The differences in pre-task planning and need to create a discourse seems to have made the composition group process the meanings of the words more deeply; it also explains the differences in the delayed post-test scores out of 20 (10 words, 2 possible points each) of a mean of 5.30 for the fill-in-the-blank group, 9.60 for the sentence writing group, and 13.91 for the composition group. Zou's study is important for those words that teachers focus on in class – although his study had only 10 words in 30 minutes.

Cobb (2016) pointed out that IEP students often have one year or less to learn many words in the 3000–9000 frequency bands, and so class time must be used judiciously. Ten words in one 'vocabulary class' meeting five times per week over three semesters might add up to 750 words being studied intensively, which is not many. Cobb also estimates that the amount of time for 'extensive reading' that is available to learners during the time that they have to prepare for academic study will provide learners with fewer than 12 exposures needed to help them learn each new word.[3] Although he discusses the large amounts of reading needed, he still concludes that instruction is important. Thus, program coordinators need to decide very carefully indeed which words to practice in any way at all in class. Finally, there is of course a difference between receptive and productive vocabulary, with productive vocabulary requiring much more time and effort.

Nagy and Townsend (2012) refer to Graves (2006), who advocated a four-pronged approach to instruction: (a) rich and varied experience (=extensive reading), (b) teaching individual words, (c) word-learning

108 *Lexical Development in an IEP*

strategies, and (d) promoting word consciousness. The second and fourth of these go beyond the 'immersion only' approach, but are all adopted in the Pitt IEP in various forms. For the Pitt IEP, promoting word consciousness forms part of an approach to word learning strategies as we focus on different forms of a word.

The subsections that follow describe various ways the IEP has implemented parts of the four-pronged approach. For extensive reading, the IEP maintains a library of readers that students are encouraged to check out and read. We have yet to carry out empirical research on this approach, but the IEP also has a book club to promote the use of the library. The first study to report on is the use of a reading tutor that was used during the portions of the period in which data were collected.

4.5.2 *Using Technology to Teach Vocabulary: The Role of Learners' Motivation, Culture, and Teachers' Perceptions*

Language programs may have students from mostly one first language or, as is usually the case in North America, from several different L1s. With learners from different educational and linguistic backgrounds, finding the right set of words to teach for each L1 or even each individual can be a challenge. Although the teachers in the Pitt IEP are well aware of the vital role of extensive reading in vocabulary learning, they felt that learners did not in fact engage in enough reading outside class. Although graded readers are valuable, they may not contain the vocabulary that will challenge learners once they begin their academic study.

The Pitt IEP faculty considered that one possible way around this problem was to adopt a personalized reading tutor that required learners to read and process words that had been selected from an academic word set. A tutor that fit this need was made available through a collaboration with the Pittsburgh Science of Learning Center, now http://learnlab.org. A team of computer scientists at Carnegie Mellon University developed a system, called REAP (www.lti.cs.cmu.edu/projects/language-technologies-education/reap-reader-specific-lexical-practice-improved-reading), which was based on texts freely available on the world wide web (Collins-Thompson & Callan, 2004; Heilman, Collins-Thompson, Callan, & Eskenazi, 2006). The researchers used a search engine that found reading passages that satisfied very specific lexical constraints, namely AWL words in texts of L1 English grades 6–8 level reading. (This level of reading was decided on because the intermediate textbook was shown to have about a US grade 7 level.) The web crawler netted a database of 50,000 documents (after filtering from 10 million), with each document about 1000 words. Because the selection was from an open corpus (the web), it satisfied a wide range of student interests and classroom needs. It had the potential to model an individual's degree of acquisition and fluency for each word in a constantly expanding lexicon so as to provide student-specific practice and remediation.

The advantage of the tutor was that each student would receive a personalized list of words to learn. Before starting the reading course at the beginning of term, the students took a YES/NO test on a list of words from the AWL (Harrington & Carey, 2009). Students had to state if they knew a word or not. The words that formed the basis of the individual students' lists for that term were derived from those words the student reported they definitely did not know. The web interface then generated a series of texts for each student that contained one to five key AWL words that the student reported not knowing. These words were highlighted in the text via hyperlink. When clicked on, the hyperlink directed the student to a pop-up dictionary entry that explained what the word meant in English and provided example sentences.

In 2007–2008, in an unpublished action research study, IEP faculty (led by Lois Wilson) carried out a quasi-experimental comparison of this automatic reading tutor with regular in-class activities.[4] The procedure for the tutor was first a pre-test to establish an individual focus word list of 100 AWL words. Then the students read texts that were selected to provide examples in context of the words they didn't know. While reading, they could choose to get help by clicking (or not) on words and looking at definitions. After the passage, there was a reading check question after reading the passage. Finally, there was a vocabulary check question. If a target word question was wrong, another passage with that word was presented right away; otherwise, the word was tested later. All words were seen at least five times: in the text, in the vocabulary questions, and in the reading check. At the end of term, post-test cloze and written output production tests were given.

In contrast, in the classroom activities only, students took a pre-test to establish an individual focus word list of 58 AWL words, none of which would appear in the REAP program. The words were chosen by the curriculum supervisor on the basis of her assessment of which words the students would know and would find useful. Students then completed interactive exercises in class, look-ups in class, and homework exercises, as part of their grade in the class. The in-class instruction was based on pair/group work, interaction, and written output practice. The final post-test was in cloze format, and there was also a final post-test of production. (We can assume based on the pre-tests that students did not know the words prior to the beginning of the instruction because the words were carefully screened.)

Over the two semesters in reading class, we compared the two approaches to vocabulary learning with the two sets of students, with a complete, combined data set for the two semesters of $n = 50$ for the cloze test and $n = 49$ for the production test (data for one student's production were missing). Because the scales on the tests were somewhat different,

110   *Lexical Development in an IEP*

we converted the scores to percentage scores in order to make two comparisons: post-test scores on receptive vocabulary tests (cloze) and on the production tests (sentence writing) in both treatments. A comparison of the scores in Table 4.3 on the post-tests shows very different scores in accuracy on the words that were taught. It is important to recall, however, that with REAP, the learners never carried out *writing* as part of the learning process – the post-test writing was an assessment only.

These results indicate that the focused instruction that was teacher led provided learners with better learning for the words that were taught for both receptive and production skills. The complete data set of reading activities is available on request from the Learnlab data repository: https://pslcdatashop.web.cmu.edu/Project?id=26.

It would be premature, of course, to assume that reading only should be abandoned. Recall that beyond the basic 2000 words, learners need to learn a substantial proportion of words in the 3000–9000 frequency band range. At a conservative estimate, this means that they need to learn 7000 words in three semesters. It is impossible to teach *in class* such a large number of words – there is simply not enough time. *This word learning task means that students absolutely have to devote time to extensive reading on their own in addition to in-class work*. No one denies this important component of vocabulary reading. Teachers and programs can help students in many ways, some of which are discussed in this chapter.

First, students must be encouraged to read materials that interest them, an issue considered by Cobb (2016). One of the advantages of teacher-led practice is that the teacher keeps the focus of the students on task – this is true in a wide range of teaching contexts, for example, in Spanish as a second language, it was shown that teacher led practice was more

Table 4.3 Results of Paired *t*-Tests on % Scores of Receptive and Productive Skills

Percentage scores	Mean/SD		Paired t test
	In class	*REAP*	
Cloze Test	84.25 (14.8)	42.00 (22.0)	$t(49) = 14.75$ $p \leq .0001$
Production Test	74.86 (14.13)	27.82 (20.04)	$t(48) = 16.45$ $p \leq .0001$
Correlation Both Receptive Tests	$r = .45$		$df(50)$ $p = .001$
Correlation Both Production Tests	$r = .36$		$df(49)$ $p = .012$
Correlations With MTELP	Cloze: $r = .48$ Production: $r = .51$	Cloze: $r = .56$ Production: $r = .30$	

effective than student group work on difficult morpho-syntactic properties of Spanish verbs (Toth, 2008). Specifically, with the REAP tutor, however, Heilman et al. (2010) showed that when using the REAP system, allowing students to select texts that were in an area of interest to them lead to greater gains in vocabulary knowledge. The role of interest has been highlighted by Krashen (1989), though the Pitt IEP does not agree that simply reading is an adequate preparation for learning vocabulary for academic study. However, given that attention is important in learning and that interest will enhance attention, it is clear that Heilman et al.'s findings support the idea that students must read articles of interest to them because this allows them to maintain greater focused attention (Schmidt, 1990, 2001). In the IEP context, this means academically oriented texts that contain words that students will encounter later in their degree programs will be of special value as long as they are not too difficult. In addition, using a system that allows translations (in moderation) can also be helpful (Saz, Lin, & Eskenazi, 2015).

However, although such intelligent tutors and online reading tutors offer extraordinarily rich opportunities for focused study at the individual level, the IEP ultimately decided that this was not the best use of class time. This decision does not mean such tutors are not valuable. Indeed, based on our research, with specific guidance, the tools can be important in helping students develop their knowledge through extensive reading. The guidance that students can benefit from emerged from several mixed-methods classroom-based studies.

Pelletreau (2006) began our review of the use of the tool. He found that some students took off-line notes while using the tutor, whereas others did not, preferring to interact with the teacher. Moreover, the topic choice was important to some students. (This was an option introduced in the system later.) Most importantly, students who were invested in the tool did best in learning, doing better on the words they were asked to focus on and on non-target words that they themselves chose to focus on. Pelletreau (2006, pp. 50–51) also notes that 'the number of target word lookups proved to be moderately correlated with non-target production task scores' and 'Provided students did not overdo the attention and the resources they devoted to non-target words, they could increase their target-word acquisition by taking a difficult vocabulary task and simplifying it with intermediate steps and a combination of bottom-up and top-down processing'.

Juffs and Friedline (2014) followed up on Pelletreau (2006). Using an activity theory framework, they confirmed that learners took an individual approach to the tool – and these approaches arose to some extent from the cultural background the students came from and their attitudes to reading as part of their vocabulary learning. Juffs and Friedline (2014) compared 41 Arabic-speaking learners with 21 Korean-speaking learners, whose cultures place different emphasis on oral interaction and reading.

112 *Lexical Development in an IEP*

Recall that the reading tutor permitted the students to click on words that were highlighted (=target words from each students' list of words they had reported they did not know) and non-target words, which were any other word the student wanted to check the meaning of. The two groups transformed the reading tutor based on their approach to learning. The Arabic-speaking learners clicked at the same rate as Korean speakers on target words – 49 on average for the Arabic speakers and 53 on average for the Korean speakers – but clicked on far fewer non-target words (74 vs. 114). In addition, in the reading check, which was a simple way to see if the learners actually read the text and not a set of comprehension questions, the Arabic speakers performed at chance (54%), whereas the Korean speakers did much better (71%).

Based on qualitative research with the learners, it was clear that the Arabic-speaking learners rushed through the readings due in part to their belief that reading was not helpful in learning vocabulary. In contrast, the Korean-speaking learners took a great deal of time, clicking on many words that were perhaps not essential to the reading, because they believed that every word needed to be understood.[5] The study concluded that learners need help in interacting with online tutors and that teachers' assumptions about the use of computer software have to be checked and reinforced carefully during the period that the software is used. Overall, the students preferred that class time be used through interactions with the teacher.

Finally, Wojcik (2009) looked at the problem of AWL list instruction from the point of view of teachers and students in an ethnographic study in the IEP. In a very detailed analysis, Wojcik looked into the IEP's instruction program of 50 AWL words during the three-month term. A pre-test and a post-test were used, requiring students to provide both synonyms and good example sentences. Core vocabulary words were focused on in all classes – not just reading class. Each week, a set of 5 words from the 50 chosen was selected for focused instruction and practice. Core words were written on the board and practiced at the beginning of every class. Other activities involved crossword puzzles, synonyms, dictation, fill-in-the-blank, and sentence writing, both in class and for homework. Teachers were encouraged to 'spontaneously' use the target words in classroom discourse, and students were noticed paying attention to the use of these words. The total amount of time across a level – reading, writing, speaking, listening, and grammar – amounted to about 2 hours per week. In this way, the IEP hoped to raise students' awareness of word families, the relationship among different lemmas (a persistent problem [Friedline, 2011]), and key usage.

However, the intent of the IEP during this period did not seem to make it into the consciousness of the students. Based on student interviews, Wojcik discovered that that none of the students knew about the AWL or why those particular words being focused on had been chosen. In general, students seemed not to realize that the words had been chosen for future use in their academic studies but seemed focused on 'every day' use and were much less interested in those technical words. Learners also seemed to think that receptive knowledge was all that they needed to know.

In interviews with the teachers, Wojcik reported that they were modest concerning their knowledge of how to teach vocabulary, although many had had training through webinars and brown bag talks. The teachers did feel that they needed more guidance, however, in coordinating the teaching in the various skills with skill-appropriate activities.

In the final measurement of vocabulary learning, Wojcik notes with some concern that more than 50% of the students were not able to accurately provide synonyms and sentences for 23 out 50 of the AWL words taught during the term. In spite of this, students improved their score out of 100 possible points by an average of 32 points.

Wojcik points out some issues surrounding the teaching of words. For example, she notes that teachers who try to discuss the differences in meaning between such words as *aspect* and *feature* can eat up a large amount of class time, and such usage might better be acquired through extensive reading. Indeed, meanings of abstract words in general are a challenge for bilinguals, as reported in the experimental literature (e.g., De Goot & Poot, 1997), a fact that is finally coming into estimates of lexical sophistication (Crossley & Kyle, 2018). Wojcik also noted that students seemed to have some knowledge already of some AWL words, for example, *method, alternative, secure, regions, obvious, target*. She noted that 42% of students showed knowledge of these words on the pretest. This is not surprising given that *obvious* and *target* are in the 1000 most frequent words on the BNC list. Wojcik (2009, p. 95) concludes that rich instruction and exposure to five words per week does not necessarily result in deep knowledge of those words. While it is true that not every word was thoroughly learned, in fact students did improve by 32 out of 100 points on average. In addition, she notes that students are gaining important awareness of vocabulary learning, which would help future learning on an individual level when reading.

Wojcik's work highlights some important issues for IEPs. First, teachers and program administrators need to communicate better with students regarding the reasons for instructional choices. This communication has the potential to raise student motivation in certain tasks and create better attention to these tasks. Second, instruction of vocabulary needs to be focused; teachers especially need to beware of eating up valuable class time with explanations of subtle differences among word meanings.

4.7 Collocations and Formulaic Sequences

One area of lexical development that is very important, but that we have not discussed, is that of collocations, 'chunks' or multi-word expressions (MWEs). In her influential paper, Wray (2000) defines formulaic

114 *Lexical Development in an IEP*

sequences broadly as set or semi-set MWEs, such as idioms, collocations, and sentence frames. These MWEs have also been called 'prefabricated routines' (Brown, 1973), lexical phrases (Nattinger & DeCarrico, 1992), and chunked sequences (Ellis, 1996). MWE, as any construction of more than one word, is the broadest term. Idioms are MWEs whose meaning is completely opaque (Manning & Schhütze, 1999). In other words, the meaning of idioms (e.g., *spill the beans, splitting hairs*) cannot be understood by the meaning of the individual words and their arrangement. It is widely accepted that idioms must be stored as a whole in the lexicon (Wray, 2000), even though their constituents can be re-ordered under some circumstances (Nunberg, Sag, & Wasow, 1994). Collocations (e.g., *strong tea*, but less acceptably **strong car*) are phrases whose meanings extend beyond the meaning of their constituents and can include compounds (e.g., *disk drive*), phrasal verbs (e.g., *look the phrase up*), and stock phrases such as *bacon and eggs* (Manning & Schütze, 1999). Collocations are considered a different type of MWE (Bannard, 2007). Although these MWEs are compositional, they can also be highly lexically idiosyncratic (Lewis, 2002).

Researchers have discussed three possible functions of formulaic language: as minimal communication, to ease production, and as a learning strategy (Weinert, 1995). First, minimal communication MWEs (e.g., *how are you?*) serve pragmatic functions (e.g., Girard & Sionis, 2003). Second, since MWEs are expected to be partially or wholly stored, speakers may use MWEs for efficient language performance (Wray, 2000, 2012) and language processing (Dabrowska, 2004). In other words, language learners benefit from MWEs, particularly in language performance fluency, because a "chunk" of language is retrieved together (Boers, Eyckmans, Kappel, Stengers, & Demecheleer, 2006; Skehan, 1998). Additionally, MWEs allow second language (L2) learners to sound more native-like (Pawley & Synder, 1983) and more proficient (Boers et al., 2006). As such, much research on MWEs has concerned the effect on speaker fluency and proficiency (e.g., Wood, 2002, 2010).

We have not yet completed extensive research on MWEs in the PELIC data. However, we feel the relationship between learning MWEs and lexical diversity could be an interesting one to explore.

4.6 Conclusion

The learning task for learners in an intensive English program who need to be ready to study their chosen academic subject in the medium of English is a daunting one. They need to have mastered the basic 2000 words of English but may not have before entering the IEP. In addition, learners need to focus on words from the 3000–6000 frequency levels. IEPs can track progress in this area of vocabulary development based on measures such as Advanced Guiraud, which is a more useful yardstick with which to measure progress than a simple diversity measure.

Lexical Development in an IEP 115

The learning of most words must ultimately come from extensive reading of materials that are of interest to the learner. However, it may be wise to endorse the view of Nagy and Townsend (2012, p. 234), who state:

> Genuine academic reading is likely to lead to very gradual gains in knowledge of large numbers of words, whereas rich vocabulary instruction aims to produce substantial gains in knowledge for a small set of words – as well as incremental increases in knowledge of the words *around* the target words.

In other words, there is a role for instruction. In class, focused engagement with word forms, concentrated practice with derivational morphology, and well-chosen subsets of words should assist learners in making maximum use of their extensive reading, as they will notice more forms as they read and will thus build up knowledge and fluency in the vocabulary that they will need.

4.8 Topics for Administrators and Teachers to Reflect On

4.8.1 Questions and Issues Mainly for Program Administrators and Curriculum Supervisors

1. Does your IEP maintain a set of vocabulary lists such as those in Appendix I of this chapter?

    a. If yes, how was the list decided on? How often is it reviewed?
    b. If no, what is the rationale behind not having a list?

2. One area of vocabulary development that we have not discussed in detail in this chapter is 'collocations' or 'chunks' (e.g., Barfield & Gyllstad, 2009). What focus in either lists or materials is put on collocations? On idiomatic expressions?
3. Does your program assess progress in lexical knowledge from level to level? If so, how does the IEP that you supervise assess progress in vocabulary knowledge from level to level?
4. The research in our IEP suggests that communication about curriculum goals is important. How does your program communicate priorities with lexical learning to teachers and students?

4.8.2 Questions and Issues for Classroom Teachers

1. What approach to vocabulary instruction does the IEP take?

    a. Are teachers encouraged to provide vocabulary lists for the students?
    b. What kinds of exercises does the IEP encourage teachers to use?

116 *Lexical Development in an IEP*

    c. Is there a vocabulary textbook?

    d. To what extent is word structure a target of instruction in your IEP? Is it systematic or based on 'focus on form' in which it is addressed when it comes up in class?

2. Consider the following words: which one among (a)–(c) might cause learners the most challenges and why?

    a. Arrive – *arriveable. [-able cannot affix to an intransitive verb]

    b. Corner-worker-faster. [-er can be part of a word, a derivational affix, or an inflectional affix]

    c. just-justice-justify [learners may not know the two homophonous meanings of 'just']

3. Learners often make the error: 'I am very interesting in this book' instead of 'I am very interested in this book'. Why do you think this might be? Is it because (a) learners are avoiding what looks like the passive; (b) the -ing form is more common in general; (c) there is confusion over the meaning of -ing and -ed adjectives; (d) learners know one word for 'interesting' and 'interested', perhaps due to their L1?

4. A great deal of research shows that collocations or chunks are very important in lexical development. (See, for example, papers in Barfield & Gyllstad, 2009; Paquot & Granger, 2013). These days, most vocabulary textbooks provide practice with collocations (e.g., Davis et al., 2015). Does your textbook have a section on this topic? Which collocations are chosen and how useful are they? Are the collocations based on frequency, such as in the lists in 5 or other sources, for example, Martinez and Schmitt (2012)?

5. Teachers may find the following resources useful:

    a. www.lextutor.ca/

        i. Tom Cobb's (2000) website. English frequency lists. Free.

    b. www.english-corpora.org/coca/

        i. Corpus of Contemporary American English.

        ii. Frequency lists by genre. May require a fee.

Notes

1. Thanks are due to Theresa English for pointing this out to me.
2. Complete details of the calculation are reported in Malvern, Richards, Chipere, and Duràn (2004).
3. Some researchers have stopped advocating a specific number of exposures. Instead, different numbers of exposures may be needed for different elements (e.g., spelling is acquired before polysemy).

Lexical Development in an IEP   117

4. It was quasi-experimental because students were not randomly assigned to treatments. In addition, not all students completed all of the tasks, and the group sizes were rather small. This research can be considered more 'action' research, as discussed earlier in Chapter 1.
5. It is worth mentioning that Juffs and Friedline (2014) did not control for biological sex of the learners. It is possible that the majority of Arabic-speaking students being male and a greater proportion of the Korean students being female had an effect on how the students used the tutor. Such effects have been found with cognitive tutors in mathematics (Arroyo et al., 2013).

References

Andrews, S. J. (2009). *Educational background as predictor of lexical richness among Libyan and Saudi Arabian ESL students.* University of Pittsburgh ETD (Unpublished). Retrieved from http://d-scholarship.pitt.edu/7505/1/SallyAndrewsThesis.pdf

Arroyo, I., Burleson, W., Tai, M., Muldner, K., & Woolf, B. P. (2013). Gender differences in the use and benefit of advanced learning technologies for mathematics. *Journal of Educational Psychology, 105*(4), 957–969. doi: 10.1037/a0032748

Bannard, C. (2007). *A measure of syntactic flexibility for automatically identifying multiword expression in corpora.* Proceedings of the Workshop on a Broader Perspective on Multiword Expressions, Association for Compositional Linguistics, 1–8.

Barcroft, J. (2004). Effects of sentence writing in second language lexical acquisition. *Second Language Research, 20,* 303–334.

Barcroft, J. (2006). Negative effects of forced output on vocabulary learning. *Second Language Research, 22,* 487–497.

Barfield, A., & Gyllstad, H. (Eds.). (2009). *Researching collocations in another language: Multiple interpretations.* London: Palgrave Macmillan.

Boers, F., Eyckmans, J., Kappel, J., Stengers, H., & Demecheleer, M. (2006). Formulaic sequences and perceived oral proficiency: Putting a lexical approach to the test. *Language Teaching Research, 10*(3), 245–261.

Brown, R. (1973). *A first language: The early stages.* Cambridge, MA: Harvard University Press.

Browne, C., Culligan, B., & Philips, J. (2013). *The new general service list.* Retrieved June 7, 2019, from www.newgeneralservicelist.org/

Bulté, B., & Housen, A. (2014). Conceptualizing and measuring short-term changes in L2 writing complexity. *Journal of Second Language Writing, 26,* 42–65. doi:10.1016/j.jslw.2014.09.005

Cobb, T. (2000). Retrieved March 2019, from www.lextutor.ca.

Cobb, T. (2006). *The old vocabulary, the new vocabulary and the Arabic learner.* Paper presented at the TESOL Symposium on Vocabulary. Words matter: The importance of vocabulary in English Language Teaching and Learning, Dubai Men's College, Dubai, United Arab Emirates.

Cobb, T. (2016). Numbers or numerology? A response to Nation (2014) and McQuillan (2016). *Reading in a Foreign Language, 28*(2), 299–304.

Collins-Thompson, K., & Callan, J. (2004, October). *Information retrieval for language tutoring: An overview of the REAP project.* Paper presented at

118 *Lexical Development in an IEP*

the Proceedings of the 27th annual international ACM SIGIR conference on research and development, Sheffield.

Coxhead, A. (2000). A new academic word list. *TESOL Quarterly, 34,* 213–238.

Crossley, S. A., & Kyle, K. (2018). Assessing writing with the tool for the automatic analysis of lexical sophistication (TAALES). *Assessing Writing, 38,* 46–50. Retrieved from https://doi.org/10.1016/j.asw.2018.06.004

Dabrowska, E. (2004). *Language, mind and brain.* Washington, DC: Georgetown University.

Daller, M., Turlik, J., & Weir, I. (2013). Vocabulary acquisition and the learning curve. In S. Jarvis & M. Daller (Eds.), *Vocabulary knowledge: Human ratings and automated measures* (pp. 185–218). Amsterdam: John Benjamins.

Davis, B., Juffs, A., McCormick, D. E., Mizera, G., O'Neill, M. C., Slaathaug, M., & Smith, D. (2015). *Academic vocabulary building in English, low intermediate* (Vol. 1). Ann Arbor, MI: University of Michigan Press.

De Groot, A. M. B., & Poot, R. (1997). Word translation at three levels of proficiency: The ubiquitous involvement of conceptual memory. *Language Learning, 47,* 215–264.

Duràn, P., Malvern, D., Richards, B., & Chipere, N. (2004). Developmental trends in lexical diversity. *Applied Linguistics, 25*(2), 220–242. Retrieved from https://doi-org.pitt.idm.oclc.org/10.1093/applin/25.2.220

Ellis, N. C. (1996). Sequencing in SLA: Phonological memory, chunking, and points of order. *Studies in Second Language Acquisition, 18,* 91–126.

Folse, K. S. (2006). The effect of type of written exercise on L2 vocabulary retention. *TESOL Quarterly, 40,* 273–293. doi:10.2307/40264523

Friedline, B. E. (2011). *Challenges in the second language acquisition of derivational morphology: From theory to practice* (PhD dissertation), Pittsburgh University Press, Pittsburgh.

Gardner, D., & Davies, M. (2014). A new academic word list. *Applied Linguistics, 35*(3), 305–327. doi:10.1093/applin/amt015

Girard, M., & Sionis, C. (2003). Formulaic speech in the L2 classroom: An attempt at identification and classification. *Pragmatics, 13*(2), 231–251.

Graves, M. F. (2006). *The vocabulary book: Learning and instruction.* New York: Teachers College Press; Newark, DE: International Reading Association; Urbana, IL: National Council of Teachers of English.

Harrington, M., & Carey, M. (2009). The on-line yes/no test as a placement tool. *System, 37*(4), 614–626.

Heilman, M., Collins-Thompson, K., Callan, J., & Eskenazi, M. (2006). *Classroom success of an intelligent tutoring system for lexical practice and reading comprehension.* Paper presented at the Proceedings of the ninth international conference on spoken language processing.

Heilman, M., Collins-Thompson, K., Callan, J., Eskenazi, M., Juffs, A., & Wilson, L. (2010). Personalization of reading passages improves vocabulary acquisition. *International Journal in Artificial Intelligence in Education, 20*(1), 73–98.

Hulstijn, J., & Laufer, B. (2001). Some empirical evidence for the involvement load hypothesis in vocabulary acquisition. *Language Learning, 51,* 539–558. doi:10.1111/0023-8333.00164

Jarvis, S. (2013a). Capturing the diversity in lexical diversity. *Language Learning, 63*(Suppl. 1), 87–106. doi:0.1111/j.1467-9922.2012.00739.x

Lexical Development in an IEP   119

Jarvis, S. (2013b). Defining and measuring lexical diversity. In S. Jarvis & M. Daller (Eds.), *Vocabulary knowledge: Human ratings and automated measures* (pp. 13–44). Amsterdam: John Benjamins.

Jarvis, S., & Daller, M. (Eds.). (2013). *Vocabulary knowledge: Human ratings and automated measures*. Amsterdam: John Benjamins.

Juffs, A. (2009). Second language acquisition of the lexicon. In W. Ritchie & T. K. Bhatia (Eds.), *The new handbook of second language acquisition* (pp. 181–205). Leeds: Emerald.

Juffs, A. (2019). The development of lexical diversity in the writing of intensive English program students. In R. M. DeKeyser & P. B. Goretti (Eds.), *Reconciling methodological demands with pedagogical applicability* (pp. 179–200). Amsterdam: John Benjamins.

Juffs, A., & Friedline, B. E. (2014). Sociocultural influences on the use of a web-based tool for learning English vocabulary. *System*, 42, 48–59. doi:10.1016/j.system.2013.10.015

Juffs, A., Petrich, J., & Han, N-R. (2013, March 13). *Tracking the development of lexical diversity in intensive English program students in the US*. Presentation at American Association of Applied Linguistics, Houston.

Krashen, S. (1989). We acquire vocabulary and spelling by reading: Additional evidence for the input hypothesis. *Modern Language Journal*, 73, 440–464.

Krashen, S. (2012). Direct instruction of academic vocabulary: What about real reading? *Reading Research Quarterly*, 47(3), 233–234. doi:10.1002/RRQ.018

Laufer, B., Elder, C., Hill, K., & Congdon, P. (2004). Size and strength: Do we need both to measure vocabulary knowledge? *Language Testing*, 21(2), 202–226.

Laufer, B., & Hulstijn, J. (2001). Incidental vocabulary acquisition in a second language: The concept of task-induced involvement. *Applied Linguistics*, 22, 1–26.

Lewis, M. (2002). *Implementing the lexical approach*. Boston, MA: Thomson, Heinle.

MacWhinney, B. (2000). *The CHILDES Project: Tools for analyzing talk. Third Edition*. Mahwah, NJ: Lawrence Erlbaum Associates.

Malvern, D., Richards, B., Chipere, N., & Duràn, P. (2004). *Lexical diversity and language development: Quantification and assessment*. Basingstoke: Palgrave Macmillan.

Manning, C. D., & Schütze, H. (1999). *Foundations of statistical natural language processing* (2nd printing ed.). Cambridge, MA: MIT Press.

Martinez, R., & Schmitt, N. (2012). A phrasal expressions list. *Applied Linguistics*, 33(3), 299–320.

McCarthy, P. M., & Jarvis, S. (2007). vocD: A theoretical and empirical evaluation. *Language Testing*, 24(4), 459–488.

McCarthy, P. M., & Jarvis, S. (2010). MTLD, vocD-D, and HD-D: A validation study of sophisticated approaches to lexical diversity assessment. *Behavior Research Methods*, 42(2), 381–392. doi:10.3758/BRM.42.2.381

Nagy, W. E., & Herman, P. A. (1987). Breadth and depth of vocabulary knowledge: Implications for acquisition and instruction. In M. McKeown & M. Curtis (Eds.), *The nature of vocabulary acquisition* (pp. 19–35). Mahwah, NJ: Lawrence Erlbaum.

120 *Lexical Development in an IEP*

Nagy, W. E., & Townsend, D. (2012). Response to Krashen. *Reading Research Quarterly, 47*(3), 233–234. doi:10.1002/RRQ.018

Naismith, B., Han, N-R., Juffs, A., Hill, B. L., & Zheng, D. (2018). Accurate measurement of lexical sophistication with reference to ESL learner data. In K. E. Boyer & M. Yudelson (Eds.), *Proceedings of the 11th international conference on educational data mining* (pp. 259–265). Buffalo, NY. Retrieved from http://educationaldatamining.org/EDM2018/

Nation, I. S. P. (1990). *Teaching and learning vocabulary*. New York: Newbury House.

Nation, I. S. P. (2001). *Learning vocabulary in another language*. Cambridge: Cambridge University Press.

Nation, I. S. P. (2013). *Learning vocabulary in another language* (2nd ed.). Cambridge: Cambridge University Press.

Nattinger, J. R., & DeCarrico, J. S. (1992). *Lexical phrases and language teaching*. New York: Oxford University Press.

Nunberg, G., Sag, I., & Wasow, T. (1994). Idioms. *Language, 70*, 491–538.

Paquot, M., & Granger, S. (2013). Formulaic language in learner corpora. *Annual Review of Applied Linguistics, 32*, 130–149. doi:10.1017/S0267190512000098

Paribakht, T., & Wesche, M. (1997). Vocabulary enhancement activities and reading for meaning in second language vocabulary acquisition. In J. Coady & T. Huckin (Eds.), *Second language vocabulary acquisition* (pp. 174–200). Cambridge: Cambridge University Press.

Pawley, A., & Synder, F. H. (1983). Two puzzles for linguistic theory: Nativelike selection and nativelike fluency. In J. C. Richards & R. W. Schmidt (Eds.), *Language and communication* (pp. 191–226). New York: Longman.

Pelletreau, T. (2006). *Computer assisted vocabulary acquisition in the ESL classroom* (Master of Arts), University of Pittsburgh, Pittsburgh. Retrieved from http://etd.library.pitt.edu/ETD/available/etd-08082006-035505/unrestricted/timothyrpelletreau_etd2006.pdf

Perfetti, C. A., & Hart, L. (2002). The lexical quality hypothesis. In L. Verhoeven, C. Elbro, & P. Reitsma (Eds.), *Precursors of functional literacy* (pp. 189–214). Amsterdam: John Benjamins.

Read, J. (2004). Research in teaching vocabulary. *Annual Review of Applied Linguistics, 24*, 146–161.

Saz, O., Lin, Y., & Eskenazi, M. (2015). Measuring the impact of translation on the accuracy and fluency of vocabulary acquisition. *Computer Speech and Language, 31*(1), 49–64. doi:10.1016/j.csl.2014.11.005

Schmidt, R. W. (1990). The role of consciousness in second language learning. *Applied Linguistics, 11*(2), 129–158.

Schmidt, R. W. (2001). Attention. In P. Robinson (Ed.), *Cognition and second language instruction* (pp. 3–32). Cambridge: Cambridge University Press.

Schmitt, N., & Schmitt, D. (2014). A reassessment of frequency and vocabulary size in L2 vocabulary teaching. *Language Teaching, 47*(4), 484–503. doi:10.1017/S0261444812000018

Sisková, Z. (2012). Lexical richness in EFL students' narratives. *Language Studies Working Papers, University of Reading, 4*, 26–36.

Skehan, P. (1998). *A cognitive approach to language Learning*. New York: Oxford University Press.

Todd, R. W. (2017). An opaque engineering word list: Which words should a teacher focus on? *English for Specific Purposes, 45,* 31–39. Retrieved from http://dx.doi.org/10.1016/j.esp.2016.08.003

Toth, P. D. (2008). Teacher and learner led discourse in task-based grammar instruction: Providing procedural assistance for L2 morphosyntactic development. *Language Learning, 58,* 237–285.

van Hout, R., & Vermeer, A. (2007). Comparing measures of lexical richness. In H. Daller, J. Milton, & J. Treffers-Daller (Eds.), *Modelling and assessing vocabulary knowledge* (pp. 93–115). Cambridge: Cambridge University Press.

Weinert, R. (1995). The role of formulaic language in second language acquisition: A review. *Applied Linguistics, 16*(2), 180–205.

West, M. (1953). *A general service list of English words: With semantic frequencies and a supplementary word list for the writing of popular science and technology.* London: Addison-Wesley Longman.

Wojcik, R. (2009). *An ethnography and analysis of the learning and teaching of academic word list vocabulary in the ESL classroom* (MA thesis), University of Pittsburgh, Pittsburgh.

Wood, D. (2002). Formulaic language in acquisition and production: Implications for teaching. *TESL Canada Journal, 20*(1), 1–15.

Wood, D. (2010). *Formulaic language and second language speech fluency: Background, evidence and classroom applications.* New York: Continuum.

Wray, A. (2000). Formulaic sequences in second language teaching: Principle and practice. *Applied Linguistics, 21*(4), 463–489.

Wray, A. (2012). What do we (think we) know about formulaic language? An evaluation of the current state of play. *Annual Review of Applied Linguistics, 32,* 231–254.

Youngblood, A. M., & Folse, K. S. (2017). Survey of corpus-based vocabulary lists for TESOL classes. *MEXTESOL Journal, 41*(1), 1–15.

Zou, D. (2017). Vocabulary acquisition through cloze exercises, sentence-writing and composition-writing: Extending the evaluation component of the involvement load hypothesis. *Language Teaching Research, 21*(1), 54–75. doi:10.1177/1362168816652418

Appendix I
English Language Institute Vocabulary List

The following word list is derived from putting the Coxhead word list through the Vocab Profiler on Tom Cobb's 'The Compleat Lexical Tutor', based on the British National Corpus (BNC) (P. Nation) [www.lextutor. ca]. From this list, ELI levels will focus on:

- Level 3–1000–2000
- Level 4–3000–4000
- Level 5–5000+

In addition to the vocabulary from this list, the students are expected to know key targeted vocabulary from various activities in all skill areas. Students are asked to keep a list of words that they studied and hand it in at the end of the semester.

Token List [↑]

BNC-1000 [fams 82 : types 82 : tokens 82]

achieve	confer	finance	obvious
affect	consult	function	odd
apparent	contact	fund	paragraph
approach	contract	furthermore	percent
appropriate area	converse	grant	period
assume	couple	identify income	plus
authority	create	individual invest	policy
available aware	debate	involve	positive
benefit	definite	issue	presume
brief	design	item	previous
called colleague	document	job	proceed
comment	economy	labour	process
commit	environment	link	project
community	file	major	range
compute	final	normal	region

Lexical Development in an IEP   123

require	scheme	similar	structure
research	section	site	tape
resource	secure	specific	team
role	sex	strategy	transport

BNC-2000 [fams 198 : types 199 : tokens 199]

access	conflict	exclude	licence
accommodate	considerable	exhibit	locate
accurate	constant	expand	logic
adequate adjust	consume context	expert	maintain
adult	contribute	factor	margin
aid	convince	feature	medical
allocate	corporate credit	fee	mental
alter alternative	criteria	flexible	method
analyse	culture	focus	minimum
annual	cycle	generate	minor
appreciate	data	generation goal	monitor
aspect assemble	define	grade	nevertheless
assess	demonstrate	guarantee	obtain
assign	deny	highlight	occupy
assist	depress	ignorant	occur
assure	despite	image	option
attach	detect	impact	overall
attitude	display	implicate	panel
behalf	distinct	impose	partner
capable	distribute	indicate	physical
capacity	domestic	initial	potential
category	draft	initiate	precise
challenge	drama	injure	prime
channel	edit	inspect	principle
chapter	element	instance	priority
chemical	emphasis	institute	professional
circumstance	enable	instruct	promote
civil	energy	intelligence	proportion
clarify	enormous	internal	prospect
code	ensure	interpret	psychology
commission	equip	investigate	publish
communicate	establish	justify	purchase quote
compensate	estate	label	react
complex	estimate	lecture	recover register
concentrate	eventual	legal	regulate
concept confirm	evolve	liberal	reject

124 *Lexical Development in an IEP*

relax	schedule	sum	tradition
release relevant	seek	survey	transfer
rely	select	survive	ultimate
remove	series	target	valid
reside	shift	technical	vary
respond	significant source	technique	vehicle
restrict	stable	technology	version
reverse	status	temporary	virtual
revise	stress	text	volume
revolution	style	theory	voluntary
route	sufficient	topic	whereas

BNC-3000 [fams 87 : types 87 : tokens 87]

adapt	external	neutral	substitute
approximate	extract	norm	supplement
author	format	nuclear	suspend
bond bulk chart	foundation	orient	symbol
classic coincide	founded	outcome	tense
collapse compile	framework	phase	terminate
comprehensive	identical	phenomenon	trace
conceive	illustrate	portion	transform
consequent	incentive	pose	transmit
contrast convert	incline	precede	trigger
coordinate core	incorporate	predict	uniform
correspond	index	principal	unique
crucial devote	intense	random	utilise
dimension	interval	restore	via
discriminate	layer	reveal	visible
dispose	manual	scope	vision
dominate	mature	sole	visual
equivalent error	medium	somewhat	welfare
export	military	straightforward	whereby
expose	motive	subsidy	

BNC-4000 [fams 98 : types 98 : tokens 98]

abandon	advocate	cease	conclude
academy	aggregate	clause	conduct
accompany	amend	commence	conform consist
accumulate	anticipate	complement	construct
acknowledge	attribute	component	controversy
acquire	bias	compound	cooperate

Lexical Development in an IEP   125

currency
decade
decline
device
differentiate
distort
duration
encounter
enhance
ethnic
evident
exceed
exploit
federal
fluctuate

formula
forthcoming
gender
globe
guideline
implement
imply
inevitable input
insert
integrate
interact
intervene
isolate
legislate
manipulate

mechanism
media ministry
mode
modify
mutual
network
notion
objective
offset
ongoing
output
overlap
overseas
participate
perceive

persist
perspective
philosophy
primary
prior
publication
pursue
refine
resolve
restrain
retain
revenue
rigid
scerlie

BNC-5000 [fams 60 : types 60 : tokens 60]

abstract
albeit
ambiguous
analogy
arbitrary
attain
coherent
commodity
compatible
comprise
confine consent
constitute
constrain
contemporary
contradict

contrary
derive
diminish
discrete
displace
diverse
dynamic
eliminate
emerge
enforce
erode
evaluate
explicit
fundamental
hence

incidence
infer
inherent
inhibit
innovate
insight
integral
integrity
intermediate
journal likewise
maximise
migrate
minimal
minimise
parallel

passive
predominant
preliminary
ratio
regime
reinforce
reluctance
simulate
sphere
transit
undergo
unify
widespread

BNC-6000 [fams 19 : types 19 : tokens 19]

adjacent
cite
deduce
deviate
entity

equate
facilitate
hierarchy
implicit
infrastructure

levy
practitioner
prohibit
radical
rational

subordinate
successor
thesis
undertake

126 *Lexical Development in an IEP*

BNC-7000 [fams 13 : types 13 : tokens 13]

append	immigrate	parameter
convene	intrinsic invoke	protocol
domain	nonetheless	qualitative
empirical	notwithstanding	thereby

BNC-8000 [fams 7 : types 7 : tokens 7]

concurrent denote
finite
ideology mediate
negate
violate

BNC-9000 [fams 2 : types 2 : tokens 2] automate hypothesis
BNC-10,000 [fams 2 : types 2 : tokens 2] ethic paradigm
OFF LIST [? : types 2 : tokens 2] administrate induce

5 Grammatical Development in an Intensive English Program

5.1 Introduction: Theories of Grammar and Learning

In second language teaching and praxis, one of the main foci over the years has been on grammatical development at the level of the clause. Although language teaching may have begun by focusing on structure, a consensus now exists that language learning and teaching must account for a variety of factors from the complexity of the code that language employs (grammar) to the ways language is used to communicate in longer stretches of discourse, especially in academic settings. At least since the 1950s, applied linguists have taken an eclectic approach to language development. For example, Norris (1964) listed as equally important the oral nature of language, the arbitrariness of symbols, the systemic nature of language patterns, their communicative use, the habits that underpin language learning, and the cultural ties that languages have to their respective speakers' societies. Ten years after that, in the United Kingdom, Allen and Corder's (1973, p. 2) influential Edinburgh Course on Applied Linguistics stated the following, suggesting alternative views of language might be useful:

> If language is knowledge, then learning it will share some of the characteristics of learning, say Chemistry; if it is skillful behaviour, it will be something we acquire through practice; if it an object, we may get to know it through descriptions or use, while if it is a social event we shall wish to participate in the social interaction in which it is manifest.

Re-reading these earlier discussions, it is striking how much current theorizing still reflects thinking of 50 years ago. However, more recently, rather than conceding that language is multifaceted and requires different tools to understand each component, some researchers seek to make their viewpoint an exclusive one rather than seeing which subpart of language knowledge and learning can be best accounted for by which theoretical approach. In part, differences among researchers reflect the diverse view

128 *Grammatical Development in an IEP*

on the nature of knowledge of language itself. Formal accounts assume that some kind of 'blueprint' for language is available to learners that prevents them from making certain assumptions about language; such accounts can also show that adult second languages are 'natural languages' and not only the products of generalized learning mechanisms (White, 2003). Quantitative accounts emphasize the role of input and general learning mechanisms (e.g., Robinson & Ellis, 2008). Sociocultural views put the onus squarely on meaning, concept development, social co-construction, and culture (e.g., Lantolf & Thorne, 2006). A reasonable approach is to accept that each viewpoint, whether language is an abstract code, acquired through input, subject to skill development, or learned through social interaction, is a part of a complete theory of language acquisition (Gleitman, 1993) and thus also of SLA. All of these approaches are relevant to language learners, teachers, and classroom praxis at different levels of knowledge detail. To some extent, differences among these approaches continue a long tradition in the debate between empiricism and rationalism (see Ochsner [1979] for some philosophical history and Toth and Davin [2016] for a more recent opinion on the need for multiple perspectives). Because these debates would take us much too far afield from our focus on intensive English programs, we will direct our attention to the data themselves, but we should bear in mind that explanations for patterns of grammatical development will by necessity rely on a variety of factors.

This chapter will focus on grammatical development at the sentence and clause level. By this term, I mean topics such as control of relative clauses, complement clauses, and grammatical morphology. This approach assumes that a useful, descriptive distinction can be made between open class vocabulary items such as *cat*, oppo*rtunity*, and *modernize* compared to closed class, functional words such as modal verbs (e.g., *could*), definite and indefinite articles, functional words such as *whether*, and inflectional morphology. Although researchers may approach knowledge of a second language from various perspectives, they generally agree that the influence of the first language in grammar and the lexicon is overwhelming, especially in the initial stages (MacWhinney, 2008; Schwartz & Sprouse, 1996). Of course, by the time most students arrive in intensive English programs, this first language influence has been attenuated by exposure to English through instruction and/or participation in an English-speaking environment.

Consideration will be given to data from both spoken and written sources and will concentrate on the developmental orders of key grammatical forms and the role of the LI (Schepps, 2014; see also Spinner, 2011) and tracking syntactic complexity (Vercellotti & Packer, 2016). Using data based on the spoken output from student monologs (recorded speaking activities described by McCormick & Vercellotti, 2013), Spinner (2011) identifies the emergence of morphemes and syntax and their

Grammatical Development in an IEP 129

relation to assessment. Readers may be interested in considering the stages that Spinner identifies in her paper based on Pienemann's processability theory (Pienemann, 2012). Section 5.3 reviews published work from subsets of the spoken data from the corpus. The spoken data derives from recorded speaking activities (McCormick & Vercellotti, 2013). Later in the chapter, based on data from the IEP students' written work, a more speculative exploration of grammatical lexical frequency of some key functional words is considered as an indication of increasing grammatical complexity.

5.2 Background: Grammatical 'Functors' in English, Developmental Orders, and First Language Influence

Well-trained ESL instructors know that English has only eight bound inflectional morphemes. For nouns, there is plural -s as in *a dog – two dog-s* and possessive -s, as in *John – John's book*. For verbs, we still have one last subject-verb agreement morpheme for third-person singular present tense 'Mary works every evening' (c.f. 'Mary and Jane work every evening'), past tense ('Mary worked hard last year'), and progressive aspect ('Mary is working hard in the factory right now'). A summary of English inflectional markers is provided in Table 5.1. Recall that some morphemes have allomorphs that agree in voicing with the final consonant of the root to which they attach or require an epenthetic vowel: hence, the pronunciation of plural -s in *dog-s cat-s*, and *horse-s* and past -ed in *dragg-ed*, *walk-ed*, and *sorted* is pronounced differently.

In addition to these bound morphemes, English has other closed class 'functional' free morphemes that do not have to be affixed to another word. These morphemes include modal and semi-modal verbs (e.g., *can-could, may-might, shall-should, will-would, must, ought [to]*), determiners (e.g., *the, a, this-that*, quantifiers such as *many, few*), complementizers (e.g., *whether, if, that*), and coordinators (e.g., *but, and, or*). The development of (accurate) production of such morphemes is taken as a measure of development in proficiency. Taken together, the bound inflectional morphemes in Table 5.1 and free closed class morphemes are often referred to as 'functors'.

Table 5.1 English Inflectional Morphemes

Noun	Verb	Adjective
-s: plural	-s: present singular third	-er: comparative
-s: possessive	-ed: past	-est: superlative
	-ed/-en: past participle	
	-ing progressive	

5.3 Acquisition Orders in Functors and L1 Influence Revisited

Informed by developmental orders in L1 English (Brown, 1973), Krashen and colleagues have claimed that the development of English inflectional morphology (including some free functional morphemes) followed a 'natural order' in both first and second language acquisition (Bailey, Madden, & Krashen, 1974; but see Gregg [1984] and McLaughlin [1987] for counter-arguments to this 'theory'). The proposed order is illustrated in Figure 5.1, with the developmental order from beginning (on the left) to the last 'stage' (on the right):

A related claim was that there was little first language influence in this developmental order. Luk and Shirai (2009) and Murakami and Alexopoulou (2016), however, have shown that L1 influence can be an important factor. With this background in mind, Schepps (2014) investigated whether such L1 influence could be found in the IEP spoken data in response to a finding from similar IEP RSA data in Vercellotti's (2012) dissertation on complexity, accuracy, and fluency (CAF). She found that L1 was not a major factor in *global* accuracy in our IEP spoken data. (See Chapter 6 for more on CAF). Schepps (2014; Schepps & Juffs, 2015) examined recordings of speaking activities from the database that were from 15 L1 Gulf Arabic speakers and 15 L1 Mandarin Chinese learners of English who had enrolled for at least two consecutive semesters during the data collection period. All learners had placed into the low-intermediate level (Level 3) and continued through at least high-intermediate (Level 4). There were no statistically significant differences between their initial proficiency at placement (MTELP, listening or writing assessments). For example, on the MTELP, Arabic speakers scored 42.07 and Chinese speakers scored 46.53 ($t = -1.29$, $p = .20$).

Each student had contributed six unscripted monologues over eight months as they progressed from a low-intermediate to a high-intermediate level of proficiency. Each monologue was recorded digitally and transcribed using PRAAT. Measures that were tracked included complexity (subordination; clauses/AS unit [Foster, Tonkyn, & Wigglesworth, 2000]), accuracy (mean error-free clauses), and Fluency (words per minute; filled/unfilled pauses) over time. Schepps (2014) found no overall between-group effect for L1 ($F(1,27) = 2.56$, $p = .121$). However, a significant interaction over time emerged ($F(1.946, 52.537) = 3.63$, $p = .034$),

Figure 5.1 Putative Universal Development Order of English Functors

Grammatical Development in an IEP 131

showing that the Arabic-speaking learners had both higher fluency scores and slightly higher accuracy scores. These findings are discussed further in Chapter 6.

Analysis of six grammatical functors (plural, articles, third-person singular present, regular/irregular past) revealed robust L1 effects, contrary to Krashen's predictions but consistent with Luk and Shirai (2009). Implicational scaling (Rickford, 2002) and Analysis of Variance (ANOVA) showed that Arabic-speaking learners were more accurate than the Chinese-speaking learners and that they followed separate developmental paths. For example, the Arabic-speaking learners were more accurate on nominal functors, third singular, and regular past, whereas Chinese learners were more accurate on irregular past.

These results are illustrated in the following rankings, providing an overview of the developmental patterns with higher accuracy to the left and then descending in order of accurate production. Not surprisingly, and consistent with all previous research, third singular -s is always the least accurate:

- *For all learners:*

- Level 3: *the* > plural -s > *a/an* > reg. past -*ed* > irreg. past > third sing. -s
- Level 4: *the* > plural -s > irreg. past > *a/an* > reg. past -*ed* > third sing. -s

If there were a natural order, we should see the same ranking at Levels 3 and 4. Separating out each group, we see that the Arabic-speaking learners followed a different trajectory than that of the Chinese learners.

- *Arabic*

- Level 3: plural -s > *the* > *a/an* > reg. past -*ed* > irreg. past > third sing. -s
- Level 4: plural -s > *the* > *a/an* > irreg. past > reg. past -*ed* > third sing. -s

- *Chinese*

- Level 3: *a/an* > *the* > irreg. past > plural -s > reg. past -*ed* > third sing. -s
- Level 4: *the* > irreg. past > *a/an* > reg. past -*ed* > plural -s > third sing. -s

Now, looking at L1 groups in greater detail, L1 effects in nominal functors are illustrated in the box plots in Figure 5.2.

Figure 5.2 shows that the Arabic-speaking learners at Level 3 produce definite articles and plurals more accurately than the Chinese learners, but by Level 4, these differences have declined.

Figure 5.3 shows the accuracy improvement for verbal functors. Note that the L1 differences are less pronounced. For the irregular past at Level 3, the Arabic mean was 46.65%, whereas the Chinese mean was

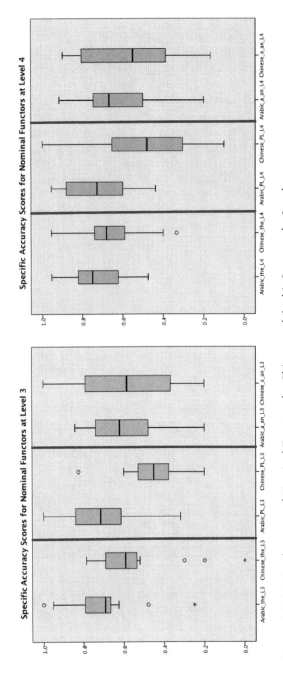

Figure 5.2 L1 Development of Nominal Functors by Chinese and Arabic Learners by Level

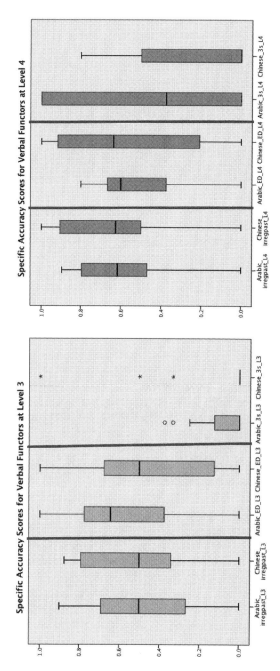

Figure 5.3 Accuracy on Verbal Functors, Chinese and Arabic Learners by Level

134 *Grammatical Development in an IEP*

51.44%. By Level 4, both were 60.7%. Chinese may be slightly better at Level 3 because the memorization of specific irregular past forms may have had an effect earlier. The overall improvement is due to exposure in an ESL environment, in which irregular past forms are more frequent than regular.

For the regular past *-ed*, Arabic speakers are 28% more accurate at Level 3. Arabic requires tense marking, but Chinese does not have bound tense morphology. But by Level 4, the Chinese are 8.85% more accurate but with less growth in accuracy than for the irregular past. The last morpheme to 'emerge' is the third-person *-s* because of redundancy (Goldschneider & DeKeyser, 2001) – the third-person *-s* is simply not needed for accurate comprehension, and in some varieties of English, this form has disappeared completely. Indeed, it is the last subject-verb agreement morpheme English has left.

Instruction effects in irregular past (either from corrective feedback or input from texts and listening exercises) for all learners, and especially regular past tense for Chinese learners, are also noteworthy. Over time, Chinese learners improved more in their accurate use of *regular* past. The L1 effects are clearest at the lower levels of proficiency, which is expected before learners converge more on the target language forms, getting further away from crosslinguistic influence.

However, there were also important individual differences, as all of the data exhibited inter- and intra-individual variation, with learners varying in how much attention they paid to form (form orientation) and risk-taking and restructuring (complexity) vs. control (accuracy) on an individual basis. This finding echoes a point made by Larsen-Freeman (2006), who noted individual paths among a small group of Chinese-speaking learners of English. In other words, although we are able to see L1 group trends, individuals within those groups may deviate from L1 tendencies.

The conclusion from these data is that the grain size of analysis might explain some previous contradictory results from similar data with regard to L1 influence. In other words, looking at global accuracy in a clause, as Vercellotti (2017) did, may lead one to think there is little L1 influence, whereas looking at specific language phenomena allows a teacher to see the influence of L1. This result suggests that researchers should consider and state clearly the level of analysis when describing developmental paths and errors with track-specific linguistic phenomena. For teachers, the implication is that for corrective feedback, an awareness of the L1 of the learner and the likely challenges they face may help in prioritizing which developmental errors to focus on in class and in written feedback. To many IEP teachers, this is not new information, of course. But the influence of Krashen's work on teaching, based on the lack of L1 effects and a so-called 'natural order', is shown to be incorrect in these data.

Grammatical Development in an IEP 135

For teachers who have followed Krashen's influence, these data may help them reconsider their views.

In addition, Bardovi-Harlig has carried out a series of longitudinal analyses of student writing and their use of tense and aspect (e.g., Bardovi-Harlig, 1992, 1994, 1997, 2000, 2004) that are relevant to IEP administrators and teachers. Bardovi-Harlig points to a range of factors that determine accuracy of tense-aspect morphological production that goes well beyond the word level to discourse and which other indicators of time are present in the clause. Unfortunately, space does not permit a detailed review of Bardovi-Harlig's work here, but it is directly relevant to development in IEP learner language.

5.4 Development of Clause Structure in Recorded Speaking Activities

Although morphological development is important, the acquisition of more complex clause structure is also crucial for students aiming to study academic subjects in English-medium schools or to work in English-speaking environments. For this reason, Vercellotti and Packer (2016) investigated types of clauses that emerged over the course of three semesters of spoken data in the IEP. They looked at various clause types that can be produced by learners (note that these are real learner data, uncorrected):

1. Main clauses: 'all around the world *they cut plants*'
2. Co-ordinate main clauses: 'a lot of people like him and listen to his singer'
3. Adverbial clauses: 'if you go there, you have a lot of fun'
4. Relative clauses: 'The aspect I liked is the winters'
5. Embedded clauses with a finite verb (Clauses with a Tensed Phrase [CTP]): 'I think I'm fine'
6. Embedded clauses: 'I always liked to play with her'

The CTP clause-type in 5 is traditionally analyzed as a complex clause, with the verb such as *think* being the 'top' or matrix clause that contains the embedded clause 'I'm fine'. However, some functional linguists have claimed that chunks such as *I think* frequently convey secondary information of the speaker's stance toward the main clause (Kaltenböck, 2013) and often function as a prefabricated formula in expert speaker and learner speech (Diessel, 2004), much like single words such as *obviously* or *maybe*; hence, in the sentence *I think I am fine*, *I think* acts functionally as a chunk like *maybe*. Further, CTP clauses can serve interactional functions, such as fluency 'fillers', such as *I think . . . I think . . . .* This view flips 'the traditional notion of "dependent clause"

136 *Grammatical Development in an IEP*

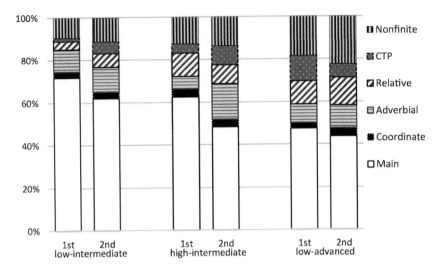

Figure 5.4 Emergence of Clause Types by Proficiency Level

Source: Reprinted from Vercellotti, M. L., & Packer, J. (2016). Shifting structural complexity: The production of clause types in speeches given by English for academic purposes students. *Journal of English for Academic Purposes*, 22, 179–190. doi:dx.doi.org/10.1016/j.jeap.2016.04.004 with permission from Elsevier

upside down, by showing that it is the matrix clause that is actually conceptually dependent' (Verhagen, 2001, p. 349). Accordingly, many CTP clauses can be considered syntactic adjuncts (not grammatically necessary) whereas the other, message-carrying, principal 'embedded' clause is required.

Without going into the theoretical differences between functional and formal approaches in more depth, the study found that the stages in complexity of clauses that were produced over time favor a formal account rather than a functional account. As illustrated in Figure 5.5, simple clauses clearly form the majority of clause types, followed by non-finite and adverbial clauses. Co-ordinate sentences, while being structurally simpler in some ways, are much less frequent.

In principle, because adverbials (in horizontal stripes in Figure 5.5) are considered more complex than embedded clauses from a functional point of view, the functional analysis predicted that CTP clauses would emerge first. However, the low number of CTP clauses did not support a functional claim that they are learned early and as a chunk. For teachers, this indicates that main clauses that contain embedded clauses could be a true indication of development of grammatical complexity.

5.5 Word Frequency Ranking Changes Reflect Morpho-Syntactic Development in English as a Second Language Writing

In the previous sections, we concentrated on free production in speaking activities. In this section, we focus on the written data from IEP students' essays. This part of the chapter is rather exploratory, consisting of a 'think-piece' regarding the usefulness of frequency in tracking morpho-syntactic development. In that sense, this is a 'new' approach and designed to prompt teachers (and perhaps researchers) to think about how lexical development might reflect the development of complexity. It is longer and more detailed than the other sections because of this novelty, and these details may be more relevant to researchers than classroom teachers, so the details could be skipped over if desired.

The analysis is based on the frequency of selected lexical items at different levels in the Pitt English Language Institute Corpus data. The main hypothesis is that tracking the use of some specific lexical items based on linguistic theory (functional categories and verbs with specific complement requirements) will make it possible to infer increases in morpho-syntactic complexity as proficiency increases in different levels. Texts from writing classes from Arabic, Chinese, Japanese, Korean, and Spanish learners in Levels 3, 4, and 5 were chosen and examined using data science tools (Python). Results suggest that tracking lexical development informed by formal theory is a useful way of approaching corpus analysis.

In second language acquisition, one advantage of formal theories is that they provide a set of clearly defined categories and 'rules' that make specific predictions about the structure and difficulty of various morpho-syntactic phenomena (see White [2012] for a recent review). This formal approach has led to the discovery of important patterns of development in second language learning in experimental studies, some of which may be relevant to instruction, for example, early work on question formation (White, Spada, Lightbown, & Ranta, 1991), recent papers in Whong, Gil, and Marsden (2013) on topics as varied as clitic pronouns in L2 Spanish and verb argument structure in L2 Japanese, and papers in a special volume of *Language Teaching Research* edited by H. Marsden and Slabakova (2019). Such approaches focus as much on internal contributions from the learner as the input the learners receive, although input remains extremely important. Formal linguistics has also been used in corpus studies but in a fairly limited way with and usually with case studies (Spinner & Juffs, 2008; Schwartz & Sprouse, 1996; White, 1987) or hand-coded sets of essays (Zobl, 1989).

As noted in the introduction to this chapter, other approaches to SLA focus much more on frequency in the input, affording learner-internal grammatical resources little or even no importance. According to Ellis

138 *Grammatical Development in an IEP*

(2002, 2016), the introduction in Robinson and Ellis (2008), and many other publications, input frequency and perception of language to and by the learner is the main determinant of acquisition. Ellis (2006, p. 102) states:

> The fact that high-frequency constructions are more readily processed than low-frequency ones is a testament to associative learning from usage. . . . Through experience, a learner's perceptual system becomes tuned to expect constructions according to their probability of occurrence in the input, with words like *one* or *won* occurring more frequently than words like *seventeen* or *synecdoche*.

Given that input frequency determines 'tuning' and therefore the development of the learners' grammar, then the output of the learner's grammar should (obviously) reflect that input. Thus, the prediction is (all things being equal – which of course they never are) that more frequent items are learned first and most accurately. Structures in usage-based theory are 'associated with particular semantic, pragmatic, and discourse functions' (Robinson & Ellis, 2008, p. 4), and *not formal categories*. For this reason, investigating formal properties without semantics at all is not theoretically supported. In fact, the problem of polysemy and individual experience makes the statistical task of creating generalizations a challenging task (Ellis, 2016, p. 44). Although other factors such as saliency, perception, attention, schema, and functional use are important, the usage-based approaches stress frequency above all else.

As was explained in Chapter 4, frequencies are determined on the basis of corpus analysis, usually native speaker corpora. Such corpora are collections of (usually) written texts consisting of millions of words, sometimes hundreds of millions of words. The Corpus of Contemporary American English provides a list of the most frequent 5000 lemmas in English (www.wordfrequency.info/top5000.asp). The British National Corpus also provides frequency bands often used by applied linguists (Cobb, 2016; Ellis, 2016). For example, COCA makes clear that *the* is the most frequent word in the corpus of English; thus, *the* is ranked number 1; *be* is the next most frequent lemma in the corpus and is ranked 2; the noun *detail* is ranked 1000, the verb *sign* ranked 1002, and so on. Given that learners might be expected to be exposed to similar frequencies as native speakers (Ellis, 2016, p. 43; but see Naismith, Han, Juffs, Hill, and Zheng [2018] for a caution on this point), it follows that their grammars should reflect these input frequencies. This claim is central to usage-based approaches to grammatical development. Naturally, a great deal of evidence exists that frequency has a large effect on acquisition, but perhaps frequency and usage-based knowledge are not the only factors.

It is explicit in usage-based frameworks that words and their properties will be acquired together and in similar fashion without regard

Grammatical Development in an IEP   139

to their formal *hierarchical* syntactic properties and that each word is learned based on functional usage in collocations (Ellis, 2016). Essentially, usage-based theories eschew hierarchy and formal categories in favor of statistical collocations for form-meaning links in fairly simple clauses. For example, Goldberg and Casenhiser (2008) discuss datives and resultatives but not attachment and embedding of additional clauses such as *I think that the weather will be fine tomorrow* or *This is the book that I talked to you about last week.*

Associative learning theorists rarely address formal syntactic theories or proposals such as claim that *the* is a determiner and the head of a functional category DP or *whether* is a complementizer and a head of complementizer phrase (CP) (Carnie, 2013). Little discussion is provided as to *why* words might be favored beyond the criteria of frequency, collocation, and 'usage'. It is suggested by associative learning theorists that formal theories have it all wrong and that no purely formal hierarchical syntactic properties are worth considering as part of the acquisition process (O'Grady, 2008; Tomasello, 2005). This section seeks to show that in a balanced approach to the use of theory in low-intermediate to more advanced development in written output, both the frequency *and* formal grammar viewpoints regarding words are useful in the context of adult English as a second language learning in an intensive English program.

The leading idea here is that the frequency of certain key function words and verbs that imply syntactic complexity should increase in frequency as the level of the students' proficiency increases. However, although frequency is important, this effect may be modulated by the complexity of syntax implied by the lexical item *and not just its frequency.* For example, we expect lexical items that can be hosted by a functional category to be markers of complexity: for example, *when* is a conjunction that introduces an adjunct in CP, and *whether* can *only* fill a functional head that introduces a complement clause embedded in a verb phrase.

In addition, many verbs in English permit either a noun phrase (NP) complement or a clause complement. For example, *know* can take either a simple NP or a clause, for example, *John knows the doctor* or *John knows (that) the doctor is reliable.* (Both can be replaced by the pronoun *her* or *that*, leading some pedagogical grammars to label the CP complement a 'noun clause'.)

However, some verbs are more likely to be followed by an NP and others more frequently by a clause, even though they permit both. At this point, frequency evidence from psycholinguistics rather than a corpus can be useful. In sentence processing research, it is assumed that sentences are parsed incrementally by both first and second language readers. When studying processing, it is important to know whether a verb 'prefers' one kind of complement over another in order to balance the type of sentence used in stimuli. In this context, Kennison (1999) carried out a sentence completion task for a range of verbs. She found that her

140 *Grammatical Development in an IEP*

participants were more likely to complete a sentence containing *recommend* using an NP complement (55% NP, 44% CP), whereas sentences with *suggest* were more likely to be completed by her participants with a clausal complement (32% NP, 59% CP). Such refinements, added to frequency ranks, suggest that development may be trackable with reference to these properties.

While usage-based theory also emphasizes verbs (Ellis, 2016, p. 44), and formal theorists would agree (e.g., Juffs, 1996, 2009), formal theory makes *a priori* predictions that can be added to information from frequency counts to track developmental patterns. In this sense, formal theory and psycholinguistic studies that adopt formal theory as a framework provide a set of falsifiable predictions that go beyond frequency predictions, which must rely on 'hundreds of millions of words to approximate usage' (Ellis, 2016, p. 44). In fact, it is hard to know, just based on a simple lemma frequency list, what *predictions* lemma frequency alone makes for acquisition of clause structure. (Collocations are much more important for this kind of analysis in usage-based frameworks, but they explain output in terms of input frequency only and not on formal representation.)

Therefore, the broad research questions in this section are:

1. To what extent do specific lexical items in the COCA frequency ranking reflect frequency rankings of those words in the IEP students' written output?
2. Are frequency ranks of lexical items related to formal morpho-syntactic complexity?
3. Can changes in frequency ranking as proficiency increases be interpreted as measures of morpho-syntactic development?
4. What useful information can researchers give teachers from such research?

The hypothesis is that in order to operationalize the construct 'morpho-syntactic complexity' in the context of lexical frequency ranking,[1] it is possible to select lexical items based on formal theoretical grounds without running statistical models on hundreds of millions of words. One way to justify these choices independently is to seek words that might indicate increasing complexity of T-units. A T-unit is 'an independent clause and any associated dependent clauses, that is, clauses that are attached or embedded with it' (Hunt, 1965), cited in Gass and Selinker (2008, p. 73). For example, *The child shrieked* is a mono-clausal T-unit; in contrast, 'the child that sat in the stroller shrieked whenever the mother took away the toy' is a T-unit consisting of three clauses, including the main clause, one subject relative clause modifying *child*, and an attached adjunct *whenever*. . . . Thus, the words *that* and *whenever* are suggestive of the presence of dependent and embedded clauses, albeit not a complete guarantee of their presence. (Note that the terms 'attached' or 'embedded' presuppose hierarchical structure, where 'attachment' refers to adjuncts and embedding refers to recursive elements in a clause.)[2] The proposal is therefore to investigate the frequency and ranking of the following morphemes:

1. Functional categories:

> Formal theories make a distinction between closed class, grammatical lexical items such as determiners and conjunctions and open class lexical items such as nouns, verbs, and adjectives. For example, determiners [Det] and modal auxiliaries [Inflection/Tense] are inserted in the syntax under functional categories. These categories contrast open class items such as *soccer* [N] and *contribute* [V], which are lexical heads and can freely admit new members. Thus, new technologies have necessitated the creation of numerous new words over the years (e.g., fax, telephone), but new grammatical words are not coined.

One hypothesis that follows from this distinction is that tracking the increasing frequency and consequently the higher frequency *ranking* (compared to other words) of functional categories could be useful. Moreover, tracking specific functional words might also facilitate tracking development of an increasing number of clauses per T-unit, which is also an indication of increasing complexity. For example, *which* and *that* indicate possible dependent relative clauses that modify a noun phrase. In addition, *if* and *whenever* introduce adjuncts; *whether* can only introduce a complement clause; these words also imply larger numbers of clauses per T-unit. (It is important to note that *which* is ambiguous. It can be a relative pronoun, e.g., *The store which closed last week* and also a question word, *Which book did you buy?* The word *that* is ambiguous in four ways: determiner [*that book*], relative pronoun [*the book* that *she wrote*], complementizer [*she said* that *they left*], and pronoun [*she saw* that]).

One interesting question concerns the most frequent word in English, that is, changes in the ranking of *the*. Increasing use that approximates the frequency in L1 texts might indicate increasing mastery of this item but not necessarily of the functional category that hosts it, namely 'Determiner', or 'D'.

2. Lexical categories: Verbs that may take clausal complements

It may also be possible to gauge development through increasing frequency ranking of certain verbs, based on psycholinguistic research (e.g., Kennison, 1999). Remember that some verbs simply require an NP

142 *Grammatical Development in an IEP*

complement and disallow an embedded clause, for example, *John hit the ball* but not **John hit that the ball he was thrown*. Other verbs are known to permit an NP or CP complement; for example, *consider* and *deny*: *The minister considered her resignation* vs. *The minister considered whether she should resign*; *the thief denied the accusation* vs. *the thief denied that he was guilty*. As was already mentioned, these verbs have been the focus of considerable research because they are considered in studies of reading, processing, and sentence ambiguity resolution. (For example, *The woman knows the doctor*. is a complete sentence, and *the doctor* can be attached as the object of *know*; in contrast, in 'the woman knows the doctor departed an hour ago', *the doctor* must be the subject of the verb *departed*. See Juffs and Rodríguez [2014, Chapter 3] for a review of this research.)

Kennison (1999, p. 168) carried out a norming study for these verbs to investigate which verbs expert speakers might prefer with which type of complement. In each case of a verb that could take either an NP or a CP complement, 40 participants were asked to write a reasonable sentence that used the predicate as a main verb in the past tense. The resulting percentages for each verb complement completion were recorded. Not all verbs in the current study were listed in Kennison (1999), so for now their complement frequency was estimated from Google N-gram, which tracks frequency in written texts rather than output by expert speakers in an output completion task.

The preferences for the predicates examined in this study are listed in Table 5.2, along with the basic BNC band list and whether the item was part of the focus words selected by the IEP faculty to focus on.

The data for this project consisted of the output of IEP students from Levels 3–5 in their writing classes that were stored in the Pitt English Language Institute Corpus.[3] Using Python, the minimum text length was arbitrarily set at a minimum of 10 words. This minimum length should have ensured that there was at least a clause-length piece of text. The Pitt ELI Toolkit (PELITK), which contains computational tools to analyze aspects of the corpus, was used to tokenize and lemmatize all words. (Lemmatization involves counting inflected forms of a word as one item and derived forms as separate items. See Chapter 4.) Subsequently, the package [nltk: FreqDist] was used to count the most frequent 3000 lemmas used by each L1 group (Arabic, Chinese, Japanese, Korean, and Spanish) at each level (3,4,5), resulting in 15 lists of most frequent lemmas in rank order from most to least frequent. (Frequencies based on New General Service List frequency bands were not used because it was desirable to have a complete frequency list by L1). Subsequently, the normalized frequency per million was calculated [permil_factor = 1/ (L1_toks_count/1,000,000)] for each word on the 3000 most frequent list based on the total word count of samples at each level for each L1. (The Python code can be made available on request.) This analysis resulted in the distributions described in Table 5.3, by L1 and level.[4]

Grammatical Development in an IEP   143

Table 5.2 Verbs and Approximate Complement Preferences (NP vs. CP) Based on Kennison (1999) or Google N-Gram if Absent (in Alphabetical Order)

Verb	COCA Frequency Rank. The lower the number, the higher the frequency.	NP Complement %	Tensed Clause Complement %	ELI Focus List? BNC-COCA K-Band
admit	1093	14	42	No. 1000
claim (v)	877	33	43	No. 2000
complain (PP 65.4%)	1874	7.7	11.5	No. 2000
conclude	1680	25	63	Yes – 3000
consider	395	93	0	Yes. 1000 ('considerable')
decide (INF, 'to': 81%)	457	2.4	7.1	No. 1000
deny	1413	78	11	Yes BNC 2000
doubt (v)	2988	45	52	No. 1000
Explain	482	82	3.8	No. 1000
Indicate	786	21.6	66.7	Yes. 2000
Know not in K 1999	*47*	*110*	*600*	*No. 1000*
Realize not in K 1999	*621*	*3*	*40*	*No. 1000*
recommend	1699	55	44	No. 2000
Suppose not in K 1999	*2180*	*0.5*	*5.6*	*No. 1000*
suggest	431	32	59	No. 1000.
suspect	2118	30	59	No. 2000
Think not in K 1999	*56*	*0*	*800*	*No. 1000*

Thus, the data are derived from 1166 students, 19,078 texts, and a total word count of 2,499,843. The samples from the Arabic Level 2 students were not included in the text or word count. The data are presented in Tables 5.4 through 5.5. The lexical items are organized from left to right according to their frequency and rank in COCA (www.word-frequency.info).

Table 5.4 shows that the word *the* never starts as the most frequent word for any of the learner groups, not even those languages that have a definite article (Arabic, Spanish). However, as proficiency increases, all language groups, with the exception of the Korean learners, show *the* as the most frequent item by Level 5. Those languages that have definite articles reach this point by Level 4. This finding reminds one of Zobl's (1982) findings for the L1 influence on article development – learners go through similar stages but develop more rapidly if the L1 has a similar category.

As noted before, the word *that* is highly ambiguous as to its category and very frequent – 12th most frequent. It is an interesting case because

Table 5.3 Descriptive Data by L1 and by Level

L1 and Level	Unique Students	Unique Texts > 10 Words	Total Words	Per Million Multiplier
*Arabic 2	14	302	9802	102.02
A3	138	2174	157,764	6.34
A4	218	3111	398,596	2.51
A5	154	2380	365,495	2.74
Chinese 3	51	775	60,208	16.61
C4	105	1625	248,334	4.03
C5	72	1999	284,185	3.52
Japanese 3	14	161	14,824	67.45
J4	39	685	110,208	9.07
J5	27	578	100,061	9.99
Korean 3	65	733	74,819	13.37
K4	120	1995	296,669	3.37
K5	87	1853	259,895	3.85
Spanish 3	13	238	19,852	50.37
S4	29	402	60,321	16.58
S5	20	369	48,612	20.57
Totals	1166	19,078	2,499,843	

* A=Arabic; C=Chinese; J=Japanese, K=Korean; S=Spanish in all tables.

Table 5.4 Frequency Rank of Functional Category Words (FCW) in Top 2000 Most Frequent Words by Language and Level. (COCA Rank in Header). Rank/Frequency per Million. (Lower Rank and Higher Frequency per Million Indicate Increased Use)

L1 and Level	1 the	12c/903r that	40 if	58 which	322 whether	2334 whenever
A2	5/28872	25/5509	25/714	0	0	0
A3	3/46062	16/8741	44/3264	122/1204	0	0
A4	1/48300	12/12203	39/3537	55/2873	1149/75	1609/43
A5	1/55410	11/15122	53/2553	27/4739	439/274	1139/88
C3	3/41406	19/7873	43/3654	207/681	1031/83	0
C4	2/40792	17/9399	28/4534	59/2533	700/161	1497/52
C5	1/52019	11/11693	36/3371	29/3881	489/264	1803/49
J3	5/34876	14/9916	49/3036	150/944	1374/67	915/135
J4	3/39425	16/8756	27/4464	47/3267	397/327	1197/73
J5	1/47881	11/12013	28/4537	32/3788	364/350	1318/80
K3	4/33160	14/9784	33/4317	111/1203	1479/67	1454/67
K4	3/35268	11/12203	27/4716	60/2548	625/185	518/229
K5	2/44553	11/12228	32/3786	31/4009	446/273	535/227
S3	2/54325	11/12291	47/2922	344/353	1064/101	0
S4	1/49552	10/15484	42/2918	65/2072	900/116	0
S5	1/56776	9/19131	40/2942	59/2016	730/165	1874/41

* COCA Ranks: www.wordfrequency.info/top5000.asp

Table 5.5 Frequency Rank of Verbs Permitting CP (V-CP), but Preferring NP or CP (Kennison, 1999) by Language and Level. Rank/Estimated Frequency per Million. (Lower Rank and Higher Frequency per Million Indicate Increased Use)

COCA RANK*	47 know NP<CP	56 think CP only	395 consider NP-93–0	431 suggest CP-32–59	457 decide – to INF	481 explain NP-82–3.8	621 realize NP<CP	786 indicate CP 21–66	877 claim 33–43 ==
A2	356/408	50/3367	0	0	258/714	0	0	0	0
A3	83/1692	47/3125	509/209	1533/44	367/317	1184/70	1007/89	0	1636/38
A4	79/1922	63/2398	298/432	968/98	305/416	743/140	738/143	1425/53	0
A5	84/1606	61/2049	168/799	1129/88	244/514	627/194	733/156	1351/68	859/126
C3	75/1927	36/4169	517/233	0	291/482	1739/33	1038/83	1292/66	1667/33
C4	76/2098	39/3515	364/358	937/109	337/383	861/121	564/209	1158/81	1745/40
C5	68/1904	46/2724	283/450	737/165	288/447	844/137	474/271	885/130	841/137
J3	117/1214	23/5801	1352/67	1130/67	348/405	1675/67	890/135	0	0
J4	86/1815	45/3312	312/417	857/127	228/608	759/145	489/254	1248/73	1912/36
J5	97/1249	39/3068	285/450	1155/90	355/360	385/340	401/330	744/170	894/180
K3	84/1510	36/4090	324/388	0	309/414	798/134	1078/94	1995/40	1502/53
K4	78/1787	47/3300	299/428	741/148	226/597	833/128	463/256	1963/34	0
K5	83/1504	44/3136	241/527	859/135	197/643	555/219	319/377	1336/73	1279/77
S3	89/1713	35/3526	868/101	0	349/353	1803/50	1906/50	0	0
S4	53/2487	33/3415	253/514	1165/83	282/464	237/547	718/166	891/116	0
S5S5	64/1707	43/2551	208/617	504/47	209/617	182/720	347/370	1354/82	692/165

* COCA Ranks: www.wordfrequency.info/top5000.asp

146 *Grammatical Development in an IEP*

it shows little development, ranking in the teens for all learner groups and frequency per millions in the high 1000s. The word *if* is also very frequent and remains stable in frequency in the whole corpus by language and by level, with frequency ranks of between the high 20s and low 50s, close to 40 in COCA. As such, they provide a baseline contrast with the other closed class items.

The word *which* is ambiguous (as already noted), but when used in a relative clause, it is clearly indicative of a complex T-unit. The frequency in COCA of 58 is very high and probably includes question forms, for example, *Which movie did you see?* In spite of this, it is well known that relative clauses are challenging for L2 learners (for a review, see Juffs & Rodríguez, 2014, Chapter 5), and therefore the prediction is that *which* will increase as the proficiency of the learners increases, as it will mark not only questions but also relative clause embedding. It is worth noting that this word is completely absent from Level 2 Arabic. In all the other language groups, the ranking increases from the 100s to the 30s–40s range from Level 3 to Level 4, with similar dramatic increases in words per million. A clear developmental trajectory is visible. These results are illustrated in Figure 5.5.

The lexical item *whether* is unambiguously a functional category head. It introduces an indirect question as in such verbs as *wonder*: *She wondered whether she should enroll in law or business school*; and *consider*: *She considered whether she should train as a lawyer or a doctor.* Therefore, the use of *whether* requires a T-unit of at least two clauses. A breakdown of use of *whether* by L1 and level is provided in Figure 5.6.

Although in COCA *whether* is ranked at 332 in frequency, for all the learners at Level 3, its frequency rank ranks are over 1000: for example, 1479 (Korean, Level 3) to 1031 (Chinese, level 3), and even 0 in Arabic, Level 3, which means that they did not use it at all. However, by the time students are at Level 5, the frequency ranks approach the mid-100s range for all learners. This steep increase in ranking and associated words per million indicates that the learners are using more complex syntax as their proficiency increases and parallels the increase in the use of *which*. Clearly *whether*, which can only be a functional head of CP introducing a dependent clause, increases with proficiency. $\chi^2(4) = 91.49$, p ≤ .0001.

Finally, *whenever* provides an interesting contrast with *if*. Unlike *when*, which can be both a question word and a conjunction, *whenever* is unambiguously a conjunction and implies the presence of two clauses in a T-unit.[5] Both words are conjunctions that introduce an adjunct: *If the weather is good, we can go to the beach/Whenever the weather is good, we go to the beach.* The semantics of *whenever* are narrower than *if*: *whenever* introduces a habitual event (past or present), can be substituted by *when*, and results in a correspondingly lower frequency rank than *if* in COCA (40 for *if* vs. 233 for *whenever*). We see this effect reflected in the L2 data: *whenever* is absent from the most frequent 2000 words for

Figure 5.5 Frequency Rank of Selected Functional Categories by Level

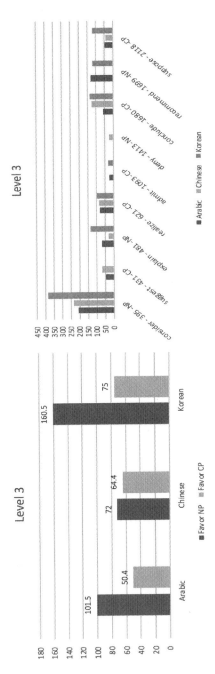

Figure 5.6 Estimated Frequency per Million of 'whether' by L1 and Level

Level 3 Arabic, Chinese, and Spanish learners, and even for the Spanish Level 4 learners. However, it increases by Levels 4 and 5, leveling off in the mid-1000s at those two levels. Thus, frequency is important for *whenever*, but its increase also indicates growth in T-unit complexity in Levels 4 and 5.[6]

In sum, we have seen that the selection of just a few words whose syntactic requirements imply complex clause structure can be used to infer the increasing syntactic complexity of student writing. This conclusion is possible because these words require sentences that contain more than one clause; thus, the rise in their frequency rank and increasing numbers per million words in the output of the learners suggest increasing complexity of T-units, which is a marker of more sophisticated writing.

Turning to the analysis of various predicates that would also indicate greater complexity, the frequency rank and numbers per million are provided in Tables 3.2 and 3.3. As with the functional categories, items are listed from left to right based on their frequency rank in COCA, which is listed in the first row of the table. In the L2 data, the frequency rank and the estimated frequency per million are provided by L1 and by level. We will consider the verbs in pairs, based on their approximate COCA frequency ranks, which are provided in parentheses after each verb (1) to help the reader keep track.

The first pair are *know* (47) and *think* (50) – very close in COCA rank. However, the ranking among the learners is very different: in fact, *know* is consistently lower in rank than *think* for all L1s and all levels. It is reasonable to assume that *think* could be a chunk that learners use for expressing opinions [*I think (that)* . . . .], which is a frequent activity in ESL classes. This assumption is confirmed by data from Juffs' (1998) analysis of Richards, Hull, and Proctor (1991): the raw frequency of *think* in that textbook series is 254 tokens, whereas *know* has 116 tokens. (Raw token counts of all NP/CP verbs in Interchange are provided in Appendix I of this chapter. Only *think, say, want,* and *know* exceed 100 total tokens in the three volumes.) Thus, the frequency of *know* as compared to 'think' in ESL materials is more likely to affect frequency in the written production data than COCA rank. This confirms a frequency account of acquisition, and it makes no real difference that *think* and *know* are respectively more and less likely to require NP or CP.

However, when we consider other NP/CP verbs, we do see some effects. *Consider* (395) and *suggest* (431) are similar in COCA rank (both also BNC-1000). However, in the L2 data, *consider* is much more frequent and higher in rank than *suggest*. This is true for all L1s and all levels, and indeed *suggest* is entirely absent from the Level 3 Chinese, Korean, and Spanish most frequent 2000 words. Given the equal frequency in common textbooks (number of tokens 6 and 7, respectively, in *Interchange* also), it is plausible that the preference for *suggest* to have an embedded CP complement clause (an indication, in fact, of its *semantic complexity*

150 *Grammatical Development in an IEP*

[Grimshaw, 1981]) is the reason it appears less frequently than *consider*, not because it is less frequent. This observation is an important point – the inherent semantic complexity of *suggest* is the reason it is used less frequently, not its frequency in a corpus. Hence, it seems that a predicate that prefers a complex T unit may be disfavored. For this reason, *suggest* appears later and less frequently than *consider* in this corpus overall, *suggest* remaining about equal in Levels 4 and 5 but not as high in rank as in COCA. One possible influence is that *considerable* is a word on the ELI list, and so it is possible classroom input could be influencing production. However, this explanation seems less likely given the use of more verbs on the IEP list, which is discussed directly.

The question is whether this semantics-syntax NP/CP effect can also be seen at lower frequency levels. The next pair, close in frequency in COCA rank, that differs according to their preference for either NP or CP is *conclude* (1680), which has preference for CP, and *recommend* (1699), which has a preference for NP.[7] Table 5.3 shows that although similar in COCA frequency rank, in this ESL corpus, *recommend* is much more frequent. This pattern is similar to *consider* and *suggest*: CP-preferring *conclude* is much less frequent than *recommend* and completely absent from the top 2000 in Japanese Level 3, Arabic Level 4, Chinese Level 4, Korean Levels 4 and 5. In contrast, *recommend* is present for all L1s and all levels. It is also noteworthy that *conclude* is on the ELI list and therefore a focus of instruction, whereas *recommend* is not. From these data, it is clear that, although taught in the ELI and almost as frequent in putative input based on COCA, *conclude* is significantly absent. The key difference between *recommend* and *conclude* is that *conclude* overwhelmingly favors complex syntax. Furthermore, *deny*, which is higher in COCA rank and on the ELI list, is also largely absent from the learners' writing.

It is interesting that, with some exceptions, few L1 differences are apparent in the verb frequency ranking. This finding suggests that it is the input frequency in materials that the learners encounter and the kinds of meanings they want to express that influence learning more than L1. However, few of the verbs are on the IEP target list for AWL. Only *indicate* and *deny* (BNC 2000 level) and *conclude* (BNC 3000 level) are on the list. *Deny* is almost never used by the students, and both *conclude* and *indicate* are used rarely by the learners and much less than *suppose*, which is lower frequency and not on the IEP list. In fact, as Wojcik (2009) noted, not even all those words focused on by the teachers in every class in every week were completely learned. Thus, frequency and saliency are clearly not the only factors that are driving the usage of these verbs.

An analysis by L1s that had large amounts of data (Arabic, Chinese, and Korean) and level for verbs favoring NP and CP reveals interesting trends. These data are illustrated in Figures 5.7–5.9, by L1, by level, and with a breakdown of verbs used in each case.

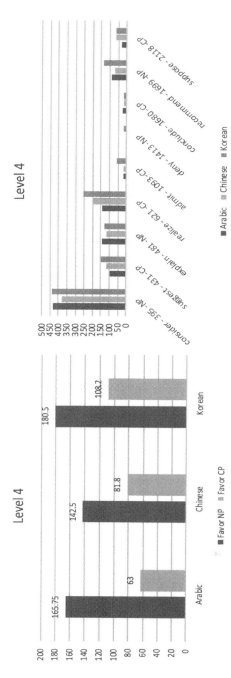

Figure 5.7 Level 3: NP vs. CP Verb Frequency per Million by L1

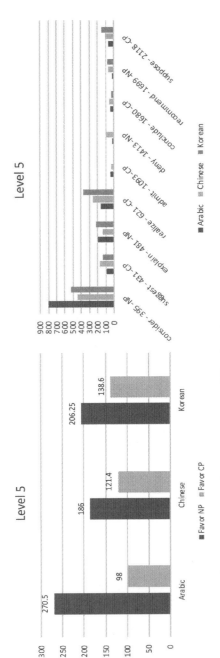

Figure 5.8 Level 4: NP vs. CP Verb Frequency per Million by L1

Grammatical Development in an IEP   153

The data show that frequency is a useful predictor but that the perspective of NP vs. CP verbs is important also. These data are summarized in Figure 5.9.

Although learners favor NP complement verbs, at each level, the numbers per million of CP-favoring verbs also increase, as do the NP complement verbs, with CP verbs doubling from Level 3 (average 64.33 per million) to Level 5 (129.73) per million. However, while increases in verbs favoring NP are reliable [$\chi^2(4) = 27.02$, p ≤ .0001], those favoring CP are not [$\chi^2(4) = 1.016$, p ≤ .91]. Regardless of NP vs. CP preference, it is clear that all these verbs do permit a CP complement and increase in frequency in the students' writing. The next step is to carry out collocational analysis to determine whether all the verbs do, in fact, increase in the number of CP complements as proficiency increases, as we would predict.

In this section, we have explored the idea that frequency, formal categories, and psycholinguistics experiments can be considered together to make *a priori* predictions and thus inferences, perhaps more nuanced than on frequency alone, about the development of morpho-syntactic complexity in writing in an IEP. We considered functional categories and the formal properties of predicates – NP vs. CP – rather than 'constructions' or frequency alone.

Frequency, operationalized by frequency rank in COCA, clearly plays an important role in the development of lexis in the students' writing: function words and verbs of higher frequency rank predictably appear earlier in the students' writing. However, by selecting lexical items that

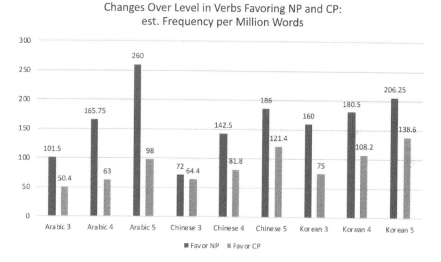

Figure 5.9 Level 5: NP vs. CP Verb Frequency per Million by L1

154 *Grammatical Development in an IEP*

represent key functional categories, such as *which* and *whether*, we were able to infer increasing complexity of T-units across proficiency levels.

In addition, by considering the subcategorization properties and making principled choices with reference to experimental psycholinguistic preference data, we were able to show that inherent semantic and syntactic complexity matters and not just frequency. Thus, not only a verb's COCA corpus frequency, but also the verb's preference for complement type, affects the use of verbs in IEP writing. This finding justifies the fine-grained semantic-syntactic analysis presented in this section. Those verbs that the participants in Kennison's study preferred to write a complement clause for are arguably more semantically complex: *deny, suggest, realize, indicate*, and *conclude*. This is because they all imply a proposition and thus are more likely to require an embedded clause (Grimshaw, 1981). Thus, it could ultimately be semantic complexity rather than input lemma frequency that is driving the acquisition sequence. In other words, for an ESL student to write a sentence with the structure 'noun verb + embedded clause', the student has to have some kind of complex discourse in mind that is to be *denied, suggested, concluded*, and so on. Such complex idea creation naturally occurs with increasing frequency from Level 3 through Level 4 and to Level 5: through the topics the students write about and the ideas they want to express. Thus, it is the type of ideas/concepts that the students want to convey that is the source of the development and not input frequency of the verb itself.

This point is actually made by Bley-Vroman (2002, p. 210) in his response to Ellis (2002). In his article, he points out that in the usage-based approach, 'the statistical structure of a corpus is essentially its own explanation. Words go together because they go together, and speakers of a language know that they go together, so they put them together'. Such statistical explanations seem somewhat circular. In contrast, if we focus on a speaker's intent to create meaning, then learners/writers/speakers choose words because of their desire to convey certain meanings:

> Language itself is thought of as a system of expression of ideas and intentions. The statistics of language use follow from the interaction of this system with the communicative intents of the users in particular contexts. To be sure, language production does have a statistical structure, but it is derivative and with little direct explanatory force.
> (Bley-Vroman, 2002, p. 2010)

One might argue that usage-based approaches would make the same predictions as generative theory based on complement frequency preferences – attested in Kennison (1999) and Google N-gram viewer (https://books.google.com/ngrams). However, Kennison (1999) and formal linguists make a theoretical distinction between NP or CP complements, which are purely *formal* syntactic categories, albeit linked to semantics. It is important to emphasize that formal approaches take the links between semantics and syntax seriously and have well-developed theories of such links (Grimshaw, 1981; Jackendoff, 1990; Juffs, 1996; Pinker, 1989). From this point of view, meaning-making is very important in the formal approach. However, verb argument structures are not 'emergent' categories that derive from connectionist patterns based on hundreds of millions of words. Indeed, one could argue that verbs that 'prefer' complement clauses should cluster more together in a usage-based network as one 'construction', yet they seem not to. However, an approach that assumes individual lexical entries are associated with symbolic options [NP] and [CP] was successful in identifying patterns in the data. It was not necessary to treat them as emergent constructions, linked in competing usage-based networks.

It is worth returning at this point to Yang's (2008)'s review of probabilistic approaches. Like Bley-Vroman (2002), he stressed that care is needed with statistical approaches, noting that probabilistic effects may in fact be the result of interaction with the categorical system of linguistic knowledge. Researchers who hold that formal linguistic categories are important can also accept the inevitability of frequency effects, but they also bring to bear the tools of formal analysis to the task of corpus analysis. In fact, formal linguists have adopted this approach for a long time, just with smaller data sets. Thus, the approach taken by researchers such as Prévost and White (2000), Schwartz and Sprouse (1996), and Zobl (1989) can be used in larger data sets such as PELIC. It is here that the value of data science tools as a methodological advance becomes important: without such tools, formal linguists cannot deploy their theoretical knowledge to large data sets. In this case, data from over 1000 students and 2.9 million words could be manipulated with ease by just one person over a very short time.

This study might also have important pedagogical implications. By the time learners enter an IEP (low intermediate Level 3), one can assume that these learners have all functional categories (FCs), including 'complement clause' functional morphology, and some control of tense and modals. By examining learner's writing, however, we can identify some gaps and lags in different levels of lexical proficiency by examining the frequency of words chosen by the researcher for purely theoretical reasons. Specific intervention to help learners achieve the complexity of syntax that they need to express nuanced opinion and sophisticated ideas could be speeded up by a focus on more lexical items that prefer CP complements. Moreover, extra work on relative clauses and embedding with *whether* could help improve the learners' fluency at earlier stages with complex syntax, setting them up for greater gains later in the program.

In addition, this approach gives teachers an immediate guide as to what to look for and teach regarding certain predicates based on a straightforward identification process for their students' writing. Asking teachers to focus on certain verbs and their derivations can be more readily implemented than, for example, asking teachers to focus on increasing the numbers of clauses per T-unit. The requirement for large corpus studies of hundreds of millions of words puts research such as that proposed by Ellis (2016) outside the reach of most classroom teachers and might end up, to use Cobb's (2016) term, being no more than 'numerology'. Thus, a formal approach allows for a principled focus on certain important verb structures that will rapidly allow students to more clearly express complex ideas in academic and professional English.

To conclude this section, Juffs (1998) argued that formal approaches to syntax-semantics correspondences in conjunction with corpus analysis was a useful way to analyze and perhaps improve learner materials by going beyond frequency in native speaker corpora. Juffs (1998) emphasized that structures that may be *less frequent* might actually be useful triggers for development. We have extended this idea to the analysis of a corpus of student writing. Selecting categories on the basis of formal linguistic properties that are provided by generative grammar as well as some psycholinguistic evidence from experiments, we were able to select from among the most frequent 2000 learner words those lexical items that might best distinguish proficiency levels and thus be indicators of development. The result was that on the basis of limited lexical choices, we were able to show evidence for the development of syntactic complexity across proficiency levels. This finding vindicates the role of formal linguistics combined with corpus analysis and constitutes a challenge for researchers who would dismiss formal linguistics as irrelevant to current concerns in applied linguistics. As such, this chapter is a step in the direction of a program that Juffs (2017, p. 28) called for: 'a characterization of symbolic meaning and frequencies in the input to create a better idea of how we can optimize instruction'.

This section has obvious limitations; we will mention three. First, we focused on only a few key words; thus, the approach needs to be validated by teasing apart the polysemy issues of *which* and *that* and other items. In this, we agree with Ellis (2016) that polysemy is a problem that needs to be addressed. However, more sophisticated data analysis of collocations in future will be able to tease apart such usages, but this analysis is based on formal theoretical predications rather than emergent categories. Thus, this first pass is a very coarse-grained tracking of morpho-syntactic complexity. Second, it would also be desirable to track the clause structure of the predicates used by the learners to research whether they use [NP] and [CP] complements in the same ways as the participants in Kennison (1999) or based on Google N-gram (https://books.google.com/ngrams) frequencies. Third, more sophisticated statistical analysis remains to be done, although the large frequency changes apparent in the descriptive data suggest that the effects are large and reliable.

5.5 Specific Structures and L1 Development: Two Case Studies

PELIC is a rich source of data for investigating the development of specific structures in the IEP. Combining training in TESOL with teaching in the IEP at Pitt allows new teachers to gain both practical and research experience. In this section, we review two studies by former MA students who used PELIC to learn more both about the structures that they chose and track development of those structures in the IEP. In the section on articles, an experimental study conducted in the IEP is also reviewed.

5.5.1 Articles

Learners find the English article system particularly challenging due in part to conditioning from context and pragmatics and in spite of it being the most frequent word in the English language (e.g., Burton-Roberts, 1976; Hawkins, 1978; Huebner, 1983; Master, 1997). A great deal of research has focused on whether corrective feedback on articles in L2 English is useful or not (e.g., Bitchener, 2017; Ellis, Sheen, Murakami, & Takashima, 2008), with some researchers arguing against corrective feedback (Truscott, 2007). As stated earlier, IEP programs are expected to provide such assistance as reasonable given that articles are so frequent and mastery of the system is a key to clear writing. We will consider two studies in our IEP that relate directly to development and instruction of the English article system. Stehle (2009) tracked students' development in article use over several semesters, and Wylie, Koedinger, and Mitamura (2009) carried out an instructional intervention in a CALL cognitive tutor with the IEP students.

Stehle's (2009) work is an MA thesis carried out on the spoken data in the IEP. It is not appropriate to provide all the details of Stehle's work here, but complete data and full details of the theoretical frameworks Stehle used can be accessed free of charge from the University of Pittsburgh electronic thesis web site. Stehle (2009) used Huebner's theory of article use as a theoretical framework for her study. Huebner's 'semantic wheel' divides article usage into four 'quarters' with the concepts of '±Specific Reference' and '±Hearer Knowledge'. Generic NPs, in which all three articles can be used, are [+SR, –HK], for example, *The tiger is a fierce animal, A tiger is a fierce animal,* and *Ø Tigers are fierce animals,* where ø = null articles. In sentences such as *The moon is bright tonight,* (unique reference) is coded as [+SR, +HR], where the NP is specific and the speaker assumes the hearer knows about the NP being refereed to. Referential indefinites, for example, *I am going to see a tiger at the zoo today,* implies that I know that I am going to see a tiger, but that the hearer doesn't know [+SF, –HK]. Finally, non-referentials [–SR, –HK] usually require the indefinite article *a,* for example, *This is a mistake.*

158 *Grammatical Development in an IEP*

Stehle also included the concept of count/non-count in her study, for example, *This is Ø/*a river-water* (non-count); 'The *rivers are wide in the Pittsburgh* (count).

Stehle (2009) intensively studied three Chinese-speaking and three Arabic-speaking learners over a period of three semesters. Chinese does not have articles (but does have equivalents of *this* and *that*), while Arabic only has a definite article. Her data came from the Recorded Speaking Activities described in more detail in Chapter 6. Overall, Stehle's analysis confirmed the advantage seen for definite article use with these three learners (see Section 5.3 for Schepps' [2014] study that confirms this with more students). However, the Chinese learners are a little better at indefinites and use them more accurately (in terms of percentage). Stehle proposes different stages of acquisition for the learners based on L1 influence. For example, although at stage 1, both groups of learners use *the* with specific reference and Ø with [–SR], at stage 2, the Chinese learners begin to master indefinite articles for [–SR], while the Arabic speakers are more accurate with *the* for [+SR, +HK] and are not as accurate with indefinites until later.

Stehle suggests that in teaching, instructional focus on the Chinese speakers' overuse of *the* with proper nouns would be helpful. For learners whose L1 does not have an indefinite article, practice with examples based on specific reference and hearer knowledge could be helpful. As would be expected in a communicative curriculum, instruction with realistic discourse contexts is very important.

In contrast to Stehle's detailed qualitative analysis of the data, Wylie et al. (2009) carried out an experimental intervention with Pitt IEP students using a cognitive tutor. A cognitive tutor is a software package that guides learners through problems and examples in order to teach them the content. Learning scientists at Carnegie Mellon University have been particularly successful in teaching mathematics (e.g., Ritter, Anderson, Koedinger, & Corbett, 2007). In such tutors, hints about the how to solve problems have been a particular focus of research, as well as asking students to 'self-explain' why certain solutions are better.

Wylie et al. (2009) focused on 'self-explanation' of English articles in their study. In research on learning science and mathematics, the authors note that learning gains had been observed for students who were prompted to 'self-explain'. Self-explanation is defined as 'asking students to speak aloud as they study and counting any utterance beyond paraphrasing material as a possible self-explanation' (https://learnlab. org/research/wiki/Self-explanation). In the case of a cognitive tutor with English articles, self-explanation was operationalized as students being asked to justify their answers through a pull-down menu or writing in their own explanation. The full details of the tutor, along with screen shots, are published in the research paper, which is available online free of charge. Sixty-one IEP students took part in the training with the

Grammatical Development in an IEP 159

tutor. Students took part in one of three conditions: pull-down menu 'self-explanation', free writing in self-explanation, and a control condition with no self-explanation. Results showed that all groups benefitted from using the tutor: instruction was effective. However, the results also showed that the time taken for the students to 'self-explain' did not lead to higher learning gains. Article use is abstract, complex, and varies pragmatically (that is, it relies on assumptions about hearer knowledge.) The authors conclude that more practice without explanation could be better for probabilistic types of grammar knowledge:

> It appears that for procedures that are difficult to explain (i.e., those for determining which article to use), receiving more practice opportunities with less reflective instructional practice (i.e., 3 times as many items in the no self-explanation condition) is better than fewer opportunities but more reflection per item.
>
> (Wylie et al., 2009, p. 1305)

5.5.2 Development of Passive in the Intensive English Program

In very general terms, the passive voice in English is used to foreground the undergoer in an event in order to focus on that particular participant in the event rather than the causer or doer. Thus, *The cat scratched the dog* can be put into the passive voice as *The dog was scratched by the cat*. However, not all verbs permit the use of passive voice, and a large body of literature exists on common errors with passive and a subtype of intransitive verb (Oshita, 2001; Zobl, 1989). These errors persist even in very advanced writers and speakers, for example, the following was printed in Soekkha (1997, p. 112) * 'The A-310 AIRBUS air-**accident was happened** during a period of important changes inside of TAROM company the national carrier' Such errors are also now addressed in ESL grammar textbooks for teachers (Lock, 1996, p. 90).

In addition, Spinner (2011, p. 553) indicates that in the speaking data from our IEP, the passive voice was one of the last structures to *emerge* in production, but it was not clear whether sufficient contexts existed for passive to be produced. In other words, Spinner suggests that passive is a structure that learners use only later in their speaking, even if they have been taught the structure.

Due to this late emergence and documented set of errors with passive, Adler (2012) examined a subset of PELIC data to look into any developmental patterns with the passive. Adler chose to focus on Arabic and Korean speakers in her analysis and used both written and spoken data from PELIC. Adler selected six Arabic-speaking students and six Korean-speaking students (three males and three females in each case) for her analysis. (Passive is reviewed in Level 4 [used in

160 *Grammatical Development in an IEP*

simple past and present only] and in Level 5 in more depth [all tenses, modals, stative passives, and 'reporting passives']). Adler's study found relatively few errors with the passive voice – in part because in Level 3, they did not produce passive. This finding is consistent with Spinner (2011). In addition, she found no errors at all with over-passivization of intransitive verbs like *die* or *happen*. In some cases, the use of passive seemed to indicate some 'chunking' such as *is/was located*. Such uses occur a great deal as a lexical chunk and may not even be a 'passive' at all, and, of course, *was born* is technically a passive but does not function as such. Adler confirmed that use of passive increases from Level 3 to Level 5 and even more in Level 5. This result might be expected in writing due to more elaborate topics in writing, but it is striking that the six Arabic learners produced 0 passives in Level 3 speaking, 14 in Level 4, and 30 in Level 5. There was also some individual variation in that in writing one learner produced only 4 passives, whereas another learner produced 50. The main error for all learners was incorrectly omitting the passive auxiliary *be*, using it more with emotional content, and chunking. Both groups of learners exhibited similar learning profiles. Adler's study confirms Spinner's (2011) study in that learners are not *producing* passive at lower levels of proficiency in either speaking or writing. Many of Adler's examples actually come from Level 5 grammar exercises.

Adler notes that Xiao, McEnery, and Qian (2006) compared English and Chinese use of passive. It may be the case that other languages use fewer passive constructions, which in turn affects the use of the structure in the L2. Hinkel (2004) reported that expert users of English used far more passive that the learners in her data and recommends a focus on the form and use of passive and active sentences. This argument has been made for the difference in production of other structures, for example, relative clauses (Kamimoto, Shimura, & Kellerman, 1992). Thus, it may not necessarily be the case that learners are avoiding grammar points due to structural difficulty but rather the form-function uses in L1 and L2 English may vary and these pairings are yet to be acquired.

5.6 Summary

This chapter has addressed learners' abilities with some grammar at the clause and phrase level. Learners' acquisition of key functional morphology and functional free morphemes are influenced by their first language either structurally (articles, past tense) or from different form-function mappings (possibly passive).

The implications for instruction in a heterogeneous student body are that teachers need to be aware not only of specific types of errors that students make but also of omissions in their production. Despite some of the more subtle L1 influences on development, some developmental

Grammatical Development in an IEP   161

orders are not radically different, and they may not follow the order in which instruction occurs. IEP teachers need to be aware of both common developmental stages and L1 influence. Knowing these aspects of development, teachers will be in a stronger position to provide focus on form during communicative activities that can be delivered at the right stage in development. This suggestion is based on hypotheses related to processing and 'teachability' (Pienemann, 2012). This means that instruction/corrective feedback may be most effective when the students have reached close to the right 'stage' in development. Even if grammar is not a separate class in the IEP, focus on form during communicative activities should make references to developmental readiness.

5.7 Topics for Administrators and Teachers to Reflect On

5.7.1 Questions and Issues Mainly for Program Administrators and Curriculum Supervisors

1. How is grammatical development viewed in the intensive English program? Is grammar instruction limited to assisting monitored output, or is grammar instruction seen as an important component of the program?
2. Are specific grammatical structures targeted at specific levels or with specific student learning outcomes?

   a. If levels are associated with grammar points, what is the rationale for making the alignment?

      i. Difficulty? If so, how is this defined? See DeKeyser (2005) for a possible framework for discussion.
      ii. Frequency? If so, where does this information come from?
      iii. Function? Are grammar structures aligned with function? If so, how?
      iv. Developmental orders? Which order has been chosen and why? What is the role of the L1?

3. Choose ONE area of grammar development that learners find particularly challenging. How could you develop an intervention and what level(s) would you choose? DeKeyser (2005) may suggest some areas where an administrator could focus attention.
4. In the section on written output, a suggestion was made to focus on verbs of different frequency levels that seem to require complex complements/noun clauses in expert user English. Could such lexical focus work in your program?
5. Adler's (2012) and Stehle's (2009) works were both MA papers written by teachers in the Pitt IEP based on data that had been collected.

162 *Grammatical Development in an IEP*

As a curriculum supervisor or administrator, what kinds of action research projects on grammar could be promoted to understand how students are developing knowledge of structure/grammar in the IEP? Should the focus only be on structure, or would it be preferable to match forms with certain functions in the IEP?

5.7.2 Questions and Issues for Classroom Teachers

1. What approach to grammar instruction does the IEP take?

    a. Are teachers encouraged to provide corrective feedback on grammar errors?

        i. In speaking?
        ii. In writing?

    b. What kinds of grammar exercises does the IEP encourage teachers to use?
    c. Is there a grammar textbook or a pedagogical grammar available to teachers?

2. Tense and aspect are some of the most challenging aspects of English grammar for L2 learners, even if they know morphemes such as *-ing* and *-ed*. How could a teacher help students understand why you can and cannot say the following:

    a. John is building a house ??in a month.
    b. John built a house ??for a week.
    c. ??Kris is liking ice cream; Kris is enjoying ice cream.

3. Stehle (2009) looked at learner errors with articles. Which L1 group of learners in your IEP might benefit more from

    a. Instruction with definite articles?
    b. Instruction with indefinite articles?

4. Explain why

    a. *be located* and *be born* might not be true passives.
    b. '*an accident was happened' and '*this chair is sitable' are ungrammatical, but 'an accident was reported' and 'this chair is stable' are grammatical.

5. Why do second language researchers focus so much attention on functors? Are these mistakes more important than confusion about word meaning and usage?

6. Download Stehle's (2009) MA paper on articles. How could you develop a similar project with a different set of L1s or a different structure at the IEP? Plan to present a brown bag at your IEP, at a local TESOL affiliate, or TESOL International.

Notes

1. Other measures of syntactic complexity are discussed in Chapter 7, including syntactic analysis proposed by Lu's work, for example, Lu and Ai (2015).
2. Usage-based theories are silent on such differences as far as I am aware. The terms 'adjunct', 'attachment', 'embedding', and 'recursion' are all absent from Robinson and Ellis' (2008) subject index. The O'Grady (2008) paper in that volume does address structure dependence.
3. We would like to thank the teachers and students of the English Language Institute at the University of Pittsburgh and grants from the National Science Foundation via the Pittsburgh Science of Learning Center (http://learnlab. org), funded award number SBE-0836012. (Previously NSF award number SBE-0354420.)
4. Descriptions of levels in PELIC are provided here: https://github.com/ ELI-Data-Mining-Group/Pitt-ELI-Corpus and in Chapter 2.
5. There are a few exceptions, such as the use in exclamation: 'Whenever shall we know the result of Brexit negotiations?!'
6. COCA lists 'if' and 'when' as a conjunction 'c', but 'whenever' as an adverb 'r'. We assume that 'whenever' is also a conjunction given its syntactic distribution.
7. 'Recommend' is BNC 2000 vs. 'conclude' BNC 3000; Interchange counts: 'conclude' (1), 'recommend' (0).

References

Adler, E. (2012). *Investigating L1 Arabic and L1 Korean acquisition of the passive voice in L2 English*. University of Pittsburgh ETD. Retrieved from http://d-scholarship.pitt.edu/id/eprint/11990

Allen, J. P. B., & Corder, S. P. (1973). *The Edinburgh course in applied linguistics. Vol. 1: Readings for applied linguistics*. Oxford: Oxford University Press.

Bailey, N., Madden, C., & Krashen, S. D. (1974). Is there a natural sequence in adult second language learning? *Language Learning, 24*, 235–243.

Bardovi-Harlig, K. (1992). The use of adverbials and natural order in the development of temporal expression. *International Review of Applied Linguistics, 30*, 299–320.

Bardovi-Harlig, K. (1994). Reverse-order reports and the acquisition of tense: Beyond the principle of chronological order. *Language Learning, 44*, 243–282.

Bardovi-Harlig, K. (1997). Another piece of the puzzle: The emergence of the present perfect. *Language Learning, 47*, 375–422.

Bardovi-Harlig, K. (2000). *Tense and aspect in second language acquisition: Form, meaning, and use*. Oxford: Blackwell.

Bardovi-Harlig, K. (2004). The emergence of grammaticalized future expression in longitudinal production data. In M. Overstreet, S. Rott, B. VanPatten, & J. Williams (Eds.), *Form and meaning in second language acquisition* (pp. 115–137). Mahwah, NJ: Lawrence Erlbaum.

Bitchener, J. (2017). Why some L2 learners fail to benefit from written corrective feedback. In H. Nassaji & E. Kartchava (Eds.), *Corrective feedback in second language teaching and learning: Research, theory, applications, implications* (pp. 129–140). New York: Routledge.

Bley-Vroman, R. (2002). Frequency in production, comprehension, and acquisition. *Studies in Second Language Acquisition, 24*, 209–213. doi:10.1017. S027226310200205X

164 *Grammatical Development in an IEP*

Brown, R. (1973). *A first language: The early stages*. Cambridge, MA: Harvard University Press.

Burton-Roberts, N. (1976). On the generic indefinite article. *Language, 52*(2), 427–448. doi:10.2307/412569

Carnie, A. (2013). *Syntax: A generative approach* (3rd ed.). Oxford: Wiley-Blackwell.

Cobb, T. (2016). Numbers or numerology? A response to Nation (2014) and McQuillan (2016). *Reading in a Foreign Language, 28*(2), 299–304.

DeKeyser, R. M. (2005). What makes learning second-language grammar difficult? A review of issues. *Language Learning, 55*(1), 1–25. doi:10.1111/j.0023-8333.2005.00294.x

Diessel, H. (2004). *The acquisition of complex sentences*. Cambridge: Cambridge University Press.

Ellis, N. C. (2002). Frequency effects and language processing: A review with implications for theories of implicit and explicit language acquisition. *Studies in Second Language Acquisition, 24*, 143–188.

Ellis, N. C. (2006). Cognitive perspectives on SLA: The associative cognitive CREED. *AILA Review, 19*, 100–121.

Ellis, N. C. (2016). Cognition, corpora, and computing: Triangulating research in usage-based language learning. *Language Learning, 67*(1), 40–65. doi:10.1111/lang.12215

Ellis, R., Sheen, Y., Murakami, M., & Takashima, H. (2008). The effects of focused and unfocused written corrective feedback in an English as a foreign language context. *System*, 353–371.

Foster, P., Tonkyn, A., & Wigglesworth, G. (2000). Measuring spoken language: A unit for all reasons. *Applied Linguistics, 21*, 354–373.

Gass, S. M., & Selinker, L. (2008). *Second language acquisition: An introductory course*. Hillsdale, NJ: Lawrence Erlbaum.

Gleitman, L. (1993). Interview comments, *The human language series. Part two: Acquiring the human language*. New York: Ways of Knowing Inc.

Goldberg, A., & Casenhiser, D. (2008). Construction learning and second language acquisition. In P. Robinson & N. C. Ellis (Eds.), *Handbook of cognitive linguistics and second language acquisition* (pp. 197–215). New York: Routledge.

Goldschneider, J. M., & DeKeyser, R. M. (2001). Explaining the natural order of L2 morpheme acquisition in English: A meta-analysis of multiple determinants. *Language Learning, 55*, 27–77.

Gregg, K. (1984). Krashen's monitor and Occam's razor. *Applied Linguistics, 5*, 79–100.

Grimshaw, J. (1981). Form, function and the language acquisition device. In C. L. Baker & J. J. McCarthy (Eds.), *The logical problem of language acquisition* (pp. 163–182). Cambridge, MA: MIT Press.

Hawkins, J. A. (1978). *Definiteness and indefiniteness*. London: Croom Helm.

Hinkel, E. (2004). Tense, aspect and the passive voice in L1 and L2 academic texts. *Language Teaching Research, 8*(1), 5–29. doi:10.1191/1362168804lr132oa

Huebner, T. (1983). *A longitudinal analysis of the acquisition of English*. Ann Arbor, MI: Karoma Publishers, Inc.

Hunt, K. W. (1965). *Grammatical structures written at three grade levels*. NCTE Research Report No. 3.

Jackendoff, R. S. (1990). *Semantic structures*. Cambridge, MA: MIT Press.

Juffs, A. (1996). *Learnability and the lexicon: Theories and second language acquisition research*. Amsterdam and Philadelphia, PA: John Benjamins.

Juffs, A. (1998). The acquisition of semantics-syntax correspondences and verb frequencies in ESL materials. *Language Teaching Research*, 2, 93–123.

Juffs, A. (2009). Second language acquisition of the lexicon. In W. Ritchie & T. K. Bhatia (Eds.), *The new handbook of second language acquisition* (pp. 181–205). Leeds: Emerald.

Juffs, A. (2017). Moving generative SLA from knowledge of constraints to production data in educational settings. *Second Language: Journal of the Japanese Second Language Association*, 16, 19–38. doi:10.11431/secondlanguage.16.0_19

Juffs, A., & Rodríguez, G. A. (2014). *Second language sentence processing*. New York: Routledge.

Kaltenböck, G. (2013). The development of comment clauses. In B. Aarts, J. Close, G. Leech, & S. Wallis (Eds.), *The verb phrase in English: Investigating recent language change with corpora* (pp. 286–317). New York, NY: Cambridge University Press.

Kamimoto, T., Shimura, A., & Kellerman, E. (1992). A second language classic reconsidered – the case of Schachter's avoidance. *Second Language Research*, 8(3), 251–277.

Kennison, S. M. (1999). American English usage frequencies for noun phrase and tensed sentence complement-taking verbs. *Journal of Psycholinguistic Research*, 28, 165–177.

Lantolf, J., & Thorne, S. (2006). *Sociocultural theory and the genesis of second language development*. Oxford: Oxford University Press.

Larsen-Freeman, D. (2006). The emergence of complexity, accuracy and fluency in the written and oral production of five Chinese learners of English. *Applied Linguistics*, 27(4), 590–619.

Lock, G. (1996). *Functional English grammar: An introduction for second language teachers*. Cambridge: Cambridge University Press.

Lu, X., & Ai, H. (2015). Syntactic complexity in college-level English writing: Differences among writers with diverse L1 backgrounds. *Journal of Second Language Writing*, 29, 16–27. doi:https://doi.org/10.1016/j.jslw.2015.06.003

Luk, P-S. Z., & Shirai, Y. (2009). Is the acquisition order of grammatical morphemes impervious to L1 knowledge? Evidence from the acquisition of plural -s, articles, and possessive s. *Language Learning*, 59(4), 721–754.

MacWhinney, B. (2008). A unified model. In P. Robinson & N. C. Ellis (Eds.), *Handbook of cognitive linguistics and second language acquisition* (pp. 341–371). New York: Routledge.

Marsden, H., & Slabakova, R. (2019). Grammatical meaning and the second language classroom. *Language Teaching Research*, 23(2), 147–157. doi:10.1177/1362168817752718

Master, P. (1997). The English article system: Acquisition, function, and pedagogy. *System*, 25, 215–232.

McCormick, D. E., & Vercellotti, M. L. (2013). Examining the impact of self-correction notes on grammatical accuracy in speaking. *TESOL Quarterly*, 47(2), 410–420. doi:10.1002/tesq.92

166 *Grammatical Development in an IEP*

McLaughlin, B. (1987). *Theories of second language learning.* London: Edward Arnold.

Murakami, A., & Alexopoulou, T. (2016). L1 influence on the acquisition order of English grammatical morphemes. *Studies in Second Language Acquisition, 38*(3), 365–401. doi: 10.1017/S0272263115000352

Naismith, B., Han, N-R., Juffs, A., Hill, B. L., & Zheng, D. (2018). *Accurate measurement of lexical sophistication with reference to ESL learner data.* Paper presented at the Educational Data Mining 2018, Buffalo, NY.

Norris, M. J. M. (1964). Linguistic science and its classroom reflections. In H. B. Allen (Ed.), *Readings in applied English linguistics* (2nd ed., pp. 346–350). New York: Appleton-Century-Crofts.

Ochsner, R. (1979). A poetics of second language acquisition. *Language Learning, 29*(1), 53–80.

O'Grady, W. (2008). Language without grammar. In P. Robinson & N. C. Ellis (Eds.), *Handbook of cognitive linguistics and second language acquisition* (pp. 139–167). New York: Routledge.

Oshita, H. (2001). The unaccusative trap in second language acquisition. *Studies in Second Language Acquisition, 23,* 279–304.

Pienemann, M. (2012). Processability theory and teachability. *Encyclopedia of Applied Linguistics.* doi:10.1002/9781405198431.wbeal0958

Pinker, S. (1989). *Learnability and cognition: The acquisition of argument structure.* Cambridge, MA: MIT Press.

Prévost, P., & White, L. (2000). Missing surface inflection or impairment in second language acquisition. *Second Language Research, 16,* 103–134.

Richards, J., Hull, J., & Proctor, S. (1991). *Interchange: English for international communication* (3 Vols.). Cambridge: Cambridge University Press.

Rickford, J. (2002). Implicational scales. In J. K. Chambers, P. Trudgill, & N. Schilling-Estes (Eds.), *The handbook of language variation and change* (pp. 142–167). Oxford: Wiley-Blackwell.

Ritter, S., Anderson, J. R., Koedinger, K. R., & Corbett, A. (2007). Cognitive tutor: Applied research in mathematics education. *Psychonomic Bulletin and Review, 14*(2), 249–255.

Robinson, P., & Ellis, N. C. (Eds.). (2008). *Handbook of cognitive linguistics and second language acquisition.* New York: Routledge.

Schepps, H. (2014). *The emergence of complexity, accuracy, and fluency as dynamic systems in the spoken output of Arabic and Chinese learners of English* (MA thesis), ETD University of Pittsburgh, Pittsburgh.

Schepps, H., & Juffs, A. (2015, March 23). *Grain-size of analysis determines L1 effects in CAF research.* Paper presented at the American Association of Applied Linguistics. Toronto, Ontario, Canada.

Schwartz, B. D., & Sprouse, R. (1996). L2 cognitive states and the full transfer/ full access model. *Second Language Research, 12,* 40–72.

Soekkha, H. M. (Ed.). (1997). *Aviation safety: Human factors, system engineering, flight operations, economics, strategies, management.* Utrecht: VSP.

Spinner, P. (2011). Second language assessment and morphosyntactic development. *Studies in Second Language Acquisition, 33,* 529–561.

Spinner, P., & Juffs, A. (2008). L2 grammatical gender in a complex morphological system: The case of German. *International Review of Applied Linguistics, 46,* 315–348.

Stehle, M. (2009). *The interlanguage development of articles in English as a second language: A longitudinal study* (MA thesis), University of Pittsburgh, Pittsburgh. Retrieved from http://d-scholarship.pitt.edu/id/eprint/7368

Tomasello, M. (2005). Beyond formalities. *The Linguistic Review, 22*, 183–197.

Toth, P. D., & Davin, K. (2016). The sociocognitive imperative of L2 pedagogy. *Modern Language Journal, 100*(Suppl 2016), 148–168. doi:10.1111/modl.12306 0026-7902/16/148-168

Truscott, J. (2007). The effect of error correction on learners' ability to write accurately. *Journal of Second Language Writing, 255–272.*

Vercellotti, M. L. (2012). *Complexity, accuracy, and fluency as properties of language performance: The development of multiple subsystems over time and in relation to each other* (PhD dissertation), University of Pittsburgh, Pittsburgh. Retrieved from http://d-scholarship.pitt.edu/12071/1/Vercellotti_CAF_v3.pdf

Vercellotti, M. L. (2017). The development of complexity, accuracy and fluency in second language performance. *Applied Linguistics, 38*(1), 90–111. doi:doi.org/10.1093/applin/amv002

Vercellotti, M. L., & Packer, J. (2016). Shifting structural complexity: The production of clause types in speeches given by English for academic purposes students. *Journal of English for Academic Purposes, 22*, 179–190. doi:dx.doi.org/10.1016/j.jeap.2016.04.004

Verhagen, A. (2001). Subordination and discourse segmentation revisited, or: Why matrix clauses may be more dependent than complements. In T. Sanders, J. Schilperood, & W. Spooreen (Eds.), *Text representation: Linguistics and psychological aspects* (pp. 337–357). Philadelphia, PA: John Benjamins.

White, L. (1987). Children's overgeneralisations of the dative alternation. In K. Nelson (Ed.), *Children's language* (Vol. 6, pp. 261–287). Hillsdale, NJ: Lawrence Erlbaum.

White, L. (2003). *Second language acquisition and universal grammar.* New York: Cambridge University Press.

White, L. (2012). Universal grammar, crosslinguistic variation, and second language acquisition. *Language Teaching, 45*(3), 309–328. doi:10.1017/S026144481200014

White, L., Spada, N., Lightbown, P., & Ranta, L. (1991). Input enhancement and L2 question formation. *Applied Linguistics, 12*, 416–432.

Whong, M., Gil, K-H., & Marsden, H. (Eds.). (2013). *Universal grammar and the second language classroom.* New York: Springer.

Wojcik, R. (2009). *An ethnography and analysis of the learning and teaching of academic word list vocabulary in the ESL classroom* (MA thesis), University of Pittsburgh, Pittsburgh.

Wylie, R., Koedinger, K. R., & Mitamura, T. (2009). Is self-explanation always better? The effects of adding self-explanation prompts to an English grammar tutor. *Proceedings of the 31st Annual Conference of the Cognitive Science Society*, 1300–1305. Retrieved from http://toc.proceedings.com/06199webtoc.pdf

Xiao, R., McEnery, T., & Qian, Y. (2006). Passive constructions in English and Chinese: A corpus-based contrastive study. *Languages in Contrast, 6*, 109–149.

Yang, C. (2008). Review article: The great number crunch. In Review of: R. Bod, J. Hay & S. Jannedy (Eds.), *Probabilistic linguistics*. Cambridge, MA: MIT Press, 2003. *Journal of Linguistics, 44*, 205–228. doi:10.1017/S0022226707004999.

168 *Grammatical Development in an IEP*

Zobl, H. (1982). A direction for contrastive analysis: The comparative study of developmental sequences. *TESOL Quarterly, 16,* 169–183.

Zobl, H. (1989). Canonical typological structures and ergativity in English L2 acquisition. In S. Gass & J. Schachter (Eds.), *Linguistic perspectives on second language acquisition* (pp. 203–221). Cambridge: Cambridge University Press.

Appendix I

Frequency of Verbs Allowing Noun Phrase or Complementizer Phrase Complements in Richards, Hull, and Proctor (1991) (Volumes 1–3) (Juffs, 1998)

Verb	Complement Type	Frequency
acknowledge	NP/CP	1
advise	NP/CP	0
allow	NP/CP	5
claim	NP/CP	5
communicate	NP/CP	1
conclude	NP/CP	1
consider	NP/CP	6
decide	NP/CP	18
deny	NP/CP	1
discover	NP/CP	11
expect	NP/CP	7
explain	NP/CP	15
know	NP/CP	116
mean	NP/CP	29
mention	NP/CP	1
note	NP/CP	2
predict	NP/CP	1
promise	NP/CP	7
pronounce	NP/CP	4
realize	NP/CP	3
report	NP/CP	15
require	NP/CP	8
say	NP/CP	154
suggest	NP/CP	7
suppose	NP/CP	1
think	NP/CP	254
try	NP/CP	61
want	NP/CP	112
warn	NP/CP	4
wish	NP/CP	5
wonder	NP/CP	7

6 Spoken Language

Pronunciation and the Development of Complexity, Accuracy, and Fluency in an Intensive English Program

This chapter will focus on some aspects of spoken language development and the influence of sound systems on spoken output in an IEP. As with previous chapters, the discussion in this chapter cannot be a comprehensive overview of speaking development in an IEP. Rather, the chapter is indicative of some questions and concerns that the Pitt IEP faculty and graduate students, as well as other researchers, have addressed as they seek to understand development and improve instruction. The goal is to provide an overview of some of the findings that have emerged that might stimulate thinking and review for IEP teachers. This chapter only briefly considers some issues in phonetics and phonological development. A complete review of phonetics and phonology for IEP teaching is obviously beyond the scope of this book, but if a review is desired, some suggestions for reading are provided.

The principal focus of the chapter is on the ability of learners to produce spoken output in the IEP viewed through the lens of hypotheses about complexity, accuracy, and fluency development. CAF research has generated a great deal of interest in the second language acquisition literature and so this chapter is an opportunity to show how these concepts have been applied to speaking in an IEP. The data on this topic are derived from recorded speaking activities described in McCormick and Vercellotti (2013). Some of these data are available free of charge at https://slabank.talkbank.org/access/English/Vercellotti.html. Additionally, we will consider research in the IEP that was specifically designed to enhance students' fluency (de Jong & Perfetti, 2011; de Jong & Vercellotti, 2016). Finally, the chapter also considers the role of morphophonology and orthography. While not directly related to speaking, the sound system of the L1 of learners influences writing systems and, as a result, can affect both pronunciation and reading. The IEP faculty, like many before them, have noticed for some learners a disconnect between high spoken/lexical proficiency and their ability to spell accurately. We review research that probes this issue using experimental techniques from psycholinguistics.

6.1 A Brief Review of Topics in Pronunciation: Phonetics and Phonology

An important concern in second language speech articulation is pronunciation, the acoustic properties of speech, and the phonological systems that influence each other in multilingual speakers.[1] The influence of the first or other languages on L2 pronunciation is often very clear even among very advanced, very fluent speakers. One obvious point about 'accent' that is worth repeating is that accent should not (always) be seen as a negative. Clearly, expert speakers of English themselves vary widely in pronunciation across the English-speaking world. Even within one country, the United Kingdom, for example, a large range of varieties exists, not to mention local, 'native' standard varieties of English in South Asia, Southeast Asia, Australia, New Zealand, and of course the Americas from Alaska, Canada, the United States, the Caribbean, and South America. Although eliminating accent completely should *not* be the goal of instruction (Derwing & Munro, 2005), contextually appropriate comprehensibility and intelligibility are very important (Derwing et al., 2014). As Derwing and Munro (2005) pointed out, the SLA literature had not provided a great deal of guidance about pronunciation instruction, which is yet another disconnect between theoretical research and classroom instruction. They stressed that reference to good research 'can help teachers and learners set realistic goals' (p. 384), given that age effects in pronunciation are almost inevitable. The point about realistic goals is important. In the Pitt IEP, instructors are encouraged to provide sensitive, corrective feedback on pronunciation, but the focus on pronunciation is made during communicative activities.

In order to provide effective feedback, teachers need to be aware of the complexity of human language sound patterns. Individual sounds may be more or less difficult depending on the L1 of the learners. One issue is that languages may appear to have similar sounds but differ very slightly in articulation and thus cause problems in sounding 'native-like'. This situation is especially true of sounds that don't involve complete closure of the oral tract: /s/ and /ʃ/ (*sip* vs. *ship*, for example) can be difficult for learners from southern China whose L1 dialect does not make the distinction or Japanese learners for whom the L1 /ʃ/ is a predictable variant of /s/ in many cases. Of course, there are well-known issues with tense and lax vowels – the often taught *ship* /ʃɪp/ vs. *sheep* /ʃip/ distinction. However, importantly, some 'mistakes' may be more crucial than others in affecting comprehensibility. For example, [d] for /ð/ in 'the' might be less problematic than [p] for /b/) in 'bit' (Derwing & Munro, 2005). Thus, teachers need to consider which segments to focus on based on how important for intelligibility sounds are.

In addition, rather than being solely a function of pronunciation of individual segments, lack of intelligibility may also reside in failure to

172 *Spoken Language*

command the supra-segmental constraints on syllable structure (Hancin-Bhatt & Bhatt, 1997; Hansen, 2004; Juffs, 1990; Li & Juffs, 2015; Young-Scholten & Archibald, 2000). For example, it is well known that speakers of L1s that limit the numbers of segments at the ends of syllables tend to delete or epenthesize oral stop segments at the ends of words in English, hence, 'bag' [bQg] becomes 'bage' [bQg´].

Language learners whose first languages are Chinese, Korean, and Japanese are particularly noted for changing syllable-final structure in English when speaking. All of those languages restrict syllable final consonants compared to English. English is unusual in that it allows up to four consonants in the coda, for example, 'sixths' [sIksθs].[2] It is important to realize that native English speakers also reduce the number in fluent speech, but epenthesis tends not to be a strategy that L1 English-speaking children use – they more often delete consonants. Li and Juffs (2015) pointed out, however, that the source of L1 influence may in fact be different and that the patterns of modification vary based on the first language. While teaching in the IEP, Li had noticed that the students from Japan, China, and Korean seemed to be pronouncing words differently even though they were predicted to make the same changes based on a simple comparison of the L1 and L2 English possible syllable structures. Li therefore looked at the RSA data, which were in .wav format, using acoustic analysis and coding using PRAAT (speech analyzing freeware) (www.fon.hum.uva.nl/praat/).

Tables 6.1 and 6.2 summarize our first analysis of the types of changes each language group makes.

Table 6.1 shows the Japanese speakers, while making a similar number of total errors, actually preserved more consonant codas than the Chinese and Korean speakers, who tend to delete more. In addition, Table 6.2

Table 6.1 Results of the Number of Preserved and Deleted Consonant Codas

L1	Preserved	Deletion	Total errors
Japanese	520 (83%)	85 (14%)	626/1104 (57%)
Chinese	373 (54%)	280 (41%)	685/1194 (57%)
Korean	309 (58%)	187 (35%)	534/1144 (47%)

Table 6.2 Results of the Number of Errors From Preserved Consonant Codas

L1	Epenthesis	Aspiration	Devoicing
Japanese	134 (21%)	117 (19%)	269 (43%)
Chinese	154 (22%)	33 (5%)	186 (27%)
Korean	95 (18%)	27 (5%)	187 (35%)

Spoken Language 173

shows that even when they preserve a consonant in syllable final position, Japanese speakers devoice that segment or aspirate that segment more often than the speakers of the other two languages. Note that both aspiration and devoicing are laryngeal features, whereas epenthesis involves adding a whole extra vowel segment.

Li and Juffs (2015) suggested that this pattern could be the result of two factors: first, Japanese is a 'mora' timed language. Briefly, this means that the timing units of Japanese at the level of syllable and mora are different. The following words in 1 exemplify how the mora and syllable are perceived differently by L1 Japanese. The word for Tokyo 'too-kyo' has two syllables, Amazon 'a-ma-zon' has three syllables, and America 'a-me-ri-ka' has four syllables; yet all three words for Japanese speakers have *four* morae (adapted from Kubozono, 2002), with the 'long' vowels in 'Tokyo' and the nasal in Amazon each having the status of a whole mora.

1. a. To-o-kyo-o   b. a-ma-zo-n   c. a-me-ri-ka

Thus, the timing units of Japanese could be influencing their retention of consonants because the Japanese speakers are using a different unit of speech organization in their L2 English. Second, devoicing of vowels in word final position is common in Japanese inflectional morphology – thus a word final devoicing 'strategy' is already available to Japanese speakers, who may utilize this in indirect transfer to make syllable final consonants easier to pronounce. The pedagogical implication of these findings is that instruction on pronunciation should take account of L1 influence, but for all learners, the role of syllable structure and intonation are important in addressing pronunciation challenges at the level of the segment. Thus, interventions that only address segments may be less effective than interventions that address the whole 'melody' of the language.

In this regard, it is important to recognize that intonation patterns in sentences may rely on different acoustic cues across languages: for example, falling pitch is used in English to indicate clause boundaries, while rising pitch is often used to indicate a question in a yes/no question: compare *Mary played tennis and John played chess*, where the pitch on *tennis* and *chess* falls; in contrast, *Did John play chess?* the pitch rises on *chess*. In both cases, *chess* means the same thing. In many tonal languages, pitch movement changes lexical meaning. For instance, in Chinese 'ma4' with falling tone means 'scold', whereas '*ma3*' with falling-rising tone means 'horse'. Tone also plays a role in many African languages and interacts with voicing of segments in complex patterns, including grammatical inflection. All of these phenomena rely on control of vocal fold vibration in the larynx; thus, languages deploy physiological aspects of speech production differently for creating meaning (e.g., lexical differences

174   *Spoken Language*

[Chinese] vs. sentential meaning [questions in English]). This physiological control of the larynx is subconscious, very finely tuned, and therefore difficult to change once it has been deployed as a key component of the sound system.

These are all just specific examples; we mention them in this amount of detail because it is important for language professionals to realize that the sound systems of human languages are complicated and can have interesting effects on the comprehensibility of students' speech. It is very important for curriculum supervisors and teachers to build in appropriate activities to address comprehensibility, but the design of activities or 'on-the-spot' focus on form feedback can only be achieved efficiently if the instructor has enough background knowledge in both basic phonetics (e.g., a sound knowledge of the International Phonetic Alphabet) and the effectiveness of interventions that can improve intelligibility throughout the sound system.

6.2 Complexity, Accuracy, and Fluency in L2 Speaking

This section addresses spoken development among the learners in the Pitt IEP through the lens of how learners improve in their (global) spoken proficiency in an activity which the IEP calls a 'recorded speaking activity'. As part of the Pittsburgh Science of Learning project (www.learn lab.org), the IEP encouraged research on spoken production, including complexity, accuracy, and fluency (see an overview of this research) and the importance of noticing and feedback (Long, 2007; Schmidt, 1990). But before delving into the CAF research, it is useful to briefly review just how complex spoken production is and how instruction in the CAF framework targets different facets of the speech production process.

Speaking is a complex skill for expert users and even more challenging for L2 speakers because it involves the coordination of many sources of knowledge in real time. In any language, speech production involves (a) conceptual planning, (b) selection of vocabulary and syntax to represent those concepts, and then (c) articulatory production that converts a non-linear order into a linear sequence, and (d) monitoring. Stages (b) and (c) can overlap, which contributes fluency in speaking as grammatical-lexical selection is occurring at the same time as articulation (Kormos, 2006, pp. xviii–xix; Levelt, 1989). Unlike writers, who can carefully revise a sentence, speakers have only limited time to check the output that they want to produce. This time pressure often results in speech errors that reveal the underlying production processes (e.g., papers in Fromkin, 1973). For example, spoonerisms, in which a sound in a word 'moves' to another word (either earlier or later) (e.g., *I have a well-boiled icicle* from *I have a well-oiled bicycle*) tell us that speech planning affects even the linear order of single sounds as well as words. MacKay (1973, p. 192) suggests that such speech errors imply that lexical items are put into a 'buffer' and broken down into the phoneme level before motor output (moving

Spoken Language 175

the mouth in real-time pronunciation). These errors explain in part how it is that phonemes (and words themselves) can be re-ordered in sentences during speech production. If speaking one's first language is such a complex process, no wonder second language learners' production can be slow and often lags behind their comprehension. The specific details of the psycholinguistics of (bilingual) speech production have been discussed in depth in Kormos (2006), and readers should be aware of the rich literature on this topic if they wish to pursue more sophisticated pedagogical interventions and understand all the processes that can influence bilingual speech production.

In a way, the CAF approach to L2 spoken proficiency concentrates on stages (b) and (c) of speech production. Although a great deal has been written about CAF, especially in the context of task-based language instruction (TBLT; see Skehan (2018) for a recent overview), the definition of each component and the best way to measure each one is not always agreed on. First, accuracy is fairly obvious as in the absence of errors, but, as we saw in the previous chapter, the grain size of the grammatical structures being analyzed and the counting of 'errors' can be a problem in accurately tracking L1 influence in development of accuracy. Overall, and perhaps surprisingly, it seems that 'error' is a term that is reserved for an error in morpho-syntax and that pronunciation errors are not considered separately. Also, the possibility that an error with phonological structure could influence morpho-syntax is also not often considered. One exception is Goad (2011), who analyses some morphological errors in L2 English as arising from constraints on phonological word formation. Moreover, the distinction between 'error' and 'mistake' is also not dealt with in depth in measuring accuracy (Towell, 2012, p. 52). Thus, even a measure as apparently straightforward as 'accuracy' turns out to be a challenge.

Fluency is operationalized in various ways, for example, as a function of the rate of speech (e.g., amount of speech within a set period); the number of pauses, both filled (*ums* and *ers* in English) and unfilled (when the speaker simply stops and silence ensues); these pauses can occur in the middle of a clause or between speech units; and, finally, the number of false starts and repetitions.

Complexity is perhaps the most challenging construct, as it may be hard to establish how complexity is determined (Bulté & Housen, 2012). The influence of the tasks on the measure of complexity can be important (Robinson, 1995, 2011a, 2011b). However, questions remain on whether complexity can increase naturally as proficiency increases or whether complexity is dependent on tasks that learners are asked to carry out. Despite such concerns, complexity is generally held to be a measure of the learner's interlanguage grammar; that is, the range of *linguistic* structures available to learners in their grammars (e.g., control of tense and aspect; noun clauses, adjective clauses; quantifiers) and how the learner demonstrates this knowledge in real-time spoken performance to

176 *Spoken Language*

achieve certain *functional* goals (e.g., describing, persuading, narrating) (Housen & Kuiken, 2009, p. 464).

6.2.1 *Recorded Speaking Activities in the Pitt Intensive English Program*

The Speaking Curriculum in the IEP during the period of data collection focused on skills that evolve from social discourse/class participation (Level 3) through discussions and presentations in formal settings (Level 5). As part of this curriculum, the student learning objectives call for a focus on key aspects of pronunciation and emphasize both accuracy and fluency. As one part of building these skills, the RSAs were developed in order to provide students with opportunities to improve in accuracy and fluency by (a) recording themselves, (b) transcribing their speech, noting any mistakes that they had made and (c) correcting them, (d) receiving feedback from the teacher, and (e) finally re-recording the speech for fluency practice.

Vercellotti (2017) reports on an analysis of the CAF features in these RSAs. She pointed out that if individual components of CAF compete for cognitive resources during speech production, it is important for teachers to know *when* to devote instructional effort to *which components* to maximize learning growth (see also Skehan, 1998) or to consider their development inseparable.[3] Vercellotti noted that various interactions among the three components of CAF have been found, with the most robust finding being that fluency is reduced when the focus is more on accuracy and complexity: here, the role of task instructions and not just the task itself can be heavily involved. Importantly, in her study, Vercellotti is able to track the same students over time (a longitudinal study) rather than comparing different groups.

Vercellotti (2012) provided much greater detail regarding speaking performance in the IEP. She chose 66 students to track over time during a whole year in the IEP. Vercellotti transcribed the learners' RSA speeches in a software program (PRAAT) that allowed her to carefully measure a range of important features, including time between utterances. She analyzed these transcriptions of the learners' RSAs and measured development using several parameters, the results of which are summarized in Table 6.1.

One point that needs to be clarified is how the RSAs were divided up and what parts of the RSA could 'count' as data and which 'units' counted for calculating errors and pauses. Foster, Tonkyn, and Wigglesworth (2000) is the standard reference for how to divide and calculate the number of 'units' in spoken language. Foster et al. (2000) proposed the 'analysis of speech unit' (AS unit), which consists of an independent clause or subclausal unit, plus any subordinate finite or nonfinite clauses. These could be subject or object clauses, complements, or adverbials.

Spoken Language 177

Hence, the following sentences would all constitute one single AS unit, even though they differ in structure: (a) co-ordinate VPs: *The girl caught the bus and then walked to the store*; (b) adverbials: *Before walking to the store, the girl caught the bus*; and (c) complement clause (relative clause in this case): *The girl who caught the bus walked to the store*. To be counted in the same AS unit, a subordinate clause must be in the same 'tone unit' as one of the clause units in the AS unit; this caveat means that the pause cannot be too long and, under this definition, ultimately depends on the coder's perception of tonic stress assisted by the PRAAT software program. 'Disfluency' features, for example, repetitions, hesitations, false starts, and so on are not usually counted but may be depending on the researcher's interests (Foster et al., 2000, p. 368 and footnote 10). The article also contains guidance on interruptions, parallel speech, and topicalization.

After carefully segmenting the RSAs into AS units, Vercellotti coded the data according to various CAF features. The most straightforward coding was accuracy, determined by the percentage of clauses that contained no errors, and then she also controlled for length of clause. Complexity was calculated using four measures: (a) length of AS unit calculated by the average number of words for each unit and (b) clause length (average number of words per clause); (c) average number of clauses per AS unit (number of clauses divided by AS units); and (d) a measure of lexical diversity, vocD, or D, which was discussed in Chapter 4. The third measure concerned fluency. Three measures of fluency were calculated: (a) phonation time ratio = total talk time/total duration (this measure is the percentage of the time spent speaking compared to the total time taken to create the whole speech [Towell, Hawkins, and Bazergui, 1996, p. 91]), (b) the number of filled and unfilled pauses that lasted longer than 200 milliseconds, and (c) average length of fluent run. (This measure is essentially the length of uninterrupted speech and is thought to reflect efficient planning and execution of speech. In other words, it is the reflection of a 'proceduralized' grammar, which is one that that can be deployed more or less automatically to execute conceptual planning.) Vercellotti (2012, p. 24) concludes that

> Therefore, a combination of these three measures (phonation time ratio, mean length of pause, and mean length of fluent run) can adequately capture differences in fluency in oral performance.

Vercellotti (2012, 2017) used sophisticated statistical analyses that will not be discussed here. Instead, a summary and interpretation of the findings are provided. This chapter's review does not necessarily reflect all the statements made by Vercellotti in her work but does largely follow her interpretation. The results are summarized in Table 6.3. The first column lists and defines the measure. The second column provides a baseline

178 *Spoken Language*

Table 6.3 Basic Statistics: Initial Measure and Subsequent Growth Rates

Measure	Initial baseline mean and SD	Rate of change (slope)	Improvement over the year? Yes/No
Accuracy 1 (Error-free clauses)	.44 (44%) (.10) (10%)	–.11 (–11%) (.01)	No – a decrease of 10% in accuracy.
Accuracy 2 Error-free clauses (Controlled for AS unit length)	.59 (.10)	.03 (.13)	Yes – a modest increase of 2.7% during the data collection period if AS unit length is considered.
Complexity 1 (Length of AS unit in words)	9.97 (1.26)	6.93 (4.67)	Yes.
Complexity 2 (Clause length in words)	5.89 .219	.786 (.96)	Yes.
Complexity 3 (Clauses per AS unit)	1.74 (0.133)	.779 (.57)	Yes.
Complexity 4	53.72 (7.48)	–26.79 (26.79) Acceleration: 53.89 (54.23)	Yes, but not linear – a decrease and then an increase. Varied by group.
Fluency Phonation Time Ratio Speech/Time of recording	.60 (.09)	.21 (.20)	Amount of speech for time available increased.
Number of pauses > 200 ms	.99 (.32)	–.49 (.52)	Pauses decreased in length. Lower pauses, higher lexical variety.
Mean length of fluent run	4.31 (.92)	2.31; acceleration: –3.32 (6.24); (8.32)	Increase but curvilinear.

score from which growth was measured. The rate of change (a proxy for growth) is provided in column three and commentary in the last column. Thus, the baseline for clause length in words averaged 5.89 words per clause and increased over time by just under one word per clause over the period of the data collection. This improvement was significant.

Taken together, the data suggest the following conclusions regarding the development of speaking ability in the IEP. First, although the initial proficiency when the student entered the program was always a significant predictor of ultimate development, no differences existed based on initial proficiency in *the rate of growth* in any of the CAF measures. In other words, all students gained at the same rate, and a higher proficiency on entry did not mean that proportionally greater gains were made. Put another way, higher entry proficiency did not result in more learning during the program. This finding is contrary to what is often called the 'Matthew effect' in which greater gains are achieved by students who have greater prior knowledge (Stanowicz, 1986). If this had been the case, different trajectories (slopes) for more proficient learners (steeper) and less proficient learners (less steep) would have been identified by the statistical models.

Second, overall, the students' separate CAF measures developed in parallel and not antagonistically. That is, as the students improved in their accuracy, they also improved in complexity and fluency, so they were 'connected growers' Vercellotti (2012, p. 29). However, longer clauses did lead to lower accuracy; this finding, of course, makes sense because the more a student speaks, the more opportunities to make mistakes there are. It is important to note that the types of errors were not examined (but see Chapter 5 for analysis of separate grammatical functors), only *how many* there were. As with pronunciation, it is important to remember that some errors may be less important than others in that they do not cause as many problems in intelligibility.

Another interesting point to mention about the data is that although individuals varied from RSA to RSA in their proficiency (for reasons that were not controlled for in the study, for example, motivation, topic knowledge), it did not appear that learners took different, individual developmental paths overall. All learners generally appeared to develop CAF in parallel; thus, it was not the case that some learners, for example, focused on accuracy at the expense of complexity or fluency. Of course, these are group data and individuals may differ in specific assignments, but statistically there were no 'different paths'. This finding is not consistent with a view that learners – even learners with the same L1 – have differing and separate paths in development (Larsen-Freeman, 2006). The finding is important for instruction because it means the design of instruction can, within reason, be more general at the program level. Individual differences are important, however, and instructors will always need to be mindful of the needs that students have to focus on at the level of each student during a variety of task-based activities.

Finally, a comment on lexical variety is warranted. The learners who had greater lexical variety were also more accurate based on the number of errors per clause. This finding is perhaps one of the most important to emerge, in my view. It supports the intuitive idea than an excellent knowledge base in vocabulary is an essential component of proficiency development, albeit not the only one. It would not be unreasonable to speculate that having many choices in vocabulary and having to select from a range of words during the stages from conceptualization to production might impede elements of CAF. Vercellotti's work shows that

180 *Spoken Language*

this is *not* the case. Indeed, a student who has a larger repertoire of word choices and also *uses* them performs better in these tasks. One might speculate that this higher level of vocabulary knowledge facilitates the stage from conceptualization to implementation in the speech production model proposed by Levelt (1989).

In previous chapters, the role of the L1 has been important. The majority of the learners during the time of data collection were Arabic speakers. Many of the students were from the Gulf region (principally Saudi Arabia) but also from Libya prior to the civil war in that country. The analysis showed that, overall, the Arabic speakers scored higher than the speakers of other language groups. Vercellotti's analysis combined those language groups, so whether the Korean, Chinese, and Japanese speakers were different was not explored. However, this result is a quantitative confirmation of a point IEP instructors know: Arabic-speaking learners tend to be more *fluent* than students from countries in east Asia (which, of course, have their internal differences and strengths). For example, in these data, these learners are also more accurate overall than non-Arabic speaking learners.

6.2.2 Do Self-Correction Notes Make a Difference?

In a separate study of students' RSAs, McCormick and Vercellotti (2013) investigated whether the notes that the students made about their own speech made a difference to their accuracy. In previous research, Lynch (2007) had pointed out that drawing attention to learners' output through transcription was a useful activity. In their study, McCormick and Vercellotti (2013) focused on whether the notes assisted the learners in noticing and correcting their mistakes because the specific goal of the transcription part of the RSA activity is to promote noticing and, as a result, improve accuracy.

Twenty-eight students from a variety of L1s were selected. Their RSAs and self-correction notes were chosen for analysis. On average, the students made 5.7 (sd 4.1) notes each, but two students made no notes at all and so the variability was very high. The majority of the notes concerned grammar (57.5%), a smaller number concerned pronunciation (12.5%), and the fewest were lexical (9.4%). The majority of 'other' notes involved meta-talk about self-evaluation or editing.

McCormick and Vercellotti (2013, p. 416) report that 84% of the grammar notes were accurate and that 50% of them were implemented in the re-speech. However, the relationship of grammar notes to the error rate was not significant by word-count in the re-speech, but it was in the number of errors per minute in the re-speech. Students with higher grades in speaking and grammar (separate classes) implemented more self-correction notes. Moreover, the authors counted *new* errors in the re-speeches and did not directly match the specific grammar points noticed

Spoken Language   181

with specific errors that were avoided or corrected in the re-speeches. Thus, while the results concerning the relationship of noticed grammar error to error in the re-speech are inconclusive, they do suggest a beneficial effect for note-taking and self-correction in error rate. Certainly, more research is needed to pinpoint effects of self-correction notes more precisely.

6.2.3 *The Development of Fluency in the Intensive English Program – An Example Intervention Study*

As part of the research on fluency in the Pittsburgh Science of Learning Center (www.learnlab.org/research/wiki/Fluency), several researchers worked to investigate techniques to target this one area of the CAF cluster. The essential insight from this area of research is that higher-level fluency and efficient retrieval must be based on sound knowledge and practice of lower-level skills. In addition, the Pittsburgh Science of Learning Center research seeks to promote learning that is 'robust'. Robust learning is defined as learning that is long-term, transfers to new contexts, and accelerates future learning (https://learnlab.org/research/wiki/Robust_learning). For learning in general, not just language learning, fluency is an important marker of robust learning. De Jong and Perfetti (2011) treat fluency as the transformation of declarative language knowledge (lexis, chunks, and 'rules') of which the learner may be consciously aware into proceduralized knowledge. Proceduralized knowledge is knowledge that has become so familiar that its use may not be at the level of conscious awareness. Deployment of procedural knowledge is faster than declarative knowledge and uses fewer memory resources and thus is the better option as a source of fluent speech. The assumption is that students whose spoken language fluency is challenged often find it difficult to increase their ability to speak – perhaps in part because they are overly reliant on declarative knowledge or at least impeded by it. Fluency training aims to promote declarative knowledge into more quickly accessible procedural knowledge. The robust learning approach, however, seeks to analyze which training types will be longer lasting and transfer to other contexts. Most research shows that interventions will lead to at least short-term gains, but the true goal of instruction is, of course, long-term development.

De Jong and Perfetti (2011, pp. 536–538) noted that specific *training in fluency* in the context of communicative and task-based language teaching has not been the target of as much research as CAF in general. In order to investigate whether IEP students could benefit from fluency training, de Jong and Perfetti (2011) adopted Nation's (1989) 4–3–2 task. In this task, students produce a narrative in 4 minutes and are then required to retell it in 3 minutes and then 2 minutes, in fairly rapid succession. This task creates an opportunity for the students to perform the

182 *Spoken Language*

speech production process several times, effectively speeding up stages 2 (selection of vocabulary and syntax) and 3 (production) of the process described by Levelt (1989).

In order to measure the effect of repetition, which is designed to facilitate the 'conceptualization-grammatical encoding-articulation-monitoring' sequence, the authors compared students who repeated monologues on the same topic with those who gave monologues on different topics. Of course, more fluency was expected with the same topic, but, importantly, the authors predicted that fluency would be higher four weeks later with different topics for those students who repeated the same narrative earlier in the study, even up to four weeks after the intervention. Equally important, the treatment was implemented as part of the RSAs described in Section 6.3. Thus, the research was integrated into the curriculum with cooperation of the teachers in the IEP.

The intervention involved raising students' awareness that fluency is not just 'speaking quickly' and reminded the students about the other elements of CAF. In addition, the students were asked to reflect on their monologues in various areas concerning word choice and number of pauses. The authors also provided feedback to the students regarding these features so that they knew how well they were doing on the various measures.

Overall, the study found an improvement in fluency for the group that repeated the same topic, not only in the repeated monologues, but also on unrelated tasks as long as four weeks later. Importantly, the findings included repeated use of key non–topic-related words in later monologues, which facilitated later RSA speeches. This 'lexical overlap' is precisely what proceduralization is – transferring of knowledge to new contexts to create fluent output. One danger, of course, is that students might become 'stuck' with using certain words and become fluent with only a restricted repertoire.

Given the importance of the lexicon in completing tasks and the concern over task effects (e.g. Robinson, 2011b), in a follow-up study, de Jong and Vercellotti (2016) looked at the role of specific picture prompts and whether the language they elicited was similar in terms of CAF measures. Their concern was that prompts that are often assumed to be equivalent in terms of complexity may actually not be the same. Pictures in a sequence, such as in a cartoon, are often used to stimulate a narrative task. The authors chose five 6-frame picture sets about a bicycle, a race, a tiger, a frog, and a turtle. The order of pictures could not be altered, so none required any causal reasoning (a feature of tasks that is manipulated in some studies), but the motivations of the participants needed to be interpreted and explained (requiring intentional reasoning, another task feature). Each set had only two characters and two locations, so the number of 'elements' was constant. Thus, in principle, the tasks were similar.

Spoken Language 183

Measures now familiar in this research type were collected: fluency, accuracy, complexity, and lexical variety. Table 6.4 summarizes the reliable differences found in the various measures. All other comparisons were not reliably different.

As can be observed from Table 6.4, differences appeared only in pauses (between the 'turtle' and 'tiger' picture stories) and in lexical variety – both in D and other measures that the authors calculated based on frequency of use of individual lexical items in the stories. For example, in the 'race' story, most students used far fewer nouns than in the other stories. Another point was that several students did not know the word 'turtle' for the turtle story and, indeed, narratives from this story received the lowest ratings overall: 'Of the five prompts, 'turtle' seems to stand out with low fluency, vocabulary difficulties, and less speech, all indicating that this prompt created a more difficult task for these participants (p. 399). The authors attribute this lower score to the need to use unknown or less frequent vocabulary in a task, which puts pressure on the learner and causes hesitation and decreasing CAF scores; they contrast this with a feature of the 'frog' story in which the frog is buried for a reason that is not clear but did not lead to difficulties. However, the authors refer to a paper that looked carefully at specific grammatical structures elicited by the stories. They suggest that 'race' elicited more relative clauses (probably as a function of fewer referential NPs – each vague NP *guy*, *man*, *person* has to be identified, e.g., 'the guy who/that . . .') and more embedded clauses, whereas 'frog' elicited more co-ordinate structures, 'the boy and the dog'.

Table 6.4 Reliable Differences Among CAF Measures on Picture Prompt*

Measure	Bicycle	Tiger	Race	Frog	Turtle
Mean pause length (secs) (No other fluency measure showed a difference)	1.13 (0.3)	1.10[a] (0.3)	1.1 (0.3)	1.13 (0.2)	1.26[a] (0.4)
Lexical variety (D)	36.7[a,b] (8.8)	41.3[b] (7.2)	47.5[a,b] (12.1)	31.9[a,b] (6.9)	36.2[a] (7.9)
Complexity (E.g., words per AS unit/clause)	No reliable differences				
Accuracy (E.g., % of error-free AS units or clauses; corrections per 100 words	No reliable differences				

*Reliable differences are co-superscripted

184 *Spoken Language*

These comments bring into perspective the need for finer-grained analyses of language in tasks.

6.2.4 *A Comment on Task-Based Language Instruction and Complexity, Accuracy, and Fluency Research*

At this point, it is useful to consider what aspects of this research mean for teachers and administrators. An important component of language teaching theory and practice to emerge out of the communicative approach has been the role of tasks and the development of task-based language teaching and learning. Although the precise nature and place of TBLT remain the source of considerable debate in language teaching (Long, 2016), tasks have become very important features of language classrooms. Long (2016) pointed out that a true task-based syllabus is constructed around students' needs and follows a learner-centered needs analysis. The idea is that the vocabulary and structure follow from real-world tasks created for the contexts the learners will find themselves in. Through interaction with other students and teachers, forms (lexical and grammatical) emerge that receive attention and corrective feedback as necessary. The reality of most IEPs, however, is that tasks and structures are more likely to be implemented in a parallel approach along lines advocated by scholars such as R. Ellis (1997), where tasks are used to promote language rather than the other way around, with an implicit structural or language-oriented syllabus that is less oriented to the 'pure' task-based syllabus advocated by Long (2016). This approach may be termed 'task-*supported* language teaching' (TSLT), although Long (2016) remains skeptical about any syllabus that is not oriented to tasks because of the developmental imperatives of the learner-internal syllabus. Long (2016) assumes that psycholinguistic developmental stages are not amenable to change by instruction, although this issue remains somewhat controversial. See Bonilla (2015) for Spanish L2 and Zhang and Lantolf (2015) for Chinese L2 instruction for contrasting views.

Bygate (2017) notes that TBLT will have to engage with classrooms and 'stakeholders' in four ways: (a) specifying precisely what is learned from a task, (b) strengthening the task-language links, (c) considering the other activities that are used in tasks, and (d) looking at the impact of a sequence of TBLT programs. Bygate's comments are appropriate for IEPs, as a 'pure' task-based curriculum is probably not a viable approach for a whole IEP. At the Pitt IEP, the curriculum is designed as one that prepares students for academic study in English (EAP), but the IEP also acknowledges that academic study is not the goal of all students. (See Juffs and Friedline [2014] for a survey on goals that students have in the IEP, from academics to everyday life.) Many IEP students come to improve their English for jobs in their home countries, for traveling, and for other non-vocational reasons. Some students are spouses of university

Spoken Language 185

students, professionals, or faculty and only take one or two courses in the IEP to help their fluency with daily life. Thus, the IEP must rely on a coherent curriculum, as described in Chapter 2.

In this context, the research from the IEP discussed in this section suggests that tasks can be designed to promote various components of CAF, not only with real-world communication goals but also with certain *structural* language properties in mind, as suggested by Bley-Vroman and Loschky (1993) and more recently by Robinson (2011b, p. 16), whose comment is worth quoting in full:

> For example, in L2 English, tasks which require complex reasoning about the intentional states that motivate others to perform actions can be expected to draw heavily on the use of cognitive state terms for reference to other minds, – *she suspected, wonders*, and so on – and in doing so orient learner attention to the complement constructions accompanying them – *suspected that, wonders whether* – so promoting awareness of, and effort at, complex L2 syntax.

We can link Robinson's remarks back to the observation from the corpus-based study of verb use in students' writing that was discussed in Chapter 5. It was noted that students use fewer verbs that require or prefer embedded clauses and so tasks that can enhance the production of such clauses, and consequently the use of complex syntax, could be targeted. We have already mentioned that the narrative task 'race' in which the participants must be identified would promote the use of adjective (relative) clauses, so a range of task types can be developed to respond to the structural needs of students whether the syllabus is a purely task-based one or not, based on the identified needs of the learners.

Bygate's (2017) suggestion that TBLT theorists engage more directly with administrators and teachers is actually a real issue but can be accommodated. As Long (2016) himself points out, the contexts of language instruction (including trained teachers and resources available) vary by location and target population: for example, training for service industries, refugees, and prospective university students. Most IEPs (and all UCIEP members), however, do in fact have trained teachers who are more than capable of engaging in action research projects to address leaner-internal syllabus needs and TSLT that can target areas where students need to develop or help students develop more rapidly. The research by our own MA students cited in Chapters 4 and 5 is a testament to this possibility. As Larsen-Freeman and Long (1991, p. 321) pointed out, instruction (a) can assist learners in the *rate of progress* through developmental stages (even if they may be difficult to skip) and (b) prevents learners from plateauing at an early stage of development – in other words, helps them *reach a higher level of attainment*. Teachers who are aware of developmental sequences, facets of CAF, and techniques to elicit and practice

186 *Spoken Language*

those facets should be able to fine-tune tasks carefully to practice *forms* that the students need in their respective communication settings. Finally, Paulston's (1985, pp. 23–24) comments on communicative language teaching bears repeating, as she noted that no matter the method, the role of the teacher in effective classroom management is of paramount importance: 'It is the teacher's job to arrange for both types of activities [learning and acquisition] in the classroom. *Good teachers make very clear what tasks and exercises they set and what the students must do to accomplish these tasks.*' This last sentence is the essence of current approaches to task-based teaching – good organization and the requirement for a product or clear end point.

6.3 The Influence of L1 Phonology and Orthography on L2 Reading and Writing

As part of the RSA transcription analysis and the sentence writing activity in the REAP tutor, it was noticed that the Arabic-speaking learners had great difficulty with spelling even of very frequently used words, for example, 'because' (See Dunlap, 2012, for a full analysis). Of course, it was already well-known that although Arabic speakers might have good fluency (due in part to the high cultural value put on oralcy in the L1 [Zaharna, 1995]), written accuracy does not always reflect this ability. Such inaccuracy in spelling is sometimes attributed to the lower exposure to print text for Arabic-speaking learners (e.g., Al-Mahrooqi & Denman, 2016). However, Martin and Juffs (in review) proposed that it is possible that even with higher exposure to English texts, part of the problem may reside in the learned decoding routines for print based on Arabic script. Arabic script is, in turn, based on the morpho-phonology of the Arabic language itself.

The morpho-phonology of Semitic languages (which include Amharic, Arabic, Hebrew, and Tigrinya) consists of consonantal roots – for example, in Arabic, 'k-t-b' means something related to writing and books. The vowel infixes indicate grammatical relations for person, number, gender, and tense: for example, *katabtu*, 'I wrote'; *aktub*, 'I write'; inflected noun forms, e.g., *kutub*, 'books'; or other derived nominals, for example, *maktab*, 'desk' or 'office'. Most Semitic languages are written with an abjad, which is a writing system that marks consonants but may only mark some vowels or use diacritics to indicate vowels. The phonetic values of the vowels are inferred from the discourse and syntactic context. Thus, when reading Arabic, L1 Arabic speakers will be conditioned to pay less attention to the vowels and focus more on the consonantal roots. Such conditioning in the decoding of Arabic script leads to a higher reliance on syntactic context rather than grapheme-to-phoneme mappings in word recognition and retrieval. Therefore, when learning to read English, which does contain vowels, Arabic-speaking learners transfer this L1 word recognition strategy to their L2 English and focus relatively more on the English consonants than other L1 groups. The result is that their lexical representations for English words may be compromised and lead not only to problems with spelling, but also to problems with reading. One anecdotal example of this effect that I noticed was when I heard a student struggling to sound out the verb 'deepened': the student could not seem to overcome the vowel cues and insisted that the word was 'depended'.

This tendency of Arabic speakers to rely less on segmental decoding and comparatively more on syntactic context has been shown experimentally with IEP students at Pitt. Fender (2003) showed that Arabic-speaking learners were better than Japanese-speaking learners at syntactic integration, but less fast and less accurate with individual word recognition. In addition, recent experiments with eye-tracking confirm that it is indeed the vowels that the Arabic-speaking learners are skipping. Martin (2011) and Martin and Juffs (in review) compared the reading behavior of native English-speaking, Arabic-speaking, and Chinese-speaking participants of sentences that included words which contained different kinds of vowel phoneme-grapheme correspondences. For example, the orthographic sequence 'ea' in English is ambiguous, as in [e] in *great*, [i] in *seat*, and [ɛ] in *wear*, whereas 'ee' is unambiguously always [i]: *glee, seed, feel*. They found that native speakers of English look at words with ambiguous vowel grapheme-phoneme correspondences longer than words in which the vowel is not ambiguous. Arabic speakers, however, showed no such effect, whereas the Chinese speakers, whose L1 has a logographic writing system in which vowels are not represented, did show some sensitivity. Martin (2015) further explored the impact of L1 orthography on L2 reading.

These findings suggest that it is not entirely an issue of culture and reading habits that leads to challenges for Arabic speakers but a psycholinguistic 'learned inattention' to vowels below the level of consciousness that is part of an explanation.

The implications for instruction are that in addition to more extensive reading (which will also help in vocabulary development), focused practice in bottom-up phoneme-grapheme decoding for Arabic speakers, and on vowel phoneme-grapheme identification in particular, would be useful in order to re-train the learners' focus on assembled phonology (phonics) as a key to word identification. Activities to promote this will include some reading aloud, dictation practice, and other noticing activities to retrain Arabic speakers' attention during grapheme decoding. These activities will assist them in creating better lexical representations.

6.4 Summary

In this chapter, we have considered several issues involving sound systems and spoken language in the context of an IEP. The Pitt IEP adopts an

188 *Spoken Language*

approach/method/technique (Anthony, 1963) view of language learning and teaching that is 'principled eclecticism'. That is, the IEP engages in instructional activities that are supported by a wide range of research findings, practice, and experience.

One aspect that the IEP emphasizes is the provision of corrective feedback on spoken language. For teachers to provide this feedback effectively, an understanding of the phonetics and phonology of human language is very important. In a communicative approach to language teaching, comprehensibility is most important. While individual sounds may be important, teachers should also know how interconnected segments, syllable structure, and intonation are integrated. Second, in TBLT or TSLT, speaking proficiency and fluency can be measured using the metrics of complexity, accuracy, and fluency. Learners seem to develop these features in parallel, so learners can afford to make errors as they try to increase the level of complex syntax and less hesitant delivery. Specific activities such as fluency training – which may not be directly related to a specific 'natural task' – may be important. Moreover, some tasks can be created to focus on particular forms that the learners might need. We have also considered the interlinked nature of morpho-phonology, writing systems, and decoding during reading.

It is important to realize that the psycholinguistics of learners – what they perceive and learn in their first language spoken and literacy practices, the input that they are able to process and produce, and developmental stages – combine to form a complex L2 system as spoken language develops.

6.5 Topics for Administrators and Teachers to Reflect On

6.5.1 *Questions and Issues Mainly for Program Administrators and Curriculum Supervisors*

1. In communicative activities, to what extent does the IEP speaking curriculum encourage teachers to provide appropriate feedback on

   a. Segments?
   b. Syllables?
   c. Intonation?

2. *How* are teachers asked to assist learners in noticing issues in pronunciation?
3. Do curriculum notes address possible trade-offs in complexity, accuracy, and fluency?

   a. Is one aspect valued more highly than others?
   b. How does your program address the need for Fluency? Accuracy? Complexity?

Spoken Language 189

4. How is reading instruction thought of in the IEP program with regard to the first language phonology/orthography of your learners?
5. How are grammar points linked to task types in your curriculum? Are they more 'pure', as in the Long (2016) approach to TBLT, or more aligned with Ellis (1997)?

6.5.2 Questions and Issues Mainly for Classroom Teachers

1. How well do you know the International Phonetic Alphabet?

   a. https://linguistics.ucla.edu/people/keating/IPA/inter_chart_2018/IPA_2018.html

      i. Go to the website and click on some sounds that are unfamiliar to you and some that you know.
      ii. Identify one to five languages in your program that have sounds that are not in English.

   b. How many vowels does the variety of English you speak have? Note that vowels are challenging for everyone and perhaps especially in connected speech.

2. Record and listen to a short segment of speech from the L1s of your students.

   a. Can you *identify* sounds that they have problems with?
   b. Can you *prioritize* any individual sounds that cause special comprehensibility problems?
   c. What impression does supra-segmental sound organization give?

      i. Can you identify issues with syllables?
      ii. Can you identify issues with pitch *movement*?
      iii. Can you identify issues with overall intonation?

   d. Develop some strategies for providing appropriate feedback in these areas to help students notice and improve.

      i. Take care not to create whole lessons but focus on form when it's appropriate during a communicative activity.
      ii. Try to find and read a recent article about L2 pronunciation and instruction by using Google Scholar.

3. Think about the writing systems that are used by the L1s in your program.

   a. How do the writing systems reflect the sound systems in the language?
   b. If they represent the phoneme-grapheme level (as English does), to what extent are they consistent?

190 *Spoken Language*

c. Compare Japanese, Chinese, and Korean writing systems by checking Wikipedia. Can you predict any differences in spelling ability based on these writing systems?

Notes

1. For very useful and up-to-date references on this topic, see Murray Munro's website: www.sfu.ca/~mjmunro/research.html.
2. Fun fact: a language of the Caucasus, Abkhaz, has 58 consonant phonemes and only 2 vowel phonemes (https://en.wikipedia.org/wiki/Abkhaz_phonology). Languages of this region in the former USSR, which include Georgian, have quite complex consonant clusters. (Most dialects of English have 24 consonant phonemes, and US English has 15–16 vowel phonemes.)
3. Robinson's (2011b) overview article also suggests that in task-based language teaching, the cognitive demands of different tasks may affect language development, may be able to target specific linguistic structures, and should be considered when designing and sequencing TBLT syllabi. A huge literature on TBLT exists (see the Benjamins' series on this topic: https://benjamins.com/catalog/tblt), and we cannot review it all here.

References

Al-Mahrooqi, R., & Denman, C. (2016). Establishing a reading culture in Arabic and English in Oman. *Arab World English Journal, 7*(1); 5–17. Retrieved from https://papers.ssrn.com/sol3/papers.cfm?abstract_id=2803981

Anthony, E. M. (1963). Approach, method and technique. *English Language Teaching Journal, 17*(2), 63–67.

Bley-Vroman, R., & Loschky, L. (1993). Grammar and task-based methodology. In S. Gass & G. Crookes (Eds.), *Tasks and language learning: Integrating theory and practice* (pp. 123–167). Clevedon: Multilingual Matters.

Bonilla, C. (2015). From number agreement to the subjunctive: Evidence for processability theory in L2 Spanish. *Second Language Research, 31*(1), 53–74. doi:10.1177/0267658314537291

Bulté, B., & Housen, A. (2012). Defining and operationalizing L2 complexity. In A. Housen, F. Kuiken, & I. Vedder (Eds.), *Dimensions of L2 performance and proficiency: Complexity, accuracy, and fluency in L2 research* (pp. 21–46). Philadelphia: John Benjamins.

Bygate, M., Gass, S. M., Mackey, A., Oliver, R., & Robinson, P. (2017). Theory, empiricism and practice: Commentary on TBLT in ARAL 2016. *Annual Review of Applied Linguistics*, 1–9. doi:10.1017/S0267190517000010

de Jong, N., & Perfetti, C. (2011). Fluency training in the ESL classroom: An experimental study of fluency development and proceduralization. *Language Learning, 61*(2), 533–568. doi:10.1111/j.1467-9922.2010.00620.x

de Jong, N., & Vercellotti, M. L. (2016). Similar prompts may not be similar in the performance they elicit: Examining fluency, complexity, accuracy, and lexis in narratives from five picture prompts. *Language Teaching Research, 20*(3), 387–404. doi:10.1177/1362168815606161

Derwing, T. M., & Munro, M. J. (2005). Second language accent and pronunciation teaching: A research-based approach. *TESOL Quarterly, 39*(3), 379–397.

Derwing, T. M., Munro, M. J., Foote, J. A., Waugh, E., & Fleming, J. (2014). Opening the window on comprehensible pronunciation after 19 years: A workplace training study. *Language Learning, 64*(3), 526–548. doi:10.1111/lang.12053

Dunlap, S. (2012). *Orthographic quality in English as a second language* (dissertation), ETD University of Pittsburgh, Pittsburgh.

Ellis, R. (1997). SLA and language pedagogy: An educational perspective. *Studies in Second Language Acquisition, 19*(1), 69–92.

Fender, M. (2003). English word recognition and word integration skills of native Arabic and Japanese-speaking learners of English as a second language. *Applied Psycholinguistics, 24*, 289–315.

Foster, P., Tonkyn, A., & Wigglesworth, G. (2000). Measuring spoken language: A unit for all reasons. *Applied Linguistics, 21*, 354–373.

Fromkin, V. A. (Ed.). (1973). *Speech errors as linguistic evidence.* The Hague: Mouton.

Goad, H. (2011). The L2 acquisition of functional morphology: Why syntacticians need phonologists. In J. Herschensohn & D. Tanner (Red.), *Proceedings of the 11th generative approaches to second language acquisition.* Somerville, MA: Cascadilla Press. Retrieved from www. lingref.com/cpp/gasla/11/index.html

Hancin-Bhatt, B., & Bhatt, R. (1997). Optimal L2 syllables: Interaction of transfer and developmental effects. *Studies in Second Language Acquisition, 19*, 331–378.

Hansen, J. G. (2004). Developmental sequences in the acquisition of English L2 syllable codas. *Studies in Second Language Acquisition, 26*, 85–124.

Housen, A., & Kuiken, F. (2009). Complexity, accuracy, and fluency in second language acquisition. *Applied Linguistics, 30*(4), 461–473. doi:10.1093/applin/amp048

Juffs, A. (1990). The role of pitch and syllable structure in Chinese learners' stress errors. *International Review of Applied Linguistics, 28*(2), 99–117. doi:10.1515/iral.1990.28.2.99

Juffs, A., & Friedline, B. E. (2014). Sociocultural influences on the use of a web-based tool for learning English vocabulary. *System, 42*, 48–59. doi:10.1016/j.system.2013.10.015

Kormos, J. (2006). *Speech production and second language acquisition.* Mahwah, NJ: Lawrence Erlbaum.

Kubozono, H. (2002). Mora and syllable. In N. Tsujimura (Ed.), *The handbook of Japanese linguistics* (pp. 31–61). Malden, MA: Blackwell Publishers Inc.

Larsen-Freeman, D. (2006). The emergence of complexity, accuracy and fluency in the written and oral production of five Chinese learners of English. *Applied Linguistics, 27*(4), 590–619.

Larsen-Freeman, D., & Long, M. H. (1991). *An introduction to second language acquisition research.* London: Longman.

Levelt, W. (1989). *Speaking: From intention to articulation.* Cambridge, MA: MIT Press.

Li, N., & Juffs, A. (2015). The influence of moraic structure on English L2 syllable final consonants. *2014 Annual Meeting on Phonology.* Retrieved from http://dx.doi.org/10.3765/amp.v2i0.3767

Long, M. H. (2007). *Problems in SLA.* New York: Lawrence Erlbaum.

192 Spoken Language

Long, M. H. (2016). In defense of tasks and TBLT: Nonissues and real issues. *Annual Review of Applied Linguistics, 36*, 5–33. doi:10.1017/S0267190515000057

Lynch, T. (2007). Learning from the transcripts of an oral communication task. *ELT Journal, 61*, 311–320. doi:10.1093/elt/ccm50

Mackay, D. G. (1973). Spoonerisms: The structure of errors in the serial order of speech. In V. A. Fromkin (Ed.), *Speech errors as linguistic evidence* (pp. 164–194). The Hague: Mouton.

Martin, K. I. (2011). *Reading in English: A comparison of native Arabic and native English speakers.* University of Pittsburgh ETD (Unpublished). Item availability may be restricted.

Martin, K. I. (2015). *L1 impacts on L2 component reading skills, word skills, and overall reading achievement.* University of Pittsburgh ETD. Item availability may be restricted.

Martin, K. I., & Juffs, A. (in review). *Eye-tracking as a window into assembled phonology in native and non-native reading.* University of Southern Illinois, University of Pittsburgh, Ms.

McCormick, D. E., & Vercellotti, M. L. (2013). Examining the impact of self-correction notes on grammatical accuracy in speaking. *TESOL Quarterly, 47*(2), 410–420. doi:10.1002/tesq.92

Nation, I. S. P. (1989). Improving speaking fluency. *System, 17*(3), 377–384. Retrieved from https://doi.org/10.1016/0346-251X(89)90010-9.

Paulston, C. B. (1985). Communicative competence and language teaching: Second thoughts. *RELC Seminar* (Communicative Language Teaching. Selected Papers from the RELC Seminar), 13–31. doi:files.eric.ed.gov/fulltext/ED266663.pdf

Robinson, P. (1995). Task complexity and second language narrative discourse. *Language Learning, 45*, 99–140. Retrieved from https://doi.org/10.1111/j.1467-1770.1995.tb00964.x

Robinson, P. (Ed.). (2011a). *Second language task complexity: Researching the cognition hypothesis of language learning and performance.* Philadelphia: John Benjamins.

Robinson, P. (2011b). Second language task complexity, the cognition hypothesis, language learning, and performance. In P. Robinson (Ed.), *Second language task complexity: Researching the cognition hypothesis of language learning and performance* (pp. 3–38). Philadelphia: John Benjamins.

Schmidt, R. W. (1990). The role of consciousness in second language learning. *Applied Linguistics, 11*(2), 129–158.

Skehan, P. (1998). *A cognitive approach to language learning.* Oxford: Oxford University Press.

Skehan, P. (2018). *Second language task based performance: Theory, research, assessment.* New York: Routledge.

Stanowicz, K. E. (1986). Matthew effects in reading: Some consequences of individual differences in the acquisition of literacy. *Reading Research Quarterly, 21*, 360–407.

Towell, R. (2012). Complexity, accuracy, and fluency from the point of view of psycholinguistic research. In A. Housen, F. Kuiken, & I. Vedder (Eds.), *Dimensions of L2 performance and proficiency: Complexity, accuracy, and fluency in L2 research* (pp. 47–70). Philadelphia: John Benjamins.

Towell, R., Hawkins, R., & Bazergui, N. (1996). The development of fluency in advanced learners of French. *Applied Linguistics, 17*(1), 84–119. Retrieved from https://doi.org/10.1093/applin/17.1.84

Vercellotti, M. L. (2012). *Complexity, accuracy, and fluency as properties of language performance: The development of multiple subsystems over time and in relation to each other* (PhD dissertation), University of Pittsburgh, Pittsburgh. Retrieved from http://d-scholarship.pitt.edu/12071/1/Vercellotti_CAF_v3.pdf

Vercellotti, M. L. (2017). The development of complexity, accuracy and fluency in second language performance. *Applied Linguistics, 38*(1), 90–111. Retrieved from https://academic.oup.com/applij/article-abstract/38/1/90/2951570

Young-Scholten, M., & Archibald, J. (2000). Second language syllable structure. In J. Archibald (Ed.), *Second language acquisition and linguistic theory* (pp. 64–102). Oxford: Blackwell.

Zaharna, R. S. (1995). Understanding cultural preferences of Arab communication patterns. *Public Relations Review, 21*(3), 241–255.

Zhang, X., & Lantolf, J. P. (2015). Natural or artificial? Is the route of L2 development teachable? *Language Learning, 65*(1), 152–180. doi:10.1111/lang.12094

7 Some Features of the Development of Writing in an Intensive English Program

7.1 Introduction

One of the main goals of students in an intensive English program is to develop the ability to write clearly and accurately. The genres in English that many students need eventually to master are the research paper, laboratory report, or examination in their academic discipline. Students who are not preparing for academic study may want to be able to communicate clearly in business or their personal lives. Academic writing tasks are very high-stakes activities because students' grades in future academic coursework will depend on the ability to communicate effectively in writing. The body of research on English for academic purposes is very large indeed, and readers are encouraged to consult key works in this area (e.g., books by well-known experts such as Hyland [2016a] and Swales and Feak [1994] as well as recent articles in the relevant journals such as the more general *Journal of Second Language Writing* [www.journals.elsevier.com/journal-of-second-language-writing] and the two more specialized *Journal of English for Academic Purposes* [www.journals.elsevier.com/journal-of-english-for-academic-purposes], and *English for Specific Purposes* [www.journals.elsevier.com/english-for-specific-purposes]).

IEP students can be a heterogeneous group, especially in IEPs that are in large cities. Even in IEPs that have a more direct connection to a college or university, such as in a pathway program (blended ESL and basic academic courses), each class may have students who plan to take a degree course in a wide variety of different subjects and at different levels (undergraduate and graduate). Because of this range of intended majors, most IEP classes cannot be too discipline specific but must focus overwhelmingly on general academic English. Given its urban setting and broad range of students, the Pitt IEP therefore attempts to guide students through basic concepts in development of paragraph structure, organization of ideas, and provision of support for statements that they make. At the same time, students receive guidance to develop their control of the grammatical structures, organizational vocabulary, and appropriate register of written English.

The chapter is structured as follows. First, we will consider briefly some key issues in second language writing as a review for the background of the instruction in the IEP. Second, the bulk of the chapter will be based on data from the writing classes in Levels 3, 4, and 5 in the IEP. We will trace the development of several individuals' writing, both quantitatively and qualitatively. Finally, based on the analysis of these selected writing assignments, we will consider how the curriculum enhanced development in different aspects of the students' written work. As with previous chapters, the final section offers areas for administrators and teachers to reflect on. The research described in Section 4.4 regarding lexical development and in Section 5.5 on grammatical development is also relevant to the students' progress in writing in the program.

7.2 Research on L2 Writing Development – Selected Key Highlights

Hinkel (2005) provides an extremely useful summary of many of the concerns in this section, and readers are encouraged to consult Hinkel's review and other recent overviews of L2 writing, for example, Leki, Cumming, and Silva (2008) and Matsuda and Silva (2014), which give broad overviews of the field as well as more recent scholarship.

7.2.1 Writing: Taking Account of the Potential Reader

Writing is an activity that can take a very wide range of forms, from literary products (poems, short stories, novels, and plays) to laboratory reports, research papers, and email. One of the key challenges for writers, including expert speaker writers, is that the writer has to make certain assumptions about what the reader already knows about a topic. Writers must have in their mind what their potential readers already know and provide enough discourse context for them to follow an argument or narrative but not overwhelm or frustrate them, either with known information or with technical details that they have no background in. We need not belabor such issues here, as IEP administrators and instructors will be well aware of the concerns of academic writing and reading that date back well over 40 years. Many of those early researchers in academic reading and writing were also successful textbook writers. For example, Widdowson (1978), especially in his Chapter 5, pp. 134–140, discussed the development of discourse units, and his 'Reading and Thinking' textbook series (Widdowson, 1979) addressed the interactive nature of reading and writing. Johnson's (1981) work was an early ESL textbook that adopted information transfer from charts and graphs as prompts for writing. Other researcher-textbook writers whose academic writing textbooks and research on writing influenced much subsequent thinking include Reid

196 *The Development of Writing in an IEP*

(1985, 1994), and Hamp-Lyons (Hamp-Lyons & Berry Courter, 1984; Hamp-Lyons, 1986, 2007).

In the mid-1990s, Ramirez (1995) summarized some of the teaching implications that had developed in writing instruction: the need to encourage a process of planning/organizing, to compose and then revise, and the need to encourage distancing from text in order to take into account the reader's point of view. He also pointed out that often poor writers were unable to focus on global aspects of the message that they wanted to convey. This is the issue of considering the potential reader because the writer knows what the goal of the writing is but often does not make it explicit enough. Finally, he re-emphasized that reading good, finished products to obtain models is an important aspect of writing instruction. Ramirez (1995, p. 280) also noted that research in L2 writing development had shown several parallels to development of L1 writing competence: learners may respond better to comments on content than form if they are unsure of their errors. Written accuracy tends to precede spoken accuracy (although with some speakers, spelling accuracy may lag behind spoken accuracy, as we have seen). In addition, successful writers engage more in higher level planning/re-writing. It is worth re-emphasizing that good texts are shaped as much by the writer's sense of their readers as they are by the writer's own characteristics.

7.2.2 *The Learner-Centered Curriculum*

In a learner-centered curriculum, Brookes and Grundy (1990) emphasized a humanistic element. By the humanistic element, they mean that the learner is the main resource for meanings (topics to talk and write about) and language (ways of talking and writing). Here, they believe that the learner should be free from imposition of language models, that self-expression should be encouraged and respected, and that this reflects the centrality of the learner. This approach is certainly true of many first-year composition classes for students in US universities and at the University of Pittsburgh (Atkinson & Ramanathan, 1995; Bartholomae, 2005). The anthology of articles in DeLuca, Fox, Johnson, Kogen, & DeLuca (2013) includes work by well-known ESL authors such as Raimes (2013) and Zamel (2013), where the dominance of particular models of 'thesis statement' and 'controlling idea' may be considered too confining in an era of post-modern approaches to education. (See Paulston (1999) for a useful overview of post-modern approaches in comparative education, which to some degree reflect ideologies in the development of first-year student writing. The theme of post-modernity is also raised in Leki et al., 2008.)

However, IEP curriculum designers need to consider the future tasks of learners in a range of disciplines, and not just in first-year composition classes. Whereas in first-year composition, the notion of 'thesis

The Development of Writing in an IEP   197

statement' and 'supporting ideas' and the five-paragraph essay may be outmoded and even rejected outright as 'wrong' (Atkinson & Ramanathan, 1995), it is clear that for many disciplines in the social sciences and sciences, writing must follow very strict models, such as the American Psychological Association guide to writing (e.g., American Psychological Association, 2010). Thus, IEPs must strike a balance between motivating students in a learner-centered curriculum and preparing them for their various social roles in writing, for example, as research writers and students in examination settings (e.g., Hamp-Lyons, 1986).

Brookes and Grundy (1990) also noted that learners need to be able to encode the perceived power inequalities between them and the interlocutor in an appropriate way and therefore be aware of, and control, register. In order to do that, learners must have a lexical repertoire in the 3000–9000 frequency bands (Schmitt & Schmitt, 2014), as was noted in Chapter 4. Brookes and Grundy (1990) also stress the integrated nature of writing with reading for ideas and that peer feedback is integral to the writing class, not least for gauging the effect on the reader.

7.2.3 Awareness of Genre

ESL writing textbooks have recognized and addressed the contexts in which students write for some time and have long paid attention to the concept of genre. Swales (1990) views a 'genre' as a standardized communicative event mutually understood by participants. He notes that knowledge of genres also sensitizes reading in preparation for writing. At the planning stage, knowledge of genre allows a writer to know what is expected. In writing a draft, the writer can focus on drawing readers' attention to macro-level features, which allows the writer to express his/ her meaning for the intended audience.

In acknowledging different genres, Swales (1990) lists various text types that IEPs might prepare students for:

1. Explanatory writing – informing, which implies the audience does not know about a topic and lacks important background
2. Persuasive writing – persuading, which implies that the audience must be convinced to do something or to believe a position that the writer takes
3. Expressive writing – clarifying, which implies various modes of presentation
4. Literary writing and writing of personal letters

The integration of text with diagrams and other visual support has also been a vital part of writing. At least since Keith Johnson's (1981) *Communicate in Writing* textbook, writing teachers and scholars have emphasized the connection between writing and charts, graphs, diagrams, and

198 *The Development of Writing in an IEP*

images. Indeed, the IELTS examinations currently require examinees to be able to carry out 'information transfer' tasks based on a chart or graph (www.ielts-exam.net/ielts-writing/).

Over many years, a consensus among researchers is that attention to both process and product are among the most important ways that writers discover ideas, formulate goals and plans, express their ideas, assess their own writing, revise, and edit their papers. The writing process involves planning, drafting, and revising to ensure that the writer is able to communicate clearly with the reader.

7.2.4 *Contrastive Rhetoric: L1 Influence in L2 Writing*

One issue that often arises in the ESL academic writing classroom is that cultural assumptions about good writing vary as much as genre styles in English itself. A mismatch between cultures and genres, together with the requirement that students follow English-language 'rules', could be viewed as English language cultural hegemony or a conflict with international students' conceptualization of 'individualism' and of what it means to 'be' a student – see Scollon (1991), which is a conference paper cited in Atkinson and Ramanathan (1995).

Cultural writing styles clearly differ (Kaplan, 2005). However, it is in EAP and ESP contexts that differences in cultural style may have a negative effect on the reader. For example, one influence of style might be that south Asian speakers transfer stylistic embellishment from their L1 (Arabic, Sanskrit, and Persian influence) to their L2 English or conversely a Farsi text may not follow English language organization, making it harder for English-speaking readers to follow (Abasi, 2012). Other learners could assume that directly quoting long passages from a well-known author is a way to show respect; they may be unaware of the prohibition in English academic writing on 'plagiarism'. Even if they are aware of it, how they deal with it may still be a problem (e.g., Li & Casanave, 2012). Indeed, IEP teachers are well aware that the relationship of one author's work to the previous writing of others and the problem of plagiarism versus paraphrasing is a very important but difficult skill to teach and learn. Some textbooks spend a lot of time practicing it; for example, Arnaudet and Barret (1984) had a particularly strong focus and many exercises on this topic. Teachers may want to reduce flowery language, or 'nonlinear' style, or confront 'cut-and-paste' plagiarism in an aggressive way. However, a process approach and a sensitivity to contrastive rhetorical styles (Hyland, 2016a, Chapter 3; Kaplan, 2005) can mitigate the tensions between cultures and genres.

Other lower-level stylistic topics that all writers may struggle with are such choices between what Wells (1960) called nominal versus verbal style. For example, verbal style in a sentence such as *The newspaper reported that Dr. Jones approved of the fact that the hens were producing eggs while ranging freely* is much more cumbersome than *The newspaper reported Dr. Jones' approval of free-range egg production*. This example is deliberately extreme, but writers do need to spend time word smithing and polishing their work, which reinforces the need for a process approach to writing.

Included in L1 influence are the issues of spelling and spacing that were discussed in Section 6.4. These problems can be mitigated with grammar and spell-checkers, as the composing and revision process has been made infinitely easier in the past 30 years with the advent of computers and word-processing software. However, teaching learners how to use this software effectively can be time-consuming. In addition, the challenges of the 'qwerty' keyboard for speakers of non-alphabetic languages need to be addressed and learners need to be able to select which spelling errors need special focus.

7.2.5 Corrective Feedback: Second Language Acquisition Research

Another perennial issue in writing instruction is the timing and amount of feedback to give to students. SLA researchers have carried out a great deal of research on feedback with specific linguistic features in L2 writing and how feedback on written output can contribute to grammatical development. One example has been the intense focus on corrective feedback with the English article system (*a/the/*no article). (See Bitchener [2017] for a recent overview of this work with regard to articles and Ferris [2011] for corrective feedback in general.) Although some researchers continue to question the effectiveness of written feedback on grammatical development on theoretical grounds (e.g., Truscott, 2007), several other researchers have emphasized the effectiveness of overt, explicit metalinguistic feedback (Ferris, Liu, Sinha, & Senna, 2013; Sheen, 2007).

However, disagreements on the role of implicit, explicit, and metalinguistic feedback given/provided at the sentence level on more narrow linguistic features should be treated cautiously. This research does not address the training that students need in cultural and genre issues with regard to rhetorical organization and content. (See Hyland (2019) for an updated overview of many important issues.) In this sense, writing development is very clearly like any other skill or knowledge base that requires instruction, feedback, and practice.

7.2.6 Corpus-Based Studies of Writing: Quantitative Measurements

Computers enable researchers to manipulate very large volumes of text and produce very large numbers of statistics with a few simple keystrokes once the data are appropriately organized. Such computing power is a huge advantage for researchers who wish to quantify populations. One drawback lies precisely in this advantage: large numbers of statistics can drown out an individual voice and make the messages the students wish to convey subordinate to statistics such as word count per clause and other frequency information. In Section 7.3, the tensions between these two perspectives are reconciled to some extent.

As discussed in Chapter 4 on the lexicon, Chapter 5 on grammatical development, and Chapter 6 on spoken language development, the advent of computers, corpus linguistics, and data science techniques has provided researchers with heretofore unprecedented ability to examine the lexical and grammatical features of learners' spoken and written production. In Chapter 4, we discussed the important work on the lexicon (e.g., Jarvis & Daller, 2013) and the complexity-accuracy-fluency approach to spoken language (e.g., Housen, Kuiken, & Vedder, 2012).

In the realm of academic writing, Lu and colleagues have carried out extensive quantitative research on the syntactic complexity of college students' compositions (e.g., Lu, 2010, 2011; Lu & Ai, 2015). They have also provided an extremely useful web-based tool for researchers to examine data from their own students' work (https://aihaiyang.com/software/l2sca/single/). This website has a web interface that IEP administrators and teachers can use without cost to analyze their students' work.

Most of Lu's work in ESL has focused on first-year composition (FYC), which is an important writing genre that IEP students have to tackle once they begin their studies. IEPs often cater to both undergraduate and graduate students and so benchmarks of complexity from FYC essays may not be an exact fit for all IEP students. However, the extensive research that Lu, his colleagues, and other researchers have carried out provides some very important quantitative measures for the development of syntactic complexity.

Before describing Lu's work in detail, it is necessary to review some preliminaries. Recall that in Chapter 6 on speaking, the AS unit was discussed as the main unit for analyzing the CAF features of spoken production. In fact, the AS unit was based on another unit of analysis, the T-unit. Hunt (1965, cited in Gass & Selinker, 2008, p. 73) defined a T-unit as 'an independent clause and any associated dependent clauses, that is, clauses that are attached to or embedded within it'. Under this definition, sentences in 1, 2, 3 are all one T-unit, but 4 is not.

1. The student resided in Philadelphia. (One simple T-unit: one independent clause.)
2. Before residing in Philadelphia, Chris lived in Pittsburgh for several years. (One complex T-unit: one independent, one attached VP (*before . . . .*))
3. Before residing in Philadelphia, the student who now studies City and Regional Planning said that he had lived in Pittsburgh for several

The Development of Writing in an IEP   201

years. (One T-unit: one independent *had lived*, one VP attached [*Before . . .*], and two embedded clauses [*who studied . . .*] and [*said that . . .'*].)
4. Before residing in Philadelphia, (Zero T-units: one VP, zero clauses.)

The question of complexity will depend on the features of the T-unit. Thus, 3 is more complex than 2 because the T-unit has, for example, four verb phrases (VPs) (*reside, study, say, live*) compared to only two verbs (*reside, live*). Item 3 also has a ratio of dependent clauses to clauses of .66, whereas in 2, the ratio is 0. (One important point to make here is that more complexity does not always mean better, clearer writing.) As Lu (2011, p. 44) points out, whether non-finite elements are considered VPs or clauses has varied among authors. He considers that VPs are not clauses. Therefore, 'Before residing in Philadelphia' in 2–4 is treated as a VP in the web-based analyzer and not a clause; because of this analysis, there is only one clause in the T-unit in 2, but three clauses in 3. Only *tensed* adverbial clauses, relative clauses, and verb complement clauses are considered dependent *clauses*. A complex T-unit must therefore contain one additional dependent clause as well as the independent clause. Note that compound tenses, for example, *had lived*, are not distinguished in complexity analysis.

The web-based analyzer actually offers a count of 9 syntactic structure measures (including word and sentence counts) and calculates 14 syntactic complexity measures, including mean length T-unit, VPs per T-unit, and so on.

The research that Lu and colleagues have carried out suggests that only a subset of these 14 available measures is important in describing the development of complexity in L2 learners' writing. Lu (2011, p. 56) reports that seven measures were most useful in tracking development in Chinese-speaking college students and grouped them together in sets. (Example mean scores for untimed argumentative essays are provided for reference only – see Lu (2011, p. 49, Table 5) for full details.) The first set of measures (and best for distinguishing among levels) consists of two that reliably distinguished two *adjacent* levels (e.g., hypothetically Low A from Intermediate B and Intermediate B from Advanced C, as well as non-adjacent A and C). These are reported in Lu (2011, p. 51, Tables 6–7). In timed essays, complex nominals per clause (CN/C) ranged from 0.94 to 1.28. Second, mean length of clause (MLC) ranged from 8.9 to 10.87. Also discriminating two adjacent levels among schools in the study were complex nominals per T-unit (CN/T), mean length of sentence (MLS), and mean length of T-unit (MLT). Finally, two measures that discriminated among non-adjacent levels (e.g., A and C, but not A and B) were coordinate phrases per clause (CP) and coordinate phrases per t-unit (CP/T). These measures are further illustrated in Table 7.1.

202   *The Development of Writing in an IEP*

Table 7.1 Lu and Ai (2015) Selected Syntactic Complexity Indices (Averaged Across Proficiency Levels)

	Chinese	*Japanese*	*German*	*English*
	Mean (SD)	Mean (SD)	Mean (SD)	Mean (SD)
CN/C Complex Nouns/ Clause	1.27 (0.325)	0.94 (0.272)	1.19 (0.372)	1.22 (0.330)
MLC Mean Length of Clause	10.17 (1.482)	8.31 (1.217)	10.62 (1.984)	10.09 (1.624)
CN/T Complex Nouns/ T-Unit	2.10 (0.545)	1.50 (0.477)	2.12 (0.713)	2.09 (0.565)
MLS Mean Length of Sentence	17.64 (3.22)	14.67 (3.574)	22.31 (5.584)	19.60 (4.321)
MLT Mean Length of T-Unit	16.15 4.111	13.12 (2.574)	18.98 (4.612)	17.31 3.210
VP/T Verb Phrases per T-Unit	2.19 0.351	2.08 (0.396)	2.54 (0.579)	2.34 (0.434)

Given that IEPs usually have students with many L1s, Lu and Ai's (2015) investigation of L1 effects in college compositions using various measures is very relevant to IEPs. They found that combining the L2 texts from many L1s and then comparing them with native speaker texts reduced the number of differences found among the measures of syntactic complexity. However, when the L1s were disaggregated, reliable differences were found in various comparisons of all 14 syntactic complexity indices, with some being lower and some higher than the native speaker group. For example, the Japanese group at the same upper intermediate level of proficiency as other L1s showed *lower* levels of subordination and complex nominals. In contrast, at the advanced level, German native speakers seemed to produce longer sentences as a result of more coordination of sentences and phrases.

Lu and Ai (2015, p. 25) suggest that 'typological' characteristics may influence syntactic choices, but they do not state what those typological characteristics might be. I speculate that there are at least three possibilities. First, basic word order in Japanese is strictly SOV, whereas German word order is mixed, with SVO or verb second in main clauses and SOV in embedded clauses. As a result, clauses may be shorter in a strict SOV language so that parsing can be resolved by reaching the key VP earlier. (In sentence processing, understanding the verb is of paramount

The Development of Writing in an IEP 203

importance because the verb determines the relationships among the noun phrases and prepositional phrases.) Second, it may be that German-speaking learners just have slightly higher proficiency; however, that would not explain why their T-units are more complex than expert speakers of English.

A third potential source of the difference is in the contrastive rhetoric of high- and low-context cultures (Hall, 1976). Copeland and Griggs (1985) identify Germany as a low-context (more information provided) culture and Japan as a high-context (less background information) culture. Thus, German writing may contain longer sentences and modifications because of the need to provide more information. However, the construct of low-context vs. high-context cultures has come under scrutiny and, in fact, has not received adequate empirical support (Cardon, 2008; Kittler, Rygl, & MacKinnon, 2011). Kiesling and Paulston (2005) do not include reference to this construct in their reader on intercultural discourse and communication for this reason, added to the fact that the pragmatics of context is highly variable *within* cultures. As a result, Kiesling (personal communication, July, 2019) states that it is inadvisable to 'reify' cultures in this way given the wide variation in pragmatic contexts.

7.2.7 The Big Picture

IEP curriculum designers and most ESL writing textbooks are well aware of the issues discussed in Sections 7.2.1–7.25, and the implications for teaching writing of these concerns is clear. ESL writing curricula should be designed to facilitate students' awareness of audience and genre. The IEP curriculum may be learner centered, not dogmatic about cultural differences, and should show sensitivity to cultural styles. At the same time, the IEP must also prepare students for the new academic cultures that the students will find themselves in. These culture-genre issues are not only the domain of English language learners but also first-year composition programs and writing in the disciplines. For example, Atkinson and Ramanathan (1995) provided a qualitative study of English writing programs just within one US university and revealed important differences between English Composition programs for native speakers and the goals of writing programs in IEPs, all of which were taught by largely 'native-speaker' teachers. Their goal (p. 539) was 'To investigate a problem: serious disjunctions . . . in the way the two programs conceptualized and taught writing'. They found that many of the routines and guidelines emphasized by the IEP writing program (in particular the five-paragraph essay) were strongly rejected by the more open and creative approach in the English Department University Composition Program (UCP). Thus, even within one single English-speaking university, differences in the expectations of readers mean that IEP programs

204　*The Development of Writing in an IEP*

must stay attuned to the future readers of their students' writing. For a collection of articles on these and other topics, DeLuca et al. (2002) is a useful resource.

The Pitt IEP's writing curriculum is designed with all of these considerations in mind. It strives to build learners' skills from sentence- and paragraph-level organization at Level 3 with personalized topics (learner centered) through various genres (comparison/contrast, cause-effect, and so on) at higher levels. Instruction in key cohesion and coherence devices is factored in and revisited at each level.

7.3 Case Studies From the Intensive English Program – Tracking Development of Eight Students Over Three Semesters

7.3.1 Review of Curriculum Goals and Background of Selected Students

The Pitt IEP is based on a solid grounding in the research reviewed in Section 7.2. After reviewing the literature in Section 7.2, it became clear that journal articles on complexity use quantitative measures of syntactic complexity and accuracy mainly from the point of view of L2 *populations* for the very good reason that inferential statistics are designed to estimate populations. This quantitative research approach is an important one and can provide IEP administrators and instructors with a guide to what a target complexity might be for the L1s of their students in planning for measures of academic readiness. But at that level of abstraction, quantitative data do not provide an insight into the writing of the students' use of paragraph structure, connecting devices, and ideas. The scope of a quantitative journal article also does not permit authors to print multiple examples of student writing that IEP instructors could read and compare with work from their own classes. This chapter allows us to take population estimates (statistical means from samples in the papers by Lu [2011] and Lu and Ai [2015]) and compare them to individual cases in a *qualitative evaluation*, which is the goal of this section.

As was discussed and illustrated in Chapter 2 of this book, the progression from Level 3 through Level 4 to Level 5 is designed to assist learners' progress through processes and products to enable them to participate in writing in English-speaking academic settings. The research methodology in this chapter is that of Hyland (2016b, pp. 119–121): observation of texts and case studies, which is a choice from a range of theoretical and methodological approaches (Hyland, 2016b, Table 4, p. 123). Unfortunately, the students have departed the IEP and are not available to question about the intent of their writing, nor can group work and peer editing be observed. The goal in this section is to identify how the IEP addresses the research issues raised in Section 7.2 with regard to (a) genre, (b) language focus related to genre, (c) student-centered work, and (d) the role of feedback in various forms.

In general, the writing curriculum in the IEP during the period of data collection can be summarized in Table 7.2. At Level 3, students are mostly focused on creating sentences and short paragraphs. The IEP seeks to introduce the idea that writing is a process and that texts may be revised. Genres at this level include definitions and narrative. In Level 4, the idea of longer pieces of writing is introduced, including thesis statements (central ideas). Genres include giving instructions and summarizing. At Level 5, which at the time of data collection was the highest level in the IEP, the research paper is introduced, with important functions such as comparison and contrast, cause-effect, and processes. The goal of this highest level is to prepare students for university writing tasks.

The Pittsburgh English Language Institute Corpus consists of many paragraphs and essays written by students. In this chapter, we will consider those texts written by individual students in the IEP who had spent at least three semesters in the program and who had contributed enough texts that their progress could be evaluated at each stage in the program.

Table 7.2 Curriculum Objectives and Features, Levels 3–5

Level	Rhetorical Development	Example Genres (See Example Topics in Table 7.8)
3	a. Compose meaningful sentences and paragraphs that focus on a central idea with appropriate support and conclusion. b. Introduce the concept that writing is a process.	Practice the basic grammar structures of: a. Informational writing b. Written definitions c. Narratives
4	a. Compose meaningful sentences, paragraphs, and essays that focus on a central idea with appropriate support and conclusion. b. Understand and use the writing process.	Practice basic grammar structures of: a. Giving instructions b. Explaining c. Evaluating d. Summarizing
5	a. Compose expository essays in preparation for professional or academic writing tasks. b. Compose a term or research paper to prepare for this academic writing task.	Essays developed according to particular organizational patterns: a. Examples b. Comparison and contrast c. Cause and effect essay d. Argumentative essay e. Classification essay (optional) f. Process analysis essay (optional)

206 *The Development of Writing in an IEP*

Included in the texts that they wrote are exercises on grammar and reading summaries, as well as their own essays following the prompts provided by the teachers. We will consider all of these texts because it can give us a complete picture of the practice they did as well as the corrections that they might have made in response to their teacher's comments at various points in the process.

Table 7.3 identifies the students on whom will we focus as cases in this chapter. There are two Arabic speakers, two Chinese speakers, two Japanese speakers, and two Korean speakers who all contributed essays to our database over three semesters. (Only two Spanish speakers who contributed data during this period spent three semesters in the program, and they did not contribute writing data in all three of those semesters. This is because Spanish speakers often test into Level 4 and spend at most two semesters in the program.) Although some students had slightly higher test scores than others, they all tested into the program at Level 3, with one Arabic-speaking student (af3) who was a false beginner at the time of initial testing and was not admitted to the IEP until she had attained a Level 3 score on the placement test. Recall from Chapter 3 that the IEP required an MTELP score of 40–59, an IEP listening test score of 11–18, and a writing sample score of two. This proficiency level is the CEFR equivalent of A2-B1: this level indicates a student whose fluency and comprehension are limited, makes many errors that lead to misunderstanding, but who can produce several sentences when required.

Table 7.3 Summary of Students in the IEP Contributing Writing With Number of Texts Over 50 Words Long

Native Language, Gender	ID	IEP listening	MTELP	Writing Sample	Level 3 Texts	Level 4 Texts	Level 5 Texts
Arabic F	af3	11 (8)	42 (27)	2.7 (1.6)	28	10	24
Arabic M	bn7	12	42	2	25	8	32
Chinese F	aq1	8	25	2.5	6	17	35
Chinese F	bl7	21	58	3.2	9	20	21
Japanese F	ay3	11	47	1.3	22	31	27
Japanese F	fw1	13	44	2.3	16	26	16
Korean M	cc4	6	56	2	9	20	32
Korean M	eq8	15	47	2.1	6	28	15

In addition, the IEP Writing Rubric (Chapter 3, Appendix) indicates that a 'two' score on the writing sample has 'Very poor writing proficiency. The writer may address one or both of the writing prompts, but only in the most general way. There is only a list of simple sentences, with many errors in grammar, word choice, and word form. There may be confusion about meaning'. By Level 5, their writing should have the characteristics of four-five or above, where five is described as 'Good writing proficiency. The writer fulfills all requirements of at least one writing prompt and at least the general requirements of the second prompt. The writing is generally organized with main points and at least some support with details and/or examples. There is a variety of sentence types. There are some grammar, word choice, and/or word form errors. There is little or no confusion about meaning'.

Thus, on entry to the IEP, the expectations for writing are rather low and the goal for the end of Level 3 is for students to reach the point at which they can write a coherent paragraph. By Level 5, students are expected to understand and produce appropriate social science discourse structure in their writing.

Learners for qualitative analysis were selected on the basis of their having contributed enough 50-word texts at each level to permit a basic quantitative analysis of their Advanced Guiraud (AG-PSL3) score, which is a measure of advanced vocabulary knowledge (lexical sophistication), and a lexical diversity measure, vocD (see Juffs, 2019; Naismith, Han, Juffs, Hill, & Zheng, 2018; Naismith, Juffs, Han, & Zheng, submitted; and Chapter 4 for in-depth commentary on these measures).

The questions about writing that arise from the review of the literature and the IEP curriculum at the time of collection are:

1. Quantitative features for the learners' lexical and complexity development:

    a. How does their use of advanced vocabulary evolve over time compared with group means for their L1 counterparts?
    b. Does the learners' writing increase in complexity measured by complex noun phrases per clause and mean clause length?

In addition to a review of the quantitative aspects of the writing samples compared to the population samples provided by Lu (2010) and Lu and Ai (2015), it is also important to investigate the texts themselves from the other points of view that are important in L2 writing. Some of the topics are listed in 2–5:

2. Qualitative measures

    a. Do the texts take account of the reader?
    b. Do the texts reflect a learner-centered approach in that learners discuss topics that they can identify with?

208   *The Development of Writing in an IEP*

   c.   Do the texts show awareness of genre?

   d.   Is there L1 influence in rhetorical organization: citations, register, and/or organization?

3.   How does the organization in the students' writing *evolve*?

4.   How does the use of coherence and cohesion devices develop over time (Halliday & Hasan, 1976)?

5.   What is the role of topic on complexity measures?

7.3.2 Quantitative Overview of the Learners' Texts

Table 7.4 lists the quantitative scores of the learners' lexical richness: AG (based on the PSL3 word list) and vocD scores for all their texts in writing classes of 50 words or more.

Each learner's AG-PSL3 (that is, Advanced Guiraud based on excluding the most frequently used words at Level 3 in the IEP written corpus so that learners do not get credit for using words that are frequent for *them* but not expert English speakers) and vocD scores can be compared with the group means for their L1. Although Juffs (2019) reported that for *groups* of Arabic, Chinese, Japanese, and Korean learners, vocD did not distinguish between Levels 4 and 5, these learners appear to improve in their vocD scores, although both aq1 and cc4 exhibit a decline in this measure to below their respective L1 averages reported in Table 7.5.

As can be observed, many of the eight participants' scores are a little higher than the means for their respective L1s, but none of them are radically different. The AG scores of student af3 (Arabic), aq1 (Chinese), and eq8 (Korean) are rather low at Level 3, indicating that their vocabulary

Table 7.4 Quantitative Scores of Learners' Lexical Richness: AG and vocD Scores of All Texts of 50 Words or More

		Avg AG psl3	*Avg AG psl3*	*Avg AG psl3*	*Avg vocD*	*Avg vocD*	*Avg vocD*
Level		3	4	5	3	4	5
L1	ID						
Arabic	af3	0.18	0.5	1	51.87	74.55	81.25
Arabic	bn7	0.38	0.46	1.06	47.66	66.77	85.92
Chinese	aq1	0.16	0.57	0.53	60.92	70.92	61.4
Chinese	bl7	0.41	0.78	1.48	61.97	70.92	80.34
Japanese	ay3	0.47	1.27	2.19	61.89	71.58	87.68
Japanese	fw1	0.36	0.07	1.29	69.99	68.2	87.34
Korean	cc4	0.19	0.63	0.75	52.73	66.11	58.44
Korean	eq8	0.2	0.62	1.12	56.27	63.5	72.09

The Development of Writing in an IEP 209

Table 7.5 Mean Lexical Richness Scores by L1 for All Writing Texts in PELIC

	Avg AG psl3	*Avg AG psl3*	*Avg AG psl3*	*Avg vocD*	*Avg vocD*	*Avg vocD*
Level L1	3	4	5	3	4	5
Arabic	0.34	0.66	0.92	52.08	68.65	73.83
	(.21)	(.31)	(.49)	(12.42)	(14.53)	(15.32)
Chinese	0.3	0.75	1.11	56.81	76.33	79.1
	(.15)	(.35)	(.56)	(15.24)	(17.83)	(18.3)
Japanese	0.33	0.83	1.27	59.47	72.71	77.34
	(.14)	(.4)	(.5)	10.04	(11.89)	(14.3)
Korean	0.43	0.72	1.02	57.7	73.98	73.41
	(.25)	(.3)	(.49)	(17.95)	(13.95)	(16.08)
Spanish	*0.32*	*0.89*	*1.21*	*51.02*	*66.76*	*75.68*
	(.14)	*(.44)*	*(.38)*	*(10.67)*	*(14.23)*	*(11.85)*

is restricted to the most frequent 2000 words used by IEP students at Pitt. By Level 4, eq8 has caught up, but aq1's AG score does not develop as much. Overall, however, the vocabulary richness scores show a clear improvement across the three levels based on all of the writing samples from the students at each level.

Tables 7.6–7.8 contain the means of the quantitative syntactic complexity scores for the two writing samples chosen for qualitative analysis for each participant from each level. Recall from Section 7.2.5 that Lu (2011) mentioned seven measures that were most useful in tracking development: three measures of length of production, two complex nominal measures, and two coordinate phrase measures. Specifically, Lu (2011, p. 56) states that five of these were particularly useful:

> The best candidates are complex nominals per clause (CN/C) and mean length of clause (MLC), both of which not only discriminated two or more adjacent levels but also increased linearly across all four levels. The next group includes complex nominals per T-unit (CN/T), mean length of sentence (MLS), and mean length of T-unit (MLT), all of which discriminated two adjacent levels and generally progressed relative to school level.

In addition, in order to account for the number of VPs per T-unit, this additional measure was included on the basis that Lu (2011, p. 56) reports that Wolfe-Quintero, Inagaki, and Kim (1998) suggested that this measure could be useful. We will thus consider six measures in our qualitative analysis for each student.

Table 7.6 Level 3 Syntactic Complexity Measures

Measure/ L1	ID	CN/C	MLC	CN/T	MLS	MLT	VP/T	Words: Avg. of Two Texts
Arabic	af3	0.79	7.43	1.17	11.30	10.88	1.69	133.00
Arabic	bn7	0.79	7.73	1.05	12.26	10.69	1.57	175.50
Chinese	aq1	0.78	7.07	1.19	15.02	11.34	1.93	171.50
Chinese	bl7	1.18	11.46	1.75	17.76	17.03	2.26	177.50
Japanese	ay3	1.43	11.77	1.76	15.79	14.40	1.91	195.50
Japanese	fw1	0.48	7.75	0.84	14.88	13.63	2.46	172.50
Korean	cc4	0.60	8.03	0.70	10.58	9.34	1.53	171.50
Korean	eq8	0.45	7.04	0.79	11.58	12.21	2.33	149.50

Table 7.7 Level 4 Syntactic Complexity Measures

Measure/ L1	ID	CN/C	MLC	CN/T	MLS	MLT	VP/T	Words: Avg. of Two Texts
Arabic	af3	1.15	10.12	1.70	16.81	14.92	2.54	301.50
Arabic	bn7	1.00	9.09	1.41	13.85	12.78	1.60	234.50
Chinese	aq1	0.87	9.86	1.23	14.51	14.51	2.34	491.50
Chinese	bl7	1.41	11.84	2.13	15.31	14.28	1.54	424.00
Japanese	ay3	1.24	10.63	1.37	12.37	11.83	1.56	278.00
Japanese	fw1	0.76	9.40	1.13	15.57	15.05	1.98	177.50
Korean	cc4	0.94	7.92	0.68	14.41	12.63	2.05	458.50
Korean	eq8	0.97	8.66	1.61	14.42	14.19	2.02	507.00

Table 7.8 Level 5 Syntactic Complexity Measures

Measure/ L1	ID	CN/C	MLC	CN/T	MLS	MLT	VP/T	Words: Avg. of Two Texts
Arabic	af3	1.31	9.43	2.39	18.60	17.28	2.66	624.00
Arabic	bn7	1.26	10.24	2.18	18.64	17.58	2.42	779.50
Chinese	aq1	0.86	7.13	1.30	11.49	10.91	1.80	431.50
Chinese	bl7	1.05	9.85	1.80	19.44	17.08	2.49	605.00
Japanese	ay3	1.34	10.71	1.92	16.14	15.37	1.90	767.00
Japanese	fw1	1.44	10.75	2.14	17.66	16.18	2.17	725.50
Korean	cc4	0.60	7.92	1.13	14.90	14.45	2.59	723.00
Korean	eq8	0.95	8.88	1.49	15.02	13.91	1.77	637.50

The Development of Writing in an IEP 211

These data show clearly that the students' writing increases from under 200 words to over 600 words from Levels 3–5. Thus, the learners are producing much longer texts, as would be expected and required in the curriculum SLOs. Figures 7.1 and 7.2 illustrate development in the two key measures that Lu (2011) identified as most useful in tracking development in *adjacent* proficiency levels. For five out of the eight learners (af3, bn7, aq1, fw1, and eq8), complexity of NP per clause is clearly a marker of increasing complexity in writing from Levels 3 to either Level 4 or 5, whereas mean length of clause (MLC) seems to be a weaker predictor,

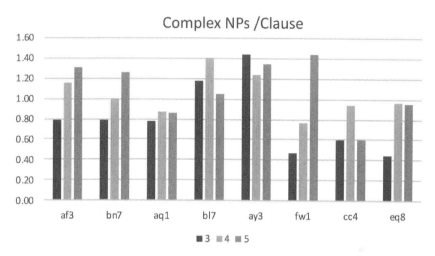

Figure 7.1 Complex NPs per Clause for Each Learner's Sample of Two Texts

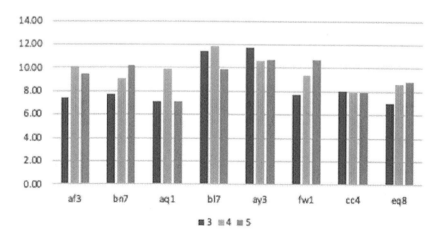

Figure 7.2 Mean Length of Clause for Each Learners' Two Texts From Levels 3–5

212 *The Development of Writing in an IEP*

with four of the eight (af3, bn7, fw1, eq8) having MLCs greater or equal in Level 3 than in Level 5.

Interestingly, none of the other measures seem to show a pattern in development over the three semesters for any of the learners. In addition, the lexical richness scores have no relation to complex NPs per clause until Level 4, and then only vocD may be strongly related to syntactic complexity. A lexical variety measure within the text that makes no connection to more sophisticated vocabulary use measured by Advanced Guiraud may make sense because syntactic complexity measures themselves make no reference to what the learners actually want to say. With a sample of only eight, however, we cannot draw any particular conclusions from these relationships but we look forward to examining these relationships in future research.

7.3.3 Qualitative Analysis

7.3.3.1 Content Evaluation

In this section, we will focus on the following:

1. Learner-centered curriculum
2. Taking account of the reader
3. Awareness of genre
4. L1 influence in rhetorical organization: citations, register, organization

Reading the 48 essays – 2 per participant for each level – the first two issues are clearly related. Scanning the list of topics, which are listed in Table 7.9, it is clear that the IEP endorses and acknowledges the learner-centered curriculum. Students are writing about their cultures (food, festivals, and traditions). These choices persist into Level 5 for aq1, who writes about a hobby of collecting coins, and bl7, who at Level 5 is writing about the Chinese New Year. Korean student cc4 addresses the challenging and controversial issue (for some) of eating dog meat. In this Level 4 essay, cc4 acknowledges the reader by conceding that many Americans will find such cultural practices shocking and upsetting. In all of the essays based on L1 culture, the students explain and expand for an imagined reader who is not from their culture, showing an awareness of audience.

The topics chosen by the students can inform the quantitative syntactic complexity measures. Comparing cc4 and bl7 in terms of the two key measures and the topics that they chose, it is immediately clear that they switched from a third-person account to a first-person account from Level 4 to 5, which may have resulted in reduced complexity. However, the two Arabic-speaking students (af3 and bn7) show a steady progression in their complexity of NP constructions from Level 3 through Level

Table 7.9 Topics Chosen by Students

Level		3	3	4	4	5	5
L1	ID						
Arabic	af3	ELI as a place to study	Fav. food	Comparing classmates (3)	Recycling (3)	Problem of children (3)	Raising the driving age (3)
Arabic	bn7	Food in SA and US	Two heads better than one	US economy (3)	Japan's ed tech (3)	Problem of children (3)	The Internet (3)
Chinese	aq1	Car comparison	Cooking	Culture shock	Success in language	Surprises about the US (I)	Hobby: Coins (I)
Chinese	bl7	Before and after leaving TW	World travel	Changing role of women	Traditional music in Taiwan	Chinese New Year (3)	Mistaken email (1)
Japanese	ay3	ELI as a place to study	Favorite food	Earth's resources	Earthquakes in Japan	Abolition death penalty (3)	Mac vs. Windows (3)
Japanese	fw1	Family pet (I)	Graduation (I)	Studying English (I)	My living room (I)	Skipping breakfast (3)	Fertility treatment (3)
Korean	cc4	Laptop comparison	Korean teens	Eating dog meat (3)	Choice of ESL program	Owning a house (I)	Military service (I)
Korean	eq8	Comparing fridges	Study habits	How to make kimchi	Exam pressure	Red Sox vs. Yankees (3)	Nature vs. nurture (3)

214   *The Development of Writing in an IEP*

5 – a progression that mirrors the topics that they chose. Aq1 does not engage with complex topics as the other students do in any of her writing assignments. It is thus arguable that her lower vocD score and complexity measures are the result of focusing on first-person topics.

The writing of the two Arabic-speaking students forms a useful contrast, both to each other and also with students from other L1s. Both students' writing improved in quantitative measures, transitioning from more personal topics (often written in the first person, e.g., 'food' and 'where to study') to ones of a larger social importance such as 'having children', 'raising the driving age', and 'the Internet'. On the face of it, these students' writing got better over the semesters based on the choice of topics that drove them to write more complex essays both in terms of vocabulary and syntactic complexity.

However, it is worth re-reading these essays in detail and comparing them with each other. The first point to note is that af3 controls and uses spellcheck better than bn7. Bn7's inability to spell *problem* ('problame') is clear, as is control of capitalization ('Convinced' 'My') and spacing between and within words ('a gree'), but he's focused on the message rather than the form at this point, even to the point of only using subject pronouns. In the second Level 3 text by bn7, many of these issues have been addressed, with the exception of the spacing problem.

Cohesion devices are already being used by the learners at this stage. Comparing food in Saudi Arabia and the United States, phrases such as *first of all* and *on the other hand* are in the repertoire of bn7, but *although* as a comparison marker is not used quite correctly: 'Although, American food is unpleasant, Saudi food is delicious'. In contrast, in her comparison letter to her parents, aq1 uses comparative markers *more* and *less*. Cc4, comparing laptops, uses only *but* and co-ordination with *and* as part of the comparison; eq8 does manage one *on the other hand* and a *however* in his refrigerator comparison. Both texts are short, so they indicate that the students are aware of cohesion devices but not fully in control at this stage.

By Level 5, eq8's repertoire when comparing 'nature vs. nurture', has not evolved to a great extent – in presenting his argument for the power of nurture over nature, eq8 chooses not to compare but rather argue one particular case instead of comparing directly as the title of the essay suggested. Thus, this is an 'argument' essay setting out a position rather than a true comparison. Ay3's essay comparing Mac OS with Windows also provides an insight into cohesion: contrasts are made through the use of *however* and comparative adjectives.

It is interesting to note that none of the essays contain the connector 'whereas', which requires a complex T-unit. Nine essays contain *on the other hand* and three essays *in contrast* (all Level 5) in sentence-initial position. Only ay3 uses both *on the other hand* and *in contrast*, which suggests that individual learners might fix on one connector to present

The Development of Writing in an IEP 215

an alternative. The phrase *on the other hand* appears at Level 3 (bn7 and eq8), so it is likely that this connector is familiar even to lower-level students.

It is worth comparing these two students' uses of *on the other hand* in some detail.

Bn7

Level 3. Saudi Arabia uses less convenience foods than the United States because the Saudi citizens used to cook but now they did not. *On the other hand*, American people used to eat convenience foods.
Level 5. Teenagers need to be restricted in using the internet in terms of proven and obvious risk. For instance, many sites EXHIBIT sexual videos and pictures which do not correspond with some people age. Therefore, internet will have a strong impact on this group of people in their behavior and future education. *On the other hand*, these people feel that this is unavoidable thing even and can educate them sex methods before getting married.
Level 5. They usually put their beautiful and awesome pictures' on this website. It can be true that people think it is quite helpful for readers for knowing where they are. As a result; their friends will start asking about the area they live in.
On the other hand, I think it might be potential dangerous in their life because of some compelling reasons. Showing any pictures in the Face book can have some negative consequences.

EQ8

Level 3. The $999 refrigerator has electronic touch temperature control, so if the refrigerator needs to lower its temperature, it changes by itself because it has a sensor. *On the other hand*, the $399 refrigerator doesn't have a sensor.
Level 4. For example, the department of liberal arts students can be pressured about a science examination, because they prefer a conversation, writing or reading than the proof of a formula or calculation. *On the other hand*, the science department student can be pressured by an examination relating to the department of liberal arts.

The first observation is that both students at Level 3 use *on the other hand* to introduce a very simple sentence that contrasts with the previous sentence. The uses in Level 4 and 5, however, connect much longer stretches of text contrasting more complex ideas, but perhaps less

216 *The Development of Writing in an IEP*

successfully. Bn7 in particular might have chosen *however*, rather than *on the other hand*, and needed to signal more strongly the change in perspective: the lead-up to the use of the connector is from an 'authority' perspective, whereas the clause introduced by *on the other hand* switches to the perspective of the teens themselves. In addition, in the second example from bn7, he begins a new paragraph with *on the other hand*, letting it do all the conceptual work for the change in perspective from 'others' to his own opinion. In contrast, eq8 uses the *on the other hand* to compare two perspectives of the same level and perspective. Thus, in the discourse, eq8 is more successful than bn7 in deploying the sentence connectors.

What does this mean? Let's take the first excerpt from bn7 in Level 5. His leading idea starts with an opinion (his?) that teenagers' internet access regarding sex should be restricted. At 'on the other hand', however, the perspective shifts to the teens themselves. It may have been clearer if the transition were 'Teenagers themselves may have a different point of view. Teens may feel that they can learn about sex from the internet'. Bn7's 'these people' is also unclear. It's possible that using a lexical contrast device 'different' instead of the ready-made chunk *on the other hand* and clarifying who the reader should assume the opinion is being attributed to would make bn7's writing clearer. The 'chunk' connectors are used at higher levels in place of connecting *sentences* that would help the reader identify when the writer has switched the points of view, answering the question 'who is talking?' or 'voice' (Elbow, 1994, p. 11).

These qualitative evaluations are not possible just by looking at quantitative data: based on the statistics, bn7 is doing well – better even than eq8 – at Level 5: CNP/C – MLC: 1.26 and 10.24 vs. 0.95 and 8.8. However, it seems that eq8 has more to say from the point of view of content and is able to expresses her views more effectively.

7.3.3.2 *Do Quantitative Ratings and Qualitative Teacher Evaluations Align?*

Many authors have sought to associate the quantitative features of writing (lexical richness, syntactic complexity) with more qualitative or holistic evaluations. For example, Daller, Turlik, and Weir (2013) found a latent growth curve using holistic ratings to measure vocabulary development. Shaw and Liu (1998) analyzed data from college-level non-native speakers over a relatively short period and thus found more development from spoken to written forms (e.g., a shift away from first person) rather than development in advanced vocabulary and syntactic complexity (p. 246). More recently, Plakans, Gebril, and Bilki (2019) found that complexity was less important than accuracy or fluency in the ratings of essays selected from the Internet-based TOEFL. (The fluency measure was simply a total word count in their analysis

The Development of Writing in an IEP 217

[Plakans et al., 2019, p. 166], which is of some concern. This choice of word count is obviously a very crude one and probably not how an IEP teacher would define 'fluent' writing. The use of this measure is of course due to the need to process text computationally.) However, in no case were either the intended meaning of the student interpreted or other features of the text (such as coherence and cohesion) considered. Ortega (2003) provided an overview of complexity and proficiency in college writing. Relevant to our discussion here is that she reiterates the warning that more complex does not necessarily mean 'better' and that the development of L2 writing involves more than just CAF features (Ortega, 2003).

In order to look at the overall human ratings of the 48 essays, three instructors from the IEP were asked to rate the essays based on the IEP rating scale (see Chapter 2, Appendix I). All the essays were anonymized (L1 and level information was removed, although of course a guess could be made about the L1 based on the content in some cases), and the essays were put into a list in random order, mixing authors, levels, and L1s. In other words, the essays were just supposed to be judged on the rubric alone. The raters were asked to simply rate the essays, not to correct them. If they desired, they were invited to make a comment but not required to do so. Each evaluator was permitted to use half points, so the scale ran from '1' = no writing proficiency to '6' = very good writing proficiency. Thus, the scale was really a 12-point scale if 0.5 points counts as points on the scale. (This was done in order to create a possible range of scores, as correlations may not be found when the range is restricted.) The three scores from each rater were averaged and used to correlate

Table 7.10 Correlations Among Average Essay Rating and Measures of Syntactic Complexity (N = 48 in All Cases)

Pearson r (p value)	Average	Words	CNC	MLC	AG-PSL3	vocD
Average	1					
Words	.41** (.003)	1				
CNC	.39** (.007)	.328* (.023)	1			
MLC	.43** (.002)	.23 (.11 ns)	.84** (.001)	1		
AG-PSL3	.34* (.017)	.65** (.0001)	.43** (.002)	.46** (.001)	1	
vocD	.25 (.08, ns)	.57** (.001)	.33* (.023)	.36* (.012)	.66** (.001)	1

(*) Significant at p = .05, two-tailed. (**); Significant at p = .01, two-tailed.

218   *The Development of Writing in an IEP*

with two syntactic complexity measures (complex NPs per clause + mean length of clause), word count, and Advanced Guiraud based on the Pitt Service List (AG-PSL3), which excludes some key frequent ESL words (see Chapter 4). Each student provided 2 essays per level, for a total of 48 essays.

These correlations indicate that a reliable relationship exists between MLC and the average essay writing score. Moreover, the number of words in the essay also correlates with the average score assigned to each essay (Bulté & Housen, 2012). However, MLC correlates very strongly with CNC (indicating co-linearity) but not with number of words. This is significant, as it suggests that MLC and length of essay contribute independently to the ratings given by the human raters. Using stepwise regression analysis (which is used when a researcher has 'no theoretical axe to grind' [Larson-Hall, 2010]), it was found that MLC and number of words together accounted for approximately 25% of the variance of the average rating of the essays, while CNC and AG-PSL did not enter the regression. (Note that vocD scores are not correlated with human ratings in these data.) This means that in judging the essays, the raters paid significant attention to both the length of clause and number of words, but the MLC of clauses was taken into consideration even in shorter texts. As an example, consider the lowest-rated text [(14) in the Appendix, score = 2.83], which is 142 words long and had a CNC score of 0.45 and MLC of 7.1, versus the highest-rated text (S in the Appendix), which received a unanimous '6' on the scale and was 695 words long and had a CNC score of 1.45 and MLC of 12.63.

Interestingly, the human raters' scores did not differ by level [means (standard deviations): Level 3 = 4.37 (.67), Level 4, 4.52 (.71), Level 5, 4.87 (.60), $F(2,45) = 2.314$, $p = .11$]. From these data, it seems that the human raters are judging the quality of the writing as if it were within the level that they assumed the student was writing, which is a topic that can be followed up on in future research. It is also worth pointing out that quantitative measures are accounting for only 25% of the variance in the average human rating scores. This result suggests that human raters are paying more attention to meaning and organization than length of essay or mean length of clause.

Although there were no statistical differences by level in grades, on reading the essays, it is possible that those essays which were written in the first person were shorter, contained lower lexical sophistication, and had lower MLC. The intuition is that if a student can rely on his or her own experience, the output that they produced may be limited to their existing vocabulary and structural style. In other words, they will not need to reach for new vocabulary and structures to explain a topic that they are less familiar with.[1] In order to explore this intuition statistically, the essays were coded either 'Impersonal' (not related to the student's direct experience and written in the third person) or 'Personal'

The Development of Writing in an IEP 219

Table 7.11 Impersonal and Personal Texts by Level in the Sample

	Level 3	Level 4	Level 5
Impersonal	5	12	11
Personal	11	4	5

(directly related to the student's own experience and written in the first person). The distribution of Personal vs. Impersonal by level is provided in Table 7.11.

Clearly, students write more texts in the first person in Level 3 and more impersonal topics in Level 5. Statistically, it is hard to separate out Impersonal/Personal topics from length of essay (words), as students write much more at Levels 4 and 5 than at Level 3. To reliably examine the effect of first-person vs. third-person texts, a selection at each level that is balanced would be necessary. Yet it is interesting to note that all five of the Personal essays at Level 5 had MLC scores of less 8.42 or less (only one Impersonal essay had a score lower than 8). Only one of those Personal essays had an AG-PSL3 score of over 1.0, while ten of the Impersonal essays had AG-PSL3 scores over 1.0.

This result is only based on a limited number of texts and must of course be treated with some caution before a larger study can be carried out. Certainly, one might want to consider further measures of lexical sophistication and diversity. Overall, it is somewhat surprising that AG scores, increasing as they do over time from level to level (see Chapter 4), did not play a key part (statistically) in influencing how the human raters evaluated the texts, although the comments on the Level 5 essays' AG-PSL3 scores suggest that they might play a role. One essay, bl7's 'Happy Chinese New Year', was the only text to receive the highest possible score of 6 from the raters. This essay was not 'academic' in the sense of other essays on social topics, but the vivid description and enthusiasm of the 'voice' of the writer come across very strongly. This observation is an important one, and such 'intangibles' cannot fully be accounted for by any quantitative measures.

7.4 Summary and Conclusion

In sum, the development of writing in the IEP not only allows the student to *develop* voice – from first-person to more 'objective' third-person writing (Shaw & Liu, 1998) – but also allows them to evolve in terms of text complexity and vocabulary sophistication.

We have seen the students increase in terms of key quantitative developmental measures of text sophistication in terms of mean length of clause and words produced during their time in the IEP, both of which

220 *The Development of Writing in an IEP*

are independently associated with higher human ratings. These quantitative metrics approach expert language users and first-year composition scores, showing that the IEP is preparing students to participate at an expert language user standard. However, human raters also consider other factors such as content and perhaps even 'voice' itself, which may be harder for a computer to identify automatically. Finally, although learners used 'chunked' cohesion devices, these essays did not evidence a wide range of such devices. The use of chunks and collocations in student writing and associating those with teacher ratings would also be of interest in future research. It may be that writing teachers need to focus more on encouraging students to broaden the repertoire of connecting devices and to write about topics that they are less familiar with in order to push output and learning.

7.5 Topics for Administrators and Teachers to Reflect On

7.5.1 *Questions and Issues Mainly for Program Administrators and Curriculum Supervisors*

1. In the IEP writing curriculum, are the level goals and objectives and student learning outcomes stated in terms of more learner-centered or more discipline-centered goals?
2. How do the IEP curricula progress from level to level such that students can be deemed 'academically ready' or 'professionally ready' for their writing assignments?
3. Does the IEP recommend a particular citation format for 'research paper'–type essays?
4. Does the IEP have a list of frequent collocations and academic vocabulary?

7.5.2 *Questions and Issues Mainly for Teachers*

1. Hillocks (1986, p. 205) reports that sentence combining is often used to increase the length of T-units:

> The sentence combining treatment is one pioneered by Mellon (1969) and O'Hare (1973), who showed that practice in combining simple sentences into more complex ones resulted in greater T-unit length – a T-unit being a traditionally defined main clause and all of its appended modifiers. That this treatment results in students writing longer T-units is hardly open to question. However, a number of critics question that it produces writing of higher quality.

Questions:

    a.   Do you use sentence combining in any of your classes? Which structures might you target for this purpose?

    b.   Why might increases in T-units not lead to better writing?

2.   Review some of the essays in the Appendix. How do they compare to essays written in the IEP where you work in terms of *topics* and *sophistication*? Where would the essays place a student in your levels?

3.   What criteria do you use to judge an essay? Do you think you are aware of the following properties?

    a.   Mean length of clause
    b.   Complex noun phrases per clause
    c.   Lexical sophistication
    d.   Length
    e.   Cohesion and coherence devices
    f.   Content – making you engaged with what the writer has to say
    g.   A subset of the above? Which ones?

4.   When choosing a textbook for your course, which factors do you consider to be most important in choosing the book?

Note

1.   Importantly, first-person writing will probably require less 'involvement load' in vocabulary use than third-person writing on a topic that is less familiar (Hulstijn & Laufer, 2001). This increased involvement load could lead to more complex vocabulary and therefore higher scores from human raters.

References

Abasi, A. R. (2012). The pedagogical value of intercultural rhetoric: A report from a Persian-as-a-foreign-language classroom. *Journal of Second Language Writing, 21*(3), 195–220. doi:10.1016/j.jslw.2012.05.010

American Psychological Association. (2010). *Publication manual* (6th ed.). Washington, DC: American Psychological Association.

Arnaudet, M. L., & Barret, M. E. (1984). *Approaches to academic reading and writing*. New York: Prentice Hall.

Atkinson, D., & Ramanathan, V. (1995). Cultures of writing: An ethnographic comparison of L1 and L2 university writing/language programs. *TESOL Quarterly, 29*, 539–568.

Bartholomae, D. (2005). The tidy house: Basic writing in the American curriculum. In *Writing on the margins* (pp. 312–326). New York: Palgrave Macmillan.

Bitchener, J. (2017). Why some L2 learners fail to benefit from written corrective feedback. In H. Nassaji & E. Kartchava (Eds.), *Corrective feedback in second*

222 *The Development of Writing in an IEP*

language teaching and learning: Research, theory, applications, implications (pp. 129–140). New York: Routledge.

Brookes, A., & Grundy, P. (1990). *Writing for study purposes*. Cambridge: Cambridge University Press.

Bulté, B., & Housen, A. (2012). Defining and operationalizing L2 complexity. In A. Housen, F. Kuiken, & I. Vedder (Eds.), *Dimensions of L2 performance and proficiency: Complexity, accuracy, and fluency in L2 research* (pp. 21–46). Philadelphia: John Benjamins.

Cardon, P. W. (2008). A critique of Hall's contexting model: A meta-analysis of literature on intercultural business and technical communication. *Journal of Business and Technical Communication*, 22(4), 399–428. doi:10.1177/1050651908320361

Copeland, L., & Griggs, L. (1985). *Going international: How to make friends and deal effectively in the global marketplace*. New York: Random House.

Daller, M., Turlik, J., & Weir, I. (2013). Vocabulary acquisition and the learning curve. In S. Jarvis & M. Daller (Eds.), *Vocabulary knowledge: Human ratings and automated measures* (pp. 185–218). Amsterdam: John Benjamins.

DeLuca, G., Fox, L., Johnson, M-A., Kogen, M., & DeLuca, G. (Eds.). (2013). *Dialogue on writing: Rethinking ESL, basic writing, and first-year composition*. New York: Taylor & Francis (Originally published in 2002).

Elbow, P. (1994). What do we mean when we talk about voice in texts? In K. B. Yancey (Ed.), *Voices on voice: Perspectives, definitions, inquiry* (pp. 1–35). Urbana, IL: National Council of Teachers of English.

Ferris, D. (2011). *Treatment of error in second language student writing*. Ann Arbor, MI: University of Michigan Press.

Ferris, D., Liu, H., Sinha, A., & Senna, M. (2013). Written corrective feedback for individual L2 writers. *Journal of Second Language Writing*, 307–329.

Gass, S. M., & Selinker, L. (2008). *Second language acquisition: An introductory course* (3rd ed.). New York: Routledge.

Hall, E. T. (1976). *Beyond culture*. New York: Doubleday.

Halliday, M. A. K., & Hasan, R. (1976). *Cohesion in English*. London: Longman.

Hamp-Lyons, L. (1986). Two Commentaries on Daniel M. Horowitz's "Process, Not Product: Less Than Meets the Eye". No New Lamps for Old Yet, Please. *TESOL Quarterly*, 20(4), 790–796.

Hamp-Lyons, L. (2007). The influence of testing practices on teaching: Ideologies and alternatives. In J. Cummins & C. Davison (Eds.), *International handbook of English language teaching* (pp. 473–490). Boston, MA: Springer.

Hamp-Lyons, L., & Berry Courter, K. (1984). *Research matters*. Rowley, MA: Newbury House.

Hillocks, G. (1986). *Research on written composition: New directions for teaching*. Urbana, IL: National Council of Teachers of English.

Hinkel, E. (2005). Analyses of second language text. In E. Hinkel (Ed.), *Handbook of research in second language teaching and learning* (pp. 615–628). Mahwah, NJ: Lawrence Erlbaum.

Housen, A., Kuiken, F., & Vedder, I. (Eds.). (2012). *Dimensions of L2 performance and proficiency: Complexity, accuracy, and fluency in L2 research*. Philadelphia: John Benjamins.

Hulstijn, J., & Laufer, B. (2001). Some empirical evidence for the involvement load hypothesis in vocabulary acquisition. *Language Learning*, 51, 539–558. doi:10.1111/0023-8333.00164

The Development of Writing in an IEP 223

Hunt, K. W. (1965). *Grammatical structures written at three grade levels*. Champaign, IL: National Council of Teachers of English.

Hyland, K. (2016a). *Teaching and researching writing*. New York: Routledge.

Hyland, K. (2016b). Methods and methodologies in second language writing research. *System, 59,* 116–125. doi:10.1016/j.system.2016.05.002

Hyland, K. (2019). *Second language writing* (2nd ed.). Cambridge: Cambridge University Press.

Jarvis, S., & Daller, M. (Eds.). (2013). *Vocabulary knowledge: Human ratings and automated measures*. Amsterdam: John Benjamins.

Johnson, K. (1981). *Communicate in writing*. London: Addison-Wesley.

Juffs, A. (2019). The development of lexical diversity in the writing of intensive English program students. In R. M. DeKeyser & P. B. Goretti (Eds.), *Reconciling methodological demands with pedagogical applicability* (pp. 179–200). Amsterdam: John Benjamins.

Kaplan, R. (2005). Contrastive rhetoric. In E. Hinkel (Ed.), *Handbook of research in second language teaching and learning* (pp. 375–391). Mahwah, NJ: Lawrence Erlbaum.

Kiesling, S. F., & Paulston, C. B. (Eds.). (2005). *Intercultural discourse and communication: The essential readings*. Oxford: Blackwell Publishing.

Kittler, M. G., Rygl, D., & MacKinnon, A. (2011). Beyond culture or beyond control? Reviewing the use of Hall's high-/low-context concept. *International Journal of Cross Cultural Management, 11*(1), 63–82. doi:10.1177/1470595811398797

Larson-Hall, J. (2010). *A guide to doing statistics in second language research using SPSS*. New York: Routledge.

Leki, I., Cumming, A., & Silva, T. (2008). *A synthesis of research on second language writing in English*. New York: Routledge.

Li, Y., & Casanave, C. P. (2012). Two first-year students' strategies for writing from sources: Patchwriting or plagiarism? *Journal of Second Language Writing, 21,* 165–180. doi:10.1016/j.jslw.2012.03.002

Lu, X. (2010). Automatic analysis of syntactic complexity in second language writing. *International Journal of Corpus Linguistics, 15*(4), 474–496.

Lu, X. (2011). A corpus-based evaluation of syntactic complexity measures as indices of college-level ESL writers' language development. *TESOL Quarterly, 45*(1), 36–62.

Lu, X., & Ai, H. (2015). Syntactic complexity in college-level English writing: Differences among writers with diverse L1 backgrounds. *Journal of Second Language Writing, 29,* 16–27. Retrieved from https://doi.org/10.1016/j.jslw.2015.06.003

Matsuda, P. K., & Silva, T. (Eds.). (2014). *Second language writing research: Perspectives on the process of knowledge construction*. New York: Routledge.

Mellon, J. C. (1969). *Transformational sentence combining: A method for enhancing the development of syntactic fluency in English composition* (NCTE research report). Champaign, IL: NCTE.

Naismith, B., Han, N-R., Juffs, A., Hill, B. L., & Zheng, D. (2018). Accurate measurement of lexical sophistication with reference to ESL learner data. In K. E. Boyer & M. Yudelson (Eds.), *Proceedings of the 11th International Conference on Educational Data Mining* (pp. 259–265). Buffalo, NY. Retrieved from http://educationaldatamining.org/EDM2018/

Naismith, B., Juffs, A., Han, N-R., & Zheng, D. (in review). *Local isn't necessarily better: The usefulness of vocabulary lists from non-program-specific learner corpora*. University of Pittsburgh, Ms.

O'Hare, F. (1973). *Sentence combining: Improving student writing without formal grammar instruction* (Vol. 15). Champaign, IL: NCTE Committee on Research Report Series.

Ortega, L. (2003). Syntactic complexity measures and their relationship to L2 proficiency: A research synthesis of college level writing. *Applied Linguistics*, 24(4), 492–518. doi:10.1093/applin/24.4.492

Paulston, R. G. (1999). Mapping comparative education after postmodernity. *Comparative Education Review*, 43(4), 438–463. Retrieved from www.jstor.org/stable/1188803

Plakans, L., Gebril, A., & Bilki, Z. (2019). Shaping a score: Complexity, accuracy, and fluency in integrated writing performances. *Language Testing*, 36(2), 161–179. doi:10.1177/0265532216669537

Raimes, A. (2013). Errors: windows into the mind. In G. DeLuca, L. Fox, M.-A. Johnson, M. Kogen, & G. DeLuca (Eds.), *Dialogue on Writing. Rethinking ESL, Basic Writing, and First-Year Composition* (pp. 279–288). New York: Routledge.

Ramirez, A. G. (1995). *Creating contexts for second language acquisition: Theory and methods*. London and White Plains, NY: Longmans.

Reid, J. (1985). *The process of composition*. Englewood Cliffs, NJ: Prentice Hall.

Reid, J. (1994). Responding to ESL students' texts. *TESOL Quarterly*, 28, 273–292.

Schmitt, N., & Schmitt, D. (2014). A reassessment of frequency and vocabulary size in L2 vocabulary teaching. *Language Teaching*, 47(4), 484–503. doi:10.1017/S0261444812000018

Shaw, P., & Liu, E. T-K. (1998). What develops in the development of second language writing? *Applied Linguistics*, 19(2), 225–254. doi:10.1093/applin/19.2.225

Sheen, Y. (2007). The effect of focused written corrective feedback and language aptitude on ESL learner's acquisition of articles. *TESOL Quarterly*, 255–283.

Swales, J. (1990). *Genre analysis: English in academic research settings*. Cambridge: Cambridge University Press.

Swales, J., & Feak, C. (1994). *Academic writing for graduate students: Essential tasks and skills*. Ann Arbor, MI: University of Michigan Press/ELT.

Truscott, J. (2007). The effect of error correction on learners' ability to write accurately. *Journal of Second Language Writing*, 255–272.

Wells, R. (1960). Nominal and verbal style. *Style in Language*, 213–220.

Widdowson, H. G. (1978). *Teaching language as communication*. Oxford: Oxford University Press.

Widdowson, H. G. (1979). *Reading and thinking in English*. Oxford: Oxford University Press.

Wolfe-Quintero, K., Inagaki, S., & Kim, H-Y. (1998). *Second language development in writing: Measures of fluency, accuracy, and complexity. No. 17* (Vol. 17). Honolulu: University of Hawaii Press.

Zamel, V. (2013). Strangers in academia: The experiences of faculty and ESL students across the curriculum. In G. DeLuca, L. Fox, M-A. Johnson, M. Kogen, & G. DeLuca (Eds.), *Dialogue on writing: Rethinking ESL, basic writing, and first-year composition* (Chapter 23). New York: Routledge.

Appendix I

AF3 Arabic L1. Writing Texts:
Errors Have Not Been Corrected

Writing 3x

Every body has favorite food. My favorite food is rice with chicken. It is delicious. It has a beautiful color, white rice and brown chicken. It is spicy. Sometimes I add some vegetables; they give it a nice color and good taste, especially if they were fresh they make it very tasty. I like it with potatoes, peas and carrot. Yellow, green, orange, white and brown, these colors make it delicious before you taste it. It is has a fresh smell. That was look my favorite food, I recommend every one to it.

Writing 4

My teacher of writing class asked us to choose one from two classmates to cooperate with him for all activities that we do in the class. For instance, when we work on editing paragraphs or analysis an essay my teacher always asks us to work in group, because that has many advantages. It was after I compared and contrasted two students, ANON_NAME_0 and ANON_NAME_1, that I finally decided to choose ANON_NAME_1 as a partner.

English Language Institute (ELI) is a good choice for students who want to study English as a foreign language. The ELI is appropriate for many nationalities. ELI enrollment as of September 12, 2008, is for example, 40 students from Korea, 17 students from Libya, 16 students from Japan, and 15 students from Saudi Arabia. 63% are male and 37% female. The ELI has a stable program. It is appropriate for every level. It has strong courses and excellent teachers. ANON_NAME_0 said, "The ELI is a good place to study because it has good courses and professional teachers." Also the percentage of the students who enrolled in five courses in the ELI is 66.67%. The courses of the ELI have many advantages for the student to become better for example they have many exercise for practice. In addition, the ELI has many activities, they are increasing every semester. The ELI is a good place to learn the English language. I recommend the ELI to every student who wants to study English.

Recycling is very important to make our valuable resource last longer. While convince the people by recycling is not always easy. There are three possible solutions to get people to recycle: educate the people about the advantages of recycling, encourage them by providing prizes or gifts, punishment them for failing to recycle.

At first, ANON_NAME_0 and ANON_NAME_1 have a lot of things in common. Both ANON_NAME_0 and ANON_NAME_1 are cooperative students. They always help anyone in the class who needs help. Also, ANON_NAME_0 is as studious as ANON_NAME_1. For example, ANON_NAME_0 always asks questions and he always does his homework. ANON_NAME_1 is a good note taker and he always tries to get perfect score on his tests. Actually, I knew these things about them because they have the same classes as me.

Although, they have many things in common, there are several differences between them. In so far as personality, while ANON_NAME_1 is shy, ANON_NAME_0 is a social person. Also, ANON_NAME_0 is from Libya, but ANON_NAME_1 is from Korea. So, ANON_NAME_0's native language is Arabic; however, ANON_NAME_1's native language is Korean. ANON_NAME_0 speaks very fast, but ANON_NAME_1 speaks slowly.

In conclusion, after I analyzed the similarities and differences between ANON_NAME_0 and ANON_NAME_1, I think I chose the right person as a partner. Working with a partner from different country, with a different culture and a different language has many advantages, such as the exchange of information about culture. The most important advantage about working with a partner is that we have to use the English language to understand each other. I found all of these things in ANON_NAME_1, so I chose ANON_NAME_1 as a partner.

First of all, educate the people about the advantages of recycling is very important to get them to recycle. For instance, everybody should be aware that there are many items causes problem to the environment. "This one of the most commonly used approaches it seems. Scare people with the facts about global warming, the mountains of west we create and the air, water and land pollution everywhere." (2007, JPDD, ¬∂2)y recycling we can protect the environment. Also, recycling useful way to save money, because the items that we recycle them we can buy them by cost cheaper than before.

Another solution to this problem, we can get people to recycle by providing prizes or gifts. To illustrate, at school we can provide gifts to students who recycle any used things at school especially, their own items. In addition, when the employees that are recycling receive rising on their salary. Consequently, that will make the employees compete on recycling.

Moreover, last solution which we can use due to being the previous solutions are not successful is scare the people by making programs in every channel on TV or radio that issue possibility of punishing people for failing to recycle. The punishment is by paying high value of money or taking them to prison for months.

In conclusion, the people should be smart enough to protecting their environment, saving money and avid spending even few hours in the prison. Hopefully, these solutions achieve our target that was getting people to recycle.

(*Continued*)

Writing 5

Life with or without children

There are different opinions about having children. Some people choose the life with children and they can't imagine their life without child while some people decide to live without children. Both have reasons for their decisions. Many people believe that the life without children is happier than it without, however, after my experience of having children many aspects revealed the opposite.

Although, many couples know that they came to the life from their parent for making the life continues, they simply decide to live without children. In fact, they always have different reasons. For instance, the most important reason for their decision is saving money they believe that having children requires spending a lot of money to meet children's needs. Another reason is they will feel less freedom after they had children. To illustrate, they can't spend a lot of time outside, they can't also travel from place to place easy. Since they have to worry about the weather of any place they will travel to if it is appropriate for their children or not. Actually, they don't want to be worried about any thing they need their life continues as the beginning of their marriage. Therefore, people with these opinions have difficulties of imaging having a child. (Children- free-living life without children).

Some people are thinking differently. They consider having a child is the most exciting event in their life. Since having a baby will change their life from a cold life to excited life. Seen their baby growing up everyday gives them a great feeling about what they did they gave life to new person to sharing them the life. So their interests are about meeting their child needs and also they don't consider they money that they spend their child is wasted money. In addition, they try to catch any chance to spend time with their child. They believe that they can make balance between their special interests and time and the time, which they spend with their child. Moreover, they think that traveling more enjoyable with their children.

Raising the Driving Age

Every day the number of accidents and victims increase. Many statistics have proved that one of the underlying reasons is driving at a young age. In fact, driving at a young age is very dangerous. It usually ends up with victims, which sometimes include the driver. Therefore, the driving age should be raised from 16 to 18.

Many scientists consider driving at 16 very dangerous 2because at this age the area of the brain called the executive branch is not developed. According to ANON_NAME_0 David, "New findings from brain researchers at the National Institutes of Health explain for the first time why efforts to protect the youngest drivers usually fail. The weak link: what's called "the executive branch "of the teen brain, the part that weighs risk, makes judgments and controls impulsive behavior. Scientists at the NIH campus in Bethesda, Md., have found that this vital area develops through the teenage years and isn't fully mature until age 25." Therefore teenagers at this age shouldn't be allowed to drive because they cannot control their behavior.

In addition, the brain's response to the stress of driving at age 18 is more responsible than the response at age 16, which is more emotion. People at age 18 can get married. Giving them this right is evidence that people at this age are adult enough to make decisions in many aspects in their lives, so it makes sense that the driving age should be raised to18.

Another reason for raising the driving age is to save more lives. The number of cases of death by accident increase every day and statistics reveal that most of these accidents were caused by age 16 drivers "On average, two people die every day across the USA in vehicles driven by 16-year-old drivers. One in five 16 year-olds will have a reportable car crash within the first year," said ANON_NAME_1. (USA TODAY)

In contrast, the life without child is more freedom but it less excited. People who have ability to have baby are not aware about the feeling of disability to have a baby. Recently, there are a lot of research to help many couples to have baby every couple waiting in hops having baby "When Pamela Mahoney and Alex Tsigdinos were married, they never thought they would have trouble having a baby. But after 11 years and many fertility treatments, they are still only a family of two" (Barrow, 2008). On other hand, the life with child is a stable life and plenty of happiness.

In conclusion, looking for appropriate style of life depends on people's opinions. People usually are different in their framework about style of life and about the future having baby is one of them. Some have desire of having baby, and some not. In my opinion, having baby has many good impacts on our life at present and in the future.

Bibliography

Child free -living life without children from WWW. ANON_ URLSITE fertility/31-child free -living-life without -children. html

Barrow, B. Tuesday, June 10 2008.F acing life without children when it is not by choice from, ANON_URLPAGE pati.13598254.html

Another point for raising the driving age is reducing the terrible impact on parents. Many parents have lost their children because of driving at 16 years old. Gayle Bell, whose 16-year-old daughter, Jessie, rolled her small car into a Missouri ditch and died in July 2003, said that she used to happily be Jessie's "ride." She would give anything to drive Jessie again. Losing children in a car accident affects their parents. Those parents live in a difficult situation; they miss their children and they regret their decision that allows them to drive early.

Despite these reasons, some people argue about raising the driving age. They consider driving at 16 ages a good idea for two reasons: one is because teenagers need to learn to drive when they are still under observation their parents. In addition, raising the age to 18 when teens have no supervision makes many events come together. At this age, they are in college and at this age the desire to try alcohol starts. The other reason for an argument is parents feel inconvenienced when they have to take their children to school or any place their children want, which will decrease the participation of children in many activities. (Clark, 2008)

However, after new research has suggested that there is a natural problem in 16-year-old's brains negates control their behavior, parents care has nothing to do with that. Even though they can control how many times their children can use their car and when, they cannot control their decisions during driving, especially when they drive alone. Therefore, refusing to raise the driving age for this reason is not a rationale.

In conclusion, after reviewing these physical and social reasons, which support the necessity of raising the driving age. After all the research also that explain why age 16 too young to drive a car, there is no reason to refuse to raise the minimum driving age. To save lives and reduce the impact on parents should be ruled that the driving age is 18.

Bibliography

Clark, D. December (2008) raising the minimum of driving age from, http:// ANON_URLPAGE

ANON_NAME_1, R. USA TODAY from, http:// ANON_URLPAGE ANON_URLSITE/newsroom/ Research _USA % 20 TODAY. PDF

Appendix II

BN7 Arabic L1. Writing Texts.
Errors Have Not Been Corrected

Writing 3

Two heads are better than one. I really a gree with this.In my opinion,you should participate with your classmate or your wife. Therefore,that gives you some help.For example,on the day I had probleme at my wedding. The probleme is conflict between myself and My wife's father. The conflict is about the weeding date. Her father's told me " we can not do it in this month." After that I told her " The apropriate date is in this month." She told me " I agee with you,I will tray to tell my father and Convinced him." Then her father is accept and he is solved I and she problames. So that,it is significant to take opinions from your wife or your father about anythings. Finally, There is wisdom in Arabic that says " The one hand does not clap."

Saudi Arabia and the United states have many kinds dishes to eat. First of all,Saudi Arabia has traditional food and so does America.For example,the traditional food in Saudi Arabia is Kapssh. Kapssh are consist of meat and rice.It is a popular dish in Saudi Arabia. An American traditional food is the Hamburger. they are contain beef, vegetables and a bun. Both Saudi Arabia and the United States use the convenience foods. Convenience food is food that is partly or completely prepared already. It is bought in supermarket. There are many kind of the convenient foods. For example, fish and chicken. Frankly, Kapssh and Hamburger are pleasant.

Saudi Arabia is different than the United States in preparation of food. First of all, Saudi Arabia uses less convenience foods than the United States because the Saudi citizens used to cook but now they did not. On the other hand, American people used to eat convenience foods. In fact, American sometimes cook and prepare foods, but there are differences between preparation of food in these countries. The most important thing is spice. Spice is a powder or seed taken from plants that is put into food to give it special taste. Although, American food is unpleasant, Saudi food is delicious.

(*Continued*)

Writing 4

America one of a lot countries which has big economic. American economic is located in the first position in economic world. In addition, It influences in the world If it lose a dealing. One years ago, America has exposure to new crises. It is called economic crises. There several effect of economic crises such as unemployment, the pries of houses or apartments and the cooperation with some countries.

A company in the US which was the biggest a airlines company all over the united states. The company had a lot of projects and money. In addition it had more than 100.000 employees to do its projects in last months, It lost many project because of economic crisis. Also, It lost a lot of money. Therefore it released many of its employees.Now, it has 30.000 employees because of this crises

The apartments and the houses used to be expensive. Three years ago, The pries of apartment was 700 $ for one bedroom. In addition, it was not with the utilizations. For instance, Electricity and Water. Also, the house was more expensive than the apartment. It is approximately 2000$ for 3 bedroom per month. Now, because of economic crises, It is cheaper more than before. The price is 450 $ for the apartments and 1300$ for the houses.

America had a huge cooperation with the world. It cooperated in a lot of aspects. For example, the science and technology. During this year, America has encumbrance to do this activities with countries because of economic crises. All the science projects stopped therefore, that will not create improvement in education level.

Last of all, this crises has effected strongly in the US. Some business men say America will pass this crises in 2012 and everything will return back to the normal level. Also it is going to be available jobs at that year, but they are not sure

Japan is the real country all over the world. Japan had been poor country in the last centuries, but now it's a big industrial country. First of all, Japan has sent some trainers to Europe world in order to learn very well and learn his country. One of these trainers succeeded and he found out how to create generator for any machine. After he came to his country, Japan established 200 colleges of technology because they want to increase ability on create products to Japan student to be creative man. Anther aspect If we look to economic development now, you will see the different numbers between the last years and Now. For example. Last years, Japan got the third position in the word. I think Japan will be the best country all over the world after couple of years. Finally. Why do not I go to this country I hope to go there as soon as possible.

Writing 5

"Children are a problem!" As we can see via the world countries, the most developed countries have changed their lives by themselves. In other words, most of countries right now try hard to not have more than 2 kids as usual Instead of having more than two in the past. Apparently, that exists in many areas in the world. An example of which is Saudi Arabia. Because of the deep-rooted traditions and culture. Most of Saudi people like to have a lot of children no matter what job you have! However, in Europe or the US, the circumstances are completely different. There are many reasons for reducing children in developed countries. Some of which are expense of life, managing or controlling on children and external factors that make parents very curious about the future. Further explanations will be provided below.

To begin with, one of the most compelling reasons of reducing the number of children in developed countries such as The U.S or United Kingdom is education. In this age, life is very expensive. People have to pay many things to survive. Therefore, these parents anticipate that will happen in the future when their income cannot cover their potential children. The second reason is the Health care which is the crucial need in our life. It has become more and more expensive fast because of the progress of medicine. Consequently, parents try to avoid having more children in the future. Furthermore, children did used to go the king radian school where they can play and study at the same time. Today, children need to have their own technological and learning things. However, some parents cannot offer these things to three or four children. The last reason is food which is source of life. It can be seen everywhere in the world that there is poor family who cannot find their daily food.

The internet is one of the world necessary tools in this time. The range of using the Internet used to be restricted in some aspects in our life such as the military sector, but the Internet has become more and more CRUCIAL thing in other aspects such as education, communication among people. It enables people to talk with anyone regardless the distance is. However, it is an INEVETIBLE fact that everything has its positive and negative effects. Therefore, the internet can wrongly educate some people bad things especially teenagers who do not have the responsibility about the potential risk. Moreover, the security of information is very important issue that we are suffering in today. Even though, the government should control on Internet: some people feel that the government should not do that and let them have completed freedom to access the Internet.

Opponents think that the internet is one of their human rights as most people in the world have. They think that Internet can exploit their free time by talking or chatting with friends or others. Once they come back from school, they open the internet to talk with unknown friends. In my perspective, Internet strongly and negatively affect youngest notably teenager who are not aware about the risk of communicating with people who have never talked to them before. It is obvious that they COMPENSATE their wasted time in doing untargeted purposes such as in communicating with friend instead of using it for educational purposes such as reading and researching in beneficial sites that offer many educational sources for students or professionals. Teenagers need to be

(Continued)

Moreover, there are some reasonable and external factors. One of which is Internet. Nowadays, the internet has become a crucial tool to deal with people and to learn or to communicate with them in many aspects such as in university or in public. But everything in our life has advantages and disadvantages at the same time. One of the disadvantages is potential tool to teach children the bad links in the internet which is Sexual site. As soon as they enter the website, they will be addicted to it. From my perspective, it is very hard to make children give up this habit, thus, parents will not be able to stop them from doing that in future.

Finally, controlling on children could be a big issue in the future when they have more than two or three kids. Having two children can be beneficial for parents, therefore they can have the opportunity to communicate and teach them when they have a chance to do that. From my own experience, my family is consisting of 6 individuals. The kids who took maintenance from our parents are only two, who are the oldest. However, the rest of them were not taught carefully by my parents

In conclusion, as I mention above, the reasons of reducing the figure of children are attributed to the expense of life in many aspect such as education, Health care and food and controlling on children. Will the community return to the traditional custom?

restricted in using the internet in terms of proven and obvious risk. For instance, many sites EXHIBIT sexual videos and pictures which do not correspond with some people age. Therefore, internet will have a strong impact on this group of people in their behavior and future education. On the other hand, these people feel that this is unavoidable thing even and can educate them sex methods before getting married.

In addition to the previous reason, opponents feel that the internet should not be monitored by the government or any authoritical organizations such as the intelligence agent. To begin with, as far as I see, there are many websites that can reveal peoples' information, let's take the Face book as a realistic example. In this site, people are able to read your profile and specific information such as the name, age, address and also your phone number. Furthermore, this websites is designed to EXHIBIT your pictures for public. Obviously, some Facebook members are professional photographers. They usually put their beautiful and awesome pictures' on this website. It can be true that people think it is quite helpful for readers for knowing where they are. As a result; their friends will start asking about the area they live in.

On the other hand, I think it might be potential dangerous in their life because of some compelling reasons. Showing any pictures in the Face book can have some negative consequences. For example, friends are capable to steal a picture of you and post it in their computers or putting the picture in their project without asking for a valid permission. Actually, it is very easy to copy the picture and put it in somewhere you prefer. In my personal view, the only one who can stop this thing is the government by controlling on this website so it can save peoples' rights. In January 2010, a lawsuit was filed against an online forum, ANON_URLSITE, by a Maldives diving charter company (see scubaboard lawsuit). The owner of the company claimed $10 million in damages caused by users of scubaboard, ANON_URLSITE, and the owner of ANON_URLSITE. Individual forum members were named in the lawsuit as "employees" of the forum, despite their identity being anonymous except for their IP address to the moderators and owners of ANON_URLSITE. This lawsuit demonstrates the vulnerability of internet websites, internet forums, and even ANON_URLPAGE local and regional lawsuits for libel and damages 1

The Department of Defense filters certain IP addresses. The US military's filtering policy is laid out in a report to congress entitled "Department of Defense Personnel Access to the Internet". 1

Another issue is that the Internet can be another tool or made product to publicize the hate among people by distorting the fact of something. To be more specific, the media has been a strong method for a long time to mobilize peoples' feelings against a group of people. As I can see, Media has been doing works against Islamic religion by making some jokes about them and sometimes makes them feel that they are MANIPULATIVE by some, so that Muslims do not become comfortable when visiting some countries. According to my experience, in particularly using the internet to communicate with foreigners, once I write in any forums that I am a Muslim, they immediately feel afraid and prefer to leave.

(Continued)

What the issue is that people generalize that all Muslims are the same which means that they all have the same quality "BAD PEOPLE". In my perspective, I do not think it is fair to say that the other religions are bad; it can be true that there are some bad people; however, we should get the relationship close. That thing can only be made by government contribution by controlling on people comments. In this way, the world can live safely!

However, when I ask the family that I live with them, they have another opinion about controlling people's comments in the internet by the government. They basically feel that it is one of their human rights to express their opinions about others via the internet. Thinking that the hate is unavoidable thing in life and you cannot dispose of it.

In conclusion, all these rational reasons of misusing of the internet lead me to agree with the concept that the government must control on the internet in all its aspects because of the negative consequences that I mention above such as publicizing the hate among people, disclosing the personal information and eventually it waste people time.

References: (n.d.) encyclopedia of Wikipedia. Retrieved form. ANON_URLPAGE

Word counts: 1022

Appendix III

AQ1 Chinese L1. Writing Texts: Errors Have Not Been Corrected

Writing 3

October, 24 2006

Dear Dad and Mom,

We moved to Pittsburgh from last October, it is nearly one year since our staying in US. Right now we live here more comfortable than we do at the beginning. We gradually feel we need to buy a car. We are considering buying a used car, it is much cheaper than a new car. We found two different cars in dealer, but we do not know much about car. We prefer Japanese model car to American model. Some friends suggest that Japanese car is less oil consuming than American car. The car price depends on the product time, mileage, model and brand. The earlier product with higher mileage are cheaper than later product and lower mileage. However, generally the Japanese car is more expensive than American car.

We still have not made final decision on choosing, we would like to get your suggestion.

Love,

Writing 4

Culture Shock

Culture shock is a period of time you need to adjust when you first come to a new country. It happens frequently for the international students. When you first come to a new country different from your own, they are forced to meet your everyday needs. If you couldnt cope with these new problems better, you will have some stress. It is also important thing how to adjust about culture shock.

My successful cooking experience

One of the things that I have been successful at was cooking. First, I always think cooking is an interesting thing. I am interested in cooking Chinese food. For example, if I tasted something good, I like to ask them how to make it, so I collected many recipes, but I had no time to try to cook, because my work was very busy when I lived in China. The second thing was that I had lots of time when I lived in Germany last year. I didnt take any work and I stayed at home. I was enjoying this period time, so I started to try to cook Chinese food using my collecting recipes, but sometimes I succeed, sometimes I failed and it didnt smell good. I wanted to improve my cooking. The final thing was that I met a friend whos good at cooking when I lived in Germany last year. I was so lucky! She taught me many useful skills and corrected some mistakes for me, I thought these were very important things and helpful for me, so I cooked Chinese food better than before.

Be a successful language learner

Learning a new language is always difficult as an un-native speaker. Different learner has different purposes of learning a new language and also different learners make use different ways to learn. About how to become a successful language learner, I have three important suggestions: get your final goal clearly in your heart, improve your learning skills and make use of the resource your around.

Climate, food, landscapes, people and language all seem strange to you. For example, when I first came to live in the U.S., I was unprepared to live here, I miss my homeland, my family and my friends, even cry a lot. Your English may not be as good as you expected, maybe you have some stress from your academic life or difficult experience. An article in WWW Sites ANON_NAME_0 said: "I had a lot of trouble at first getting adapted to living in the USA. What frustrated me most was that I did not know how even this simplest things worked!

If you feel this way, it is important not to panic. Culture shock is a normal reaction to face new surroundings. Getting over culture shock depends upon you. As you become adjusted to the U.S. culture and attitudes and begin to know your way around, you will start to adapt to and understand your new surroundings and way of life.

If your English may not be as good as you expected, it is unreasonable to expect to do things perfectly the first time, no matter how much information you read or how well you speak English. Just do your best. Just give yourself some time and things would gradually get easier (Nawuma).

If you have some stress from your academic life, you need to open your mind to experience the unknown. You don't think of the U.S. culture as better or worse than your native culture, you will be more willing to try new things. When I studied English in ELI, I try to experience many new things for me, such as taking part in many ELI activities.

Finally, don't worry about making a mistake. Just keep a positive attitude. For example, the simple things like temperatures and measurements were difficult to understand because Americans do not use the Metric system as in my country. Sometimes I felt silly and it made me sad. But after awhile, I could do all these things. I guess I just had to give myself a bit of time to learn.

First of all, it is important to know your goal of learning language. Some learners want to pass the language test, while others are only interested in learning language. According to your final goals, you will have to choose different materials to meet your requires.

The second suggestion is to get your own learning styles since people always learn in different pathways. Someone has to see it to believe it and others prefer to listen first. Someone takes notes, someone draws in their notebooks. Others like to discuss in small groups. If your learning can follow your learning styles, then you can improve your learning efficiency.

The final is using environment around. You can find many native speakers beside you. You should try to communicate with them. You will get more practice and know more deep about the new language. That is important and useful approach for language learning.

I believe it is hard to grasp a new language. You will feel more confident in being a successful language learner when you keep trying and improving.

Be a successful language learner

Learning a new language is always difficult as an un-native speaker. Different learner has different purposes of learning a new language and also different learners make use different ways to learn. About how to become a successful language learner, I have three important suggestions: get your final goal clearly in your heart, improve your learning skills and make use of the resource your around.

First of all, it is important to know your goal of learning language. Some learners want to pass the language test, while others are only interested in learning language. According to your final goals, you will have to choose different materials to meet your requires.

(Continued)

After my adjustments, I feel my life in the U.S become more familiar to me and day to day life become easier. I can live with the differences and confusions but still enjoy myself.

Source: Dinan, Bulgaria. Culture Shock by the Bureau of Educational and Cultural Affairs, U.S Department of State. ANON_URLPAGE

Nawuma, Republic of Togo. Culture Shock by the Bureau of Educational and Cultural Affairs, U.S Department of State. ANON_URLPAGE

Writing 5

Before coming, we usually have many images about a new country's culture. For example, Having been the U.S, I have found two things to be different and a similar thing from what I magic: the necessity of a car and the low price of goods.

The first thing that gave me a shock is the necessity of a car in the U.S. Before coming, I thought the U.S was an advance and modern country. It was not important and necessary for having a car. The public transportation must be convenient. There were many kinds of transportations which are quick and convenient. Such as subway, train and bus. Even I thought I could take either subway or train or bus if I had only a ticket at the same day. In contrast, when I came to the U.S., I was disappointed to the public transportation. Train and subway arent important transportations.

The second suggestion is to get your own learning styles since people always learn in different pathways. Someone has to see it to believe it and others prefer to listen first. Someone takes notes, someone draws in their notebooks. Others like to discuss in small groups. If your learning can follow your learning styles, then you can improve your learning efficiency.

The final is using environment around. You can find many native speakers beside you. You should try to communicate with them. You will get more practice and know more deep about the new language. That is important and useful approach for language learning.

I believe it is hard to grasp a new language. You will feel more confident in being a successful language learner when you keep trying and improving.

Everyone has a different hobby. People who enjoy sport spend time and strength on doing exercise and watching sport race. People who enjoy reading read many books in their free time. Similarly, some like to save stamps, dolls, ever toys. However, I enjoy saving coins. I think saving coins is a worthwhile hobby. In fact, saving coins are not only valuable memories, but also enrich your knowledge.

First of all, I think saving coins helps you remember special occasions. Every country has its own coins. For example, in 2004 I lived in Germany. When I first went shopping I was attracted by different kinds of coins. Later I knew 15 countries began using the Euro in 2002, so Euro in 2002 has special meaning. found each country has eight coins with different face value.

Bus is a popular transportation, but it isnt convenient. For example, the bus in Pittsburgh has been thought more convenient than the bus in other city. But on Saturday and Sunday some buses run, it is difficult for shopping on Saturday or Sunday. The shopping Malls are built far away. So if you dont have the car, you wont comfortable in your life.

The second thing was the price of goods. Before I came to the U.S., I thought the price of goods was high. When I came to the U.S., I found it was not true. I was surprised. I remember I had bought nice pants for only 2 dollars. I couldnt believe it. However, it was really happened. Gradually, I understood if I knew some tricks, I bought the goods at the low prices all the time. For example, usually on Holiday, there are many stores have a big sale. Sometimes there are not only 75% off, but also there are extra 30% – 50% off. I was surprised by the low price of goods. It was interesting and amazing thing..In spite of these differences. However, I found similar to images. Before coming, I thought the American people were friendly. It was true. If you meet someone who dont know each other, they usually give you a smile or say hello. Your feeling is comfortable. If you have a trouble, you ask someone help, they often give you on time. I remember one day I went to see my doctor, but I lost my way at the hospital. I asked someone, at the beginning he told me direction. lately, he found I was confused, he took me go to the doctors office. He is very friendly.

In conclusion, when you come to a new country different your images, you should open your eyes and adjust your attitude.

I wanted to begin to save coins. I found each country has eight coins with different face value. It was very difficult to save a complet set of coins of a country. The process of saving coins was a full of fun and valuable memories. I remembered, in 2005, I got a chance to visit Holand. In order to save this countrys coins, I had to buy many postcards several times for getting their coins. Each time, when I am looking at those coins that I saved from different countries I had ever visited. Those coins reminded me the wonderful time I spent in their country.

In addition, saving coins can increase your knowledge. Different country has different culture. Coins are always designed for special meaning. Some are famous places or person, some are special events. You are attracted and willing to know their culture and their country. You can learn some history. For example, there is always a head statue of president on the coins of American. Different period history has different president. Why was this president selected? What happened in this period? What did the special or important matter mean? Saving coins is not only make you are interested in their countrys history and open your eyes to the world, but also teach you many knowledge.

In conclusion, saving coins broaden your insight and enrich your experience. I am very glad to have this hobby and I usually share my pleasure and knowledge with my family members. Here I strongly recommend collection of coins to you and hope you can have fun from this process.

Appendix IV

BL7. Chinese L1. Writing Texts: Errors Have Not Been Corrected

Writing 3

Before I came to the United States, I used to live in my home country, Taiwan. For two years, I used to work for a Taiwanese opera company in Taipei. Also, I used to teach traditional Chinese musical instrument to junior and senior high school students. I used to go to work by subway everyday, even on the weekends. Although I used to work so hard, I enjoyed my busy working life.

Now I am improving my English skills at ELI. I cannot work and also don't go to school everyday. I have a lot of free time to do the things that I wanted to do long time ago, such as watching all the episodes from FRIENDS, taking a walk in the sunny afternoon and spending all day in a huge shopping mall. After I can use English skills fluently, I want to find a job in the United States because I love to work with other people.

Writing 4

The Changing Role of Women

Woman's role in this society has changed dramatically in the last century. More than 100 years ago, most women were treated as only housewives. Their life's goals included staying at home all day, doing house chores, having a large family, and raising the children. However, in most countries today, many women not only perform very well in their education and their occupation, they also share the same responsibilities as men.

I have already traveled to several beautiful cities, such as ANON_NAME_0, Lyon (France), Madrid (Spain), Venice (Italy), Wolfsburg (Germany), Innsbruck (Austria), Mexico City (Mexico), Johannesburg (South Africa), ANON_NAME_1 ANON_NAME_2, Beijing, Yunnan (China) and New York. I have walked on the most fantastic Avenue des Champs Elysees and shopped like a crazy woman. I have taken a Gondola through the rivers in Venice. I have been dead drunk with the famous Germany's beer in a pub in Wolfsburg. I have seen the most amazing beautiful Swarovski crystals in Innsbruck. I have stood on the top of the ANON_NAME_3 Pyramid and felt the magic of ancient culture in Mexico. Although I have gone to many places, but I still want to go to some places that I have never seen with my own eyes. I would like to see the blue sky and the green Aegean Sea in Greece. I would like to have an adventure in wild Africa. I would like to touch the mysterious pyramid with my own hand in Egypt. The whole world is very big and I hope I can remember all the sceneries that I have seen in my mind.

Traditional Chinese Music in Taiwan

Traditional Chinese instruments have been around through thousands of generations during more than 5000 years of Chinese history. Chinese instruments were used for Traditional Chinese orchestra performances, theater, opera, and other musical activities. In the modern Chinese society, the rise of Western instruments such as piano and violin caused some decline in people's interest in Chinese instruments. About 20 years ago in the 1980's, several city governments in Taiwan decided to provide money to raise the interest once again. The city governments' actions 20 years ago had 3 main effects; including forming several music schools, raising talented music students in challenging competitions, and reviving people's interest in Chinese music today.

(Continued)

Many women today have very high educational degrees. Families today think that not only their sons need to go to school. 100 years ago, it would not be very easy to receive degrees for women. Most women today have at least university degrees, and some even have Master's degrees or Doctor's degrees. They have degrees in many difficult fields, such as engineering, computer, astronomy, and medicine.

Many women today also have very high paying occupations. There are women in many kinds of professions. Many big companies have female businesswomen. Many doctors, engineers and astronomers in science today are also female. A lot of women have also become influential politicians in many countries. This is very different from 100 years ago, when most women stayed at home to cook and raise children.

Women today share the same responsibilities as men. Many husbands and wives today share house work at home. Some husbands sometimes even cook for the family. Today's women also work hard to earn money for their families. Husbands are not the only authority in most families anymore.

The role of women in today's world is very different from the role they had 100 years ago. Women today work hard in school to receive high level degrees. Women today also do well in many jobs that only men could do 100 years ago. Finally, today's women share a lot of family responsibilities with men. Most of them do not just depend on their husbands anymore. The role of woman will keep changing and improving and women will have even better roles in the future.

Before 1988, there were already students studying Chinese instruments in elementary school. However, there were not many students. The city government of Kaohsiung City, Taiwan, my hometown, started to spend money and consequently formed a music school called Experimental School for Chinese Music. The government wanted to see how people reacted to the formation of this school. Therefore they called this experimental school. Not only my school was formed, but several other schools also followed. I was one of the first students to join in this experimental school for Chinese music.

As a result of the formation of the schools, the schools started to hire Chinese musical instrument teachers and recruit and raise students. The students applied to the schools, took an IQ exam, and performed an instrument, usually piano or violin. Students who were recruited learned to play different Chinese instruments. The instrument I played was called Pi-Pa. After years of practice, I competed in individual competitions and won championships several times in Taiwan because of my hard work. Students also formed Chinese orchestras and performed in city and then national competitions. In 1992, my school orchestra won the championship in the whole Taiwan, as a consequence of our teachers' great teaching and our excellent team work.

The city governments' investment 20 years ago has also revived the interest in Chinese music for Taiwanese people today. People in Taiwan now think learning Chinese instrument is as important as learning Western instruments. If someone can play a Chinese instrument, it is actually a very special thing, due to so many people playing piano or violin. Talented Chinese musicians now perform in many concerts, both solo and as an orchestra. Chinese music is now a large part of Taiwanese culture.

20 years ago, experimental schools for Chinese music were first formed. Today, there are many more elementary schools, junior high schools, senior high schools, and even universities that have Chinese orchestras. Because of the rising number of students who decide to learn Chinese instruments, every year there is a lot of competitions for different levels, from elementary school to university. Just like China, there are many talented Chinese instrument players in Taiwan now. The government did a very wonderful job and now Chinese music is a very important part of Taiwanese culture.

Making Your Own Luck

Making Your Own Luck

2 (When I woke up the next morning, I was surprised to find that I had overslept and would be late for work. As I rushed down the stairs to eat a quick breakfast, I tripped over my cat and) tried to ignore his crying sounds as if he needed my help. However, I suddenly discovered that he got his whole body wet because he broke the vase on my computer desk, and the water spilled over my laptop, too! All I could do was to forget about my breakfast and to dry my cat off with a hair dryer and my poor, expensive laptop with a towel. At the same time, I figured out that I was going to be late to work.

3 (On my way to work, I decided to take a shortcut through an old part of town.) I have passed the path once before, but I was not sure I could find the correct direction. However, I had to save time, so I turned left and entered the path which was covered with dense trees. After 10 minutes, I finally admitted that I lost my way. I have never felt so much frustration before, and I really wanted to go to hell if I could. I called my older brother and asked him the direction, but he couldn't understand my location that I described to him. Oh! Somebody help me, please! I couldn't do anything but call the police, and I finally found the way to work.

Writing 5

Happy Chinese New Year!

Imagine a situation where there is a huge, evil, and vicious monster that always comes to your hometown to disturb and eat livestock, or even people, once every 365 days. What would you do to survive in this situation? Thousands of years ago, according to the traditional Chinese legend, the Chinese people had to face the monster "Nian." The monster was called "Nian", meaning "year", because the monster came once a year. During the periods that the Nian monster appeared, the ancient Chinese people discovered there were three main things that it was very afraid of. They used the color red, loud sounds and bright lights, and stayed in the house together and made noise as weapons to scare Nian away every year. This is the reason why Chinese New Year celebrations ever since then include using red decorations and envelopes; lighting firecrackers, bright torches and red lanterns; and keeping all family members inside the house together.

(Continued)

Each year before Nian came, on Chinese New Year's Eve, the first thing that ancient Chinese people needed to do was to prepare red decorations and paste them on walls, windows and doors of the house to scare Nian away. Also, they would prepare the red envelopes with a little money, called "lucky money", to give to elders and children, not only to protect them from Nian, but also to keep them healthy and safe for the entire next new year. Even today, the red decorations people install have become the "spring couplets". These are paper scrolls and squares inscribed with blesses and auspicious words, such as good fortune, wealth, happiness and springtime. Also, the paper squares are usually pasted upside down, because the Chinese word for "upside down" is a homonym of the word "arrival". Thus, the spring couplets represent the arrival of spring and that a whole new year is coming. In addition, the red envelopes with money have become the most important part of Chinese New Year for children.

The second thing that would be done before Nian came was to light firecrackers all day and night to drive Nian away. The ancient Chinese people would also light bright torches and red lanterns and then hang them around the house. Today, people still light red lanterns and firecrackers, especially a huge barrage of firecrackers to symbolize the family's everlasting fortune. However, lighting bright torches is no longer necessary. Instead people keep lights on for the entire night and also try to stay up all night to welcome the New Year. It was long believed that by doing so on New Year's Eve, the elder generation will live a longer life.

4 (When I arrived at work, I found a note on my desk from my boss. She wanted to see me right away. I took a deep breath and walked into her office. As I stepped inside, I noticed a scowl on her face.) I searched my mind very quickly and tried to recall if I forgot to do anything that she assigned to me, and fortunately, the answer was no, I thought. Then, she looked at me and spoke chillingly, "Do you know what time it is? What do you think you're doing?" I felt a cold breeze through my back and I had no idea what I could say. Before I answered, she spoke again, "Are you crazy? What is this you sent to our most primary, significant customer yesterday?" She threw a piece of paper at my face. When I saw the title, I thought that was a copy from the e-mail I sent to Mr. Richest yesterday. However, after I read the details, I thought today will be the last day at my job. It was not the proposal that I wanted to e-mail to Mr. Richest, instead the sorry e-mail that I sent to my boyfriend! "My dear, dearest Paul honey, I'm so sorry for yelling at you last night just because you forgot to wash my underwear. . . " I couldn't read it anymore! The only one thing I could say was I promised that I would fix it right now and fled out her office.

The most important thing before Nian came was to keep all family members in the house together. The ancient Chinese family members would stay in the house and talked loudly to each other. It was not only to scare Nian away, but also the members would have more courage when they stayed together. Now, people living far away from their families will always begin to prepare for their journey home several days before Chinese New Year's Eve. Then, everybody reunites and enjoys a magnificent dinner together. The dinner tends to be especially lavish and every dish regarded as symbols of good luck are served. During the most important meal of the year, family members talk about the past year's events that happened to each of them and the new hope for the next new year. During Chinese New Year's Eve, spending time with family members is the most important thing after people worked hard during the past year.

Today, people keep these traditional habits and events to continue the most significant festival for Chinese people around the world. The red decorations and envelopes, firecrackers, bright torches and red lanterns, and keeping all family members in the house together are all symbols that "tradition" and "family" play very important roles in Chinese people's notions and lives. No matter what changes may occur during this time, the notion of staying together with family will always connect the hearts of family members and Chinese New Year celebrations.

(*Continued*)

Appendix V

AY3 Japanese L1. Writing Texts: Errors Have Not Been Corrected

Writing 3

The ELI is a good place to study English as a foreign language. I would like to point out 3 major reasons for that. First, because students of the ELI came from more than 14 different countries all over the world, each student has to use English to communicate each other. If most part of students came from single country, students likely spoke their own mother language to communicate among the students. In this case, English progress of the students would be inhibited, since they loss their opportunity to speak English. " I can make a friend from many countries, and I can get an opportunity to speak English," ANON_NAME_0 said. Second, the activities outside the campus offer the students much an opportunities to learn English. In fact, there are many activities in the ELI, and the activities are just on the increase. Finally, the ELI has not only a single course like speaking but, all of English learning course including speaking, listening, writing, and grammar courses. This is an important point to note that Taking all these 5 courses would lead the students to fair and non-biased English progress. Actually, the largest group of the students, 66.67%, took all of 5 courses at a same semester. For these three reasons, it is naturally led to a conclusion that the ELI is on of the best institutes to study English as a foreign language.

My favorite food is vegetable soup, because I would like to improve my health. I really want to keep a balanced diet. I'd like to share with you the recipe of vegetable soup. First, lightly peel and slice a carrot in four 1cm thick round shapes and boil them. As in the case of the carrot, precook a white radish and a potato. Second, boil spinach in salted water. Drain and lightly squeeze out of water followed by cutting them into 5cm pieces. Next, slice chicken fillets into 2cm and boil them for about 5 minutes. Finally, add the carrots, the spinach, other vegetables and the chicken fillets to the soup and season the soup with soy sauce, pepper, and salt. Garnish with a lemon peel. It would be plain in tastes and nourishing broth. The soup contains a lot of vitamins and other essential nourishment. I will enjoy good health when I continue eating it.

(Continued)

Writing 4

There is limit to the Earth's resources. We will cause exhaustion of resources if we continue using of the resources. We must ensure effective utilization of limited resource. To that end, we have to learn of recycle method. The three most commonly proposed solutions to this Earth's resources problem are a garbage reduction, carry around eco-friendly goods and setting trash bin by category.

The first solution, we have to reduce as much as possible of the trash. For instance, we have to pay when take out the garbage. In doing so, we may stop wasting consumable goods such as tissues and paper dishes. Also, when we buy merchandise, we may carefully examine merchandise to check whether really necessary. This solution is taking good care of Earth's resources.

Another solution, we must carry around eco-friendly goods. For example, when we go to shopping, we use eco-bag and we refrain from using plastic bags. As a result, the amount of garbage will has also been dramatically reduced. Also, most of Japanese supermarkets, we have to pay money for plastic bags. According to the Japanese government, since the introduction of system, the number of plastic bags used has decreased by 60 percent. We must think about switching from waste of resources to eco-friendly alternative.

The best solution, we have to separate the garbage. More specifically, it is increase the use of renewable Earth's resources. Pet bottles, aluminum cans and paper can be recycled. We may save Earth's resources by separating recycle from no recyclable trash. Cyclical use of resources is the most important solution.

As a conclusion, current our life styles rely on mass production, mass consumption and mass disposal. There will be depletion of the Earth's natural resources. We have to bequeath a beautiful environment and valuable resources to subsequent generations. Therefore, we must lead environmental lifestyles. We need to incorporate recycling into daily life.

Japan often experiences natural disasters such as an earthquakes and typhoons due to its geographical and meteorological characteristics. In recent years in particular, many earthquakes and floods have struck the country. For this reason, people have become more anxious about natural disasters. The effects of the earthquake are a change our lifestyle and psychological damage.

Our lifestyle will be destroyed by the earthquake because a large number of houses destroy, and many people will force to evacuate their homes. The earthquake will have also cause serious damage to electric, gas and water supplies. The earthquake sometimes generates a tidal wave that crashed ashore and touch off mudslides. Therefore, it has blocked many roads and methods of transport. As a result, the earthquake will be transformed our lifestyle.

Most important effect, many people will be brought face to face with death. The earthquake causes sudden death of familiar person, relatives and pets. In consequence, victims suffer a great loss and psychological damage. In addition, victims are frightened by an aftershock. Thus they can't go on grieving forever. At worst, these states of mind lead to post-traumatic stress disorder.

As a conclusion, direct damage from the earthquake exist in large numbers. Many people in Japan live in dread of earthquakes because Japan is prone to earthquakes. We predict the widespread damage from the large earthquake, and conduct an evacuation. We want to minimize damage when an earthquake occurs.

Abolition of the Death Penalty

Currently, About 60 countries provide a capital punishment system. In other words, more than two-thirds of the countries in the world have now abolished the death penalty in law or practice. Furthermore, this latter figure has been increasing each year partly due to efforts by the European Union, which has been trying to persuade countries to show greater respect for human rights. Many people think that the death penalty should be abolished in the world. Capital punishment should not be justified for any criminals.

In addition, the Japanese government has conducted an opinion poll on the country's criminal law system. The research focused on capital punishment. More than 80 percent of the respondents accepted capital punishment. This is a 2-point rise from the last poll. It is the first time the number has exceeded 80 percent. These people said criminals should sacrifice their lives in return for the crimes they committed. On the other hand, only 6 percent disagreed with the system, saying criminals should continue to live and make reparations for their crimes. Many Japanese need to shake off conventional wisdom.

The first point, our faith in fundamental human rights should be reaffirmed. Every human has fundamental human rights. According to the Universal Declaration of Human Rights (1948), "Everyone has the right to life, liberty and security of person" (Article 3). It should not be allowed for anybody to deprive us of our right to live. In addition, the Universal Declaration of Human Rights (1948) found, "No one shall be subjected to torture or to cruel, inhuman or degrading treatment or punishment" (Article 5). Consequently, capital punishment must be regarded as homicide.

The Difference between Macintosh and Windows

Which operating system (O/S) do you use now? Why did you decide to use it? Currently, there are two kinds of O/S for our personal computers. One is Macintosh O/S, and the other is Windows O/S. When I bought my current computer, which is the Macintosh O/S, I seriously worried about which O/S was easily accessible for me. Ultimately I chose Macintosh over Windows. Because of the penetration rate, vulnerability to computer viruses, designs, and price.

First, according to Market Share (2009, May), the market share of Windows was 87.75% in May 2009, while that of Macintosh was only 9.81%. Based on this data, it is feasible to say that Windows has an apparently stronger share in the world. However, once we focus on share trends, interestingly, Macintosh's share has been increasing and Windows's share has been decreasing over time. Macintosh's share was 4.43% in 2006, 6.48% in 2007, 7.83% in 2008, and 9.81% in this year. On the other hand, Windows's share was 95.07% in 2006, 92.90% in 2007, 91.08% in 2008, and 87.75% this year.

Second, damages from computer viruses are seen as a threat to both types of computers. Once a virus attacks a computer, the cost is high to retrieve the data. According to C. Andrea, (2006, August 9), "About one in four Internet users said a virus infected their computer in the past two years, costing victims a median $109 to fix the problem, with some consumers reporting losses in the thousands of dollars. About one-third of those hit by viruses said the infection forced them to reformat their hard drives, 16% said they lost important data, and 8% had to replace hardware." Therefore, vulnerability to computer viruses is one of the most important aspects for a computer. Based on this performance, Macintosh has an advantage compared to Windows. Because the share of Macintosh is small, viruses designed to attack Macintosh are rare. Thereby, it is possible to conclude the Macintosh has less possibility to be attacked by viruses.

(Continued)

How can you sentence a suspect to death? There are no perfect people. Therefore, the ruling handed down on the defendant is not always correct. It may be a false accusation unless there is a 100% guarantee or God needs to judge instead of humankind. No one can pronouncement of a perfect judgment. According to Burnett (2002, p. 19), some adjudication might be determined by police misleading investigational results and judges may have bad judgments. Capital punishment should not be administered even if there is a 1 in 100 chance of a false accusation. There is no mending, after someone was killed. This means that it is impossible to recover lives taken away by executions resulting from a miscarriage of justice.

Moreover, some people have assumed that the death penalty has a deterrent effect on a crime. In contrast, some people have claimed that abolishing capital punishment will not necessarily increase the number of serious crimes. Up to now, many experimental studies have been accomplished about capital punishment and the change in the crime rate in the U.S.A. However, the relation has not been established between the capital punishment system and the crime rate. In short, although retentionists argue that capital punishment is meaningful as a criminal policy due to its threatening power and deterrent effects on crime, there has been no scientific evidence for this argument. Moreover, according to Goertzel (2004), "The value of this research is shown by its success in demonstrating that capital punishment has not deterred homicide." Furthermore, someone may commit a crime for the purposes of the death penalty. Therefore, if the death penalty is intended to prevent crime, it should be abolished immediately.

In addition, simple and sophisticated design is one of the fundamental features of the Macintosh machine. The weak point of the Macintosh machine is that only Apple Company can produce and assemble the Macintosh machine. However, many companies all over the world provide many varieties of Windows machines. Consequently, we are able to choose our Windows machines from a large selection. It means that we can choose a Windows machine from a variety of them between low through high level design. Nevertheless, Macintosh machine I think has more sophisticated design than Windows machine on an average. However, this is purely subjective matter.

Finally, the consumer price of a computer is also one of the most important factors for consumers or end users. The prices of Macintosh machines are evidently higher than that of Windows machines with the same function. Though Macintosh has many advantages such as resistance to viruses and sophisticated design, this higher price is an important disadvantage, which cannot be passed over. We can easily find several Windows machine at a very cheap price.

As a conclusion, we have to put the advantage and disadvantage of both machines on a scale to decide which machine we will purchase. Windows machine has advantages in terms of a price and penetration rate. While, Macintosh machine has advantages of viral resistance and sophisticated design. One has advantages, which are the other's disadvantages. I eventually chosen Macintosh as my personal computer, because of its viral resistance and sophisticated design.

In another point, capital punishment definitely and inevitably takes away human life and dignity. No matter how it may be carried out, capital punishment itself can be said to be cruel. Everyone should have respect for human dignity. That means nobody can play God with other people's lives. However, people are gone forever by use of government power. According to the Universal Declaration of Human Rights (1948), "Everyone has the right to recognition everywhere as a person before the law" (Article 6). Even the most hardened criminal must be endowed with inalienable rights. It is impermissible to kill someone who is categorized as a devil. No one has the right to kill anybody for any reason. Moreover, some do a revision when they cannot grow worse. We do not deprive someone of a chance to go straight. Therefore, all countries should not allow the death penalty.

Finally, if a government abolishes the death penalty, they may fall short of satisfying the victim's emotional request for a harsh penalty. In addition, it may not understand the pains of the victims. However, according to Bingham (2009), "Living by the motto an eye for an eye and a tooth for a tooth makes people less happy and successful." The death penalty will trigger never-ending cycle of retribution and offer no solutions. Ultimately, the death penalty may leave the family of the victim in immeasurable grief. According to Japan Federation of Bar Associations (2002), efforts to prevent recurrences by studying the causes and background of crimes and preventive measures as well as supporting victims by giving economic assistance, mental care and appropriate involvement in criminal justice procedures will possibly mitigate the sufferings of the bereaved and open a way to ease their feelings, including retributive and revengeful feelings, (p. 386).

In conclusion, capital punishment should be abolished in the world. Everyone has to think about the morality of capital punishment. Humans do not allow the life of humans to claim. The capital punishment is not the answer to solving problems. Therefore, everyone must discuss alternatives to capital punishment. Capital punishment system constitutes a violation of fundamental human rights. The use of the death penalty must not be authorized in any situation.

Appendix VI

FW1 Japanese L1. Writing Texts:
Errors Have Not Been Corrected

Writing 3

Our pet, a Japanese dog, was one of the important family members. When my daughter was 3 years old, we had a small Japanese dog for her because she was our only child and we hoped to educate her to pet him. After he became our family member since he was 3 months old, our life was changed well. She and my husband went walking with him every morning and evening. I had to feed him my handmade food because a Japanese dog could live on plain food. He was always playful with us and behaved so funny and lovely, and we enjoyed to spend time with him every day. I liked to feed and train him because he was simple and never said things against my will. As he was in his house outside, he protected us from strangers by barking. Also, I often brought him to the doctor for Filaria or some kind of vaccine and sometimes for his illness. For those reasons, he was more submissive to me than others. Finally, he finished his life after 17 years in my having him while my daughter was an university student in another city. I was very sad to miss him and I often cried when I thought about him.

Writing 4

While I live in the U.S. studying English is a lot of benefits. If I couldn't understand English, I can't live here, because sometimes I have to spent alone without my husband. I have several experiences about starting to study English such as at the musium, on the phone, and communicationn with people and aloso I can know American caltures through English. First of all, when I went to the musium,which was glass exibition,with IWAP member, I couldn't understand the tour guidance at all. After that, I was asked by the guide woman what was the most favorite, I couldn't answer. Secondly, sometimes I have to catch a call, and I couldn't understand their pronounciation and what they said.

Graduation is next month! I need to make some plans now because when exams start, I won't have any free time. What am I going to do when I finish school? My roommate is going to take a vacation before she looks for a job. I won't do that because I need to earn some money soon. I think that after I graduate, I am going to take a word processing class. As soon as I learn word processing, I will look for a job as a bilingual office assistant. It's hard to find full-time jobs, though. Part-time jobs are easier to find. Maybe I'll take a part-time job after I find a good full-time one. Or maybe I'll take a workshop in making decisions before I do something!

My living room facing the slope on the hill is bright and sunny. When I sit down on the sofa in the living room, I can see colorful nature trees outside and I can see some pictures of my grandchildren and my paintings on the wall. So, this room always cheers me up. I have an extra lamp from Japan in this room. It lights the wall up nicely with small shapes of crescent moons, stars and flowers. Last month, I turned our TV around so that I can watch TV from the kitchen because I would like to watch the news every day. At the same time, I turned the sofa and a coffee table around too. But it has made the living room feel narrow. I should try out another way.

(Continued)

And Once I missed important imformation for me. In adittion, it was difficult to communicate with peoplr. Last, I can know many interesting American calture through English study.

In conclusion, I can get a lot of information through studying English.

Writing 5

Skipping Breakfast

Why do some people skip breakfast? Recently, people who do not take breakfast are increasing, especially among the young people. It might say rather popular than increasing. When I ask my classmates whether they take breakfast every morning or not, most of them answer that they don't take breakfast and just drink a cup of coffee. However, it is said that breakfast is the most important meal of the day. There are several arguments for skipping breakfast, despite the fact that skipping breakfast causes unhealthy life style, so that people should realize the importance of breakfast.

First, some people skip breakfast because they are too busy in the morning, and have no time to make or eat breakfast. Most of them sleep too late and awake late, so their stomachs do not accept any foods. My classmate said that if she eats something in the morning, she gets sick. She is unhealthy! To make their brains clear, most people who skip breakfast drink a cup of coffee. But skipping breakfast is likely to become tired when their brain and body run with low energy. Also, some parents put these situations in their children's life styles. According to Bowden, "Eating breakfast correlates with better performance and concentration at school and work, better energy and improved well-being," (2009). If we consider figuratively our body as a car, the car engine does not work without fuel, so breakfast is important fuel that we need to get body going and starting our lives of the day. In addition, as French states, "Breakfast is not the meal to miss, especially when you feel stressed, since it can set the mood for entire day," (2008).

I felt that my living room was being a little bit cold last winter. So I am going to take down the blinds and put up the curtains on the window this winter. I have to pick out their color from now. It will end up with being more comfortable and refreshed in my living room.

Fertility Treatment

New advances in fertility medicine have created some social problems recently.

At the end of this January, Octomom was reported at the California hospital. It was almost certain that the woman was undergoing fertility treatment. There are enormous risks that fertility medicine will cause: increasing in multiple births, and birth defects.

First, due to the fertility medicine, multiple births are increasing. Multiple births have led to enormous risks on medical problems and development troubles for babies. As a result of these risks, the family has to be put under great emotional strain, including financial problems. For example, a mother of multiple births can not care them by herself. It is obvious that she has to depend on others. In fact, Octomom has already depend on her mother to care other six children, and her mother has been tired and felt so stressful about caring her multiple grandchildren. Although new babies has been caring by six nurses to gain weight faster now, imitating the way of the mother to hold babies, the family is put in the nervous situations. Moreover, the family spends much money for their daily diapers, clothes, and food, also for medical treatments. By the way, it was reported that they need about 23,000 diapers a year, which is the number of eight times diapers per a baby.

I agree with these opinions. We need more energy, clear brain, and concentration for studying hard. Also, if parents want their children to do better at school, it is better to make their lifestyles eating breakfast. Think about how to retain our healthy conditions not only a day, but also for a long term. Moreover, the communication with family through breakfast affects good beginning to start the day.

Secondly, skipping breakfast is considered as a common strategy for losing weight, especially among women. Some people believe that they will loose weight if they skip meals. In this point, breakfast is an easy target to skip. But it is not true. In fact, I have an experience that if I skipped only a meal, my weight decreased a little bit soon, but my body fat didn't decrease. Some experts say that eating breakfast is rather good for weight loss. According to Campbell, "In fact, data from the National Weight Control Registry, an ongoing study of over 5,000 people who have lost weight and maintained a weight loss of at least 30 pounds for one year or more, shows that one key factor for these people's success is that almost all eat breakfast. On theory is that eating breakfast kick-starts your metabolism, helping your body start burning food for fuel," (2007). Also, as Gardner states, "An estimated 12 percent to 34 percent of children and adolescents skip breakfast on a regular basis, a number that increases with age. Previous studies have linked breakfast skipping with a great tendency to gain weight," (2008). We can imagine that if people made arbitrary skipping breakfast, there is a possibility that they might run too much eating for lunch as a reaction or tend toward having high sugar foods. If so, it causes unbalanced eating habit. As the result, they become to gain weight. Furthermore, it could be lead to obesity. We need good balanced eating habit to maintain our weight without skipping breakfast.

In addition, there is a possibility of birth defects because of multiple babies. Most of them are tiny and premature birth for protecting mother's health condition. Embryos have to share the situation in mother's womb, only one of them is blessed with the quality to live in mother's womb normally, so some babies are involved in a lack of enough nutrition or oxygen through their mother. Therefore it is inevitable that multiple births cause the birth defects. As Fernandez states, "Infants conceived as a result of infertility treatment are two to four times more likely to have certain types of birth defects than children conceived naturally, according to one of the nation's largest studies on the issue (2008). The study shows that the defects includes heart problems, cleft lip, cleft palate and abnormalities in the esophagus or rectum. The Octomom has already three birth defects and a new baby who is in the serious condition from the beginning. Birth defects also result in medical problems and development troubles for babies for long term; Consequently, caring for babies depends on many social programs.

In brief, new advance in fertility medicine have caused serious risks instead of benefiting infertile couples. Increases in multiple births and birth defects imply that family and social have to compensate with tremendous tasks.

Works Cited

ANON_NAME_0 Fernandez. More birth defects seen with fertility treatment. Nov. 18, 2008
<ANON_URLPAGE>

(Continued)

On the other hands, some people who have health problems have to skip breakfast. As additional Campbell states, "It's not uncommon for dietitians to hear patients say, 'If I eat breakfast, I'm hungry all day.' Like wise, many people skip breakfast in an effort to lose weight. Some people with diabetes don't eat breakfast because they wake up with high blood glucose readings in the morning. What are your reasons for no eating break fast?" In addition, "Even the name "breakfast" implies that you are breaking the long overnight fast with a nourishing meal to help you face the day," (2007). However, some people who don't eat breakfast show their healthy conditions. If they continue to keep skipping breakfast, are their bodies accustomed to being good conditions? Then, why do most experts insist the importance of eating breakfast?

If we consider about the mechanism of our body, skipping breakfast is not inherent for our body, because there is a mechanism of body functions. In the thinking way of oriental medicine, I learned about it very long ago, human's functions such as five solid organs and six hollow organs have the best time to work vigorously a day. For example, the liver works in midnight actively, the lungs work at cockcrow etc. Although we have adaptability to a new situation, skipping breakfast disobeys the natural stream of body functions and it will cause some different changes to the body in the future. I believe that it is better to follow to natural stream of our body functions.

Finally, most people of skipping breakfast feel nothing about
the importance of eating breakfast, and persist their life styles
unconsciously. But breakfast is very important issue, as most
experts recommend. Of course, it should be balanced meal. At
the same time, Most people are tend to take dinner as the main
meal in a day, but I think that it is better to eat the most balanced,
qualified breakfast for energy in a day. Someday, an ELI teacher
gave us a homework that we should take enough sleeping and
good breakfast before a day taking a final test, because these are
very important for keeping clear brain, especially for language.
Sleeping gives our brain rest and good breakfast gives our brain
enough nutrition. We should know these real clues for studying,
also other people who skip breakfast too.
Briefly, a lot of people skip breakfast, but skipping breakfast can just
save time in the busy morning, and has no benefits for our healthy
life style. People who don't eat breakfast should recognize that
breakfast is very important.

Works Cited
Jonny Bowden. Eating breakfast is only half the story. Feb.02.2009
<ANON_URLPAGE>
Gerri French. Making time for breakfast. Sep. 22, 2008
<ANON_URLPAGE>
Amy Campbell. Getting off to a good with breakfast: part 1.
May 14, 2007
<ANON_URLPAGE. . . >
Amanda Gardner. Skip breakfast, pack on the pounds. Mar. 03,
2008
<ANON_URLPAGE>

(Continued)

Appendix VII
CC4 Korean L1. Writing Texts:
Errors Have Not Been Corrected

Personal Letter
March 20, 2007
Dear Father,
Hi, my father! How are you? I'm very fine. I want to buy laptop for studying.
 I have compared between the Toshiba and the LG laptop for a week.
The Toshiba laptop price is $1020, but the LG laptop price is $840. The
 Toshiba is more expensive than the LG. The Toshiba can put in more files
 than the LG because the Toshiba has 160 GB, the LG only has 60GB. Both
 have the same memory. The Toshiba and LG are different in screen size. The
 Toshiba has a 14 inch and The LG has a 15 inch monitor. The Toshiba is easy
 to move anywhere because the Toshiba is smaller than the LG. The Toshiba
 CPU is Intel dual core 2 and the LG CPU is dual core, so the Toshiba is faster
 than the LG. In my opinion, the most important thing is CPU if someone
 wants to buy a laptop. It was difficult to choose between the Toshiba and the
 LG, but I have decided to buy the Toshiba.
I miss you. I want to go back to my country. You wait for me this December.
Take care for your health. Good-bye!
Warmly,
Your son

Korean Teenager Culture
In Korea, teenagers have their own unique culture. First,
 they have highly buying power. Most of their parents
 pay for items, but teenagers choose items because
 they have good ability to find good items through
 the internet. So, most of the advertisements focus on
 teenagers.
Secondly, teenagers think fashion and appearance are
 very important. That is, they care about appearance
 and fashion. They want to impress other people. For
 example, teenagers want to wear clothes well and buy
 many clothes at once.
Lastly, teenagers are a part of the digital generation. For
 example, most of them don't read newspapers but use
 the internet and watch TV. They also like video games,
 but they don't like to read books and newspapers.
Therefore, teenagers have a specific character unlike any
 other generation.

(*Continued*)

Writing 4

In Korea, many people eat dogs. There are many dogmeat restaurants in Korea. Dogmeat is one of Korea's traditional foods. However, some foreigners such as the French criticize Koreans for eating dogmeat. They regard Koreans as barbarians because Koreans eat dogmeat. For example, in 1999, the French actress Brigitte Bardot criticizes Koreans for eating dogs. She sent the message to Korea that Koreans have to stop eating dogmeat if they want to open the 2002 world cup because many foreigners who would visit Korea in the 2002 world cup think that eating dogs is awful. But, Koreans are not barbarian for eating dogmeat. There are three reasons why Koreans are not barbarians: Dogmeat is a part of cultural heritage, we never kill dogs with cruel method, and all dogs do not become dogmeat.

First, eating dogmeat is a part of cultural heritage. In the ancient society, we were starving and finding something to eat. That is why Koreans came to eat a dog at that time. They started to eat dogmeat from B.C 3000. The French missionary Daren stated that the most delicious Korean food was dogmeat in 1847. Also, in the Sagi, which is a history book, Koreans ate dogmeat in the special day and gave it Korea's king. In other words, Koreans have traditionally eaten dogmeat so far.

Second, Koreans do not use a cruel method when they kill dogs. They use an electric shock now. They do not want to kill dogs with a cruel method. If someone in Korea wants to kill dogs with cruel method, most Koreans will accuse someone of killing dog with that method.

Lastly, all dogs do not become dogmeat. Koreans think that dogs are divided into two parts "for eating or for a pet". If a dog is for a pet, they never eat a dog. They eat just a eating dog. This means that some dogs are specially bred on food and pets are never eaten.

Some foreigners criticize eating dogmeat and regard Koreans as barbarians.

In Korea, when I was a freshman in my university, a majority of examinations and books are written in English. It was very difficult for me to read books and take examinations. I sometimes gave up a course I attended because I could not read English books well, and I even lost interest in my major because of English. At that time, I realized that English is a very important thing for me. That is why I decided to learn English in the U.S. I could select from many cities such as Los Angeles, Chicago, Boston, etc. However, I decided to study English in Pittsburgh. There are three main reasons why I decided to learn English in Pittsburgh: the rate of Korean students, prices, and the environment in Pittsburgh

The first reason I decided to learn English in Pittsburgh is the rate of Korean students. There are few Korean students in Pittsburgh unlike other cities. Before I came to Pittsburgh, I thought that the rate of Korean students was crucial for learning English. If there are many Korean students in city, people who go to that city have fewer opportunities to speak English. For example, in Los Angeles Koreans don't have to speak English because there are many Koreans in Los Angeles and Korean shops. This fact means that it is hard to talk with native speakers in Los Angeles. On the other hand, since there are few Koreans in Pittsburgh, Koreans have to speak English to communicate with native speakers when they want to buy something in the market and ask questions to other people.

Koreans are obtaining a bad image because of them. However, dogmeat is Korean
tradition and Koreans are inheriting their traditional heritage. Therefore, foreigners should not call them barbarians.

Another reason I decided to learn English in Pittsburgh is prices. The prices in Pittsburgh are very cheap compared with other cities. For instance, in New York, Mcdonald Big Mac Hamburger's meal price is about $7, but in Pittsburgh, the hamburger's meal price is about $5. And the housing price is cheap as well. Even the housing price is much cheaper than in Korea. I can save money while I am studying English.

The last reason I decided to learn English in Pittsburgh is the environment. First of all, Pittsburgh is very safe. If people live in a dangerous place, they might always be nervous whenever they come back home. And Pittsburgh also has a good surrounding for studying. There are few playing places around university such as pubs, bars, karaoke, etc, so the students can concentrate only for studying. The University of Pittsburgh has good libraries and museums as well. These surroundings inspire students to study very hard. Furthermore, the public transportation is convenient, and the main places such as universities, downtown, museums, and parks have bus stops and subway stations. People who live in Pittsburgh can go anywhere.

Due to these three reasons, I selected Pittsburgh to study English. I believe that Pittsburgh is a best city for students who want to study English. After I learn English in Pittsburgh, I will be able to read English books and take English lectures well. That is why I would be able to get good grades and a job after graduation. Also, my dream is to be a banker who deals with foreign customers. Therefore, the experience that I learn English in Pittsburgh would be the most important experience for my dream.

(Continued)

Writing 5

The Real Value of My House

Do you live in your own house? If you live in your own house, you must be a lucky person. When I was in my country, Korea, I had never worried about housing because I lived with my parents. After I came to the U.S, I had to manage to find a house by myself. Fortunately, as soon as I arrived in the U.S, I was able to live with an American family. However, I was very nervous whenever I came back home from school because the neighborhood was dangerous. Eventually, I decided to move out and had to find a new house. At that time, I thought that it was easy for me to find a house. However, I could not find my apartment and house easily unlike my expectations. When I realized that I had no house to stay, my eyes were getting darker. Also, while looking for a new house, I had to go through pain.

First, when I decided to move out from the house which I lived, I had to find a new house. That is why I started looking for a homestay because I wanted to live with an American family to improve my English skills. Fortunately, as soon as I applied to a homestay company, I was able to get a homestay house. Also, it was very close to school. In my case, I was absolutely lucky, so I was very happy. The day before I was supposed to move in, I packed my luggage and finished preparing the move-in. However, that night the homestay host suddenly had a heart attack, so he had to go to the hospital. At that time, I was in a panic. I could not believe that I did not have a house. Where would I sleep after tomorrow? Would I have to sleep on the subway or in a street? No, I couldn't! At that time, luckily, one of my friends let me live in his house. While living in his house, I had to find a place to stay again. Hopefully, I found an apartment which was close to school when I was searching the internet.

Korean Men's Obligation: The Military

Imagine a man who is your lovely brother, son, or lover. He must go to the military because going to the military in his country is mandatory even if he does not want to go there. How would you feel if he must go to the military? In most countries, people do not have to go there. However, men in Korea must go to the military. Because I am Korean, I had been there for two years. Many people think that men in Korea who must go to the military waste their time there, and are afraid for their lovely brother, son, or lover to go there. But, it was valuable experience for me. After I finished the military service, I was able to obtain three worthy things: Leadership, independence and responsibility.

The first thing which I was able to gain after I finished the military service is leadership. There are many works which soldiers must do in the military. That is why soldiers cannot do by one person and should cooperate with each other. Due to this, a sergeant who is a soldier of the highest position should lead a team which consists of privates who are soldiers of lowest position and succeed works which the team must do.

For example, when I became a sergeant after I spent one year and three months, I had to lead my privates and order them to work to succeed my work. As a private did not want to follow me, I had to make

I called the apartment's host. He permitted me to live there because the host had to go to another city as soon as possible. Because I was able to have my house, I was really happy. I started to pack my luggage again as I kept whistling. After that, I called the host. However, the host did not answer the phone. I tried to call him again, but he never answered the phone. What happened to me? Something must have been wrong. I could not believe it! He might have changed his mind, but I did not have enough time to blame him for changing his mind because I had to find another house.

I started looking for another house or apartment. From then on, I did not care any more whether the house was close to school or not. I just wanted to live in "my" house. When I saw a leaflet about a house sublet in school, I called the host. The host wanted to meet me, so we made an appointment. However, this time I did not pack my luggage because I guessed that I would have experienced a situation like last time. After all, my guess was right. He did not show up at our meeting place. At that time, I was very frustrated and sad. What should I do? Will I be homeless? I really wanted to go back to my house in my country. Suddenly, my phone started to ring. My friend called me and wanted to show me a house in which his friend lived. I met his friend as soon as I hung up the phone. Fortunately, he permitted me to live in his house. I immediately contracted with him to live there. Also, he was so kind and the house was close to the school. Finally, my unfortunate story had a happy ending and I was able to live in "my" house.

I really appreciate my roommate and my friend who introduced me to him. If my friend had not introduced him to me, I would have slept in a street or on the subway. Now, I live in "my" apartment happily. There is nothing more valuable than the house for me. I will never forget the hard time. Also, I hope that other international students will not experience the suffering of finding a place to stay.

him work. The way which I make him work is just to persuade him. At that time, I persuaded many privates and realized that persuasion is the most important of leadership. Because of these experiences, I was able to gain leadership from the military.

The second thing is independence. It was first time for me to live alone without parents. I had to do everything by myself. For example, I had to wash my laundry, clean my room, and wake up at 6 A.M everyday. And as a sergeant who has the highest position of soldiers ordered me to work, I had to finish the work by myself at any situation although I did not want to work. In addition, as I became a sergeant, I had to do my work without other person's help. Nobody was able to help me because I was in the highest position at that time. While I was being in the military, I had to tell me two words 'by myself' in my mind.

Lastly, the thing which I was able to gain after the military service is responsibility. In the military, sergeants manage their team which consists of privates. If their team fails to work or mistake something relating to the work, sergeants have to bear the responsibility for their team because they are the soldier of the highest position in the team. That is why, as soon as I became a sergeant, I had to take the responsibility instead of other soldiers. For instance, I was an army driver in the military. As other army drive committed a car accident, I had to explain its

(Continued)

situation in front of all soldiers instead of my private who committed a car accident. Also, I had to take them to the army hospital and treat them to recover health if they were injured by the car accident. In other words, I had an important responsibility to take care of my soldiers.

In Korea, people who must go to the military feel desperate before they go to the military. However, it is a best opportunity to grow up by themselves in the military. To summarize, I could get to grow up because I gained Leadership, independence, and responsibility from while I was being in the military. During the military time, people in Korea who must go to the military would have a precious experience which they cannot experience again in their lifetime. Also it would help them adapt to work in company, every organization, and anywhere.

Appendix VIII

EQ8 Korean L1. Writing Texts:
Errors Have Not Been Corrected

Writing 3

Class: 3F
Date : Jan 29/07
My Writing Habits
How I study is very important to how I learn English. I've never studied in my bedroom because I learned that the place where I study influences my concentration. I prefer a quiet place. A quiet environment influences my concentration, too.
I like to sleep in late, so I prefer to study in the evening. Sometimes, if I can't think about what to write, I take time to rest until I am ready to write again. For example, I smoke and watch TV. When I finish my homework, I want to drink a beer.
When I do all of these things I believe my studying is more effective.

Class: 3F
Teacher: ANON_NAME_0
March19,2007
Dear Father,
Long time no see. How have you been? These days, I really miss Korean things, especially Korean food like ANON_NAME_1-chee. You know, if I want to keep ANON_NAME_1-chee, I must buy a refrigerator. I found two advertisements for refrigerators in a magazine. I can't decide between the $399 refrigerator and the $999 refrigerator. The $999 refrigerator has electronic touch temperature control, so if the refrigerator needs to lower its temperature, it changes by itself because it has a sensor. On the other hand, the $399 refrigerator doesn't have a sensor. Also, the $999 refrigerator has more space than the $399 refrigerator. However, the $399 refrigerator is cheaper and costs less to operate than the $999 refrigerator. I wish I could buy the $999. However, I don't have enough money to buy it. I decided that I'll buy the $399 refrigerator. If I buy a refrigerator,could you please send me some ANON_NAME_1-chee? Before sending ANON_NAME_1-chee, please call me please. My phone number is: 412–555–5555. Thanks, Father.

Love,
Your son.

Writing 4

Every county has a representive food. For example, Saudi Arabia has Kap-sa, Japan has ANON_NAME_0-ANON_NAME_1, America has burgers or hot dogs. My country, Korea, has Kim-chi. Korean people always love to eat Kim-chi, with their meals. Today, I'm going to introduce "how to make Kim-chi". Before making Kim-chi the gathering of friendly people is important. Because we only make it a couple of times a year, we have to make a lot of Kim-chi at once. Thus people spend a lot of times making Kim-chi. This time is spent not only making Kim-chi but also deepening friendship. It is easy to make Kim-chi if you follow these three steps.

First of all, make a decision on what kind of Kim-chi. Kim-chi has much different kind of types. To choose each different Kim-chi, it needs different ingredient. Kim-chi has three types in common. If there is one thing we have enough of, it is cabbage Kim-chi. Regardless of area in Korea, we can find easily everywhere with Korean meals. If you see Kim-chi advertisement, it is almost cabbage Kim-chi which contains red pepper. Second, we have water Kim-chi. It is not contains red pepper and can see north areas in Korea. It is easy to distinguish other Kim-chi because it looks white and has soup. Sometimes, we eat water Kim-chi when someone shocked. Third, we have scallions Kim-chi. It is different from cabbage Kim-chi. It is mainly based on scallions, not cabbage. It is common in south areas in Korea. Otherwise, depend on different types Kim-chi; they have different recipes each other. I want to introduce about cabbage Kim-chi.

For most students, the pressure of examinations can be very painful. I've seen many people who are in pain over an examination. When I was a high school student, many students tried smoking because of the stress of an examination. Especially, an important examination, such as a S.A.T, a test for graduate school, or an interview for a job may make people uncomfortable. A famous Korean writer, Bi-ya ANON_NAME_0, said "Examination makes me grow up," but this is true only if someone really likes learning. Except for these people, most students don't like examinations. Whenever I had a test or examination, I could see each person's features under pressure. I think the pressure of an examination relates to age, area of study and finances.

In accordance with a student's age, pressure can have different meaning with an examination. For example, teenagers, who have a school examination, can feel pressure of a parent's expectation for the S.A.T to go to college. They can not see the big picture for their future. They just feel the pressure of their parent's scolding and are interested in going to a good college. In addition, an adult, who has a college examination or an interview for a job, also feel pressure to get good grades for graduate school or to satisfy a job. Even though they are more grown up than a teenager, they are getting more responsibility for themselves. We can find one feature in regard to a student's age, each have different pressures.

(*Continued*)

After make a decision on what kind of Kim-chi, you gather the ingredients. Before gathering ingredients, you decide that how much Kim-chi to make because Kim-chi is fermentation food. If you make too much, it is easy to make sour. Then you choose fresh vegetable. Cabbage Kim-chi needs the ingredients, such as cabbages, radishes, scallions, garlic, ginger, onions, powdered red pepper, pickled baby shrimp, oysters, salt and sugar. If you do that, you are ready.

Before make a Kim-chi, you should go though due exactly formalities. If not, it makes different taste. After you gathered all the ingredients put the cabbage sections in salt water for 10 hours, drawing out the water. The next thing you do is slice the radishes and add 2 cups of warm water to the red pepper powder. It is mixed well when the red color is set. Then you should add the scallions, garlic, and ginger and mix well. Combine all the ingredients with pickled baby shrimp, add the radishes and mix well. Then, pack the ingredients in the cabbage leaves. Finally cover the top with some of the trimmed green outer leaves of cabbage and spread salt over it. Let it sit for some time until completely fermented.

In conclusion, whenever I miss Kim-chi, I buy Kim-chi. However, I can't feel flavor which my mother's Kim-chi. No one make my mother's Kim-chi because my mother put the whole mind to Kim-chi for her son. That is; it is easy to make Kim-chi if you follow these steps but most important is Kim-chi has to contain mother's devotion. Kim-chi has a lot of spicy so you eat first time it is hard to eat Kim-chi. However, if you become accustomed, you will like it.

Second, different areas of study influence different pressures with examination. For example, the department of liberal arts students can be pressured about a science examination, because they prefer a conversation, writing or reading thanthe proof of a formula or calculation. On the other hand, the science department student can be pressured by an examination relating to the department of liberal arts. That is, if a student has an exam different from their major, they can feel pressured by it.

Finally, different financial status can make pressure for each group of students who have an examination. For instance, when poor students prepare an examination, they want to succeed on the examination so they may have pressure from the examination. However, when rich students prepare an examination, they have to worry about keeping their parents property or reputation. It doesn't matter if someone is rich or poor. They just have different kinds of pressure.

In conclusion, although there are different kinds of pressure from examination related to age, area of study and financial situation, students suffer from the examination. However, if we can become more mature by examination, it will not make pressure anymore.

The Red Sox & The Yankees

There are a lot of rival sports teams in the world. For example, the Boston Red sox & the New York Yankees, the Real Madrid & the Barcelona, the Manchester United & the Arsenal and the LA Dodgers & the San ANON_NAME_0 Giant are announced renowned rival teams. Fans do not like each other when their rival team plays a game opposite other rival team. Moreover, they refuse see each other during playing game. Actually, I am at the Boston Red Sox fan, I always interested in the article which is related to the Red Sox and the Yankees. Even though there two teams look nothing in common, they have several similarities: popular teams both of them in the U.S, relating to Babe ANON_NAME_1 and Having good players and coach.

First of all, both of them are popular teams in the U.S. the Red Sox found in 1901 and they have been a strong team in American League for a long time. Also, they have a lot of fans in the U.S even Japan and Korea. During baseball season, you can easily watch the Red Sox game by TV, because a big broadcasting station such as Fox or ABC gets a high program rating. Also, the Boston Red Sox for getting fans made their broadcasting station. The Yankees is also one of the popular team in the U.S. In the survey of "ESPN" which is a sports channel, the Yankees is the most popular them in the U.S. Yankees has been great team and got a lot of World Series Championship. They found in 1901 like the Red Sox. If you travel in the U.S cities, you can see people who wear the cap of the Yankees logo everywhere. People want to watch the Yankees games because they have a lot of stars and plays well, hence broadcasting station want to broadcast Yankees game. They also have their broadcasting station name of "YES".

Nurture or Nature

Have you ever heard a Chinese legend about Mencius? Mencius, who was a very famous philosopher in Asia, wrote a lot of books and he impacted on the Asia culture. When he was young, his mother wanted him to grow up well, so she moved many times because of his education. First, she moved to a nearby department store and then he had imitated a clerk's acting. Second, she moved to a nearby a religion area. By then, the he had imitated about shaman's acting. She was thought that there were not suitable places. Finally, she moved to a nearby school, by then he had studied too much and he was going to be a famous philosopher. This story gives us a lesson that intelligence is mostly the result of the interaction between people and their environment regardless of nature. I support that nurture is more important than nature. There are three reasons why nurture is more important than nature: Man is a social animal, people can get intelligence from effort and sometimes genius is ruined.

First of all, an Aristotle, a Greek philosopher, said "Man is a social animal." People should depend on social environment. People can not live alone. Otherwise, people have influenced by societal environment. People were taught, think and speak in their environment. Even though a genius was born, sometimes environment makes a person who is a genius change stupid person because of bad an environment.

(Continued)

Second, both of them relate to Babe ANON_NAME_1 who was the greatest baseball star in the baseball history. Even though Babe ANON_NAME_1 was renowned a Yankees star, at first, he had played in the Boston Red Sox. When he was playing in Boston, he was good pitcher and batter. Because of him, the Boston Red Sox could win many games. At that time, the Boston Red Sox got World Series Championship as many as four times. Unfortunately, executive people of the Red Sox decided to sell Babe ANON_NAME_1 to the Yankees for building new stadium name of "Pen Way Park". Since then the Boston Red Sox had not gotten World Series Championship for 86 years old. However, the New York Yankees has gotten World Series Championship as many as 26 times since Babe ANON_NAME_1 was traded from Boston. Since then, people called that "Bambino's curse." Whenever people talk about the Boston Red Sox and the New York Yankees, Babe ANON_NAME_1's story is one of the most important issues.

Finally, both of them have a lot of good players and good coaches. In Red Sox, Many ANON_NAME_2, David ANON_NAME_3, Josh Becket, Curt Schering and Mike Lowell are famous stars in the Major League Baseball. A lot of people buy a ticket to see them. Terry Franconia, who is a Red Sox coach, is great coach. He finished 'Bambino's curse? two years ago. He controls well his team. For making popular team, owner of the Boston Red Sox always invests a lot of money. Yankees has also a lot of good players and good coach. Derik Jeter, A-rod, ANON_NAME_4 Posada, Jason Jiambi and Mariano Rivera are very famous players. ANON_NAME_5 Torre, who is a Yankees coach, is one of the greatest coaches in Major League Baseball history. He got three times World Series Champion Ship. Yankees owner also invests a lot of money for his team.

In conclusion, although the Red Sox & the Yankees look nothing in common and dislike each others, there are remarkable similarities popular teams both of them in the U.S, relating to Babe ANON_NAME_1 and Having good players and good coach. In the Red sox fan's point, having rival team is good for me because it gives me more interesting and enjoy it. I can not imagine the Red sox without the Yankees.

Second, people can get intelligence by effort. Edison, who was a famous inventor, said "Genius is one percent inspiration and 99 percent perspiration." Sometimes, people do not know the maximum. People lose a lot of opportunity in their life. People think "I can not do this. I am not a genius. Maybe a genius is going to do this one." they give up their job even though they really want to do it. We can get everything we want. We can fight what really we want to do. If our life is already destined by God, we can struggle against fate and then achieve our new destiny. I have a motto in my life that "Effort can not abuse in my life." Even though I do my best, if I did not get my job that I want to do, then I did not do my best.

Lastly, sometimes genius can be ruined. I know a friend who was my schoolmate in high school. He was a great baseball player. Most people thought he was going to be great baseball player and envy his talent of baseball. Actually, ANON_NAME_0 ANON_NAME_1, the Korean baseball team, nominated him in a draft. However, his environment was not good because he had a lot of friends who liked to drink alcohol. Since he was nominated by the baseball team he had not practiced baseball and had started to drink many days. In the end, he lost his job. Today he is working in a restaurant. He could have played baseball. Even if he practices his job, he would be great baseball player.

In conclusion, this essay has presented three reason of why nurture is more important than nature: Man is a social animal, people can get intelligence by effort and a genius is ruined. Therefore, as in 'Nike' advertisement, 'just do it' regardless of nature.

8 Epilogue

8.1 The Wider Context of the Intensive English Program

An intensive English program depends on the collaborative efforts of a large team of professionals in understanding the IEP's role in the setting it is located in (the country, the state/local government area, the community, and the institution). In the United States, government policy since 9/11/2001 has been a constant factor in decisions regarding how to recruit and track students during their studies. In admissions and recruiting, these policies must be understood, implemented, and documented. Another major issue in the United States is maintaining quality that will ensure continued accreditation. Having reliable placement and progress score data (Chapter 3) and keeping records on reliable measures of progress in vocabulary (Chapter 4) and writing (Chapter 7) will assist the IEP in documenting compliance in this area.

The administration of an IEP also relies on a team of people who collaborate effectively to plan and implement curricula in different skills areas at different levels. They ensure the appropriate placement of those students in the right classes and monitor the progression from level to level. The IEP will more often than not rely on a diverse group of faculty administrators who teach and supervise instructors and part-time instructors and perhaps graduate students. This mix of personnel helps maintain new ideas in the IEP. When required to explain curricula to new experienced teachers and inexperienced trainee teachers, administrators will reflect on their curricula and make changes. At Pitt, the administrative faculty meet regularly with teachers to evaluate the curriculum and materials and to suggest changes. As a result, the IEP described during the period of data collection is not the IEP you would find if you visited the Pitt IEP today in October 2019. For example, in response to a partnership with a university in Asia, we now have a 'false beginner' Level 2 in order to accommodate students who might test in lower than our previous cut-off. This adjustment also allows the IEP to offer instruction to students who previously were not proficient enough for the low intermediate class. The IEP also now has a Level 6 – Advanced in order to

274　*Epilogue*

provide extra assistance to students who need more time to prepare for academic study. Changes are not limited to the number of levels. Changes also occur in individual curricula. For example, at the higher levels in writing, the IEP no longer offers 'narrative' as a genre in order to encourage students to seek more topics they are less familiar with.

8.2　Tracking Development: Providing Quantitative Support for Qualitative Judgments

This book has attempted to document how learners in one IEP progressed in their mastery of aspects of English that they might need to succeed in their academic programs or in their professional lives. The book has tapped into a rich source of data, the Pittsburgh English Language Institute Corpus (https://github.com/ELI-Data-Mining-Group/Pitt-ELI-Corpus). Although qualitative judgments of experienced teachers will always be important, we have seen that quantitative measures can also be very helpful in supporting these qualitative judgments.

In measuring vocabulary development, a measure of lexical sophistication (Advanced Guiraud) seems to be the most useful in distinguishing levels in our data as long as students are not given undue credit for less frequent words they already know based on their home cultures. By the time students reach the upper proficiency levels, their writing should be reaching a score of 1.0 or above.

In grammatical development, we have seen that although functional morphology seems to be controlled in speaking activities roughly along the lines of some morpheme order studies, there is nevertheless an effect of the first language. This effect was found in differences among Arabic- and Chinese- speaking learners with regard to articles and regular and irregular past tense marking. At the level of clause structure, it appears that learners progress steadily with complex embedded clauses but that judicious choice of some key verbs and other functors may in the future speed up the development of complexity and enable students to express complex ideas more fully.

In speaking, the data from PELIC, classroom experiments, and additional experiments with the IEP students enabled researchers to investigate L1 influence in pronunciation and L1 morpho-phonological influence in reading decoding. Furthermore, the development of complexity, accuracy, and fluency was documented as a set of skills that develop together rather than being in a trade-off relationship. Experiments also showed that fluency could be developed by certain kinds of focused practice in speaking.

Finally, in writing, the data show that learners developed according to statistical measures that were found to inform college student L2 writing. By Level 5, the learners were producing texts with Advanced Guiraud scores above 1 and mean length of clause above 10 when they were writing longer, more impersonal texts. However, some Level 5 students were not being pushed in their output and so the curriculum has been amended at Level 6 to include more academic writing tasks and focus on longer reading texts. In addition, the sampled essays showed that learners need help with varying the cohesion devices and not restricting themselves to some well-tried connectors. More recently, Dorolyn Smith (personal communication) notes that the IEP has started having students in writing classes keep track of their word count and include it in their essays at the end, but learners could also be encouraged to use more sophisticated online tools for this purpose. In Levels 5 and 6, the IEP requires students to note increases in their word counts from one revision to the next, especially when they had received a comment from the teacher to 'expand this section' or 'give more details'. Being aware of word count is one method the IEP is using to get students to increase their output.

8.3 Aspects Not Covered

There are two areas of development that we have not documented in this book. The first is the development of students' academic speaking ability, which is possibly one of the most challenging aspects of participation in English-speaking academic culture. A so-called 'foreign accent' can be a barrier to being comprehended and thus a threat to the students' success that must be being taken seriously. In the Pitt IEP, speaking classes require presentations, but we do not have data to analyze based on those classes. It is a gap in our understanding of how students develop in this area.

In addition, we have not provided any quantitative analysis of how many learners progress to the next level (pass rates) or a complete set of rubrics that the IEP used to evaluate students in their various skills. These data exist and are reported to the Commission on English Program Administration but reporting on these data goes beyond the scope of this book.

8.4 Prospects for Intensive English Programs

8.4.1 *In the United States*

Throughout the United States, IEPs are housed in a variety of administrative units: reporting to provosts directly, in Schools of Education, and in academic departments. Other IEPs are now part of Pathways Programs that are wholly or partially owned by outside entities. One of the themes that emerges consistently from meetings of directors of IEPs in the university and College Intensive English Program consortium is that IEPs that are well integrated into the academic life of the institution are likely to have a more stable future (Hoekje & Stevens, 2017). The Pitt IEP is

276 Epilogue

fortunate to be a core component of the Department of Linguistics and well integrated into the administrative life of the university through testing of matriculated students, instruction of credit-bearing courses for a variety of schools of the university, and serving as a partner in research and graduate student training in second language teaching and acquisition. These synergies are an important part of the vitality of a college- or university-based IEP and a key component in establishing 'academic credibility' in the institution.

However, IEPs in smaller population centers and smaller institutions may be at risk in the future as countries seek to develop their own IEP cultures in order to gain access to academic and professional advancement. In these situations, making links across campus will help programs in being recognized by their institutions in their role in international education.

8.4.2 Around the World

As of October 2019, the CEA list of accredited sites (https://cea-accredit. org/accredited-sites) reports that IEPs have been accredited by the US-based CEA across the globe: one in Egypt, one in Greece, one in Iraq, three in Kuwait, one in Mongolia, three in Peru, three in Qatar, six in Saudi Arabia, and four in Turkey. These data suggest that countries are increasingly setting up IEPs in order to train their citizens in English before they go overseas to study. This list does not include IEPs in other countries that have their own regulatory bodies. Obviously, the point is that as English remains the lingua franca of science, technology, commerce, and international politics, not just for English-speaking countries but among other countries, as well as economic and political organizations, the importance of IEPs around the world will increase.

It is hoped that this book may inform and generate debate at IEPs both in the United States as well as other countries, as long as the local conditions are taken into account.

Reference

Hoekje, B. J., & Stevens, S. G. (2017). *Creating a culturally inclusive campus: A guide to supporting international students*. New York: Routledge.

Index

AAIEP *see* EnglishUSA
academic vocabulary list *see* word lists
Academic Word List *see* word lists
accent 20, 171, 275
accreditation: of IEPs 2, 20, 42, 46, 76–78, 90; of IEPs internationally 276, 291
accuracy 130–131, 174–177; measures of 177; in Pitt IEP data *133*, 134, **178**, 178–179, **183**; and self-correction notes 180; *see also* CAF (complexity, accuracy, fluency)
acquisition *vs.* learning 10–11
Adler, E. 159–160
administrative structure of Pitt IEP 23–26
Ai, H. 200, 202, 204
Alexopoulou, T. xvii, 130
Algren, M. 4
Allen, J. P. B. 127
American Association of Intensive English Programs *see* EnglishUSA
analysis of speech (AS) unit 130, 176–177; in data analysis **178**, **183**
Anderson, T. 12
Anthony, E. M. 1, 21, 187–188
approach, method, technique 21, 106; and Pitt IEP 187–188
articles 157–158, 292; and corrective feedback 157; definite 138–139, 143, **144**; and instruction of 158–159; L1 influence on 143, 274; and learner development 158; taught in Pitt IEP 32–33, 41–57
assessment 58–59; change from discrete point to task-based formats 62–63; decisions affected by 59; historical overview 60–63; and program evaluation 59;

quantitative *vs.* qualitative measures 216–219; used in SLA research 62
associative learning theory *see* usage-based theory
AS unit *see* analysis of speech (AS) unit
Atkinson, D. 31, 196–198, 214–216, 221
audiolingualism 8, 10

Bachman, L. 60, 62, 73
Bailey, N. 130
Bartholomae, D. 196
basic interpersonal communication skills *see* BICS (Basic Interpersonal Communication Skills)
Bazergui, N. 177
bell curve *see* normal distribution
Berry Courter, K. 196
best practices 22; in Pitt IEP 36–37
Biber, D. 11, 61, 70
BICS (Basic Interpersonal Communication Skills) 9, 73
Bley-Vroman, R. 154, 155, 185
Bloomfield, L. 8
BNC (British National Corpus) 68, 98, 102, 103, 116–123, 138; and frequency bands 122–126
bookmark method *see* cut scores, methods of determining
borderline method *see* cut scores, methods of determining
boxplot analysis 70; of Pitt IEP placement data 74, 80, 83
British National Corpus *see* BNC (British National Corpus)
Brookes, A. 196–197
Brown, J. D. 59, 69
Brown, R. 114, 130

278 *Index*

Brumfit, C. 10, 61
Bulté, B. 100, 175, 218
Bygate, M. 184–185

CAF (complexity, accuracy, fluency) 130, 170, 174–185; analysis of Pitt IEP student development **178**, 177–180, **184**; coding methodology of 176–177; interactions among components 176; and L1 differences in 180; and tasks 182–186
Callan, J. 108
CALP (Cognitive Academic Language Proficiency) 9; and Pitt IEP students 73
CaMLA EPT *see* Michigan EPT
Canale, M. 21, 61
Carey, M. 59, 68, 69, 109
Castagnaro, P. J. 8
CEA (Commission on English Language Program Accreditation) 2, 5, 14, 24; curriculum standards 28–29; faculty standards 26; and international accreditation 276; placement standard 58; Student Achievement Standards 58–59, 72
central tendency *see* data visualization
classes: Pitt IEP 19
clauses: attached 140–141; development and structure of 128, 135–136; embedded 140–141; in Pitt IEP curriculum 30, 32–33, 43, 49–50, 56–57
cluster analysis 67, 70–71; *see also* k-cluster analysis; two-step cluster
Cobb, T. 100, 106–107, 110, 116
COCA (Corpus of Contemporary American English) 99, 116, 138, **143–145**; discussion of complementizer/verb rankings in 146–154
cognitive and academic language skills *see* CALP (Cognitive Academic Language Proficiency)
cohesion devices 31, 208; in Pitt IEP curriculum 44, 49–51, 204; in student writing 214–217, 220
Collins-Thompson, K. 108
collocations 113–114; in Pitt IEP assessment 86; in usage-based theory 139–140
Commission on English Language Program Accreditation *see* CEA

(Commission on English Language Program Accreditation)
communicative competence 21–22, 61–62
communicative language teaching (CLT) 10–11, 20–22, 61–62, 184, 186, 188
complementizers (*if, which, whether, whenever*) 129, 139, 140–141
complements 139–141; clauses *vs.* noun phrases 141–142, **143**; predicate preferences for 141–154, **143–145**
complexity 130–131, 175; and frequency 154; semantic 154; *see also* CAF (complexity, accuracy, fluency)
complexity, accuracy, and fluency *see* CAF (complexity, accuracy, fluency)
Conrad, S. 11
Corder, S. P. 8, 62, 127
corpus linguistics 11–12, 137–140, 156
Corpus of Contemporary American English *see* COCA (Corpus of Contemporary American English)
Corrigan, A. 61
Cortes, V. 11
Coxhead, A. 11, 95, 98–99, 102, 122
Cumming, A. 12, 59, 195
Cummins, J. 9, 73
curriculum 29; horizontal articulation in Pitt IEP 38–57; and methods of Pitt IEP 19–22, 29–33
cut scores 66–67; methods of determining 67–68; in Pitt IEP placement 66

data collection of Pitt ELI Corpus xvi
data science tools 155
data visualization 69–71
Davies, M. 11, 99
de Jong, N. 170, 181–182
dePetro Orlando, R. 3
developmental order 130; of functors in Pitt IEP data 131–135; L1 influence on 130–135
Ding, C. 71
disfluency features 177
Duolingo 6

EAP (English for Academic Purposes) 9, 11–12, 184, 196
Ellis, N. C. 9, 114, 128, 137–140, 154, 156, 163n2

Ellis, R. 184
ELLPCT *see* placement assessment, Pitt IEP in-house listening test
English as a second language *see* ESL (English as a second language)
English for academic purposes *see* EAP (English for Academic Purposes)
English for specific purposes *see* ESP (English for specific purposes)
English Language Institute, University of Pittsburgh *see* Pitt IEP
EnglishUSA xvii, 2, 26
Eskenazi, M. 108, 111
ESL (English as a second language) 1; academic writing classes 198, 200; curriculum decisions 99; effect of environment on language-learning 134; and markets and accreditation 5; and online companies 6; in PELIC 150; textbooks/materials 11, 149, 159, 196–197, 203
ESP (English for specific purposes) 11–12
expert speaker 15n2, 20, 85, 135, 142, 171, 174, 195, 203, 208; word lists and corpora of 98, 100
extensive reading 99, 106–108, 110–111, 113, 115, 187; and online tutors 111; in Pitt IEP curriculum 41, 48, 54–55, 108

faculty in Pitt IEP 22–26, **23–25**, 33
Feak, C. 11, 194
feedback 36–37, 84, 134, 176; on curriculum 22, 171; on grammar 157, 161, 184; in Pitt IEP 30, 32, 171, 188; on pronunciation/speaking 171, 174, 176, 182, 188; and rubrics 84; on writing 197–199, 205
Fender, M. 187
final exams in Pitt ELI 85–87
fluency 130–131, 175, 177; and robust learning 181; training 12–13, 181–182; *see also* CAF (complexity, accuracy, fluency)
Folse, K. S. 97, 99, 106–107
formal linguistic theory 8–9; and corpus analysis 156; and predictions of complexity 140; and syntax-semantics connection 155; in tracking lexical development 137

formulaic sequences *see* MWEs (multi-word expressions)
fossilization 10
Foster, P. 130, 176–177
frequency and learning 137–138; and development of grammatical complexity 139, 150–156; *see also* formal linguistic theory
frequency bands 68; and word lists 97–100
Friedline, B. E. 9, 96, 111–112, 117n5, 184
Fries, C. C. 1, 61
functors 129; acquisition order of 130; development of in Pitt ELI Corpus 130–135, *132–133*, 141–146, 157–159; research and pedagogical implications 155–156

Gardner, D. 11, 98–99
Gass, S. M. xvi, 9, 12, 140, 184
Goodrich Andrade, H. 85
Graddol, D. 3, 6, 15n2
grammar instruction 2, 32–33; implications of research for 160–161
Graves, M. F. 107
Grimshaw, J. 150, 154–155
Grundy, P. 196–197

Hamp-Lyons, L. 88, 195–197
Han, N-R. 62–63, 101–105, 138, 207
Harrington, M. W. 59, 62, 68–69, 109
Hawkins, R. 177
He, X. 71
Heilman, M. 108, 111
Herman, P. A. 106
Hijikata, Y. 84
Hill, B. L. 62–63, 101–105, 138, 207
Hill, K. 94
Hinkel, E. 9, 160, 195
Hoekje, B. J. 3, 4–6, 275
Housen, A. 100, 175–176, 200, 218
Hull, J. 149, 169
Hulstijn, J. 95, 106–107, 221n1
Hunt, K. W. 140, 200
Hyland, K. L. xvi, 9, 11, 194, 198–199, 204
Hymes, D. 21, 61

iBT 3–4, 28, 60–61, 67; CAF and 216–217; effects of ESL *vs.* EFL study of 60; *see also* TOEFL
idioms 114

280 *Index*

IELTS (International English
Language Testing System) 4, 61, 63,
68, 88n4, 198
IEP (intensive English Program) xv,
1–13; economic benefits of 6;
outsourcing of 6; *see also* Pitt IEP
Inagaki, S. 209
inflected forms *see* morphemes
input 9, 32, 62, 128, 134, 156,
188; frequency of and acquisition
137–138, 140, 150, 154
instruction: explicit *vs.* implicit 10–11,
22, 33, 106; and learner progress
185–186; in writing 196, 199
intensive English program *see* IEP
(intensive English Program)
international campuses 5–6
International English Language
Testing System *see* IELTS
(International English Language
Testing System)
international students 3–6; history of
in IEPs 26–27; in Pitt IEP 27
internet-Based Test *see* iBT
INTO 6, 7
intonation patterns 173, 188
involvement load hypothesis 106–107

Jackendoff, R. S. 155
Jarvis, S. 100–101, 200
Johnson, K. 61–62, 197
Juffs, A. 1, 8, 9, 101–103, 104, 111,
130, 137–138, 140, 142, 146,
149, 155–156, 172–173, 186–187,
207, 208

Kaplan, R. 198
k-cluster analysis 68, 71; of Pitt IEP
placement data 75–76, **76**, 77–79,
80, *81–83*
Kennison, S. M. 139, 141–142, **143**,
145, 154, 156
Kim, H-Y. 209
Knoch, U. 84
Koedinger, K. R. xiv, 157–158
Krashen, S. D. 10, 22, 106, 111,
130–131, 134–135

language conceptualizations 20,
127–128
language teaching 5–7, 10, 20, 184, 276
language testing *see* assessment
Lantolf, J. 9, 21, 184

Larsen-Freeman, D. 9, 10, 11, 20,
134, 179, 185
Larson-Hall, J. 70, 218
Laufer, B. 94, 95, 106–107, 221n1
Learnlab.org (Pittsburgh Science of
Learning Center) xiv, 19, 108, 110,
158, 181
lemma 95–96, 98, 99, 106, 112, 138,
140, 154; lemmatize 142
Levelt, W. 180, 182
lexeme 95–96; in Pitt IEP vocabulary
instruction 102
lexical diversity 100–101, 102,
103, 114
lexical items 95; closed *vs.* open class
141; used to infer grammatical
complexity 137–138
lexical measures 100–101; Guiraud
vs. Advanced Guiraud 101–105;
vocD 100–103, 177, 207, 208,
208–209, 212, **217**
lexical richness 100, 105; analysis of
student data 208–212; diversity *vs.*
sophistication 102–104
lexical sophistication 101; role of L1
and L2 experience 103–106
Li, N. 172–173
Lidster, R. 67–68, 83
Lightbown, P. M. 8, 62, 137
lingua franca 2–3, 7, 276
Long, M. H. 8, 9, 10, 11, 22, 32, 62,
174, 184–185
Loschky, L. 185
Lu, X. 200–202, 204, 209
Luk, P-S. Z. 130–131

Mackey, A. 10
Madden, C. 130
Marsden, E. 33, 137
Martin, K. I. 186–187
McCarthy, P. M. 101
McCormick, D. E. 30, 84, 87,
128–129, 170, 180
McEnery, T. 160
McManus, K. 33
measures of dispersion *see* data
visualization
Melitz, J. 3
Michigan English Language Test *see*
Michigan EPT
Michigan EPT 66; as assessment tool
for placement in Pitt IEP 72–84;
and cut scores **66–67**

Michigan Test of English Language Proficiency *see* MTELP (Michigan Test of English Language Proficiency)

Mitamura, T. 157

monitor model 10

morphemes 95–96, 129 (derived, inflected, bound, free)

morpho-phonology of Semitic languages 186

morpho-syntactic complexity *see* complexity

MTELP (Michigan Test of English Language Proficiency) 61, 64–66, 102, **110**, 130, 206

multi-word expressions *see* MWEs (multi-word expressions)

Murakami, A. 130

MWEs (multi-word expressions) 113–114

NAFSA 2

Nagy, W. E. 106–107, 115

Naismith, B. 62, 101–102, 103–105, 138, 207

Nation, I. S. P. 94, 95, 97–99, 122, 181

National Science Foundation (NSF) xiv

native speaker *see* expert speaker

natural approach 10

normal distribution 69–70, *70*

Norris, J. M. 59

Norris, M. J. M. 127

Nunan, D. 22

O'Grady, W. 139, 163n2

online tutors 108–109, 111–112, 117n5; cognitive 157–159

Ono, M. 84

Open Doors 3, 5, 6

orthography *see* spelling

Oshita, H. 159

outliers *see* boxplot analysis

Packer, J. 135, *136*

passive voice 159–160; in Pitt IEP curriculum 33, 50, 57

pathway programs 6, 194, 275

Paulston, C. B. 8, 10, 21, 22, 61, 186, 203

PELIC (Pitt English Language Institute Corpus) 142, 137, 155, 157,

159; descriptions of levels 163n4; numbers in *27*; student data from **209, 274**

PELITK *see* Pitt ELI Toolkit

Pelletreau, T. 111

Pennington, M. C. 4–6

Perfetti, C. xiv, *95*, 181

phrases 12, 96–97, 106, 114, 214; noun 32–33, 203, 207; verb 68, 201, **202**

picture prompts 182–184

Pitt ELI Toolkit 142

Pitt IEP 1; curriculum and methods 19–22, 29–33

Pittsburgh ELI Corpus *see* PELIC (Pitt English Language Institute Corpus)

Pittsburgh Science of Learning Center *see* Learnlab.org (Pittsburgh Science of Learning Center)

placement assessment: data analysis of Pitt IEP 71–84; Pitt IEP in-house listening test 65–66, 72, 78–83; Pitt IEP in-house writing test 65, 76–83; process in the Pitt IEP 63–66; and student stages of development 60

polysemy 96, 99, 116n3, 138, 156

predicates 142, **143**; and frequency/complexity of complement 149–150, *151–153*, 153–156

principled eclecticism 10, 20, 188

proceduralized knowledge 177, 181

Proctor, S. 149, 169

proficiency levels: historical view of 61; as measured by CAF 188; Pitt IEP 19; speaking and RSA 174

pronunciation 171–172; effects of L1 phonology on 172–174; in Pitt IEP curriculum 30, 39, 40, 46, 53

Qian, Y. 160

Ramanathan, V. 196, 198, 203

Ranta, L. 62, 137

reading and L1 Arabic-speakers 186–187

REAP *see* vocabulary, use of technology in teaching

Recorded Speaking Activity *see* RSA (Recorded Speaking Activity)

Reid, J. 195–196

Reppen, R. 11

research: design-based 12–13

Richards, J. 101, 116n2, 149, 169

282 *Index*

Robinson, P. 9, 128, 138, 163n2, 175, 185
robust learning 181
Roche, T. 59, 68
RSA (Recorded Speaking Activity) 30; in Pitt IEP curriculum 87, 176; in research 130, 171, 172, 174, 176–177, 179, 180, 182, 186
rubrics 72, 84–85; for writing 65, 93

Schepps, H. 128, 130, 158
Schmitt, D. 95, 100, 197
Schmitt, N. 95, 100, 197
second language acquisition *see* SLA (second language acquisition)
Selinker, L. 62, 140, 200
Shattuck, J. 12
Shawer, S. F. 59
Shin, S-Y. 67–68, 83
Shirai, Y. 9, 130–131
Skehan, P. 22, 114, 175, 176
SLA (second language acquisition) 7–8; approaches toward 7–9, 10, 128, 137; research on pronunciation, writing and testing 171, 199, 62
Spada, N. 11, 22, 62, 137
speaking: CAF in 174–184; components in 174; curriculum in Pitt IEP 19, 30–31, 32, 37, 39–57, 64, 86–87, 176; and pronunciation 170; and TOEFL 61
spelling 95, 116n3, 196; and influence of L1 72, 186–187, 199; and Pitt IEP curriculum 42, 49, 56, 65
Spinner, P. 62, 128–129, 137, 159–160
Starfield, S. xvi, 9
Stehle, M. 157–158
STEM fields 11
Stevens, S. G. 3, 275
supra-segmentals *see* pronunciation
Swain, M. 21, 61
Swales, J. 11, 194, 197
syllable-final structure *see* pronunciation
syntactic complexity 127; development of and theory 137–141, 9, 149, 153–156; measures of 200–201, 209; and web-based analyzer 200–201; in writing 200–203, 209–212

Task-Based Language Teaching (TBLT) 22, 33, 62, 175, 179, 181, 184–186, 190n2
Task-Supported language teaching *see* Task-Based Language Teaching (TBLT)
teaching English to speakers of other languages *See* TESOL
TESOL 1–2; and higher education xvi, xvii; and Pitt IEP faculty 26, 157
Test of English as a Foreign Language *see* TOEFL
Thorne, S. 9, 21
TOEFL 3–4, 67, 84; components of 61; historical view of 60–61; and Pitt IEP entry 28; *see also* iBT
Tomasello, M. 139
Tomita, Y. 11, 22, 62
tone 173–174, 177
Tonkyn, A. 130, 176
Towell, R. 175, 177
Townsend, D. 106–108, 115
T-unit 140–141, 146, 149, 156, 200–201, **202**, 209, 214
two-step cluster 71, 80
type/token ratio 100–101

UCIEP 2, 26; and guidelines 28, 185
University and College Intensive English Program *see* UCIEP
University of Michigan 1, 66; ELI (English Language Institute) 1
usage-based theory 138–140; and collocations 140; *vs.* formal linguistics 139, 154–155; and frequency of input 137–138

verbs *see* predicates
Vercellotti, M. L. 30, 84, 128, 129, 130, 134, 135, *136*, 170, 176–181
visa regulations 27, 28
vocabulary: historical role in language teaching 94; implicit *vs.* explicit learning 106–110; instruction in Pitt IEP 112–113; instruction of 106–108, 115; interaction with accuracy 179–180; and student motivation in learning 110–111; use of technology in teaching 108–113
vocabulary recognition method *see* cut scores, methods of determining

Weinert, R. 114
West, M. 97
White, L. 8, 9, 15n1, 62, 128, 137, 155
Widdowson, H. G. 11, 62, 195
Wigglesworth, G. 130, 176
Winke, P. 68, 83–84
Wojcik, R. 112–113, 150
Wolfe-Quintero K. 209
word *see* lexical items
word family 95–96, 99, 112
word frequency 97–98, 137; learner *vs.* native speaker differences 98
word lists: AVL 99; AWL 98; general service list 97; New General Service List 97; Pitt IEP core vocabulary 102; Pitt IEP frequency list 104; Pitt IEP Vocabulary List 122–126
Wray, A. 113–114

writing 194–199; curriculum in Pitt IEP 31, 203–206; development of in PELIC 206–208, 212–216; L1 influence on and differences in 198–199; samples of Pitt IEP students 225–272; university composition programs 196–197, 203–204
Wylie, R. 157–159

Xiao, R. 160

Yamanishi, H. 84
Youngblood, A. M. 97, 99

Zheng, D. 62–63, 102, 138, 207
Zobl, H. 143, 155, 159
Zou, D. 107
z scores 71; in Pitt IEP placement data 76, 80, *81–83*, 83–84
Zwicky, A. 1

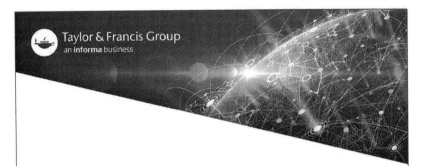